SLIDE**GUITAR**
SOLOING COLLECTION

Master Delta Blues, Soloing Techniques & Licks in the Style of 20 Slide Blues Greats

LEVI**CLAY**

FUNDAMENTAL**CHANGES**

Slide Guitar Soloing Collection

Master Delta Blues, Soloing Techniques & Licks in the Style of 20 Slide Blues Greats

ISBN: 978-1-78933-191-2

Published by www.fundamental-changes.com

Copyright © 2020 Levi Clay

The moral right of this author has been asserted.

All rights reserved. No part of this publication may be reproduced, stored in a retrieval system, or transmitted in any form or by any means, without the prior permission in writing from the publisher.

The publisher is not responsible for websites (or their content) that are not owned by the publisher.

www.fundamental-changes.com

Twitter: @guitar_joseph

Over 11,000 fans on Facebook: **FundamentalChangesInGuitar**

Instagram: **FundamentalChanges**

For over 350 Free Guitar Lessons with Videos Check Out

www.fundamental-changes.com

Cover Image Copyright: Star Singer Slides. Used by permission.

A huge thanks to Dolfinn at **www.starsingerslides.com** for making some of the best sounding and coolest looking slides on the market! (check out that cover!)

Foreword

Welcome to the **Slide Guitar Soloing Collection**. This compilation brings together three bestselling books that will help you master slide guitar – from the authentic roots of the Delta Blues to the styles and techniques of the modern slide blues masters. Here's what's inside:

- **Delta Blues Slide Guitar**
- **Slide Guitar Soloing Techniques**
- **100 Slide Licks for Blues Guitar**

There is no more comprehensive guide to slide playing!

Delta Blues Slide Guitar

A complete guide to the techniques and music of "bottleneck" acoustic blues – a genre that can be traced back over 100 years to the Mississippi Delta – where blues guitar was first heard over 60 years before Led Zeppelin, Eric Clapton and others brought it to the masses. This ground-breaking book teaches the art of flawless Delta slide guitar technique through hundreds of exercises which help you master each skill in a musical, confident way. Learn licks in the style of the Delta Blues slide pioneers, such as **Robert Johnson, Son House, Bukka White** and **Tampa Red**, and three complete songs with performance notes and guidance.

• Master the two most common tunings of Delta Blues: Open D and Open G

• Perfect your slide fretting technique to develop a solid foundation and build great tone

• The secrets of great vibrato and how to use it to create expressive melodies

• Emotive slide guitar techniques for powerful solos

• Accurate pitching and intonation. Play slide guitar in tune – every time!

• The best scales to use for slide guitar soloing, presented in easy to read diagrams

• Hundreds of authentic slide guitar licks and tricks

Slide Guitar Soloing Techniques

Slide guitar is currently enjoying a huge renaissance thanks to contemporary players like **Derek Trucks, Joey Landreth, Brett Garsed, AJ Ghent** and **Jack White** – great innovators who are carrying the flame for the next generation. Learning how to play slide guitar is one of the few techniques can change your whole approach to the guitar, so much so that it becomes a whole new instrument. In this book, you will master the art and technique of modern electric slide guitar playing.

• Essential open tunings for slide, & scale shapes for innovative soloing

• Advanced guitar techniques such as playing behind the slide, false harmonics & legato

- Slide guitar licks in style of **Duane Allman, Ry Cooder** and **Johnny Winter**
- Modern techniques from **Derek Trucks, Dan Auerbach, Joey Landreth** and **Brett Garsed**
- The rarely taught skill of playing slide guitar in standard tuning!

You'll discover how to play with a full range of expression and emotion while mastering the most useful chords, inversions, and playing positions used by the world's best players. As well as learning slide guitar in all the common open tunings, we've even included chapters on how to transfer any open tuning lick to standard tuning so you can grab any guitar and instantly make incredible music.

100 Slide Licks for Blues Guitar

100 Slide Licks for Blues Guitar goes further than other lick books. Here you will find a complete breakdown of the playing style of the world's most important slide guitarists. You won't just copy parrot-fashion, you'll internalize the language of the slide guitar masters and incorporate it into your everyday playing.

Along with extensive biographies, the musical style and language of the 20 greatest slide blues guitar players is discussed and analyzed before 5 defining "in the style of" licks are broken down, note by note. Learn slide in the style of:

Duane Allman, Ry Cooder, Brett Garsed, A.J. Ghent, Billy Gibbons, Warren Haynes, Son House, Elmore James, Robert Johnson, Sonny Landreth, Joey Landreth, Bonnie Raitt, Chris Rea, Tampa Red, Gary Rossington, Derek Trucks, Joe Walsh, Muddy Waters, Bukka White and Johnny Winter.

* * *

Along the way, we'll also discuss the important technical aspects of slide playing, such as choice of slide, which finger to wear it on, string action, amp setup and tone and more!

Finally, do make sure to download the audio files that accompany this book. A lot of effort went into recording every single lick for your study, so don't forget to spend time carefully listening to the audio, as well as studying the musical examples. One of the incredible things about slide guitar is that it doesn't lend itself well to the conventional Western system of notation or tab. There's no effective way to illustrate the microtonal options slide provides, so listen to the recordings and do your absolute best to imitate them carefully!

Good luck!

Levi

Get the Audio

The audio files for this book are available to download for free from **www.fundamental-changes.com.** The link is in the top right-hand corner. Simply select this book title from the drop-down menu and follow the instructions to get the audio.

We recommend that you download the files directly to your computer, not to your tablet, and extract them there before adding them to your media library. You can then put them on your tablet, iPod or burn them to CD. On the download page there is a help PDF and we also provide technical support via the contact form.

For over 350 Free Guitar Lessons with Videos Check out:

www.fundamental-changes.com

Twitter: **@guitar_joseph**

Over 11,000 fans on Facebook: **FundamentalChangesInGuitar**

Instagram: **FundamentalChanges**

Contents

Book 1: Delta Blues Slide Guitar

Introduction	2
Chapter One – Slides and Guitar Setup	5
Chapter Two – Fretting With The Slide	9
Chapter Three – Sliding Between Notes	16
Chapter Four – Vibrato	21
Chapter Five – Open Tuning Scales	25
Chapter Six – One String Scales	31
Chapter Seven – Open Position Playing	41
Chapter Eight – Saint Louis Blues	49
Chapter Nine – Melodies And Bass	52
Chapter Ten – Changing Chords	63
Chapter Eleven – Fretting Notes Using Fingers	75
Chapter Twelve – Solo Blues	84
Chapter Thirteen – Blues Rag	92
Conclusion	98

Book 2: Slide Guitar Soloing Techniques

Chapter One: An Introduction To Slide Playing	101
Chapter Two: Getting in Tune	105
Chapter Three: An Introduction to Using the Slide	110
Chapter Four: Single String Exercises	122
Chapter Five: Single String Solo	135
Chapter Six: Changing Strings	138
Chapter Seven: Slide Guitar Scales	148
Chapter Eight: Chord Inversions	154
Chapter Nine: Advanced Techniques	167

Chapter Ten: Open E Solo	180
Chapter Eleven: Standard Tuning	188
Chapter Twelve: Standard Tuning Solo	197
Conclusion	205

Book 3: 100 Slide Licks for Blues Guitar

Introduction	207
Chapter One – Duane Allman	210
Chapter Two – Ry Cooder	216
Chapter Three – Brett Garsed	221
Chapter Four – A.J. Ghent	226
Chapter Five – Billy Gibbons	230
Chapter Six – Warren Haynes	235
Chapter Seven – Son House	240
Chapter Eight – Elmore James	244
Chapter Nine – Robert Johnson	250
Chapter Ten – Sonny Landreth	255
Chapter Eleven – Joey Landreth	259
Chapter Twelve – Bonnie Raitt	264
Chapter Thirteen – Chris Rea	268
Chapter Fourteen – Tampa Red	272
Chapter Fifteen – Gary Rossington	276
Chapter Sixteen – Derek Trucks	280
Chapter Seventeen – Joe Walsh	285
Chapter Eighteen – Muddy Waters	289
Chapter Nineteen – Bukka White	294
Chapter Twenty – Johnny Winter	298
Other Books by Levi Clay	303

DELTA BLUES SLIDE GUITAR

A Complete Guide to Authentic Acoustic Blues Slide Guitar Technique

LEVI CLAY

FUNDAMENTAL CHANGES

Introduction

The history and development of slide, or *bottleneck* guitar can be traced back over 100 years across multiple continents. The basic idea can be seen in the "diddley bow" in early colonized America. West African slaves would stretch a single string across a wooden board and use a glass bottle as a bridge. A piece of metal would then be pressed against the string to change its pitch.

Similarly, as the Spanish guitar made its way to Hawaii, the natives began to detune the strings to an open chord (commonly referred to as *slack-key* guitar), then play the guitar on their laps, using a steel bar to fret the strings. This Hawaiian *steel guitar* sound quickly spread, with innovators like Joseph Kekuku becoming a big hit in early 1900s American vaudeville shows.

As time went on, performers in the Mississippi Delta began using other hard objects – such as knives, medicine bottles, copper pipes and the necks of glass bottles (bottlenecks!) – as tools to create a more expressive sound with their instrument. Using a slide, they were able to more closely imitate the way the human voice can smoothly slide from one pitch to another, and capture all the microtones found between the well-established twelve tone pitch system of the West.

The first recordings of this style were played by Sylvester Weaver in 1923. His *Guitar Rag* and *Guitar Blues* would heavily influence the evolving blues scene in the Mississippi Delta, along with the music of many travelling musicians who weren't fortunate enough to be recorded. From this scene would emerge iconic names such as Robert Johnson, Son House and Bukka White – all of whom are well respected by fans and historians alike.

Over time, the blues scene began to take a backseat to rock, jazz, and other styles that became popular in the dance halls. It wasn't until young musicians in the UK began to get their hands on imported records from the Delta that a new explosion of blues took the world by storm. While the big names of British blues like Peter Green, Eric Clapton, Jeff Beck, Jimmy Page etc, aren't best known for playing slide, it's certainly something they were influenced by and picked up from time to time.

This book will focus on the Delta blues style before the rise of amplification and electric guitar soloing, but it's worth pointing out that slide guitar has never died out. While there are still some incredible musicians around like Keb' Mo', keeping the original Delta spirit alive, slide guitar has been taken to extraordinary heights by the likes of Ry Cooder, Derek Trucks, Sonny Landreth and Bonnie Raitt. Slide guitar has also appeared on legendary recordings by the likes of Led Zeppelin, Derek and the Dominos, The Allman Brothers Band and The Beatles

It's no secret that blues purists are very specific about their area of expertise, so it's important to clarify that this book will focus on the Delta blues roots. From this style evolved the various American blues subgenres that include Chicago blues, Country blues, Texas blues, Jump blues and more, up to the British blues revival of the 1950s.

What this means is that this book focuses on playing the Delta music as authentically as possible. You won't find many twelve-bar blues progressions here. It's not a lick book and it's important you understand the essence of the Delta sound before jumping in. Early Delta music was normally played by a single musician using riff-based, repetitive figures on the guitar to accompany their voice. Any licks were simply fills between the rhythm guitar parts that were, again, repetitive and largely functional.

Before you get started, check out the artists listed below and make sure you're familiar with their music and style.

If you're expecting a book on twelve-bar slide guitar playing in the style of Duane Allman or Derek Trucks, in the words of Lemony Snicket, look away now! This book is a journey to the first vestiges of the blues that began to appear almost 60 years before Led Zeppelin and Eric Clapton brought blues to the masses, and decades before it was first recorded in 1920.

One final thing to remember: this style was popularised by the music of impoverished African Americans who sang about the unbelievable hardships they and their parents had faced, and were still enduring. I'm not saying you need to have a real understanding of slavery to "get" the blues, but it's worth remembering that the people playing this music were not academics. They had very little, if any, education and even less when it came to music. That said, to teach anything we need to break it down into individual concepts and ideas and some of the material in this book will need to be analysed in terms of "Western" music theory, simply so I can explain what's going on and how to recreate it.

Theory is something that's written down *after* the music has been made so we can explain it to others. It's simply one way of talking about sound. I use simple music theory in this book to communicate with you about how to recreate Delta music on your guitar and it's not my intention to turn to roots of the blues into a rigid, academic subject. Once I've described what's going on in the music, please try to get the *sound* and *feeling* of the examples into your head and forget as much of the academic stuff as possible. It's so important to download the audio examples.

This style isn't about learning and applying theory, and can never be processed in a cold, clinical manner. It's all about attitude and playing from the heart. So don't overthink it, just play!

Levi

Recommended listening:

- Sylvester Weaver – Complete Recorded Works in Chronological Order Volume 1
- Robert Johnson – The Complete Recordings
- Son House – Son House Library of Congress Recordings 1941 – 1942
- Bukka White – High Fever Blues: The Complete 1930 – 1940 Recordings
- Blind Willie Johnson – The Spiritual Blues
- Blind Willie McTell – King Of The Serpent Blues
- Tampa Red – You Can't Get That Stuff No More
- Charley Patton – The Definitive Charley Patton
- Blind Boy Fuller – Get Your Yas Yas Out
- Leadbelly – The Very Best of Leadbelly
- Elmore James – The Sky Is Crying
- Muddy Waters – The Chess Singles Collection
- Lightnin' Hopkins – Dirty House Blues

Get the Audio

The audio files for this book are available to download for free from **www.fundamental-changes.com.** The link is in the top right-hand corner. Simply select this book title from the drop-down menu and follow the instructions to get the audio.

We recommend that you download the files directly to your computer, not to your tablet, and extract them there before adding them to your media library. You can then put them on your tablet, iPod or burn them to CD. On the download page there is a help PDF and we also provide technical support via the contact form.

For over 350 Free Guitar Lessons with Videos Check out:

www.fundamental-changes.com

Twitter: **@guitar_joseph**

Over 10,000 fans on Facebook: **FundamentalChangesInGuitar**

Instagram: **FundamentalChanges**

Chapter One – Slides and Guitar Setup

I'm sure you're eager to get to the music, but it's important to begin with some equipment and technical discussion. In the first four chapters we will discuss the best setup for slide guitar, how to play a note in tune with the correct *intonation*, how to move between notes, and finally one of the most crucial playing techniques: *vibrato*. Vibrato is an essential tool for any type of slide guitar playing and it's one of the most defining factors in creating an authentic, pleasing sound.

Slide choice

There is endless debate about what material works best for a guitar slide. Ultimately, it should be about what gives you the sound you desire.

The two most common materials are glass and metal. I have a collection of slides made from many materials, including glass, ceramic, brass and steel. They all have a different sound and I use them for different things. Personally, I find I like heavier, thicker slides, so I'm fond of brass or glass. Brass slides tend to have more treble in their tone and, because they are rarely as smooth as glass, are a bit noisier – which is ideal for a rootsy Delta sound.

Most of the recordings that accompany this book were recorded using a Dunlop 222 Medium Brass slide. It's nothing fancy, but it gets the job done. If you want something a little bit more boutique, The Rock Slide (www.therockslide.com) offer a great selection of slides made from different materials and with features such as tapered interiors and finger rests. They also come personally recommended!

Guitar setup

When it comes to slide playing, the main factor in making it as easy as possible is your guitar setup. The essence of slide technique is pressing the slide against the strings so that it acts like a fret. We want to avoid a situation where the pressure of the slide pressing against the string causes it to make contact with the fretboard. A higher action will make playing slide guitar much easier.

"Action" refers to the height of your strings from the fretboard. A lower action results in less effort being required to fret a note, but the compromise is that minor inconsistencies in fret height can result in spots where the strings buzz against the frets when plucked. A higher action means that the guitar requires us to work a bit harder to play it, but generally results in a purer tone from the instrument.

On most electric guitars, there are ways to raise the action at the bridge, but this has most impact higher up the neck and less impact at the nut. For an ideal setup, you might consider having a new nut fitted that's a little taller than the factory setup. This isn't essential (I've personally never changed the nut on my electric guitars), but it can help if you're struggling to get used to the lightness of touch required for this technique.

Acoustic or resonator guitars generally come out of the factory with a higher setup than electric guitars, so if you're using one, you will most likely be OK. Don't forget, however, that as your playing develops, fine-tuning your guitar setup can help to enhance your playing style.

Most players will use the slide in conjunction with fretted notes, so your action shouldn't be so high that fretting notes lower down becomes a Herculean task. If, on the other hand, you plan to use the slide only, there are some great products available such as the Grover Perfect Nut. This is a metal nut cover that sits over the top of your existing nut to raise the action of your strings to lap steel height.

Plucking the strings

Then there is the question of how you will use your picking hand. It is possible to use a pick, but using the thumb and fingers enables us to have much more control over techniques such as muting strings and controlling the tone being produced. When playing fingerstyle, it's possible to use the flesh of the fingers, or a combination of thumb pick and finger picks. Again, it all comes down to sound and feel. Using any sort of pick will give you a brighter attack on each note which may, or may not, be more desirable for your personal goals. As always, experiment and don't be afraid to stick to what works for you.

For reference, I recorded most of the audio for this book using a Tanglewood TMR Tricone resonator guitar. The heavy steel body results in a wonderfully unique tone that's hard to achieve on a traditional steel string guitar. The guitar was strung with D'Addario .013 – .056 gauge 80/20 Bronze strings, and was recorded with Shure SM57 and SM7b microphones.

Wearing the slide

While it's possible to adapt any of the ideas in this book to use a steel bar, it's assumed that 99% of readers will be playing with a slide designed to be placed on a finger. The first dilemma any aspiring slide player faces then, is which finger to place it on! For reasons that will become apparent when we get into the exercises, the index finger is not a good choice. That leaves the middle, ring and pinky fingers. I could name notable players as evidence of the superiority of each finger, but the truth is, there is no clear winner. Each option has its pros and cons and you'll quickly become comfortable with whichever you choose.

The sensible option is to try your slide on each finger and go with the one that feels most natural. I would suggest that, for the Delta blues style, the pinky is probably the wisest choice. It frees up three fingers to perform other tasks as needed.

I learned with the slide on my ring finger, then switched to my middle finger for many years. For the last 18 months or so I have tried to make my pinky finger the default. Nothing is set in stone and once you understand the technique required for slide, you should find adapting relatively simple.

Tuning

The final consideration for the aspiring slide guitar player is the tuning of the guitar itself. Playing slide guitar in standard tuning is perfectly possible, but a trickier prospect for the beginner, since you can't fret the slide and strum all six strings at once to make a pleasing sound. For this reason, early blues musicians opted for the classic *slack-key* open tunings, where the six strings are tuned to the notes of a chord. This way, when strummed, all of the notes are in key.

While it's possible to become proficient in many open tunings, it's more common for players to choose one to master. In this book we will focus mostly on open D, but we'll dabble in open G too. These are two of the most popular tunings amongst Delta blues musicians.

"Open D" tuning means that the strings are tuned to the notes of a D Major chord. D Major contains the notes D, F# and A. You can tune your guitar to open D as follows:

- Begin with standard tuning – E A D G B E
- Tune the low E string down a tone to D
- The A string stays the same (already in a D Major chord)
- The D string stays the same (already in a D Major chord)
- Tune the G string down a semitone to F#
- Tune the B string down a tone to A
- Tune the high E string down a tone to D

You're now tuned to open D tuning – D A D F# A D

It would be worth practising this by taking a guitar with standard tuning, tuning it to open D, then putting it back into standard tuning several times. This way you're getting an understanding of what the tuning name means and how to create it.

Here's an example of the six strings tuned to open D, played individually and then as a chord.

Example 1a:

Now that you understand how to tune to open D, open G should be fairly easy to achieve. A G Major chord contains the notes G, B and D.

- Begin with standard tuning – E A D G B E
- Tune the low E string down a tone to D
- Tune the A string down a tone to G
- The D string stays the same (already in a G Major chord)
- The G string stays the same (already in a G Major chord)
- The B string stays the same (already in a G Major chord)
- Tune the high E string down a tone to D

You're now tuned to open G tuning – D G D G B D.

Example 1b:

With that knowledge under your belt, it should be possible to tune your guitar to almost any chord by taking the notes of that chord and tuning your strings to the nearest pitch. For example, an E Major chord contains the notes E, G# and B, so open E tuning is E B E G# B E, and so on.

There are no rules for tunings, only what's common. When you hear someone say something like, "I tune to open C" this could mean different things to different people. Many players would assume it means C G C G C E, but I can think of players who tune to C G C E G C. Both are perfectly valid "open C" tunings.

Because of these possible tuning variations, I've opted to label everything in this book based on the string number rather than the note it's tuned to. This way there's no confusion when switching between tunings. Referring to the F# string in open D confuses me and I've been playing for a long time!

In this book, the highest tuned string is labelled the "first string", the next is the second string, then the third, and so on.

Chapter Two – Fretting With The Slide

This section teaches you great slide technique and how to produce clean, sustained notes. The lessons here will affect every single note you play, so work slowly through each example and try to match your sound to the downloadable audio tracks.

The first thing to understand is how to produce a note with the slide and make sure it's in tune. To do this, we must fully understand what the slide does and how it creates a pitch.

When I began playing slide, I assumed you used the slide to press the string down, as an alternative to the fretting finger. This couldn't be more misguided!

When fretting a note, we push the string down so that it comes into contact with the fret. The string will then vibrate from the fret to the bridge. The shorter this distance, the faster the string will vibrate and the higher the pitch it produces. When we fret a note with a finger, we can apply pressure anywhere between the adjacent fret wires and the string will touch the fret. But when we are using the slide, it must be placed exactly above the fret wire.

Using a slide is like controlling a moveable fret. The slide makes contact with the string and applies enough pressure so that the string vibrates between the slide and the bridge. I'll say it again: for a note to be in tune, the slide must be placed *exactly* over the fret.

In Example 2a I play the high D string open, then fret with the slide at the 12th fret – D an octave higher. To be in tune the slide must be positioned right where the string would touch the fret.

Example 2a:

Now listen to Example 2b. It's notated the same way, but on the audio I have positioned the slide halfway between the frets.

Example 2b:

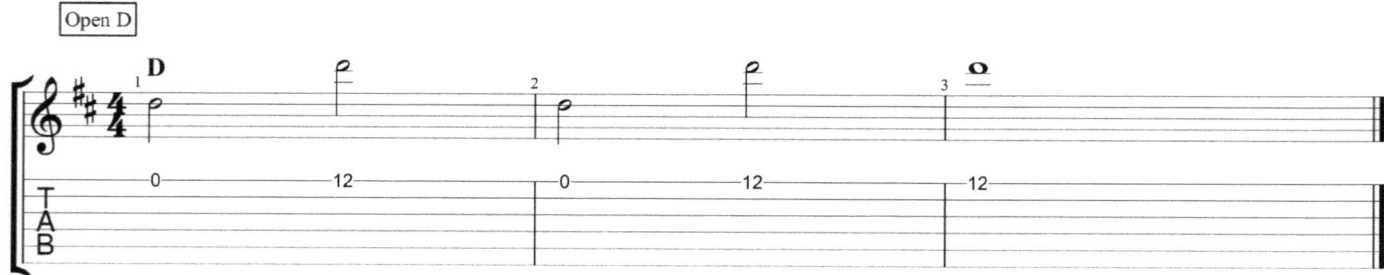

Now I'll address how I fret this note with the slide and what my other fingers are doing. When playing with a slide it's possible that the strings can vibrate between the slide and the bridge, *and* the slide and the nut. These "sympathetic" vibrations can occasionally be used to great effect, but 99% of the time they're undesirable. Therefore, it's important to use the fingers behind the slide as a mute by resting them on the strings to stop any unwanted vibrations.

Here's an example chord played at the 12th fret. I'll play it twice without any muting, then twice muting the strings behind the slide.

Example 2c:

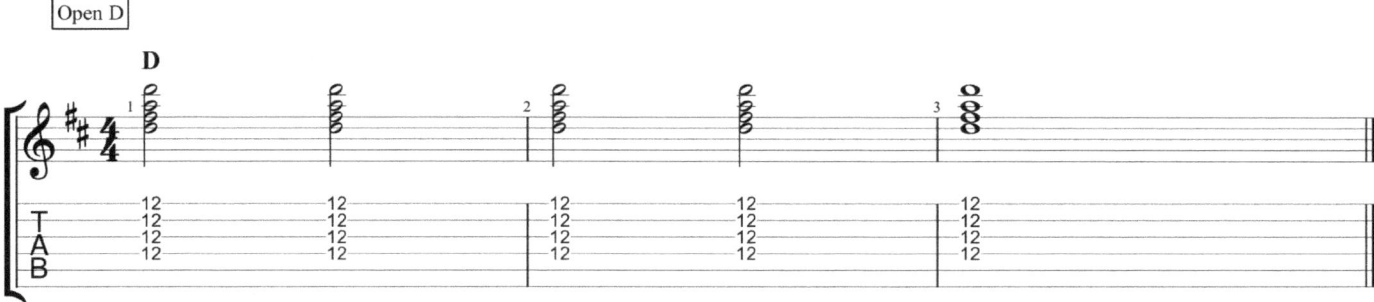

In this instance, the sympathetic vibrations are perfectly fine because the chord is played at the 12th fret – the halfway point of the neck – so the string will produce the same frequency in front and behind the string.

Now listen to this same exercise with a chord played at the 8th fret. The chord is lower, but the strings vibrating behind the slide are higher in pitch and clash with the notes we want the audience to hear. In this case muting is essential.

Example 2d:

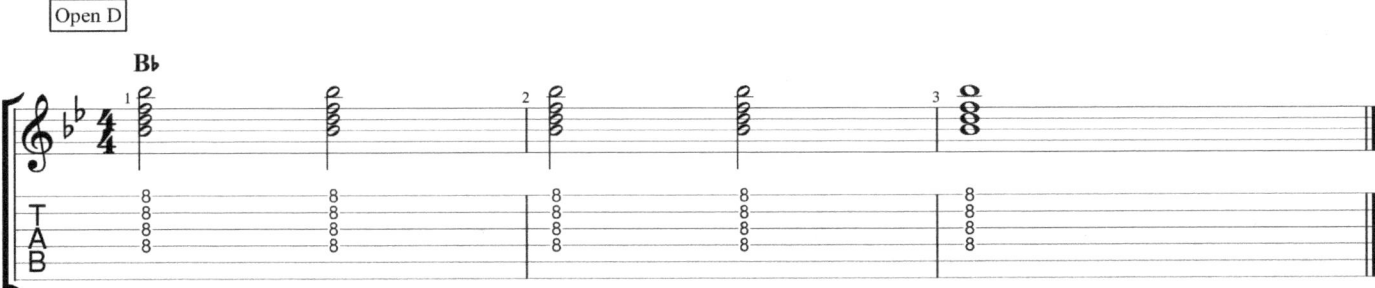

Muting behind the slide is an essential technique. It's not a rule, and some players would throw it right out the window, but muting will give you a cleaner, more focused sound. Not muting will result in a more raw, rough around the edges sound. But playing music is about expressing yourself, and it's great to have all the tools at your disposal.

Now you understand how to play notes that are in tune, the next step is to play a series of notes.

Example 2e moves between the 12th and 10th frets. At this stage, we are primarily concerned with the pitch accuracy of the notes. Listen to the audio and pay attention to exactly what it sounds like. Play the first note twice, then move to the next note by lifting the slide off the string. When doing this, use the plucking hand to mute the string so that the transition is clean.

Example 2e:

Here's another example, this time playing the full D Minor Pentatonic scale (D F G A C) on the high D string. (Obviously, this isn't particularly representative of Delta blues playing, but exercises like this are extremely valuable as they force us to concentrate on achieving good intonation. They're a valuable use of your time, so don't skip them!)

Example 2f:

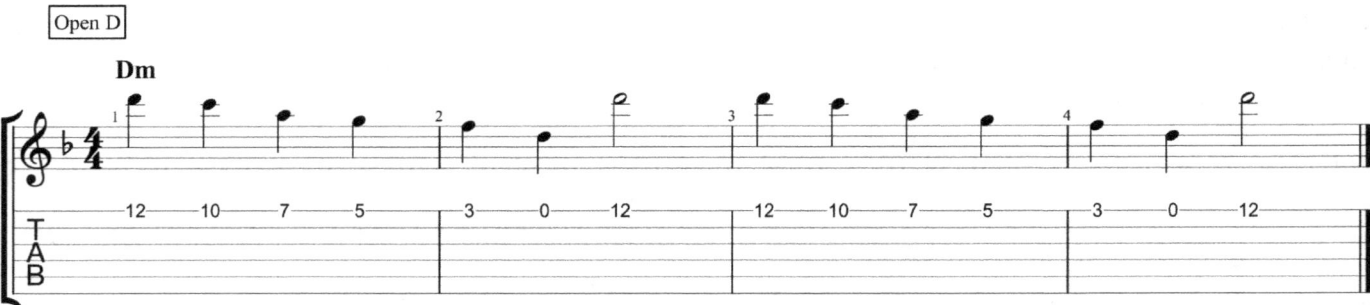

When playing an example like this I angle the slide so that it *only* makes contact with the high D string and avoids any extraneous noise from other strings.

In Example 2g, the same exercise is played on the second string. Here, the slide should be parallel to the strings and resting on most of them. Mute the surrounding strings to play this cleanly by resting the middle finger of the picking hand on the first string, and the thumb across the lower strings. Use the index finger to pluck the second string. This way it's impossible for any notes to ring out other than the one intended.

Example 2g:

The next example combines notes on the first and second strings. Here I use my thumb to mute the lower strings when playing on the high D string, and move the muting pattern over when changing string.

Example 2h:

Here's a lick that combines open and fretted notes with the slide. The difficulty here is getting used to the pressure required to make the notes sound clearly. Too little pressure and you'll get a buzz; too much and you'll be fretting the note on the fingerboard.

Example 2i:

Finally, here's a similar idea, but playing chords across four strings.

Example 2j:

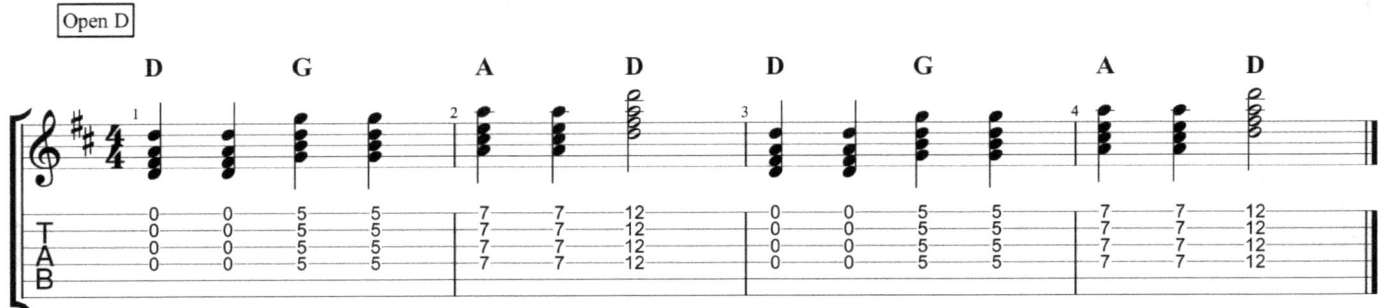

Spend some time moving around the neck and playing random notes, making sure they're in tune and sound clean. The skill you're learning here is helping to develop a feel for how much pressure is needed to get a good, clear note out of the guitar. It can take time, but it's important that this feels automatic.

Let's turn these exercises into a Delta-style riff. Remember, Delta songs were built around riffs like these that repeated for many bars (measures) without many chord changes or variation. It was very much a vocal style and the guitar simply provided a harmonic "bed" for the lyrics.

At first this might seem confusing, but when broken down, you'll notice that there's a driving eighth note rhythm being played, and the chords fit around the open, 5th and 7th frets (the I, IV and V respectively).

To make it sound more musical, I've added a D chord at the 12th fret and a bluesy chord at the 3rd fret when playing on the D chord. This isn't treated as a new chord, but used to add some melodic shape to the example.

Example 2k:

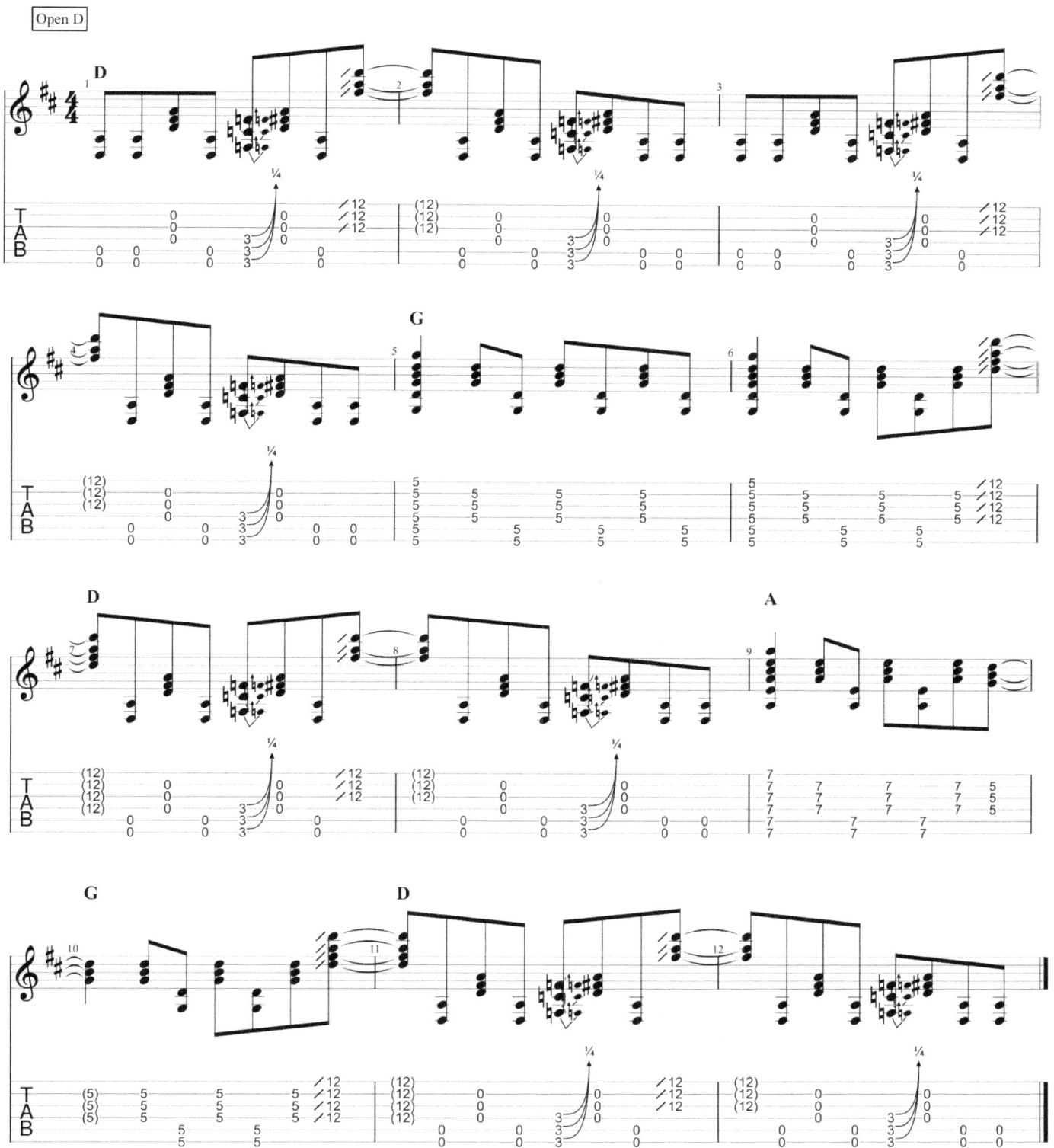

This next example is based on one of the many variations of an eight-bar blues. As the 12-bar hadn't become the norm yet, there was so standard form for a blues – it wasn't uncommon to find 11-bar blues progressions – the chords just tended to follow wherever the vocal led.

Here I've opted for a simple I, IV, V progression where the I is played for four bars, before moving to the IV, V and I for a bar each.

To keep you on your toes I've added a walk-up from the 2nd to the 5th fret in the fourth bar of the repeat. Small details like this can turn something that sounds like an exercise into something resembling music!

Example 2l:

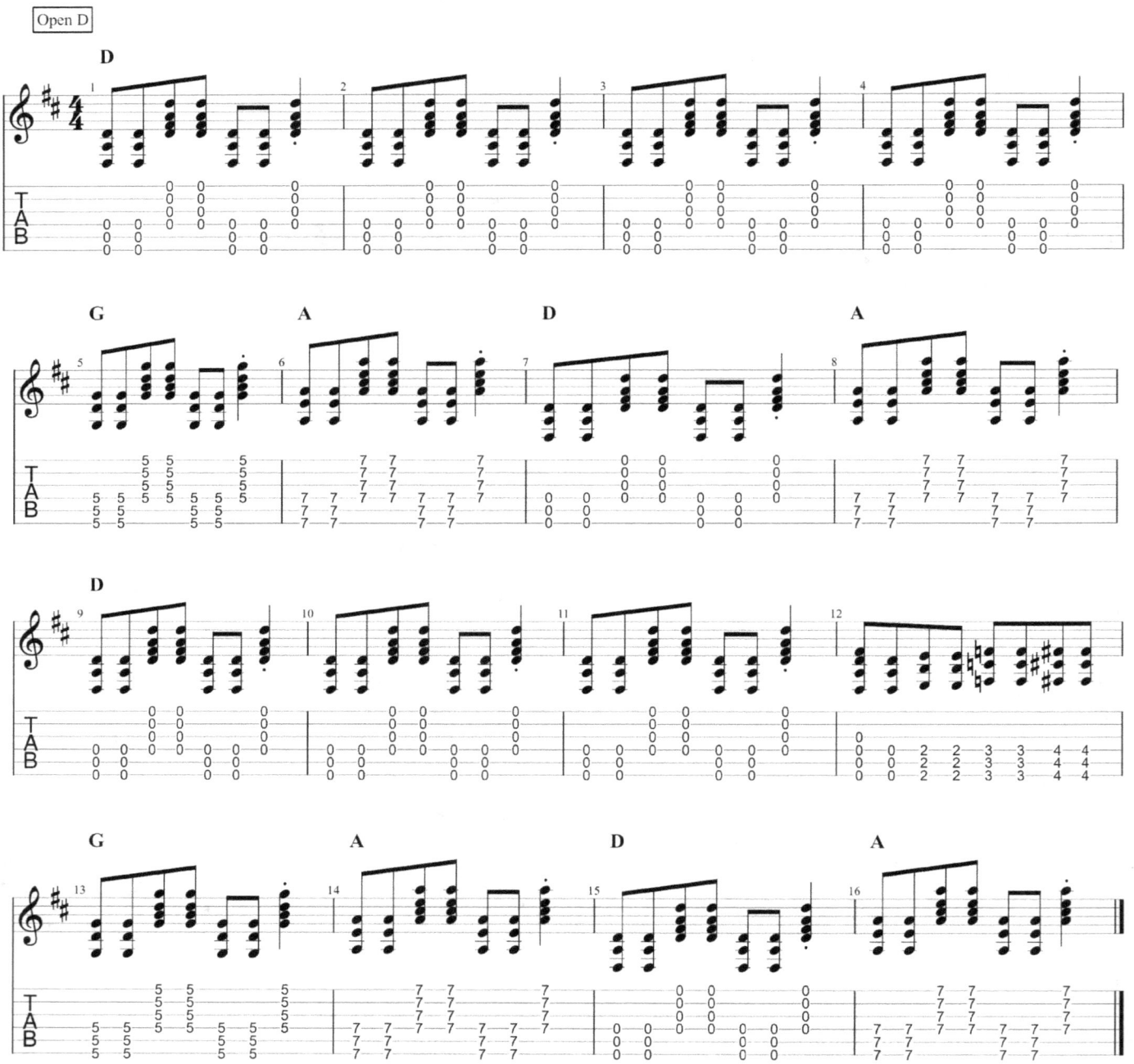

These two riffs were very basic and lacking a bit of finesse. In the next two chapters we'll look more at how to slide between notes cleanly and add the all-important vibrato.

Chapter Three – Sliding Between Notes

Now we've looked at the basics of fretting notes with the slide, we need to get to grips with the mechanics involved in sliding between notes.

It's important to keep applying pressure with the slide as you shift from one note to another. Don't squeeze the neck with your thumb, as the movement up and down the neck requires the whole arm to move, not just the wrist or finger.

Here's an example where I play a barred chord at the 3rd fret and slowly slide it up to the 12th. This slide can be played at any speed, but for technique practice, begin slowly and get used to the pressure required on the string to keep the note even. This example highlights one of the more nuanced aspects of slide guitar and shows how standard notation can be lacking when describing it. There's no way to indicate quickly you should slide, so use the audio recording as a guide to how it should sound.

Example 3a:

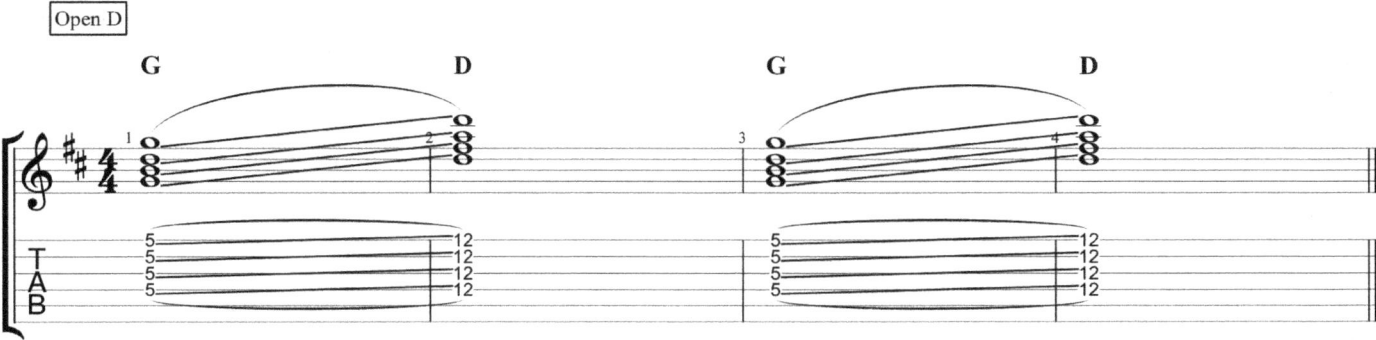

In the following single note lick, I slide between the notes quite quickly. Scalar ideas like this are common among slide players. The slide lends itself to playing lines that move up and down one string, rather than across many strings.

Example 3b:

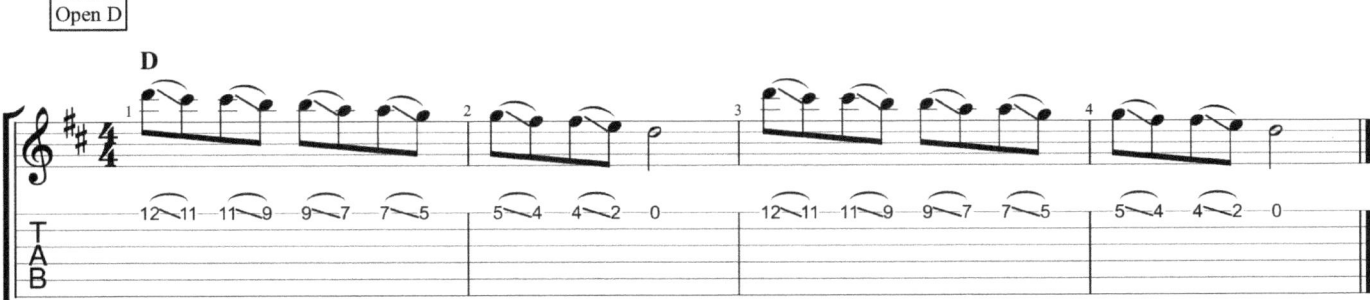

Here's a similar idea, but one that makes bigger shifts around the neck and has notes going both up and down.

Example 3c:

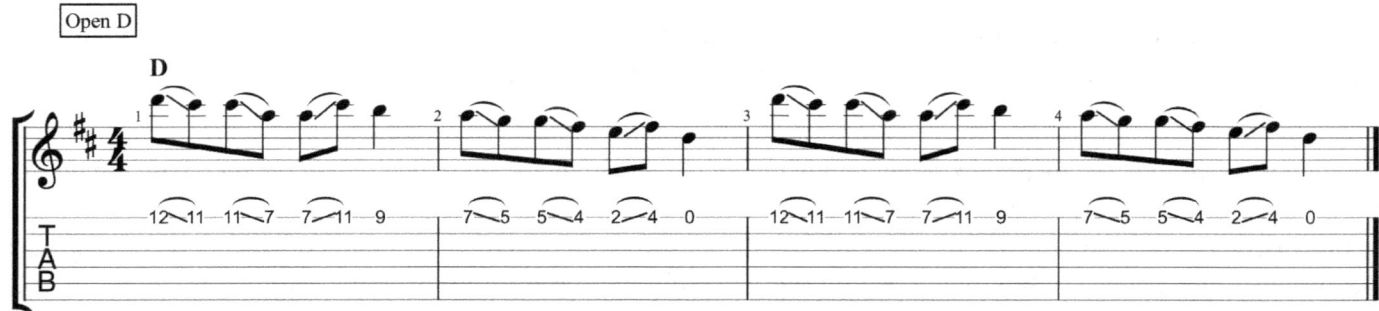

The next example begins with a *grace note* – a quick note played just before the main note. In this case, the 10th fret is played, followed by an immediate slide up to the 12th. Grace notes are a great way to add expression and note articulation.

Example 3d:

To demonstrate how grace notes can bring a melody to life, here's a melody played without any articulation. This example has a gospel hymn feel to it – something that will have been common in the Delta at the time.

Example 3e:

Now here is the same melody with added grace notes to make it considerably more expressive.

Example 3f:

Slides can be used in a similar way to bending fretted notes. They allow us to start taking advantage of the microtonal options offered by a slide.

When notating these in tab, I'll use the bend symbol for illustration purposes, but we are using the slide to raise the pitch of the note. In the following example, play the 3rd fret, and then gradually slide the note so that it's a little sharp. This creates an authentic bluesy quality.

Example 3g:

Here's another idea with those bluesy slide bends played on several strings. Focus on keeping the muting as tight as possible at first, but then just go for it when playing and let some of the notes ring out.

Example 3h:

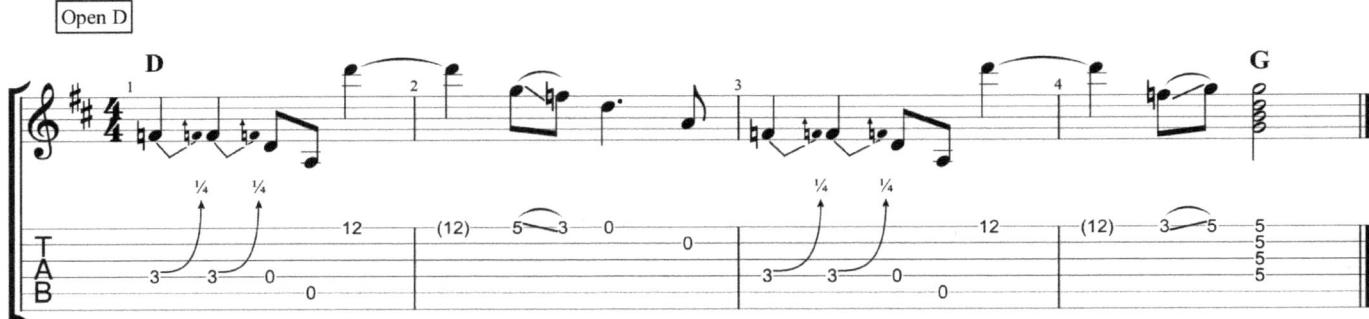

Another common sound you'll hear from any slide player is a wild slide from below into a note or chord. This is slightly different to a grace note, as the pitch you are sliding from isn't specified and may begin anywhere on the neck.

In the following example, strike the strings with the slide anywhere low on the neck and slide up to the 12th fret.

Example 3i:

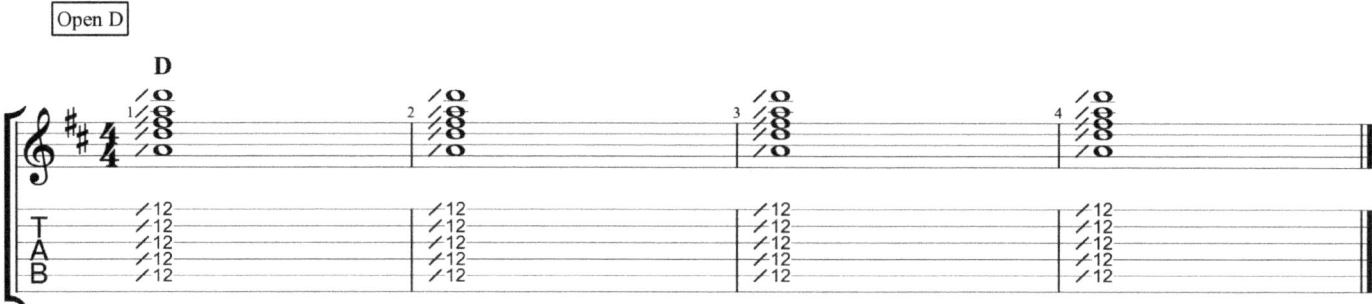

Here's a melody at the low end of the neck that slides up to the 12th fret. After repeating this idea three times, the lick ends by sliding into an A Major chord at the 7th fret.

Example 3j:

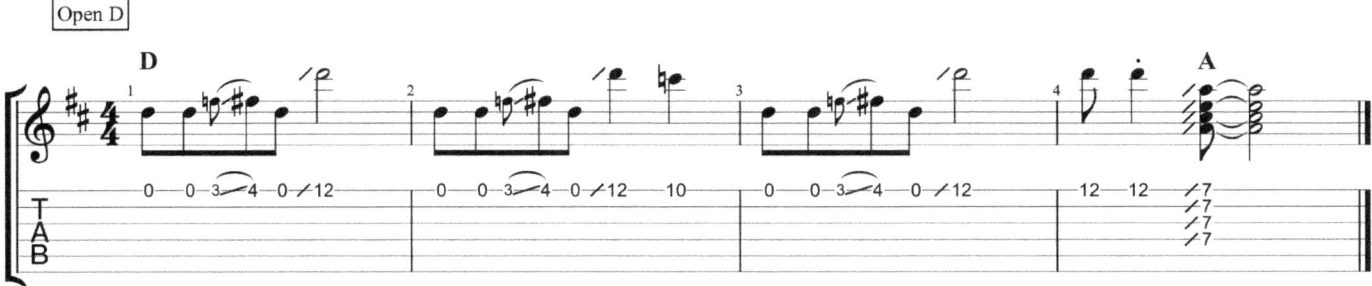

These subjects will be revisited in much more detail throughout the book, but the examples in this section will help you get the fundamentals of the style down, so that musical ideas can be fully formed later.

Now, let's jump into the wonderful subject of vibrato.

Chapter Four – Vibrato

The word *vibrato* comes from the Italian word for vibrate and refers to any variation of pitch applied to a note. As a tool, vibrato helps to give a performer a way of adding personal expression to a note, and the importance of this can't be understated.

On an instrument such as piano, vibrato isn't an option and every note is mechanically in tune (assuming you have a good piano tuner!). With slide guitar, however, it's easy to play notes that are slightly out of tune – and a note that is slightly out is often much worse than a wrong note. One of the benefits of vibrato on slide guitar is that any minor pitching inconsistencies are masked.

So far we've been working on playing notes with no vibrato and there is a good reason for this: our aim is always to apply vibrato to a *good note*, not use it to hide the fact that we can't find the note we're aiming for!

Think of the notes you play as your speech, and the vibrato as the accent you use. Other people may use the same words as you, but the way in which *you* say them is unique. Similarly, you will develop your own style of vibrato that is unique to you; your calling card.

The technique used to apply vibrato is the same as sliding up and down the neck, but this time limited to a smaller area.

In Example 4a I begin with a full chord without vibrato then, as the note progresses, I begin subtly shaking my arm from left to right, gradually moving it wider as the note continues. This isn't the way all vibrato should take shape, but it's a good way to begin practising and understanding the technique.

Example 4a:

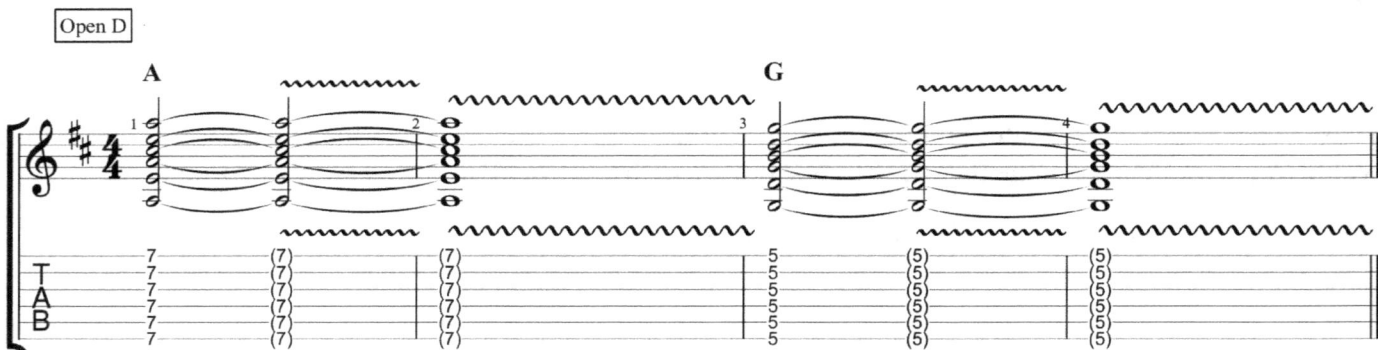

Here's a riff-based idea that begins on the lower part of the neck with a bluesy bend at the 3rd fret. It then slides up to the 12th fret on the higher strings with some wild vibrato. Playing something like this without the vibrato would sound sterile. In fact, after hearing these types of ideas *with* vibrato, the ideas in the previous chapters may sound a little off!

Example 4b:

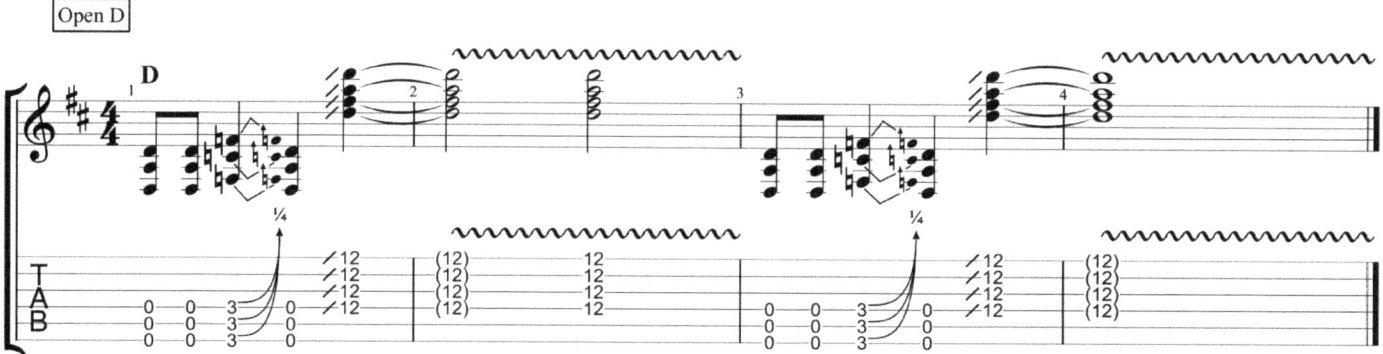

To demonstrate this, I've rerecorded Example 2n, but added a lyrical vibrato on the longer notes. Now it's starting to sound like real music.

Example 4c:

Vibrato is an extremely difficult subject to cover in text form, as it's hard to conceptualize and demonstrate. In fact, it's often overlooked even when learning by ear. When describing vibrato to students, I find it best to help people to visualise it.

The following diagrams demonstrate this idea. The straight line represents the intended pitch, and the wavy line shows how the vibrato looks around the pitch.

This first diagram illustrates how vibrato sounds when played with the fingers on guitar. It's not possible to lower the pitch below the note you're fretting, so the vibrato rises above the note, then returns to pitch, and the pattern continues.

On the other hand, if vibrato was applied using a tremolo arm, the pitch would dip, then return.

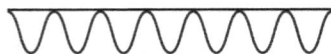

When playing with a slide, however, it's possible to apply vibrato that goes both *above* and *below* the main pitch, which might look something like this.

When you listen to a great singer, you'll notice that the voice tends to dip below the pitch before settling, then goes a little over the pitch before repeating. Imitating this using a slide results in an extremely musical vibrato that "surrounds" the note, without abandoning the vocal-like quality we hear from great soul singers, for instance.

In the following example, I demonstrate the difference between these vibratos. It's subtle, so it may take a while to really spot the difference.

Example 4d:

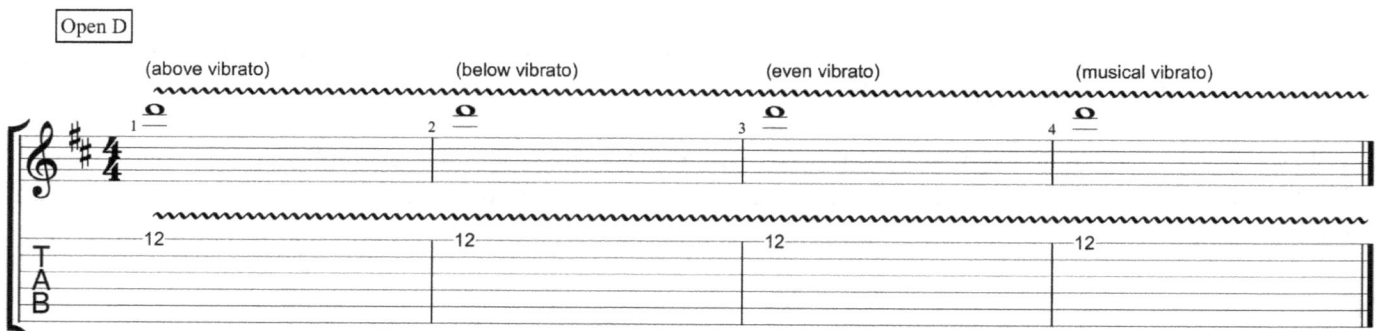

So far we have only scratched the surface of what's possible. There are many variables at play in vibrato and it's impossible to discuss each eventuality. We've looked at how vibrato can be used to *surround* the pitched note. How wide and fast our vibrato should be depends on the musical context in which it's being used.

Adding vibrato also comes down to taste. Some players have a naturally wide, slow vibrato, while others use a narrower, fast vibrato. Some will only apply vibrato to longer, sustained notes, while others apply a frantic vibrato to every note! It's all about experimentation and finding what you like the sound of.

These concepts aren't something I constantly think about when playing – it's a technique I practised in isolation until it became automatic. Now, vibrato is something I add to notes when I feel it's needed. The main thing is to focus on how *musical* your vibrato sounds. Listen to the great players and try to sound more like them.

Chapter Five – Open Tuning Scales

One of the quickest ways to learn an open tuning is to understand how each string functions in relation to the chord the guitar is tuned to. This makes it easy to transpose riffs and licks into new keys.

In open D tuning, the guitar is tuned to a D Major chord that contains the notes D (the root), F# (the 3rd) and A (the 5th). We can view the note on each open string according to its interval in relation to the root:

6th string D = Root

5th string A = 5th

4th string D = Root

3rd string F# = 3rd

2nd string A = 5th

1st string D = Root

Here's that information displayed in notation and tab, with the interval indicated above the notation.

Example 5a: (Notes at 12th fret are identical to notes on open string)

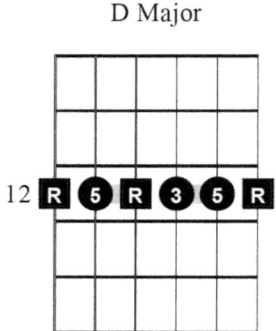

Playing the open strings or placing the slide directly over the 12th fret allows you to access all the "safe" notes of the chord. But what other notes can we add to this diagram to make music?

With a bit of knowledge about which scales best create the sound of the Delta blues, we can start to piece together a "map" of notes on the guitar that shows the best notes to use in our playing. This map can be used to construct riffs, licks and fills, and as the basis for your own song writing and improvisation.

Early Delta pioneers were probably not thinking about scales, but if we reverse-engineer their music we find that most of what they played was formed from what we now think of as the Mixolydian mode and the Blues scale.

Bear with me while we work though a little bit of music theory to create a useful map of the best notes to use when playing Delta blues. If you want to skip ahead, you'll see a diagram below that you can use immediately.

The D Blues Scale has the formula R b3 4 b5 5 b7 and contains the notes (D F G Ab A C)

D Mixolydian mode has the formula R 2 3 4 5 6 b7 and contains the notes (D E F# G A B C)

By combining these scales formulas we can create a hybrid-scale of intervals, all of which will work well over a D7 chord. They are:

R 2 b3 3 4 b5 5 6 b7 (D E F F# G Ab A B C).

All these notes sound great in the context of a Delta blues.

When we place some of these extra notes onto the guitar neck, something very interesting happens; they all lie two frets below the original "home" barre chord slide position.

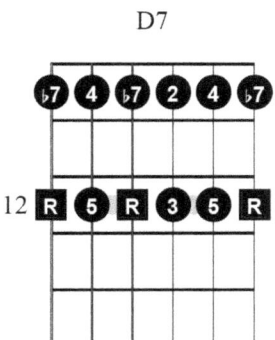

So, when playing a song in open D, we can place the slide at the 12th fret, and all the notes two frets lower are available as melodic embellishment when improvising or writing.

Here's a lick that uses this concept in its most basic form, using the 12th fret as "home" and sliding from two frets below.

Example 5b:

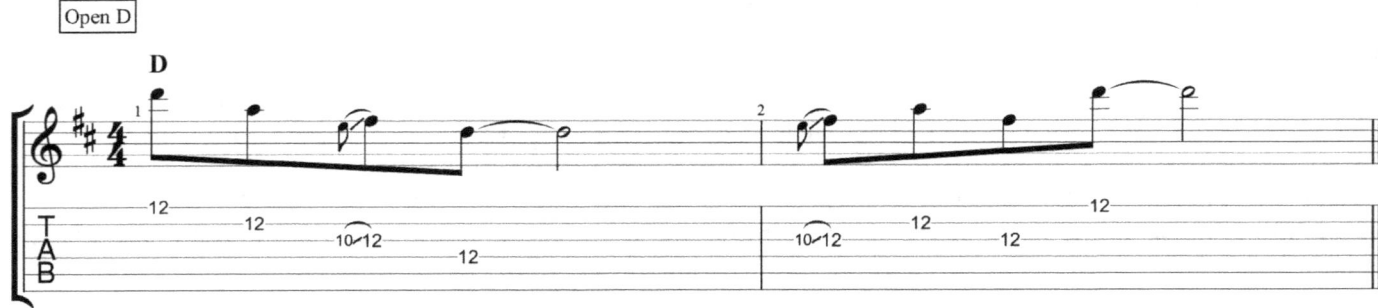

This concept makes it easy to outline chord changes, as demonstrated in the next example.

The "home" slide position can be moved onto any fret to outline any major chord. If you place it on the 7th fret you will play an A Major, and if you place it on the 5th fret you will outline a G Major chord.

In open D tuning, it's useful to remember that the root notes of chords on the sixth string are two frets above where they would be in standard tuning.

Example 5c:

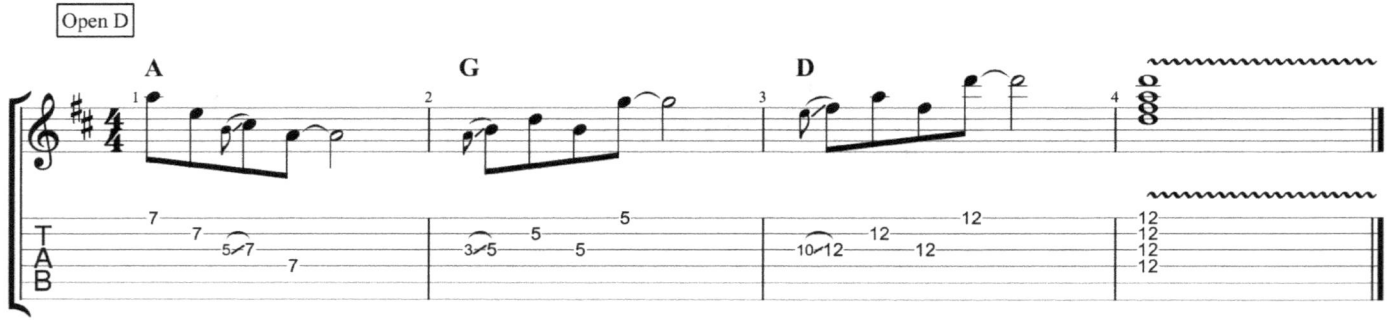

Here's another lick that uses slides on the top three strings.

Example 5d:

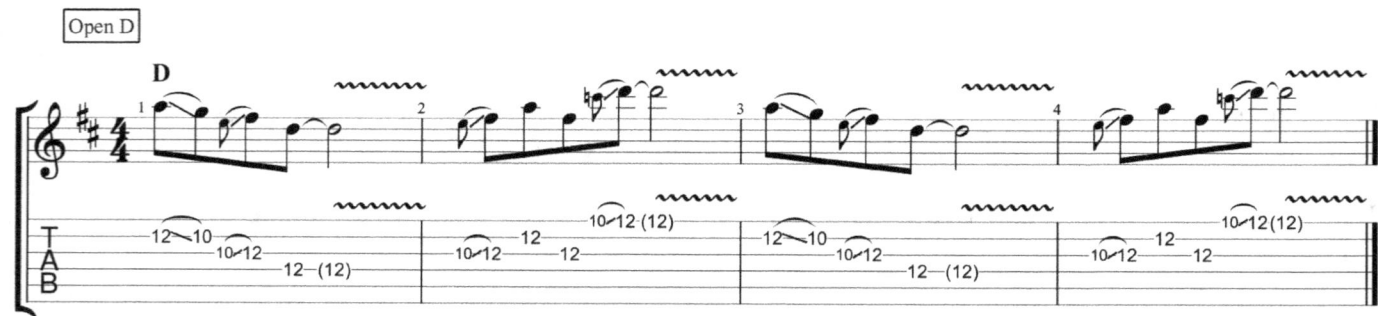

The secret to using this pattern effectively is understanding that the upper slide position is "home" and the notes two frets lower are used embellish the chord. It's rarely pleasing to rest on the lower notes. Instead, they should be viewed as tension notes which are then resolved by sliding up two frets.

Obviously, this idea can easily be expanded by adding more notes above and below the home position, but it's incredible to see just how little the real Delta blues players needed to do that. There's plenty of music to be found just using this box pattern.

Melodic Notes in Open G Tuning

Now we've had a brief look at open D, let's jump to open G tuning and see if there's any common ground we can take advantage of.

As discussed in the first chapter, open G tuning from low to high is:

D G D G B D

G Major is made up of G (Root), B (3rd) and D (5th). The intervals of open G tuning are:

5 R 5 R 3 5

Here's that information displayed in notation and tablature.

Example 5e:

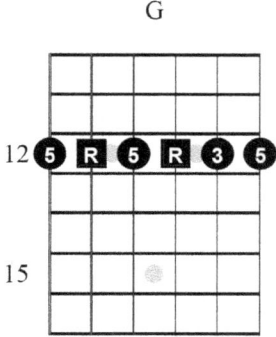

Again, all the notes of the chord are available as a barre with the slide at the 12th fret. Notice that the intervals are in a different order from open D tuning.

The interesting thing about open G tuning is that the lowest string isn't the root of the chord but rather the 5th. For this reason some players, such as Keith Richards of The Rolling Stones, have opted to remove the sixth string altogether.

Again, we can add some of the notes from the hybrid scale and once again, they appear two frets below the home chord.

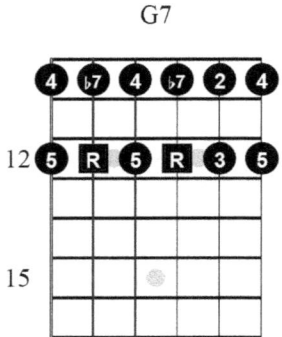

There are obvious similarities between open D and open G when compared in terms of their intervals. The two tunings are almost identical, but open D has an additional high note and open G has an additional low note.

I personally prefer open D over open G. It provides a little more low range (as the root is lower in pitch than in open G), and it also contains a root on the first string can give a great resolution to Delta blues melodies.

That said, it's easy to adapt to open G tuning quickly if we understand the intervals.

To demonstrate, here's the lick from Exercise 5d, but now played in open G tuning.

In the second bar, we don't have the option to jump up to the root on the high string, so this same note is played an octave lower on the third string.

Example 5f:

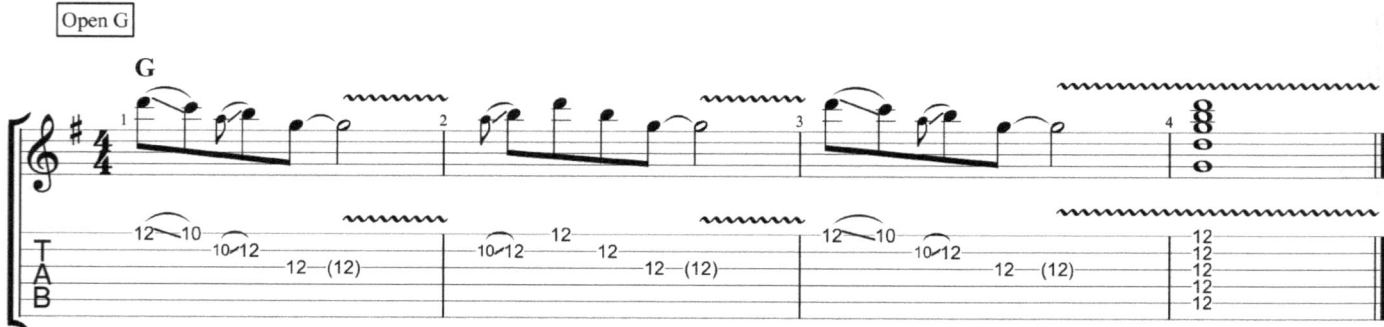

Let's extend the notes in open G tuning with another note from the hybrid scale, the 6th. The 6th is one tone higher than the 5th and sounds great when added above the highest note.

Let's also add the 4th above the 3rd on the second string.

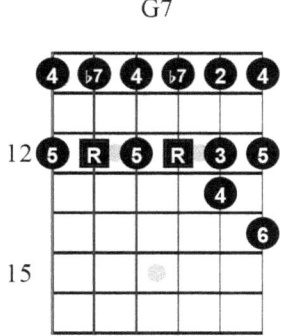

Here's a lick that uses these notes. As with earlier examples, the additional notes are used to create melodies that resolve to home notes of the chord on the 12th fret.

Example 5g:

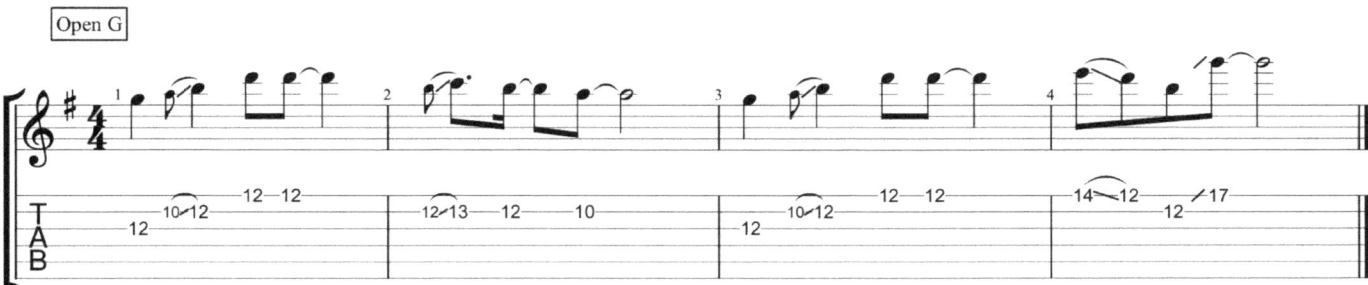

This idea can be expanded to build up a box patterns akin to those you probably visualize when playing fretted guitar in standard tuning. There is some benefit to this, but it's more common to play up and down one string rather than across the neck.

You may have noticed that we didn't really use the b3 or b5 of the hybrid scale in this chapter. These notes will come into their own as we start to explore the more traditional slide approach of one string playing.

Chapter Six – One String Scales

A useful way of getting to grips with slide technique and phrasing is to practise scales on a single string. While the ideas start off as exercises, they quickly become musical and applicable to Delta blues playing.

While this can be done anywhere, it's best to begin on the strings tuned to the root of the chord. Here's the D Major scale (D E F# G A B C#) played on the first string in open D tuning. Make sure you're playing directly over each fret and muting behind the slide. Play along with the audio track to check your intonation.

Example 6a:

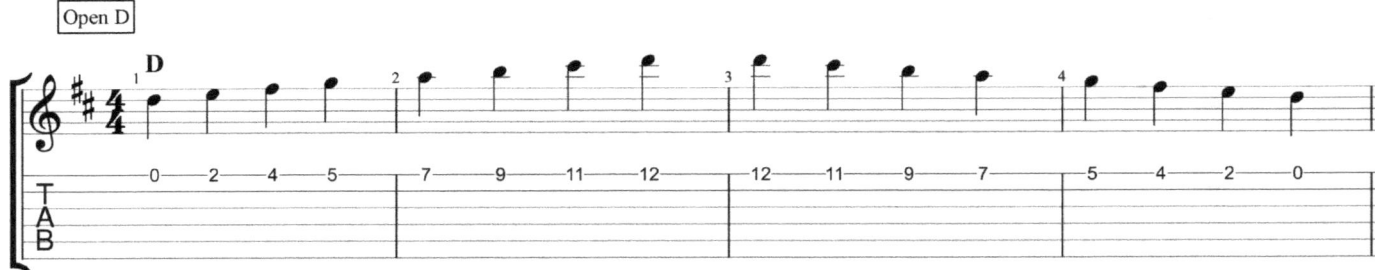

Here's the same scale played using a little more slide phrasing and articulation.

Example 6b:

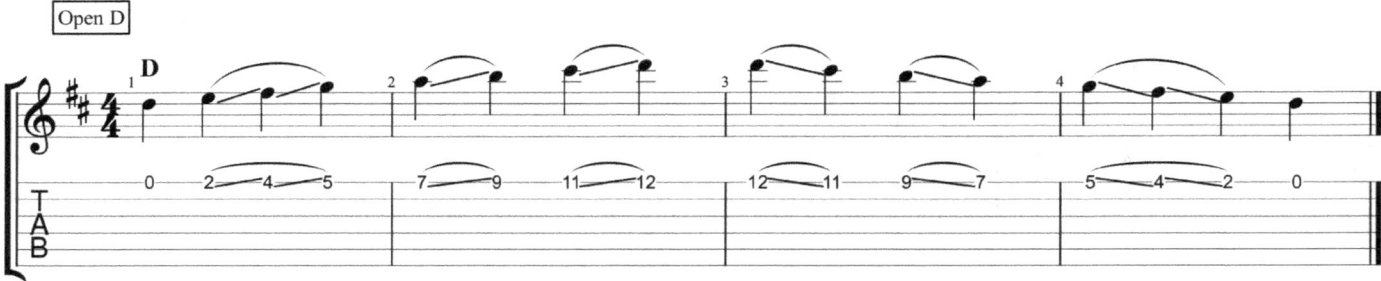

This same pattern will work on any string tuned to the root of the chord, so in open D, the same thing will work on the fourth string.

Example 6c:

The same fingering will also work on the sixth string.

Example 6d:

The Major scale is useful, but the Mixolydian mode is a scale that is suitable for playing Delta ideas over a Dominant 7 chord. It has the formula 1 2 3 4 5 6 b7.

Here's the D Mixolydian mode (D E F# G A B C) played on the first string. The only change from the Major scale is that the 7th degree of the Major scale is lowered by a semitone.

Example 6e:

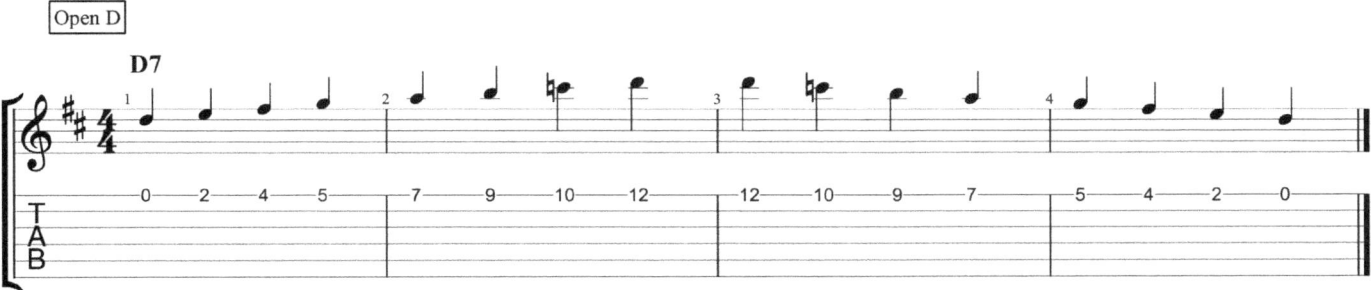

This pattern can be played on each open D string. Here's the first and fourth string combined and played as octaves. This is a common approach among Delta blues players but don't forget to practise each string individually too.

Use the thumb and index finger to pluck the notes together in a pinching motion.

Example 6f:

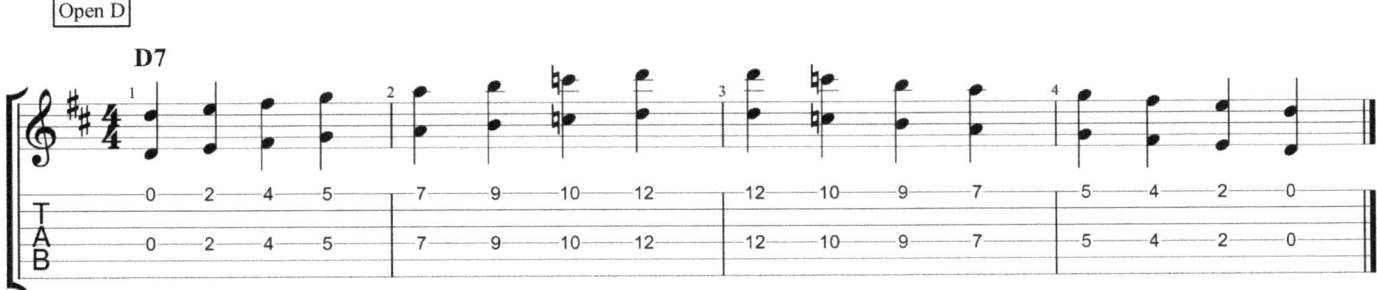

Another common sound in Delta blues is the Major Pentatonic scale. This is a five-note scale consisting of the Root, 2 3 5 and 6. (D, E, F#, A and B in the key of D)

As it's missing that dark sounding b7 (C), the Major Pentatonic creates a softer sound that's heard in music all over the world.

Example 6g:

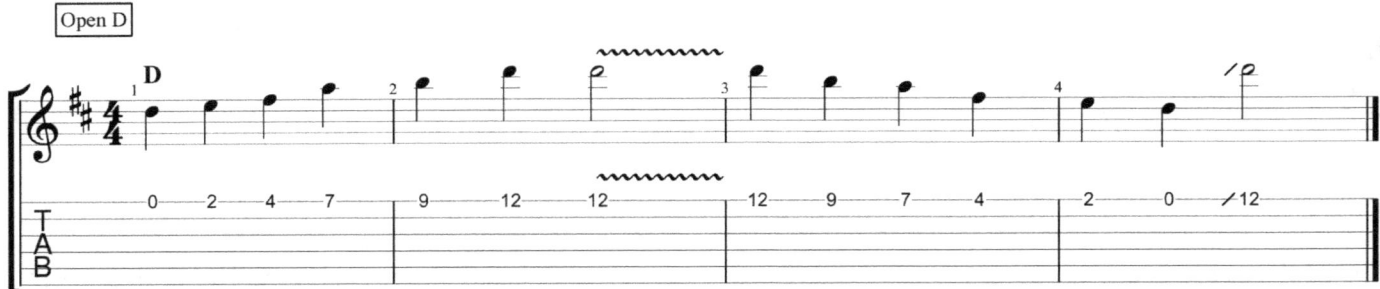

In the previous chapter, we built a hybrid scale that contained a b3 interval. It's common to add the b3rd (F) to this Major Pentatonic scale as a bluesy approach to the natural 3rd (F#).

Example 6h:

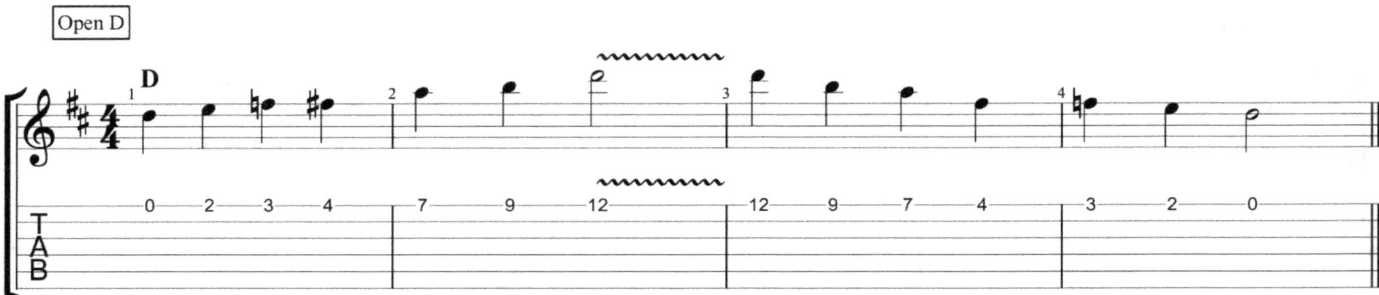

Here's a lick using the Major Pentatonic scale with the added b3. A common approach is to descend to the b3 (F) and move up to the natural 3 (F#). This makes the F# (a note that's in the chord) feel specifically targeted after playing the b3 (F) which isn't in the D Major chord.

Example 6i:

This difference between the darker b7th (C) and the sweeter 6th (B) is a subtle, but one that can be used to control the mood of the music.

For example, the following lick is the same as Example 6i, but plays the b7 instead of the 6 in bar three.

Play both of these ideas and compare the difference in sound. There are no right answers, it's all about building your own understanding of how your note choice affects the music.

Example 6j:

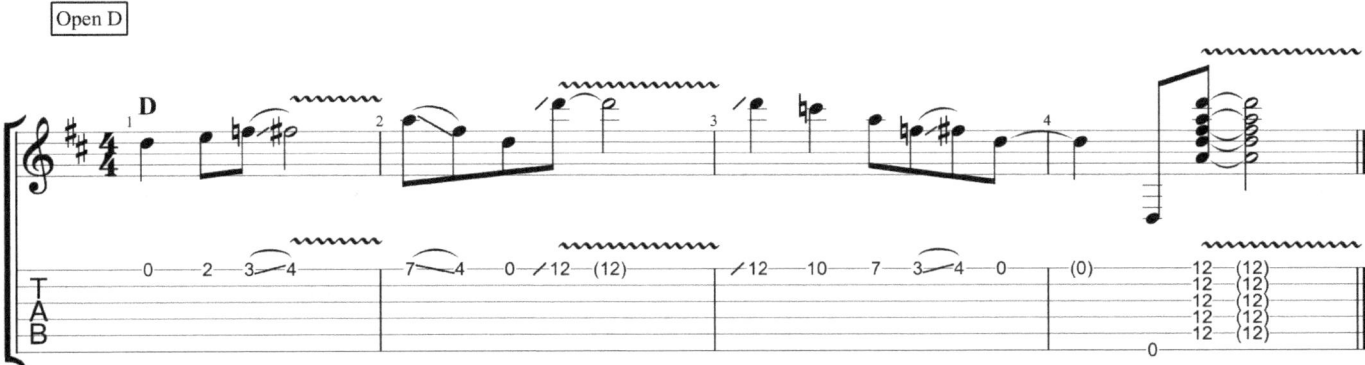

The Minor Pentatonic scale is very common in blues music. Like the Major Pentatonic scale, it is also a five-note scale, but with a different set of intervals. This time it's Root b3 4 5 b7 (D F G A C).

Here's that scale played on the first string. This scale "fits" a D Minor chord, but it's still a common choice on a major or dominant chord, where it has a rootsy, blues sound.

Example 6k:

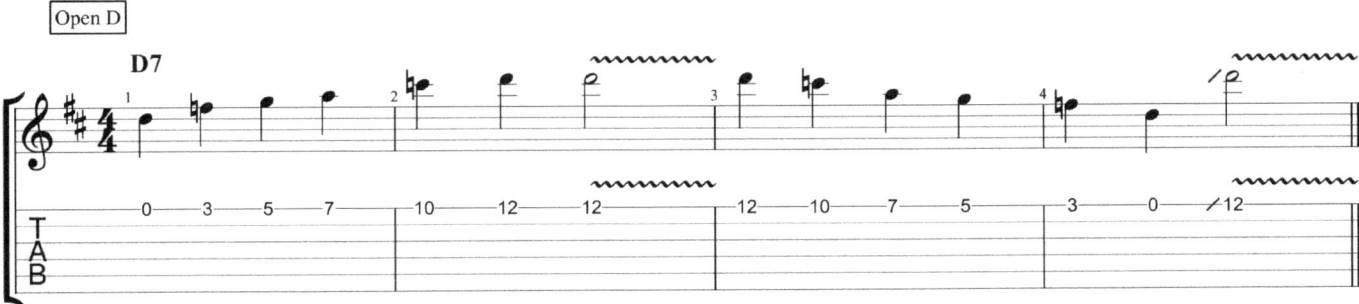

It's common to add a quarter tone bend (often referred to as a "blues curl") to the b3rd in a blues. This puts the note somewhere between the F and F#, which is an important blues idiosyncrasy. It hints at the b3 to natural 3rd movement we discussed in Example 6i.

Play the scale with the added blues curl by moving the slide slightly up the neck towards the 4th fret after playing the 3rd. Don't go all the way to the 4th fret though, just hint at it.

Example 61:

An important exercise you can practise with single-string scales will develop your control of *pull-offs* from notes fretted with the slide to an open string. The idea is to pull-off with the slide and sound the open string.

As the slide can't pull off from the note in the same way as your finger tip normally would, the secret is to flick the slide downwards off the string towards the floor.

Take this example slowly because getting this technique accurate will be extremely useful down the road. Listen to the audio so you know what sound you are aiming for.

Example 6l2:

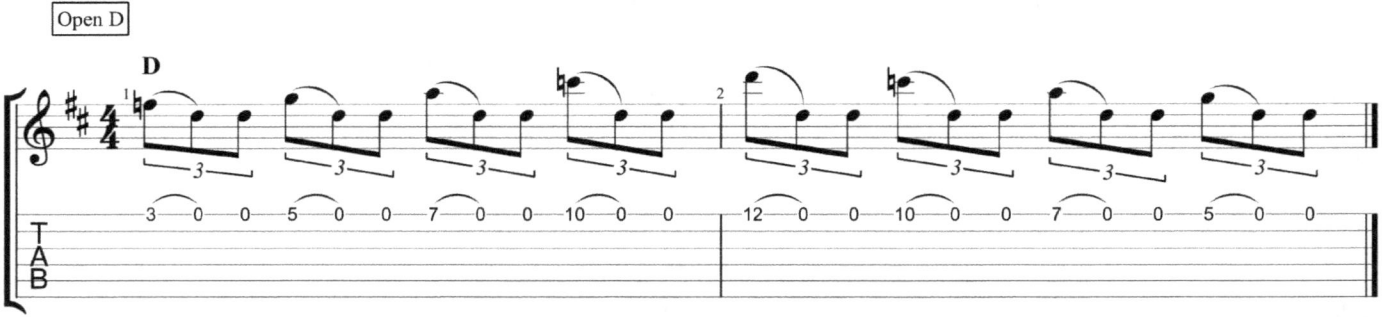

While playing slide in open tunings is a lot easier and more common, many Delta players (including Robert Johnson) also played in standard tuning occasionally. All the ideas in this section can be applied to standard tuning too. For example, playing Example 6l in standard tuning will result in the E Minor Pentatonic scale.

Example 6m:

The Blues scale is a common scale created by adding a b5 to the Minor Pentatonic scale: 1 b3 4 b5 5 b7. The b5 was included in our hybrid scale in the previous chapter.

Here's the Blues scale played on the first string in open D tuning.

Example 6n:

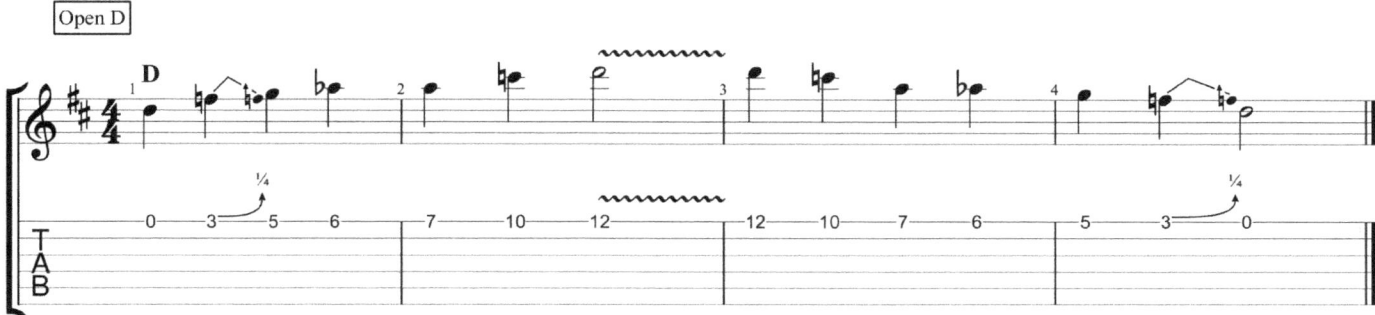

The next lick uses the Blues scale. Listen out for the b5 at the end of the first bar. This Blind Willie Johnson style lick uses the b5 blues note to imitate what the voice is singing.

As you become more comfortable with the idea, hum along as you play. This will connect your ears and fingers, and aid your musical expression.

Example 6o:

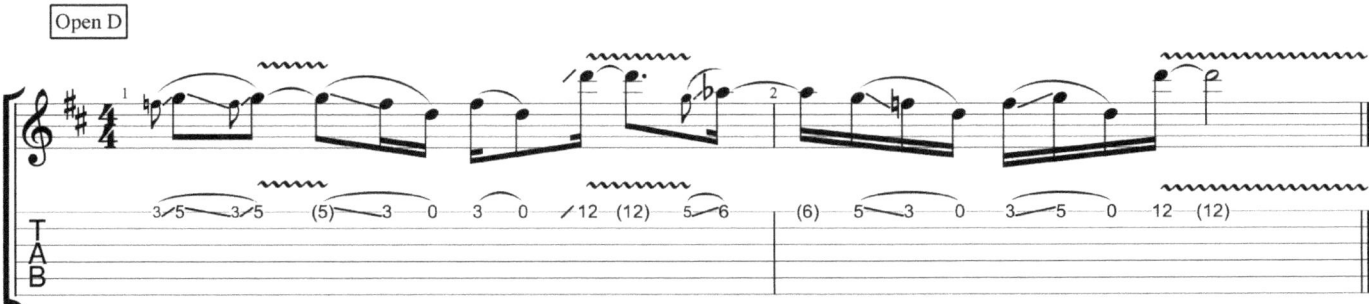

Here's a second lick on the first string using notes of the D blues scale. The possibilities are endless!

Example 6o2

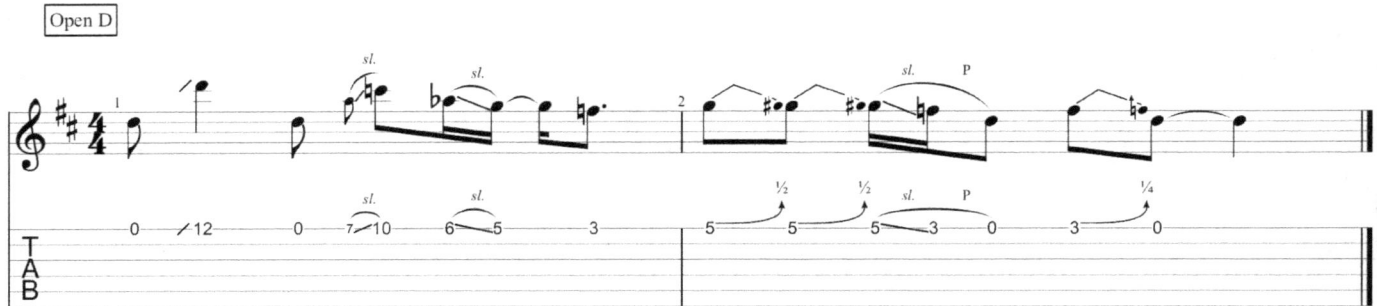

Come up with your own phrases using the D Blues scale on one string.

Next, I've written a lick inspired by Tampa Red. While there are fewer notes here, there are some rapid shifts from the 12th fret to the 3rd that need to be handled with care. You don't want to overshoot the slides as no amount of vibrato will cover that up.

Example 6p:

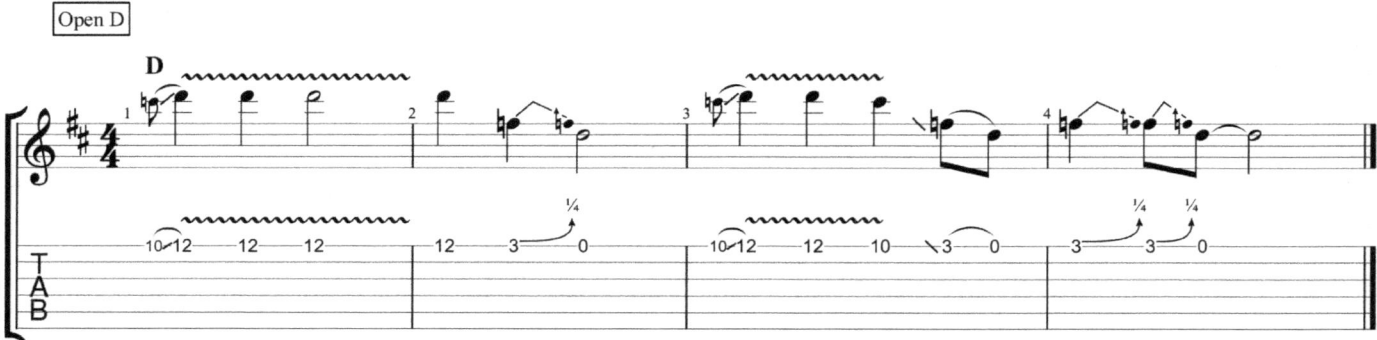

The final line in open D is a Bukka White-inspired lick that adds the open second string.

The hardest part comes in the second bar where we're required to slide from the 5th to the 7th fret, then to the 3rd fret before pushing that note slightly sharp. Again, a bend like this is created by moving the slide very slightly up the fretboard.

Listen to the audio recording and it will all make sense.

Example 6q:

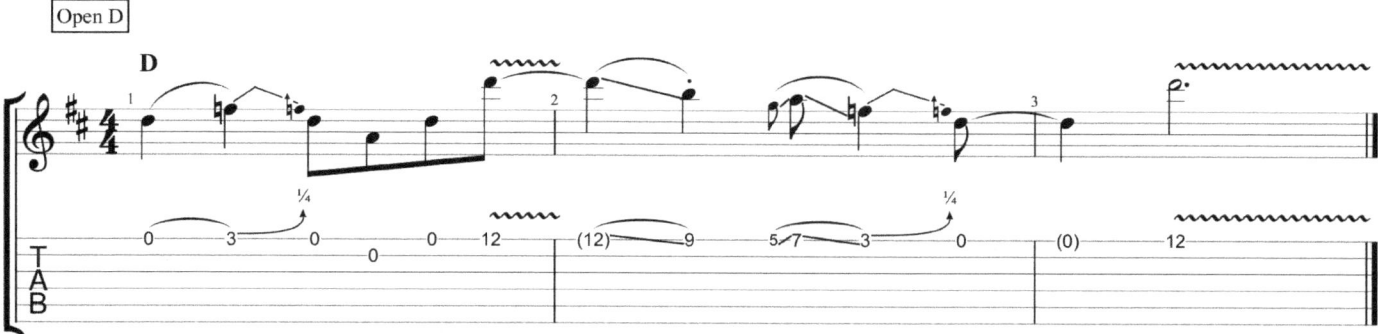

With some open D vocabulary under your belt, let's look at some single-string open G lines too.

The first thing to get used to in open G is that the root note now sits at the 5th fret on the first string. This is great because you can now play the root note and add some expressive vibrato.

Example 6r:

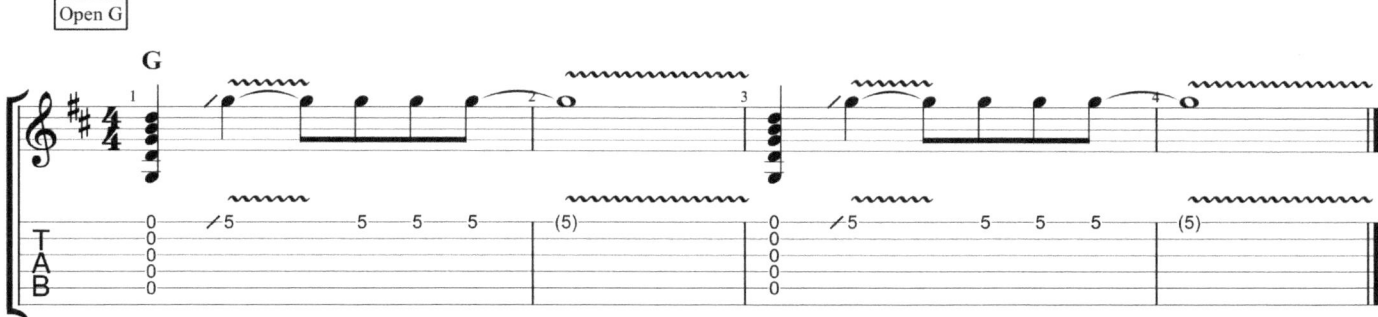

The b3 is three frets above the root and the b7 is two frets below the root. These two notes are integral to the sound of the Minor Pentatonic scale and are extremely expressive.

Example 6s:

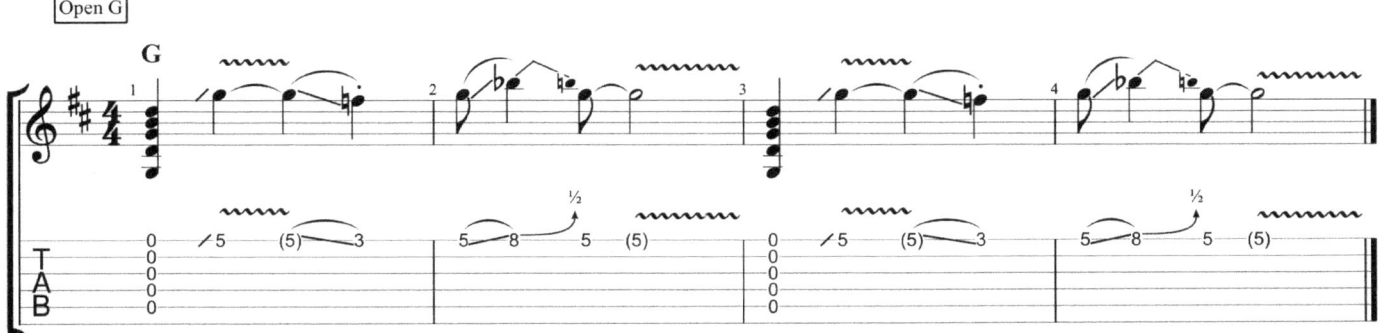

Sliding up to the 5th of the chord on the 12th fret is another strong, commonly heard sound in Delta blues. In the following example I move from the 5th to the b5 and back to really milk that powerful blues quality.

Example 6t:

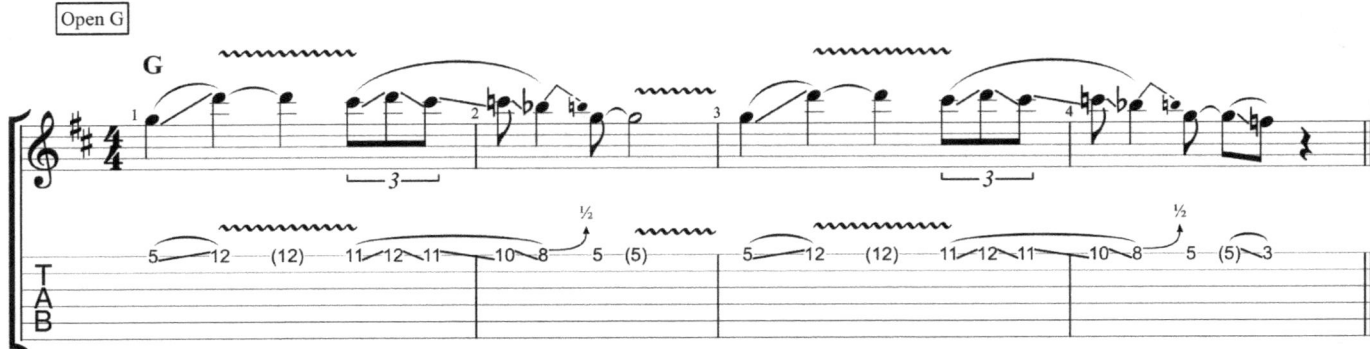

Here's another idea that ascends the first string while sliding into each note. Listen closely to the recording as this melody is all about the slides rather than perfect intonation and accuracy.

Example 6u:

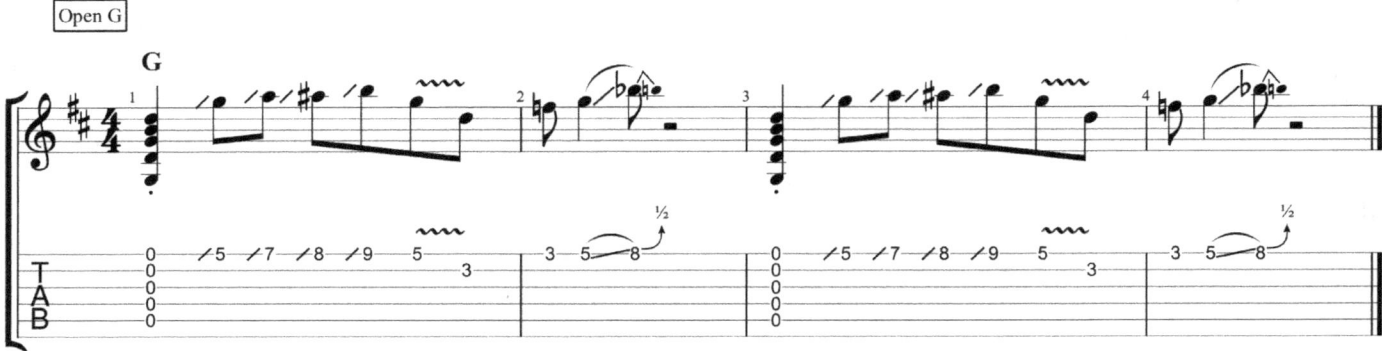

Finally, here's a lick in G Major that uses most of the notes at your disposal over the entire span of the octave. Take it slowly and experiment with the articulation to make it expressive and personal.

Example 6v:

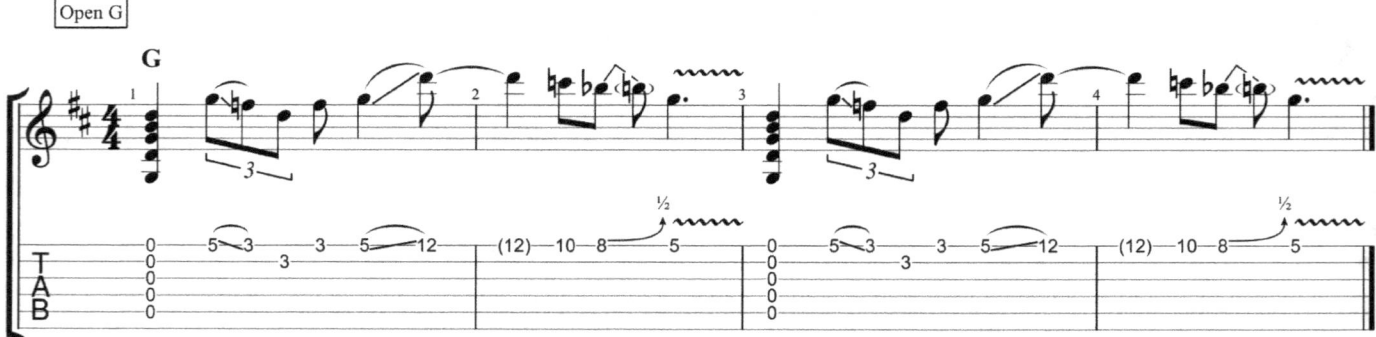

As you continue through this book, you'll find many more examples of licks that move up and down a single string, and all of them are derived from the handful of scales covered in this chapter.

Keep adding more licks to your arsenal and get an idea of how you can categorize them in your mind. Using the blues note (b5th) makes a lick instantly unsettling. The 6th gives a lick a sweeter feel, compared to the b7th, which has a more serious vibe. This is just my opinion. Playing Delta blues is all about how these notes make *you* feel. If you keep exploring these sounds and listening to the early masters, you'll quickly develop a strong connection between your ears and fingers.

Chapter Seven – Open Position Playing

Having focused on playing up and down a single string, we will now look at playing across the strings. In the Delta blues, this approach is used to create riffs that last for a whole song, often using just one, or maybe two chords.

One of the most utilised areas of any open tuning is the area around the open position. Here is a diagram in the open position, showing some of the commonly used notes in this area.

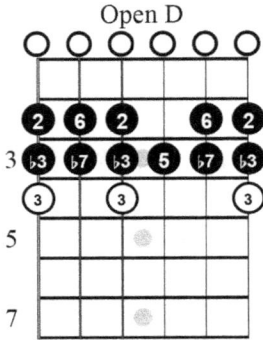

To move from an open string to a note fretted with the slide we have to place the slide down on the string. This can be a bit messy and create some unwanted noise unless you master the correct technique. It's a bit like playing a normal hammer-on, but the string is not pressed all the way down to the fret.

As with fretted guitar, pluck the open string, then lower the slide onto the string so that the new note sounds. Remember to place the slide directly over the fret and mute the strings behind it. Be firm, but not so hard that you cause the string to touch the fret wire.

This exercise is all about learning the amount of pressure required to sound the note clearly without pressing the string to the fingerboard. If you really struggle, you may want to consider having a new nut fitted that is a touch higher, or place a small shim under your current nut to raise the action.

In my picking hand, I use my thumb to play the 5th string, and my index finger on the 4th string. Alternating between these fingers allows you to mute strings more effectively if you need to.

Example 7a:

Here's the same idea, but this time hammering onto the 6th interval (B) on the fifth string to hint at that sweeter major pentatonic sound.

Example 7b:

The next example uses this hammer-on idea in a blues riff and adds a bluesy bend on the fourth string. Ideas like this often form driving rhythm patterns behind a vocal part, so dig in and let it ring!

Example 7c:

This idea can be repeated in a higher octave by moving it over to the second and first strings. I've turned the previous example into something that's more of a lead line by adding some melodic embellishment in the second and fourth bars and playing it on the higher strings

Example 7d:

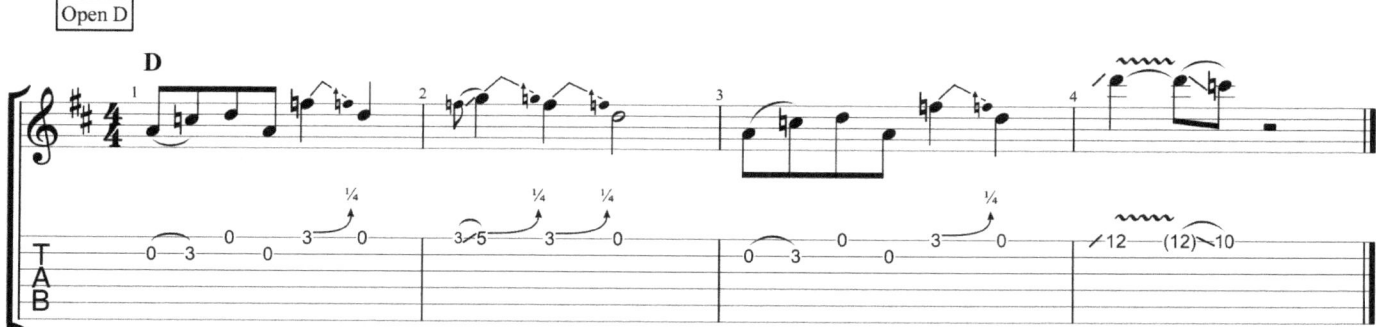

The previous two ideas, and the lines in the rest of the chapter, are perfect to use as accompaniment to a solo vocal in the true Delta style. Of course, you can use them in regular blues playing or in a band, but the authentic approach is to sing a melody over a riff and play a lick in the gaps between each line.

The next line adds pull-offs. These are tricky with a slide because there's no real way to pull off the string. Unlike a regular, fretted pull-offs, you can't just lift the slide off the string. The secret here is to *flick up* the string as you leave it, to sound the open string a little louder.

Example 7e:

Again, we can move this idea over to the second and first strings to create something more akin to a solo.

Example 7f:

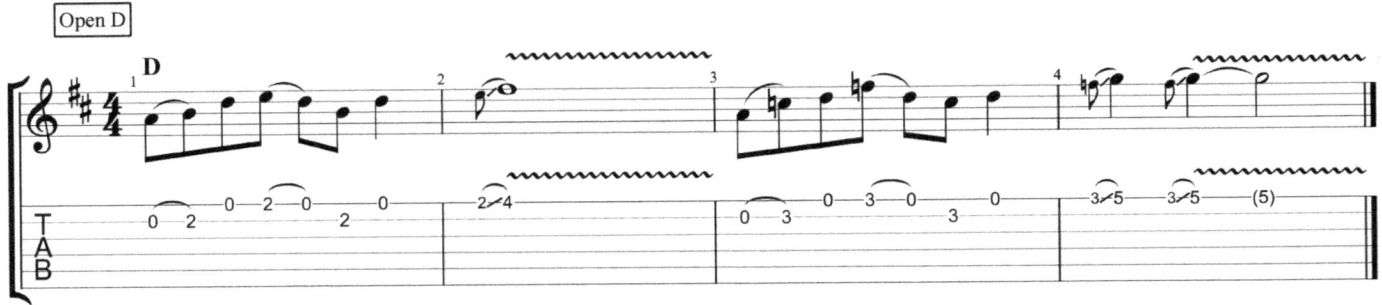

Here's another lick using bluesy bends on the b3rd on both the first and fourth strings.

Example 7g:

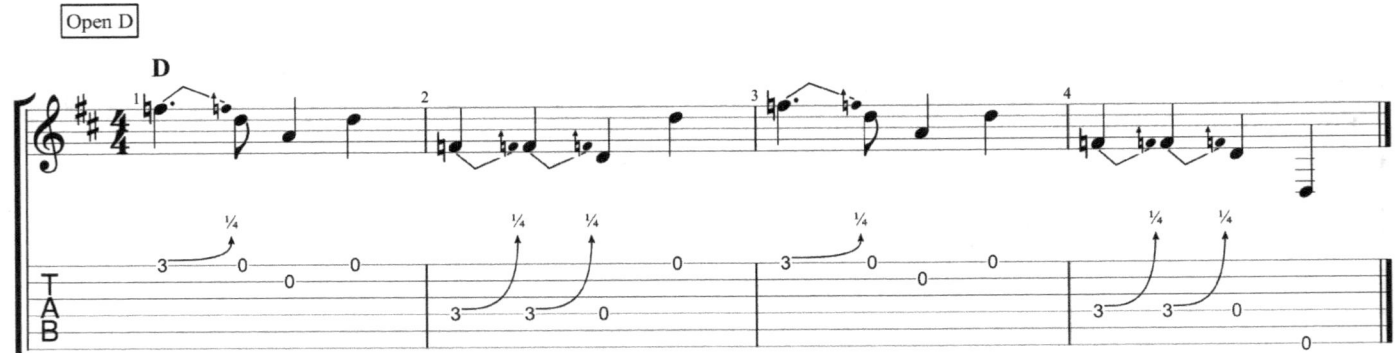

When you begin to dig in with the thumb pick or thumb, you will quickly find that hitting more than one string often works well when playing slide, because all the strings are tuned to the same chord.

Example 7h is based on the previous idea, but adds some grinding double stops on the fourth and third strings, along with a slide up to the 12th fret.

Example 7h:

Here's another example based on the same riff with some quicker grace note slides. Ideas like this are difficult to express perfectly in standard notation, so listen to the audio to hear the nuances.

When recording this lick, I began by playing it as cleanly as possible, but as time went on, I found it sounded better when it was given some attitude and when the notes were allowed to ring out along with a few extra strings.

This lick has such attitude because it includes the b5th (Ab on the 2nd fret, third string). The interplay between the b5th and the 5th (open second string) gives it a particularly dark sound.

Example 7i:

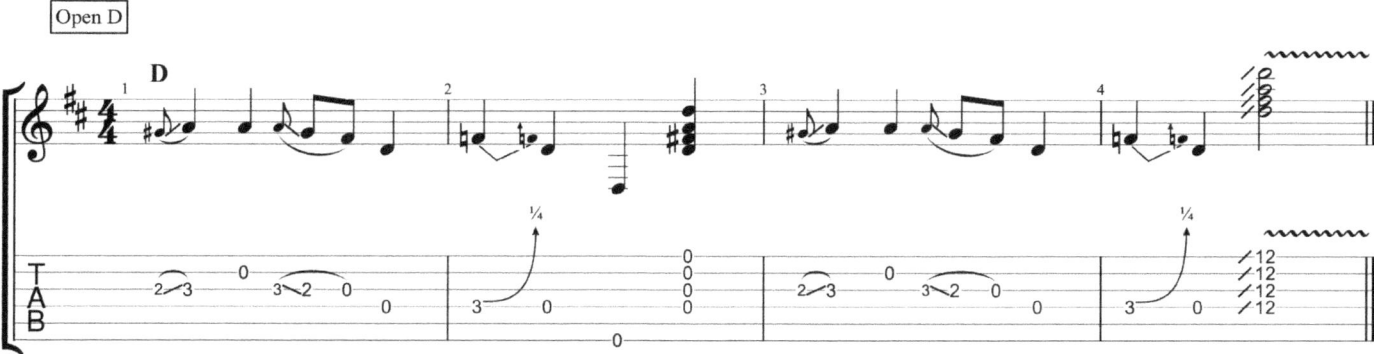

The following example uses several of the notes around the open position, along with double stops for a more aggressive sound.

Example 7j:

Here's another example, this time a little longer. It combines a single string idea with notes added in the open position.

This is the approach many slide players take, as playing across the strings in other positions can be awkward. Using the open strings means you can let any note ring out and it's going to be in key since the guitar is tuned to a chord.

Example 7k:

As you continue to explore the style of the Mississippi Delta legends, you'll find the same melodic ideas coming up again and again, regardless of tuning. This is due to the similarities in the tunings that we discussed in Chapter Five.

Here's a scale box that you could think of when tuning to open G. Notice how similar it is to the open D tuning box I showed you earlier.

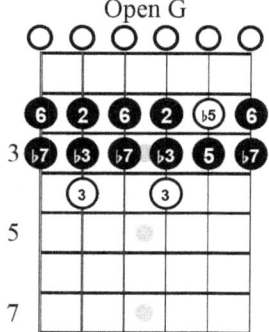

With the guitar tuned to open G, we quickly notice that the licks don't feel too different to the ones in open D. In the following lick, the most notable addition to the diagram is the root note (G) played at the 5th fret on the first string. This high-octave root allows us to add vibrato to that note – something we couldn't do if it was played on the open string, like in open D tuning.

Example 7l:

Here's another lick that uses triplets for a faster, more driving effect. Learn this one slowly as the position shifts are tricky at speed.

Example 7m:

The next line crosses five strings in the open position. Pay careful attention to the rhythm in bar two which features more syncopation (playing notes on the upbeat) to grab the listener.

Example 7n:

You can also add double stops for a bit more aggression. As always, listen closely to the recording to get a feel for the articulation and vibrato.

Example 7o:

Example 7p incorporates a double stop idea at the 3rd fret.

Example 7p:

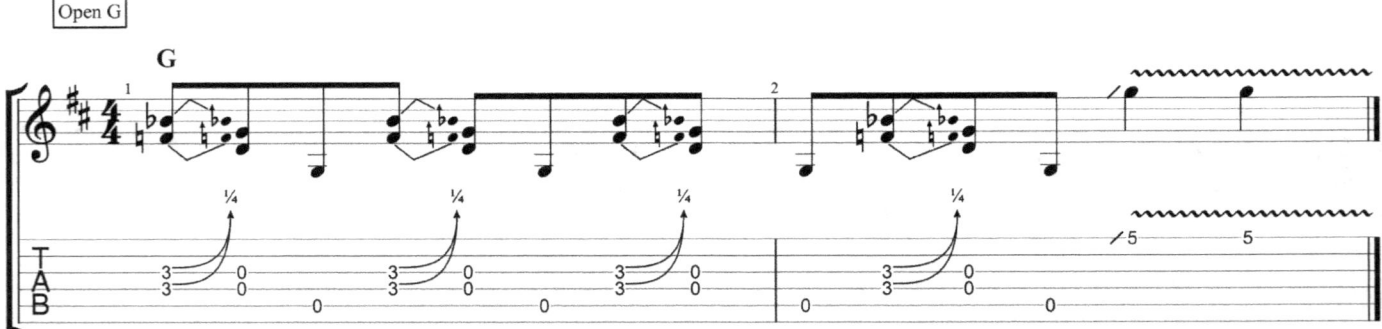

To finish the chapter, learn this tricky 1/16th note idea using a fast slide between the 5th and b5 on the second string. This can be played a little "rough around the edges", with each note ringing out, or a little more cleanly by adding more muting.

Example 7q:

Don't be afraid to experiment and combine these ideas to create your own phrases. The blues is about expressing yourself, even if that expression comes from a limited pool of notes. The only way to be completely free to do that is to exhaust these concepts and find what works and what sounds good.

When you're comfortable with these ideas, move on to the next chapter where I've written two solos using these ideas on a Delta blues tune.

Chapter Eight – Saint Louis Blues

In this chapter you'll learn a full 12-bar solo in open G tuning, based very loosely on the 1914 W. C. Handy blues standard, *Saint Louis Blues*. Over the years, this song became common in the repertoire of jazz pioneers like Louis Armstrong, Count Basie, Glenn Miller and Bessie Smith, although it's nothing more than a 12-bar blues in D.

Consisting of just the I, IV and V chords in the key of D, the first step is to learn the rhythm guitar part.

To keep it simple, I've written the rhythm guitar in standard tuning, so the chord voicings will be familiar to you, and you'll be able to play it more easily with a friend who isn't a slide guitar/open tuning specialist. Of course, you can play the chords with the slide in open D tuning if you wish.

Example 8a:

While the song is in the key of D, the soloist is actually tuned to open G. This seems counterintuitive at first, but the reason is so that the soloist can use the note B on the second string when the chord changes to G Major. (The B note is the 3rd of G Major – a very strong note to target on the chord).

Learn this solo slowly and listen carefully to the recording to get an idea of the feel. It should sound bluesy, not robotic. Bend the notes to taste and add vibrato when it feels right.

Example 8b:

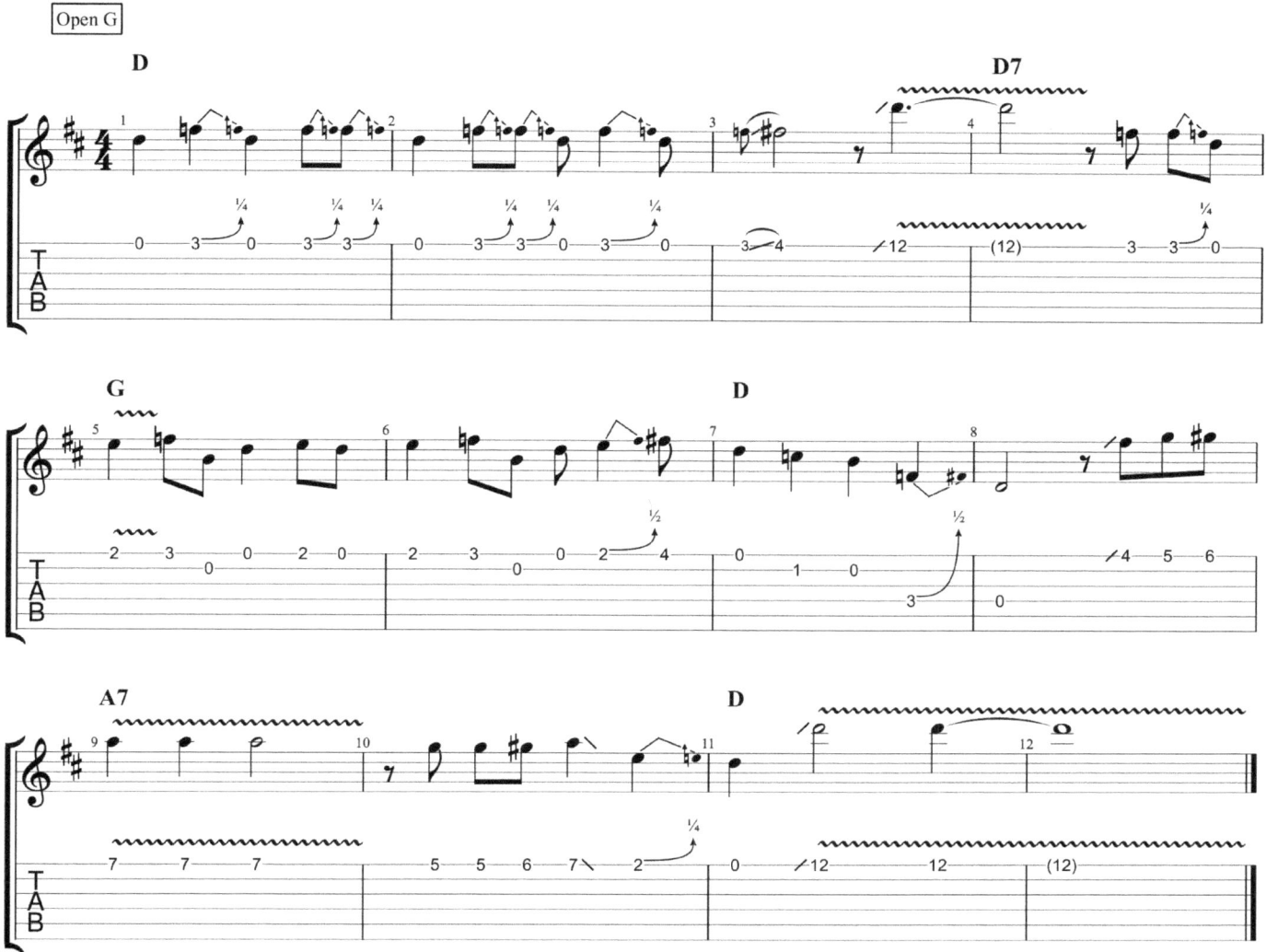

Here's one another 12-bar solo in open G tuning, this time based more around the fourth string (D).

The defining aspect of this solo is the repeating ascending chromatic parts. This is a great example of how this style of playing doesn't need to be perfectly in tune.

For example, in bar two we move up chromatically from fret 4 to fret 7. The authentic way to play a lick like this isn't to play precisely on each fret. Rather, we slide from 4 to 7 while picking the string four times.

Example 8c:

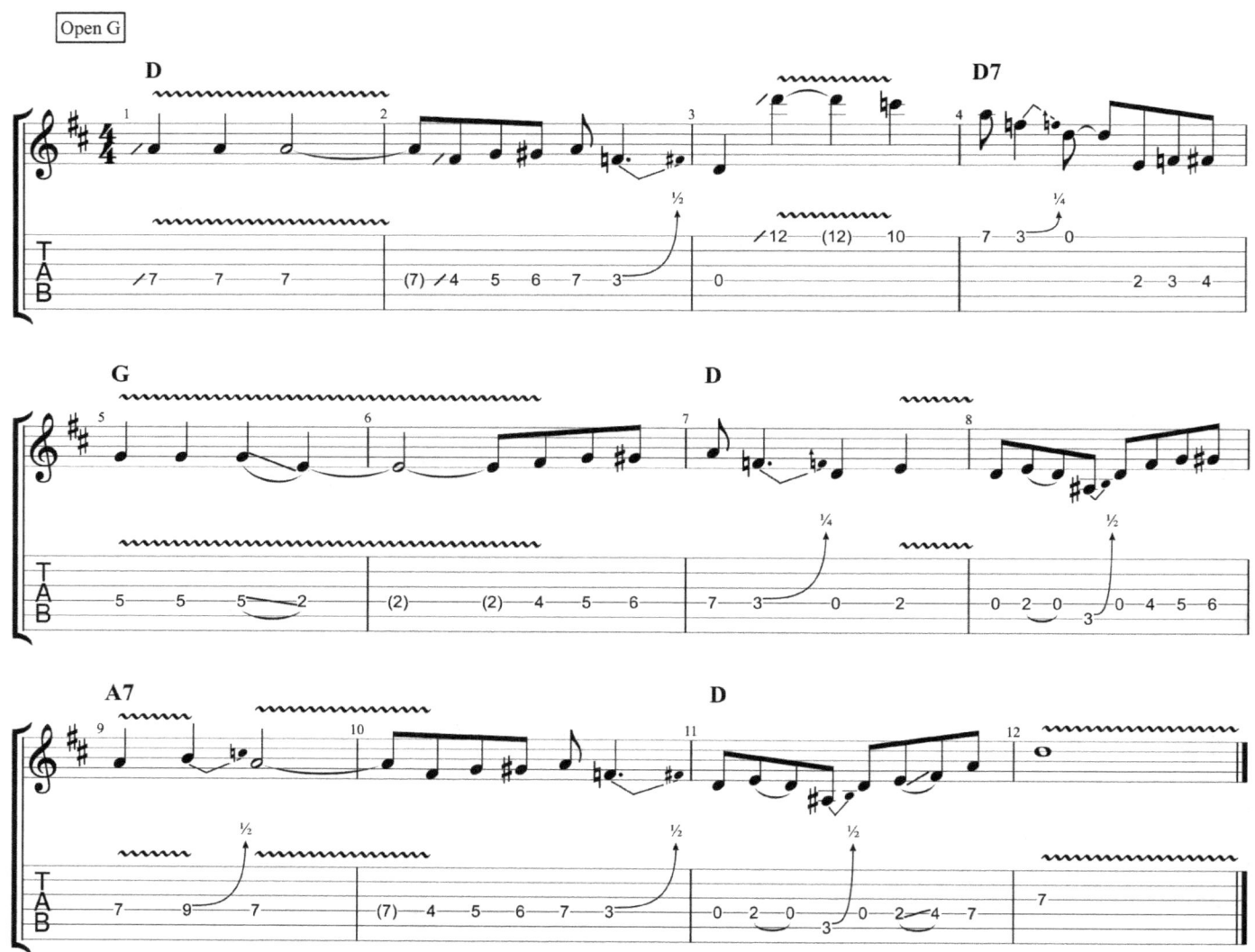

Once you've got this example under your fingers, work on playing the two solos back to back. As mentioned at the start of the chapter, examples like these are great fun to play with a friend, as the rhythm guitar part is something even a beginner could learn quite quickly.

When you're able to play this piece comfortably, your next port of call should be spending some time listening to the greats playing this song (Spotify has many different versions). The more idea you have about how an experienced musician plays over a tune like this, the more you'll be able to express yourself freely in your own playing.

Chapter Nine – Melodies And Bass

While Delta blues guitarists often stick to playing isolated melodies, solo guitar players often play both rhythm and lead guitar parts together. This approach is extremely common among acoustic guitarists who play without a slide. In open tuning with a slide, things become trickier.

To play rhythm and lead together you must develop independence between the thumb and the fingers of your picking hand.

We'll begin in open D tuning with a repeating quarter note on the sixth string. Use the thumb to play this note with a solid downstroke motion.

Example 9a:

When this becomes comfortable, the next step is to add a single note held over the top.

Slide up to the 12th fret on the first string and hold this note while adding vibrato. Keep playing the driving bass part with the thumb.

Example 9b:

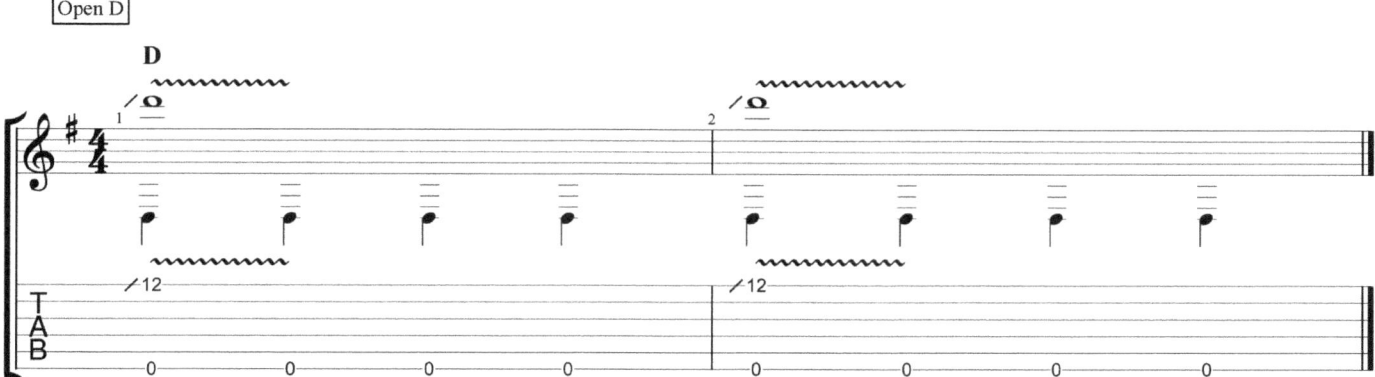

This same exercise can be repeated with a three-note chord ringing on top. Use the index, middle and ring fingers to pluck the chord, while playing the bass note with the thumb.

To play this exercise cleanly, we have to be careful with the position of the slide. Here, we need to fret several strings while keeping the low string open. The slide cannot cover all six strings.

Example 9c:

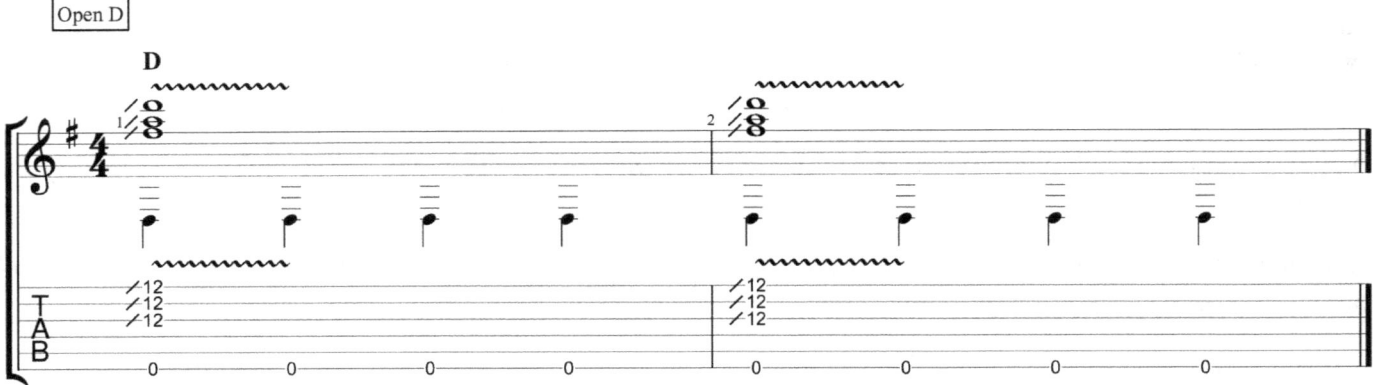

Example 9d includes some *offbeat* notes. The first melody note is played in tandem with the bass using a pinching motion, then the melody note is repeated on its own.

To mix it up a little, I've also changed the melody slightly in each bar.

Example 9d:

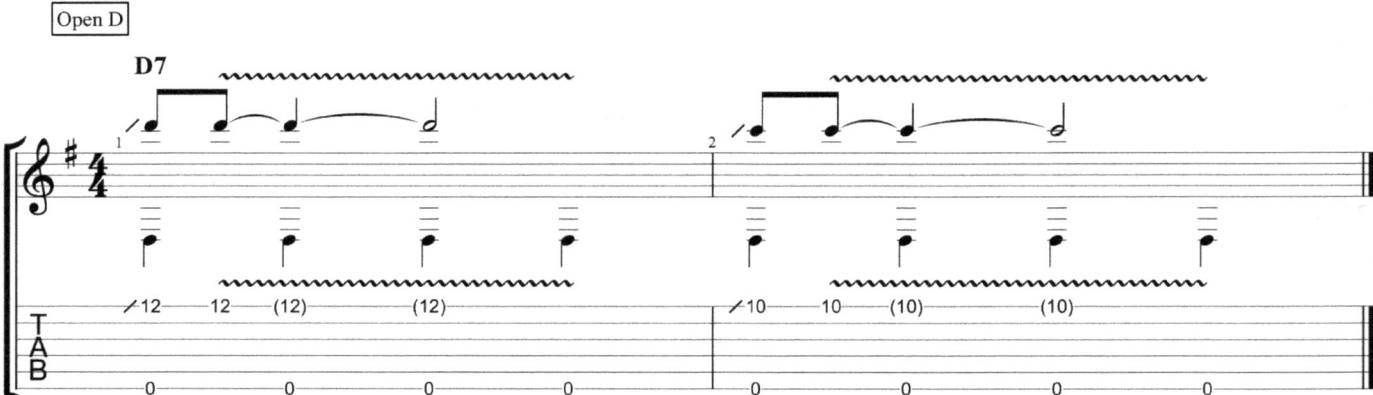

When this begins to feel normal, alter the melody in the middle of the bar. In this example the melody note changes from D to C on the "&" of beat 2.

Example 9e:

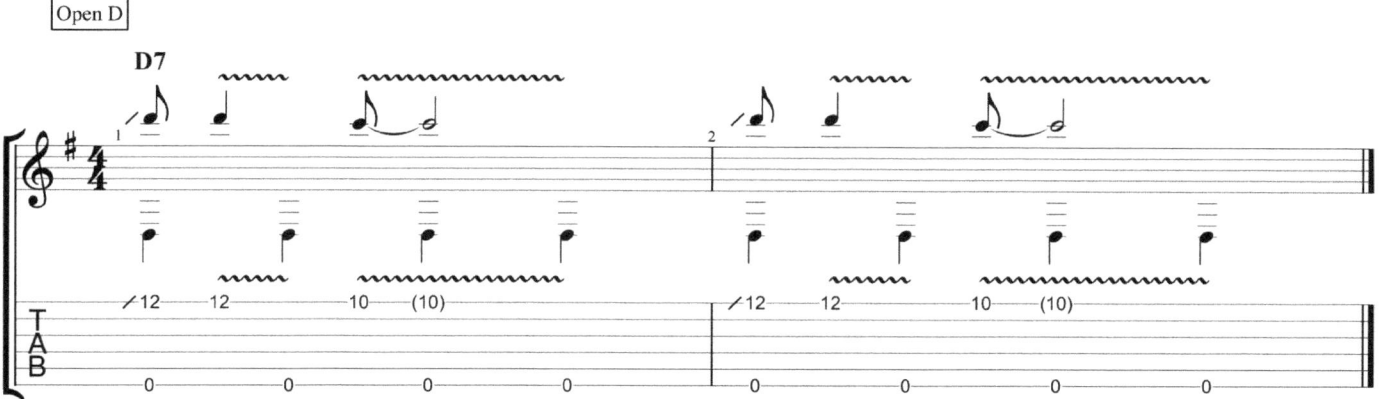

Now that the right-hand mechanics have been introduced, you are free to add more notes with the slide to create a stronger melody.

The following example develops the previous idea into a descending melody.

Example 9f:

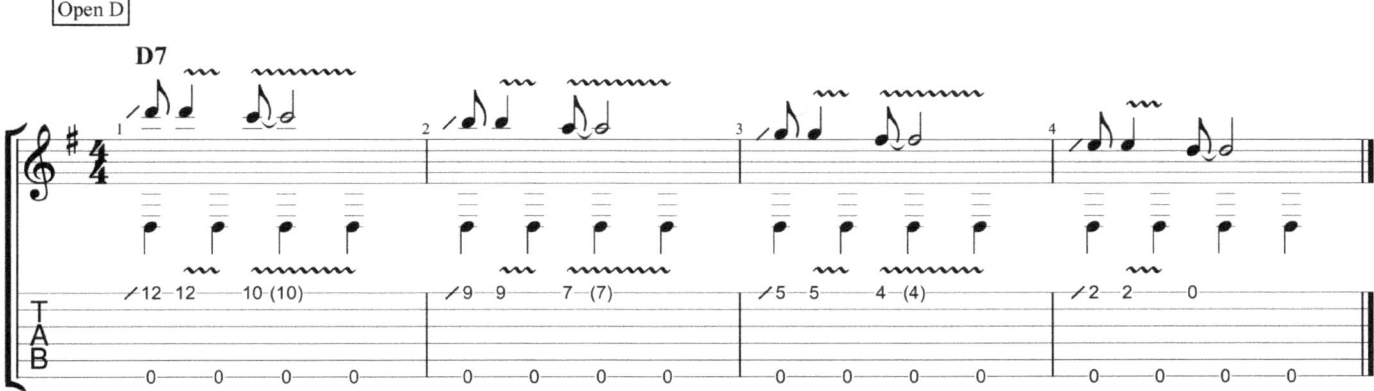

With this concept under your belt, it's possible to start creating some really musical ideas using just the notes of the D Minor Pentatonic scale over the driving bass part.

Example 9g:

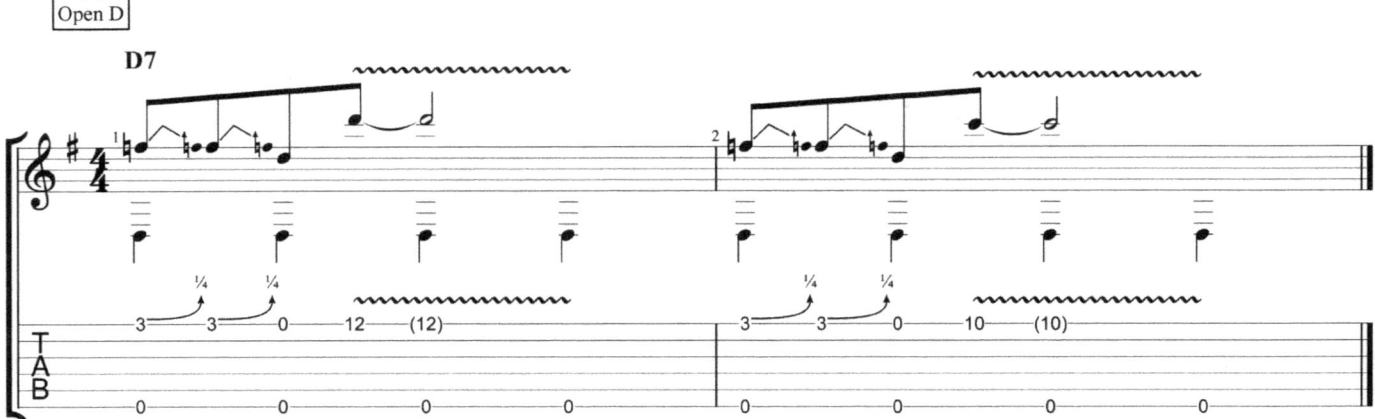

The next example builds on this idea by playing the motif in bar one and shifting to an open position lick in the second bar.

Learning to keep these bass notes ringing out as you move across the strings takes time, so be patient.

Example 9h:

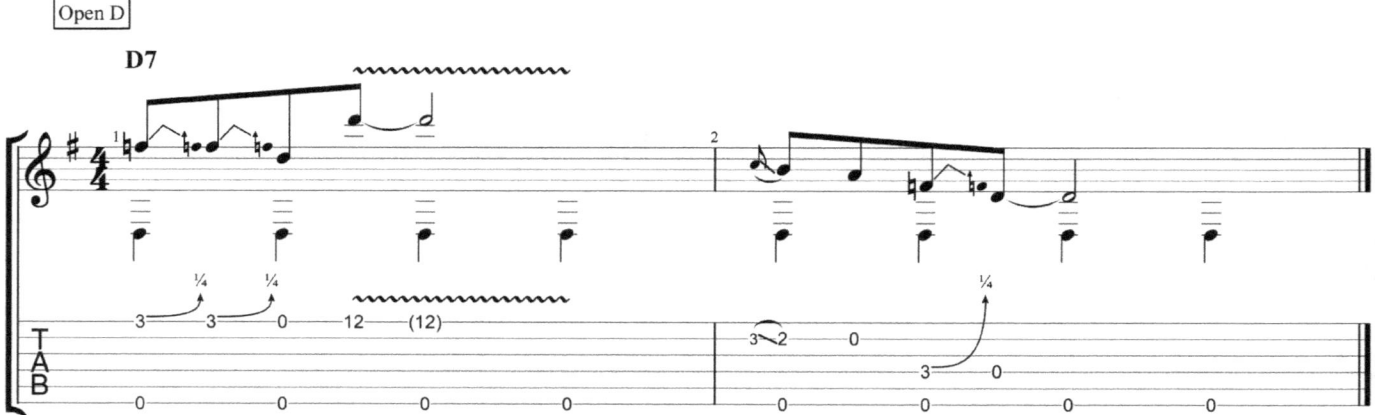

Developing this idea further, we can start to mix phrases played in the open position with notes that we slide up to. This puts us in Son House, *Dead Letter Blues* territory. Ideas like this sound best when played fast and loose.

Example 9i:

This final idea combines notes in the open position with added vibrato at the 12th fret.

Example 9j:

It's also possible to play an 1/8th note pattern with the thumb, as shown in the following example. Ideas like these are most commonly played with a swing feel.

Example 9k:

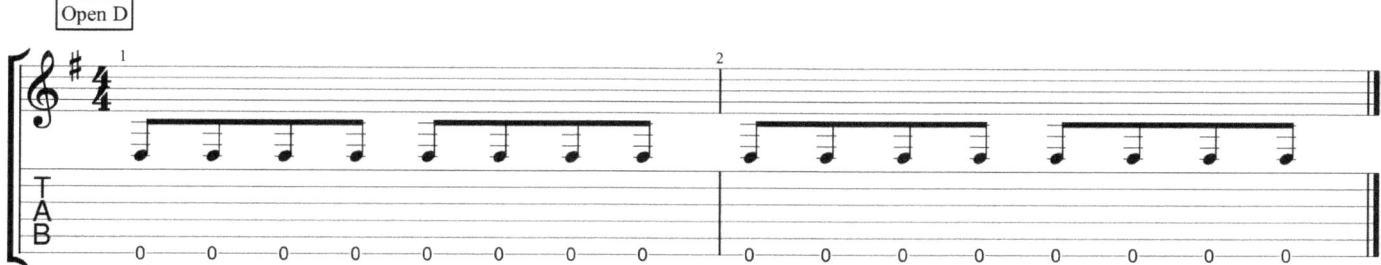

As with the 1/4 note bass pattern, it's possible to have one melody note ring out while the thumb plays a steady bass part.

Example 9l:

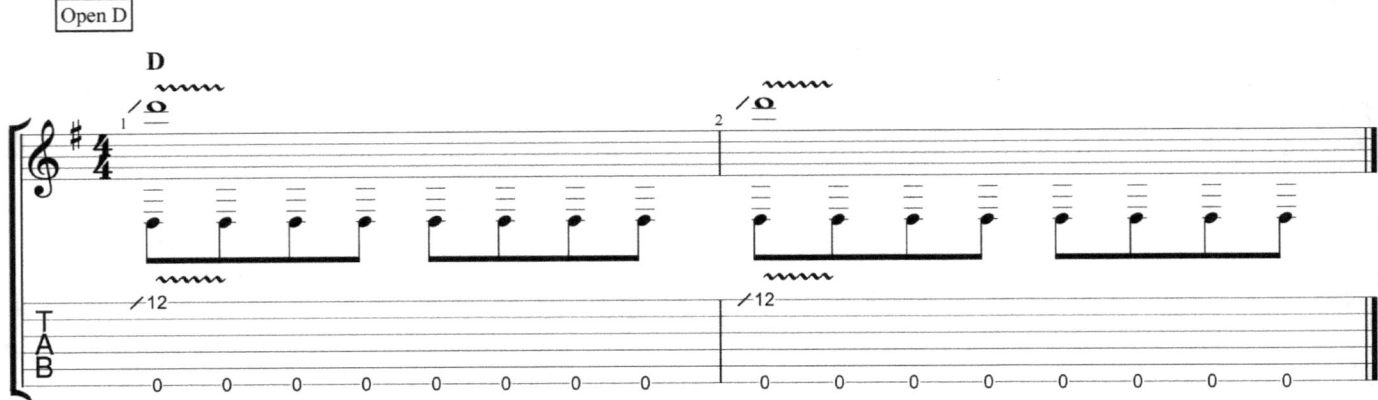

When you add 1/8th note melodies, each note is played simultaneously with a bass note in a pinching motion. To demonstrate this, here's an idea that uses open strings and the 12th fret played with the slide.

Example 9m:

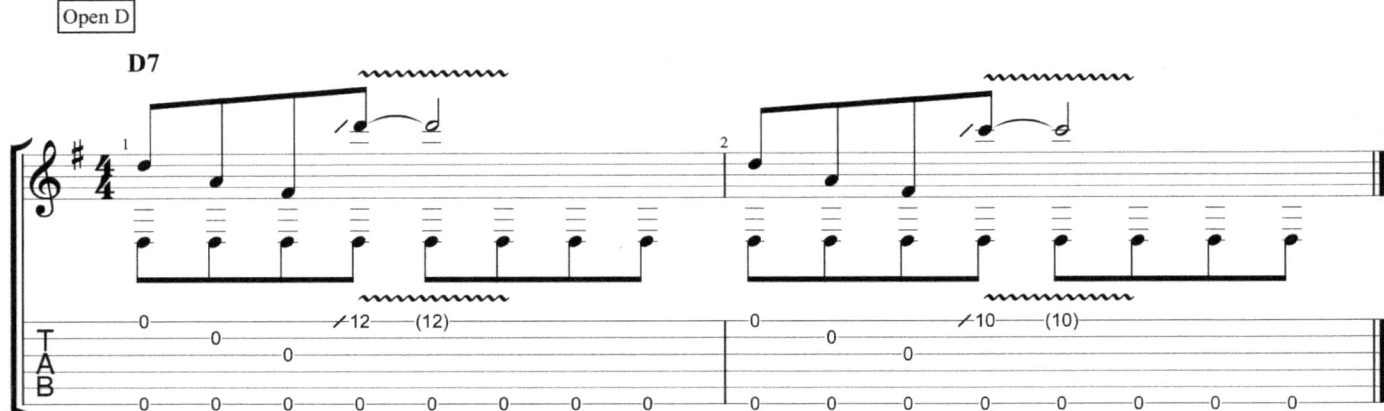

Here's a similar rhythm, with a melody played on the first string using notes of the D Blues scale against a driving 1/8th note bass part.

Example 9n:

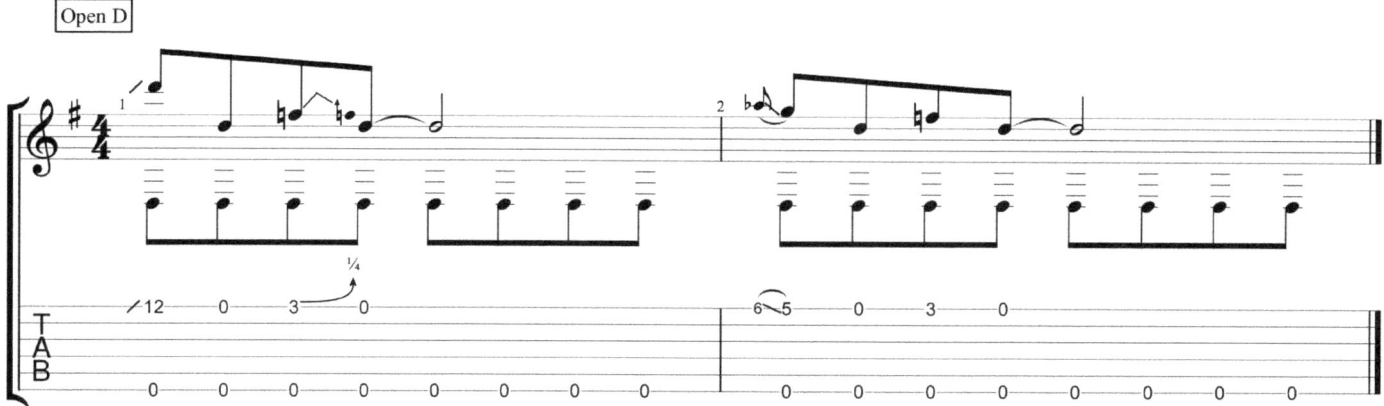

As with the 1/4 note bass part, it's worthwhile to practise open position licks with these bass parts. When listening to the audio, you'll notice that I play the slides quite slowly on this lick – they just feel right that way!

Example 9o:

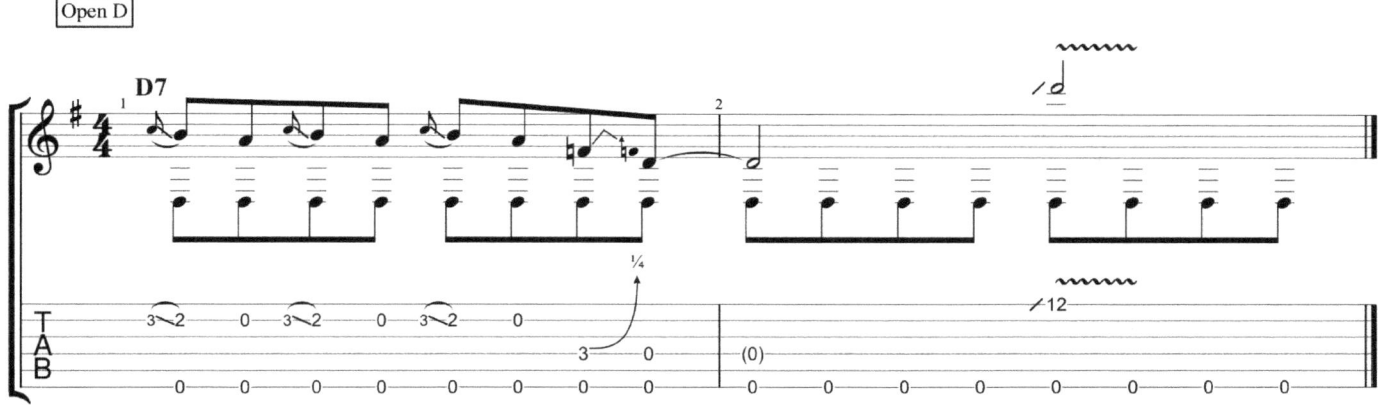

Another great idea is to split the melody and bass in a triplet rhythm.

Example 9p:

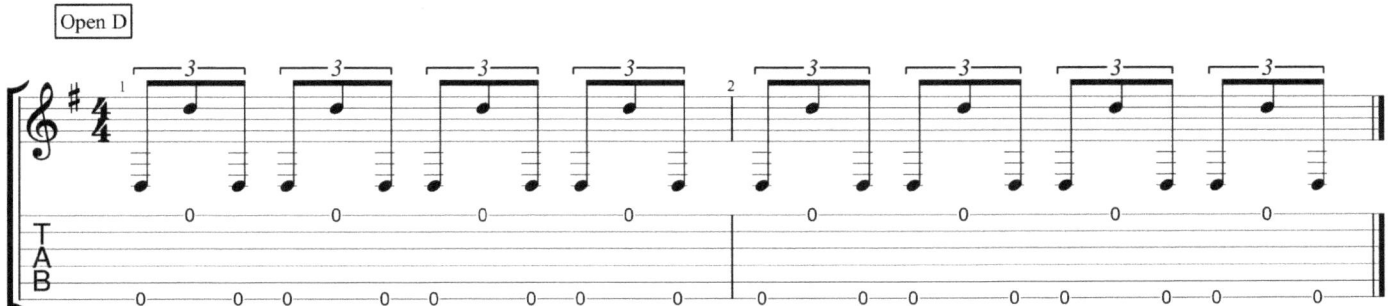

Here's the same idea, but notated more correctly with an upper and lower voice. This is a convention in two-part music where the bass line is written with downward stems and the melody is written with upward stems.

Example 9q:

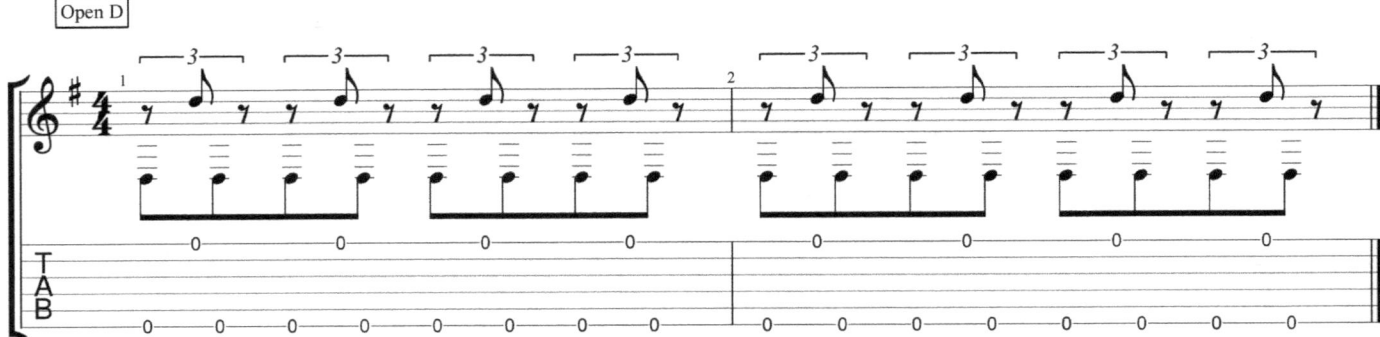

The following example features melody notes played on both the strong beats and these offbeat triplets. This looks more complicated than it is, as long as you've mastered the previous example, so listen to the audio to get the timing.

Example 9r:

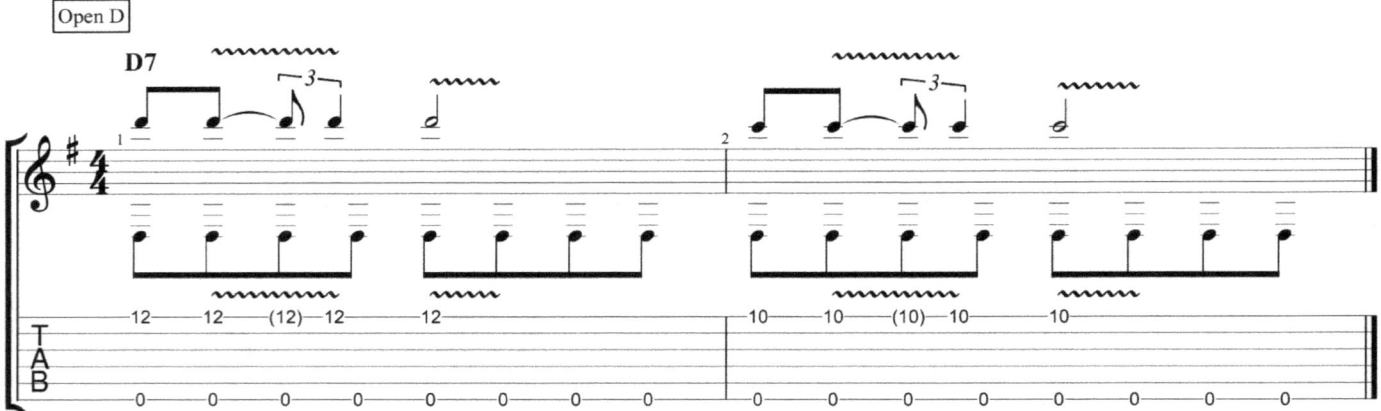

The following two-bar phrase combines open-string licks, position shifts and off-beat triplets.

This is probably one step beyond what you'll hear in authentic Delta blues playing, but it's great for your creativity and technical ability to work on ideas like this. Anything simpler will be a walk in the park when you can play this example!

Example 9s:

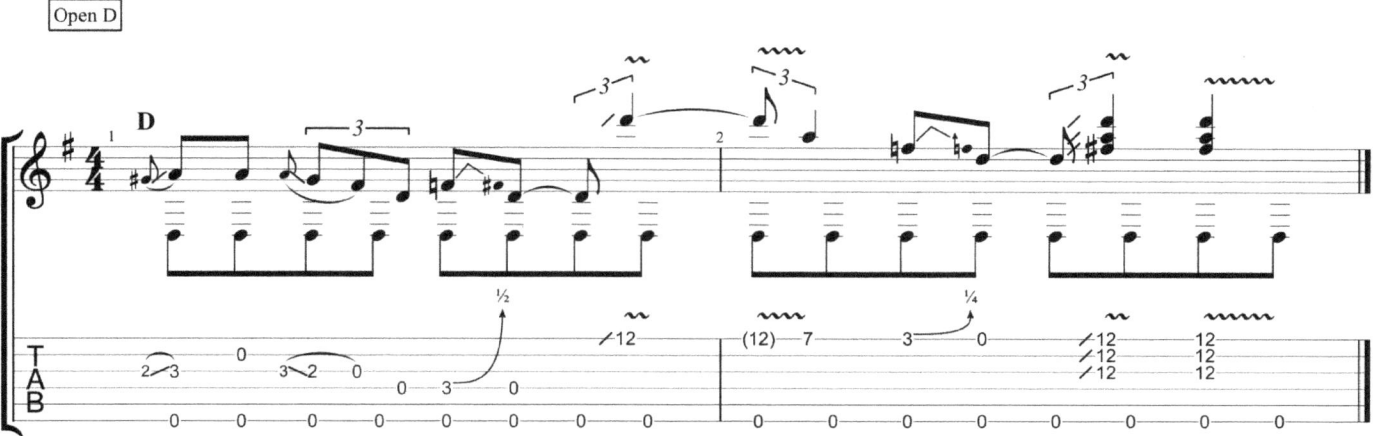

This final idea will prepare you for the blues solos in the final chapters and introduces an alternating bass pattern played by the thumb.

In open D tuning, both the fourth and sixth strings are tuned to D, so alternating between them gives a nice driving octave pattern as a framework for our melodies.

Example 9t:

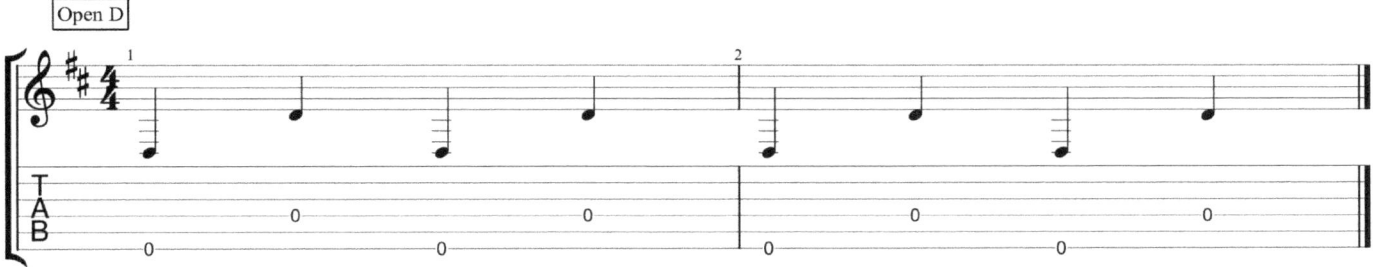

These types of alternating bass patterns are common in the country fingerstyle genre (check out my book Country Fingerstyle Guitar for more!) and must be practised until they're completely automatic in the thumb before you start adding melodies over the top.

Example 9u combines the alternating thumb pattern with a descending scale on the first string. Phrases such as these are the basis of classics like Blind Willie Johnson's *Dark Was The Night, Cold Was The Ground.*

Example 9u:

This technique can be also used in rhythm guitar patterns, as shown in the next example.

Keep the alternating pattern in the thumb, but now add the second and first strings on the 1st and 2nd beats respectively. These chords are played with a pinching motion between the thumb and index finger.

Example 9v:

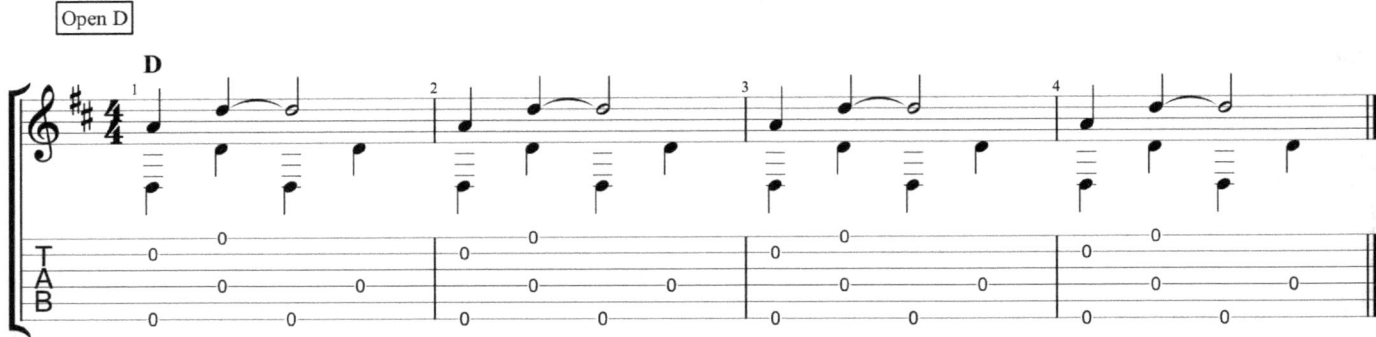

When you add notes on the up-beat, you start to create something that sounds engaging and complex without doing much hard work.

This example is the same as the previous one, but adds an additional plucked note on the & of beat 3.

Example 9w:

These picking concepts could be expanded almost infinitely, but I don't want to stray too far from the subject at hand. Let's move on now you have the basics under your fingers.

With these rhythmic picking ideas on one chord nailed, let's explore some licks that outline the chord changes of the blues.

Chapter Ten – Changing Chords

When playing in an open tuning, the guitar naturally lends itself to playing in the key of the tuning – i.e. it's very easy to play in the key of D on a guitar in open D tuning. Of course, songs don't stay on the same chord forever, so we need to learn to play and solo over other chords too. Overcoming this hurdle is one of the biggest challenges you'll come up against in this style.

Before we get into changing chords, let's take a quick look at playing in different keys. For example, how do we approach playing in the key of E if the guitar is tuned to open D? Imagine getting on stage to find that the singer can only sing in E and you don't have time to retune your whole guitar.

One way to approach playing in the key of E while tuned to open D is simply to move your perspective of where the "home" position is. E is one tone (two frets) above D, so instead of the open strings and the 12th fret forming the tonic chord, you now view "home" at the 2nd and 14th frets instead.

Example 10a:

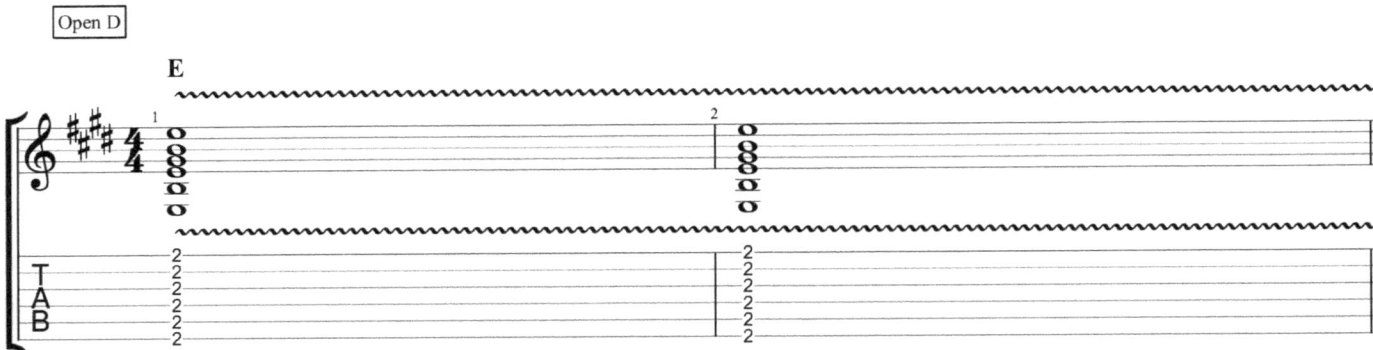

This concept opens up other options too. With the home position at the 2nd fret you can, for example, play notes below the barre that you couldn't access before. As the following example demonstrates, this results in some unique ideas that would be impossible in the key of D.

Example 10b:

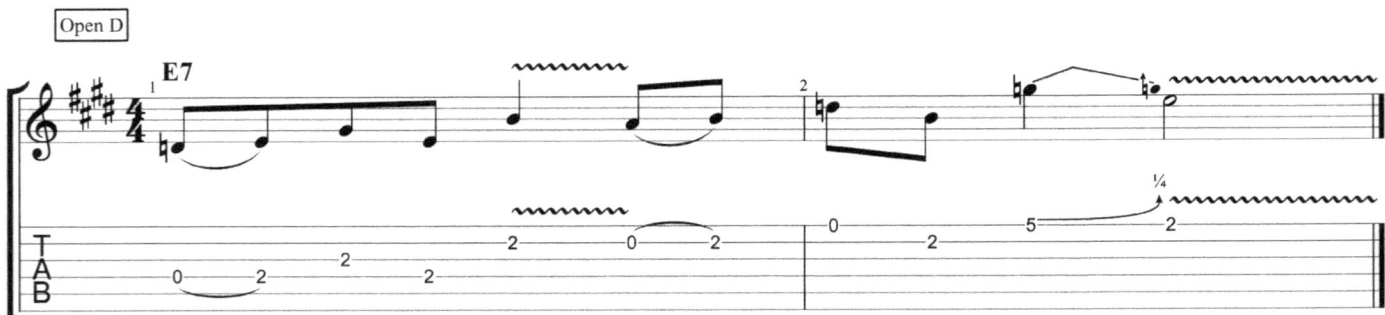

The drawback with this approach is that any open string licks you had in your arsenal are now unavailable. In the key of D, all the open strings were "strong" notes, but in the key of E they are "weak". Not "wrong", because technically they are all in key, but they don't sound as good.

There is an easy solution though, and that's to use a capo. Placing a capo at the second fret puts the whole guitar into the key of E and makes all the open-string licks you've already learned available again.

Example 10c:

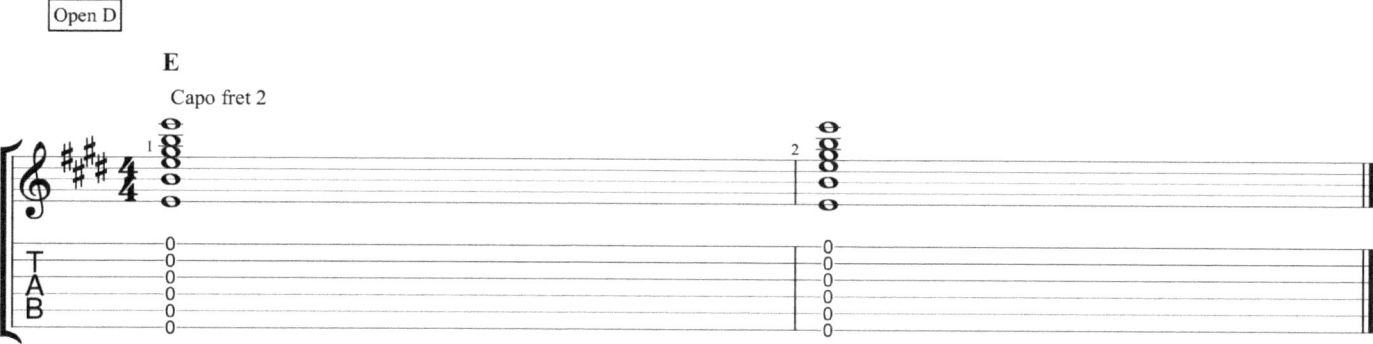

Here's Example 7i, but now played with a capo at the 2nd fret to change the lick from the key of D to the key of E.

In this example, sliding up twelve frets with the capo at the 2nd fret, means you're actually playing at the 14th fret. If you are playing a resonator guitar where the neck joins the body at the 12th fret, this can be awkward, so sometimes you'll have to adapt your vocabulary accordingly.

Example 10d:

Key changes aside, most Delta blues is formed from just three chords, the I, the IV and the V (D, G and A in the key of D). As each chord is often played for an extended time, we can adjust our thinking to treat each chord almost as if it's in a different key.

Generally speaking, in Delta blues style, each chord is treated as if it's a dominant 7 chord.

The simplest way to deal with these chord changes is to use the strength of the open tuning, and to treat each chord change as a new "home" position.

In open D tuning:

- The open strings / 12th fret barre forms the (I) chord, D Major
- A 5th fret barre forms the IV chord, G Major
- The 7th fret barre forms the V chord, A Major

Example 10e:

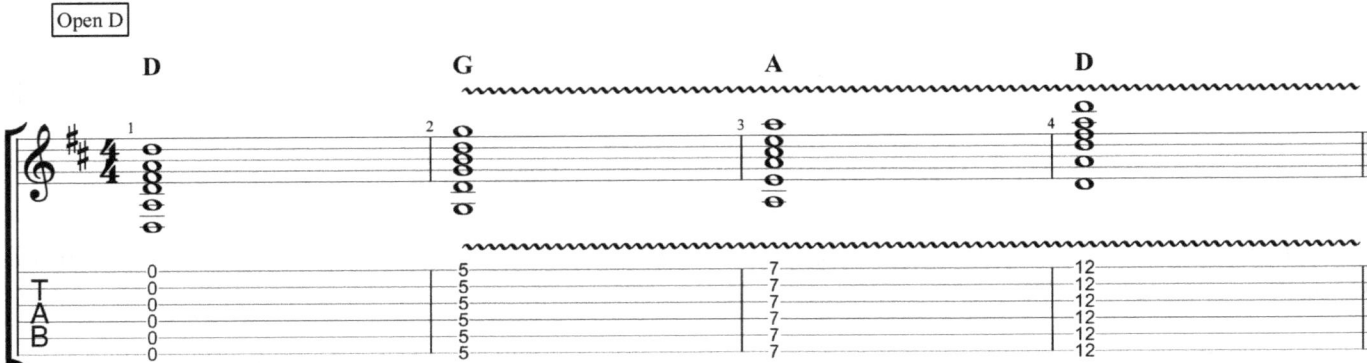

The beauty of this system is that the concept of the "home barre chord" works perfectly for each chord. The notes that work over the G Major and A Major chords form the same pattern on the neck as the D Major position we've discussed at length. You can see this in the following diagrams.

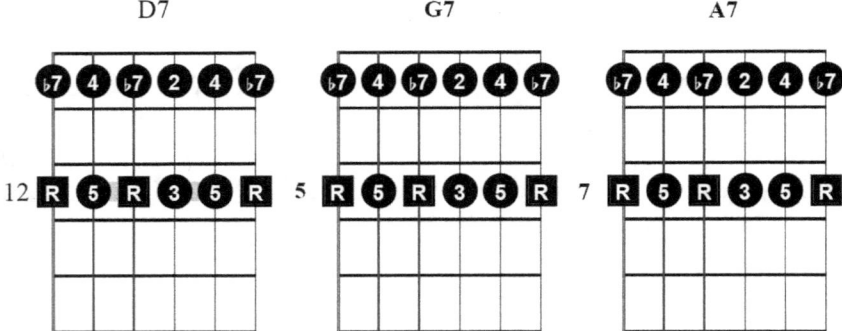

The following example uses a lick on the D chord for four bars, then transitions to the G Major (IV) chord by moving to a barre chord at the 5th fret. This is an easy way to outline the chord change and it works very well.

65

Example 10f:

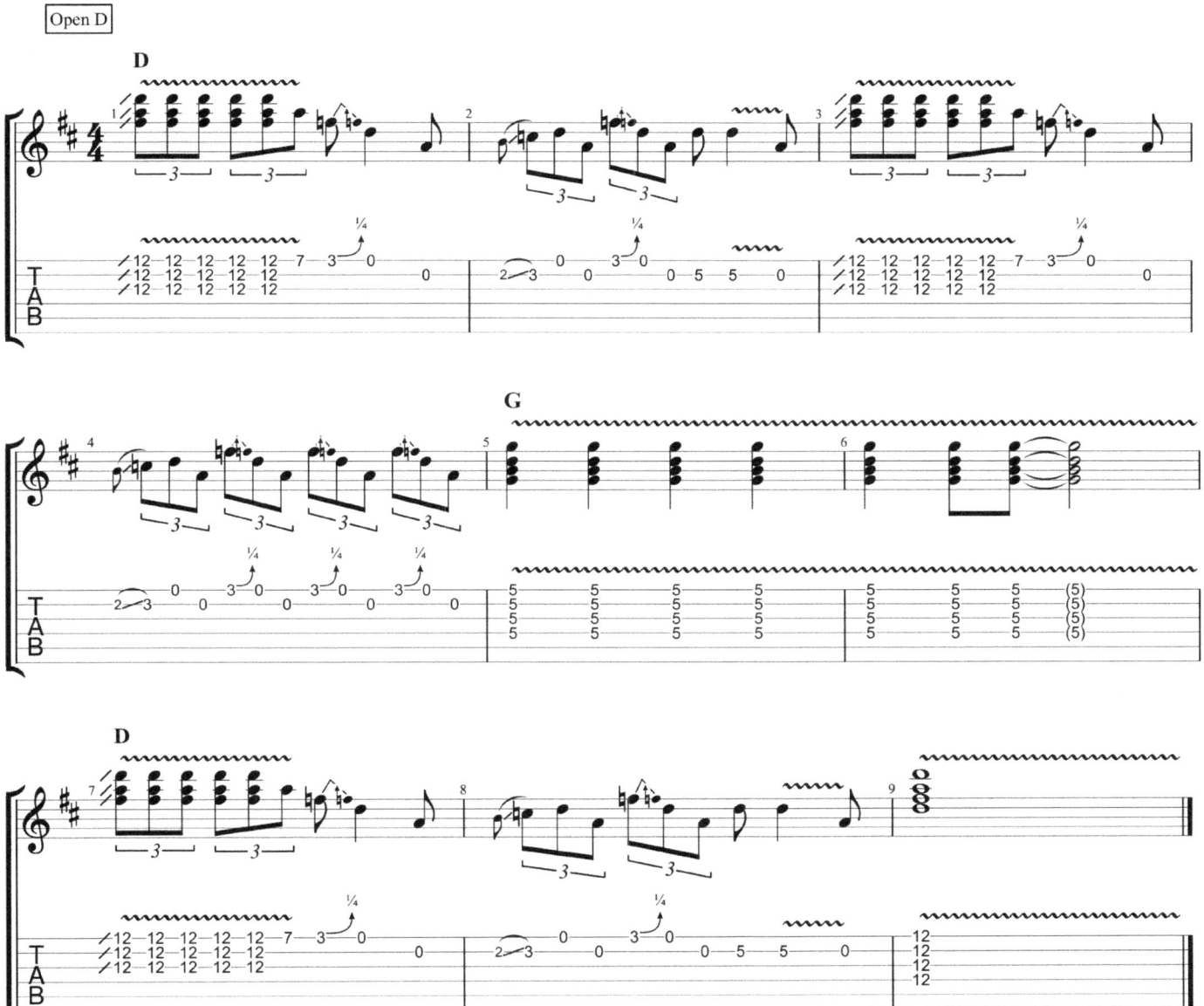

The same approach can be used for the final four bars of the blues to outline the V chord (A Major) at the 7th fret, and the IV chord (G Major) at the 5th fret, before returning to the open position for the I chord (D Major).

Example 10g:

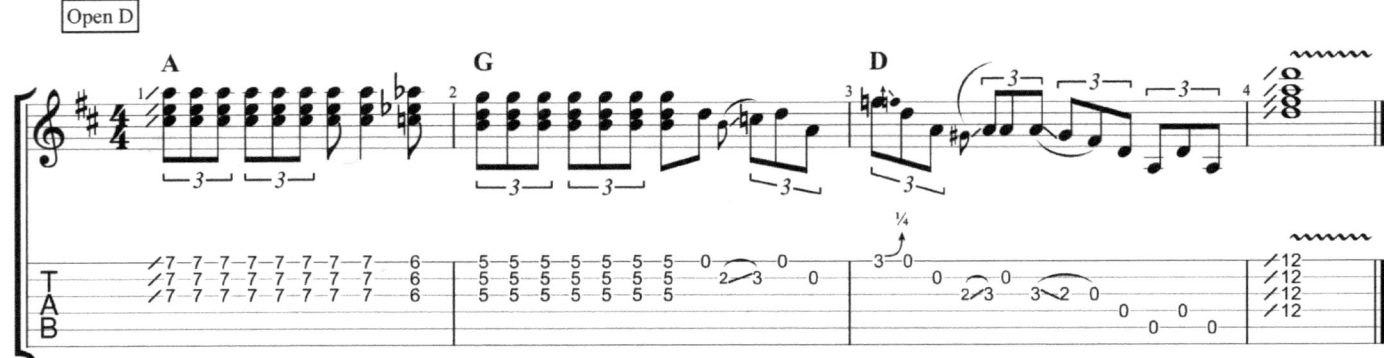

In the following example, I've written a simple melodic lick moving between A, G and D, using the simple pattern presented in example 10f.

Example 10g1

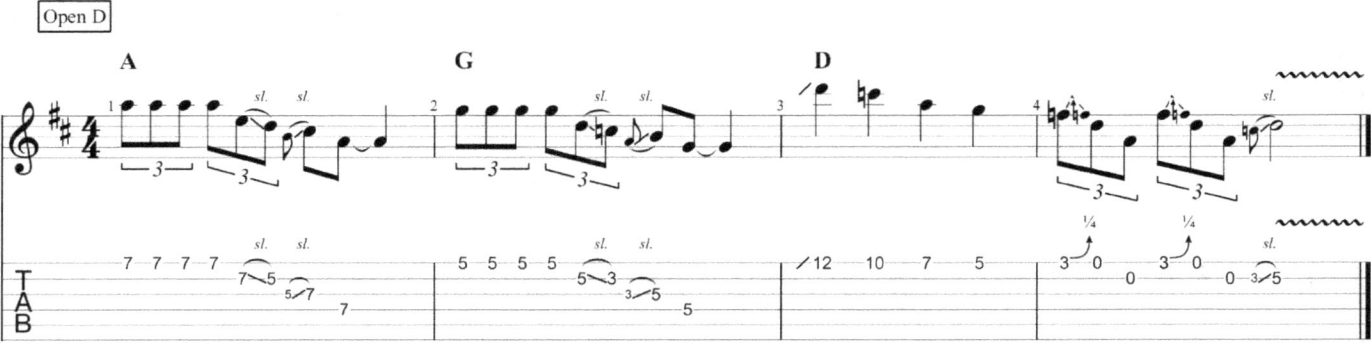

Here's another idea based around the same concept. Ideas like this are used often, and may appear fairly basic, but they're extremely effective at adding something interesting to a solo or rhythm part.

Example 10g2

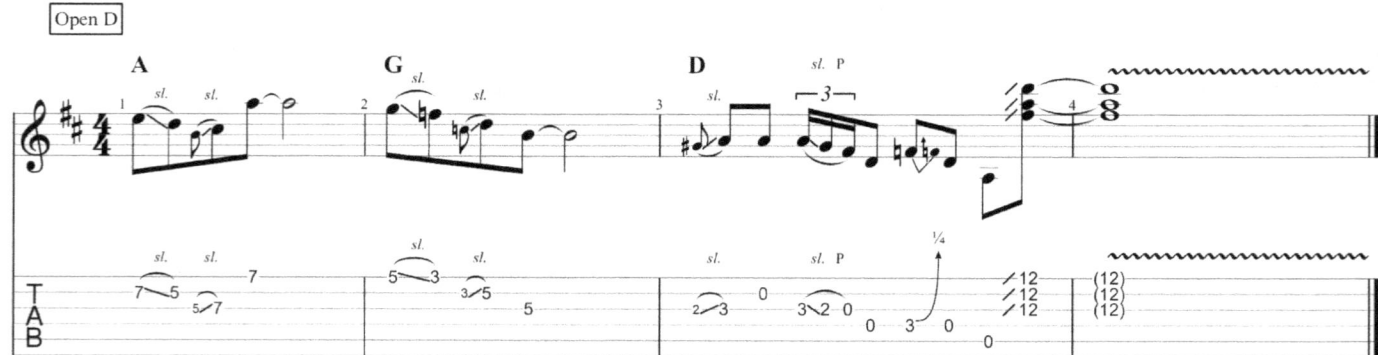

This is a common approach to navigating the blues. In Chapter Thirteen you will see this concept in use in the *Guitar Rag* example piece, for any chord that isn't played in the open position.

While shifting positions is a great strategy, it's important to have some single string and open position options at your disposal for the chord changes.

The following example plays an ascending hybrid scale in D, then the same idea in G at the 5th fret.

Example 10h:

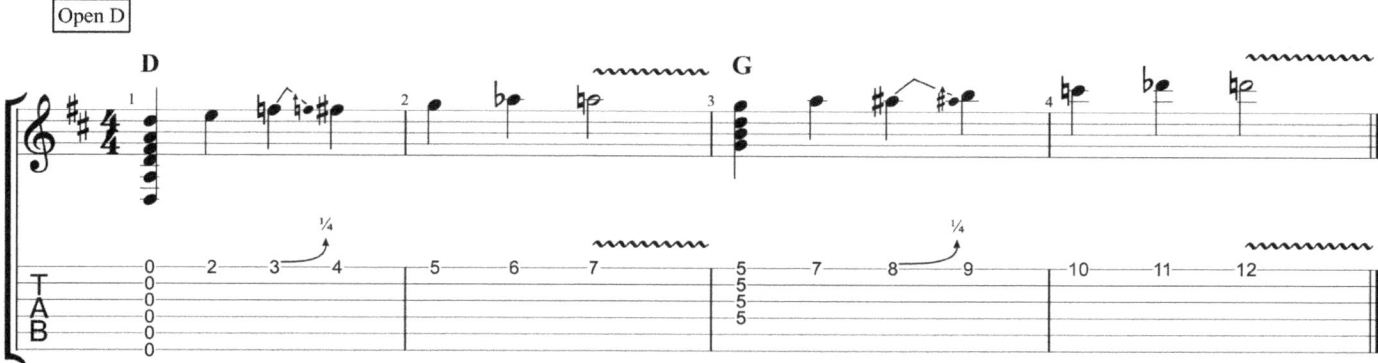

Now try this lick that moves between G Major and D Major and uses these two patterns in a more musical manner.

Example 10i:

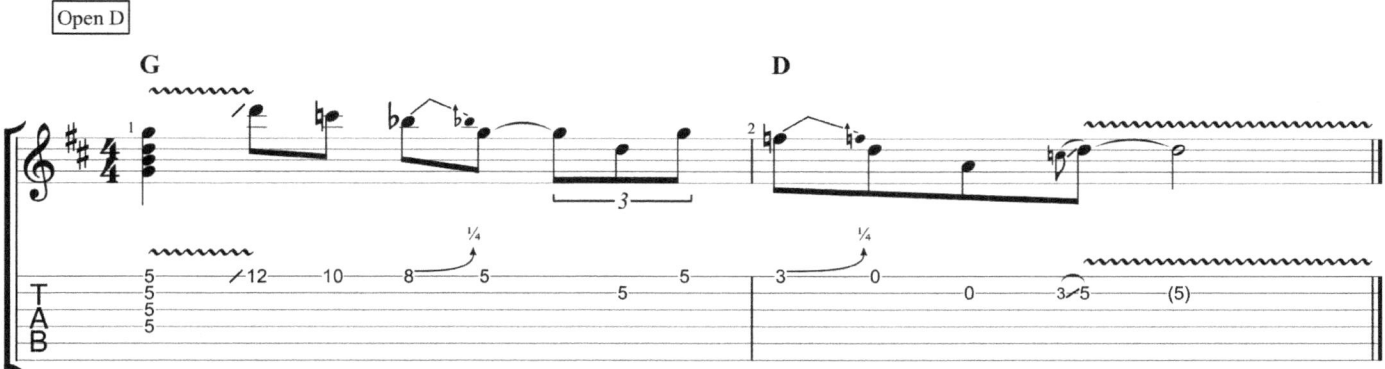

Here's a different lick, using the same concept of a single string scale for both the G and D chords.

Example 10j:

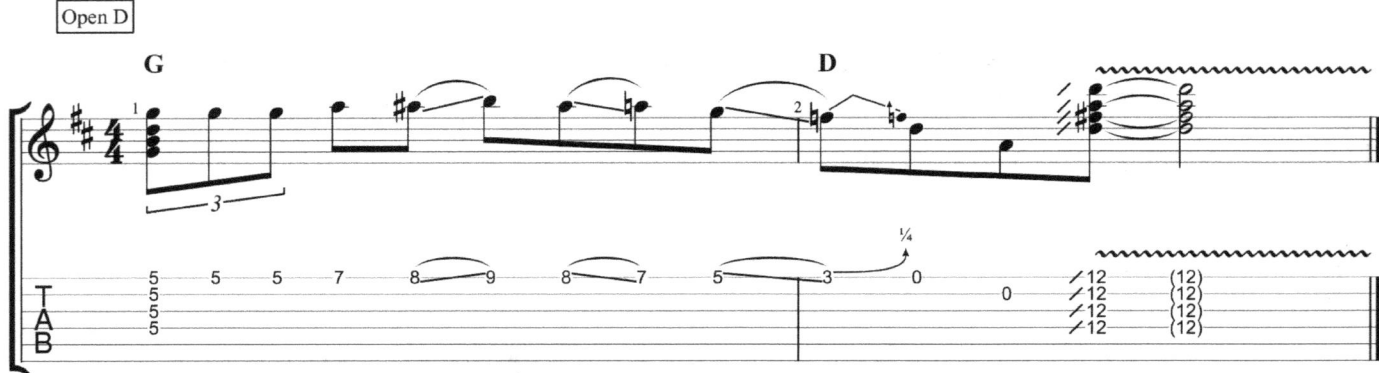

Another benefit of seeing the home position of each chord in different places on the neck is that you can play notes behind the slide which would be impossible in the open position.

In the following example, I play notes behind the G and A barres (at the 5th and 7th frets).

Example 10k:

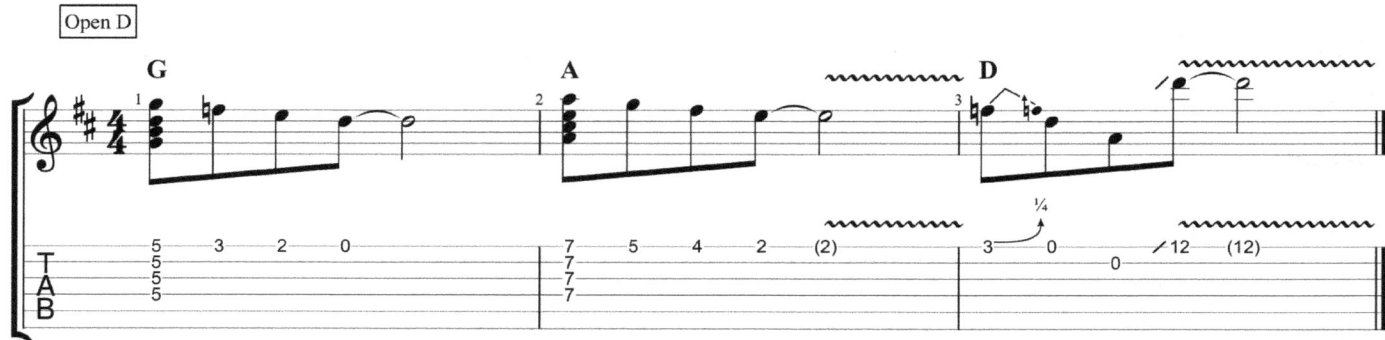

Now let's add notes around the barre position on other strings, as covered in Chapter Five.

Here's a lick repeated on G and A chords. Remember, these licks are very logical when you see the barre chord position as home.

Example 10l:

In the context of a blues, it's possible to create some melodic ideas without using much material. These ideas work because each chord is surrounded closely by the melody.

Example 10m:

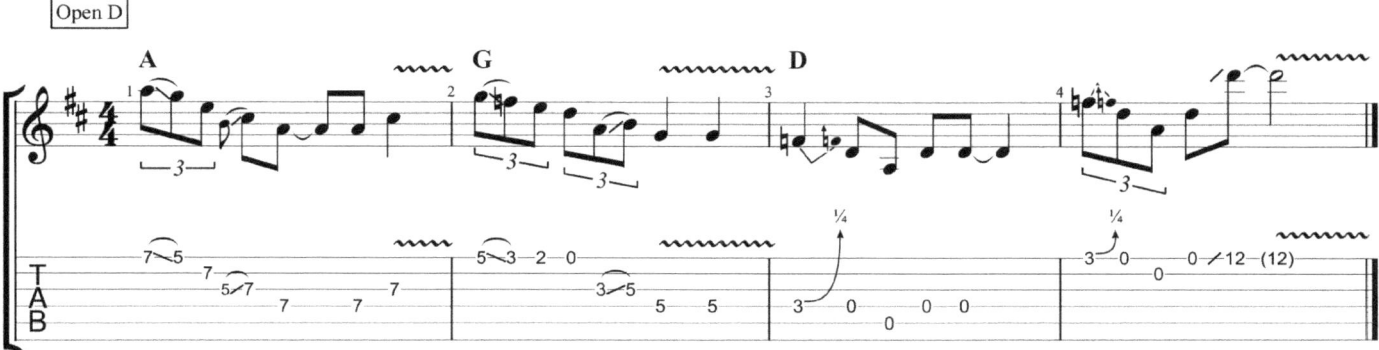

With those ideas under your fingers, it's time to explore some open position soloing for each chord.

The next example gives you four short open-string licks for G7 in open D tuning.

Example 10n:

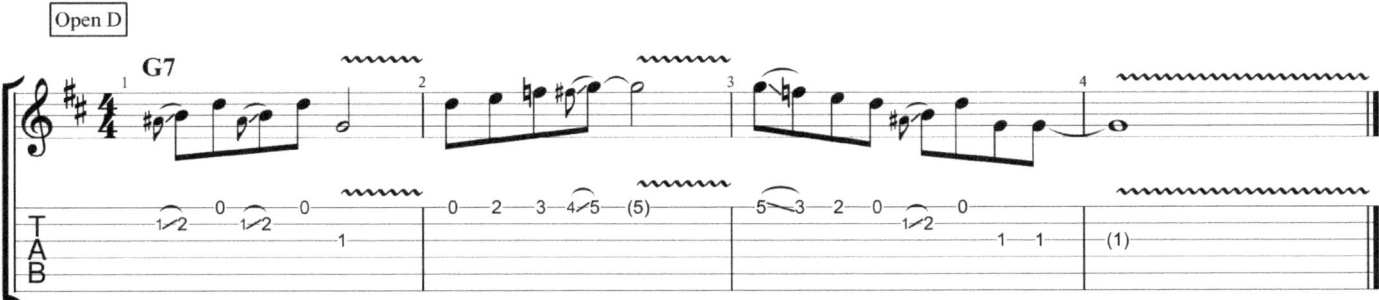

Of course, you should explore this concept further to develop your own language, so here's full neck diagram that shows the "home" position of G Major with the notes available in the open position.

I've also ascended the neck on the first string to help you explore the higher range of the guitar. Strong chord notes are shown in black and the tension notes are shown in white. The rule of thumb is normally to resolve from a tension note to a strong chord tone.

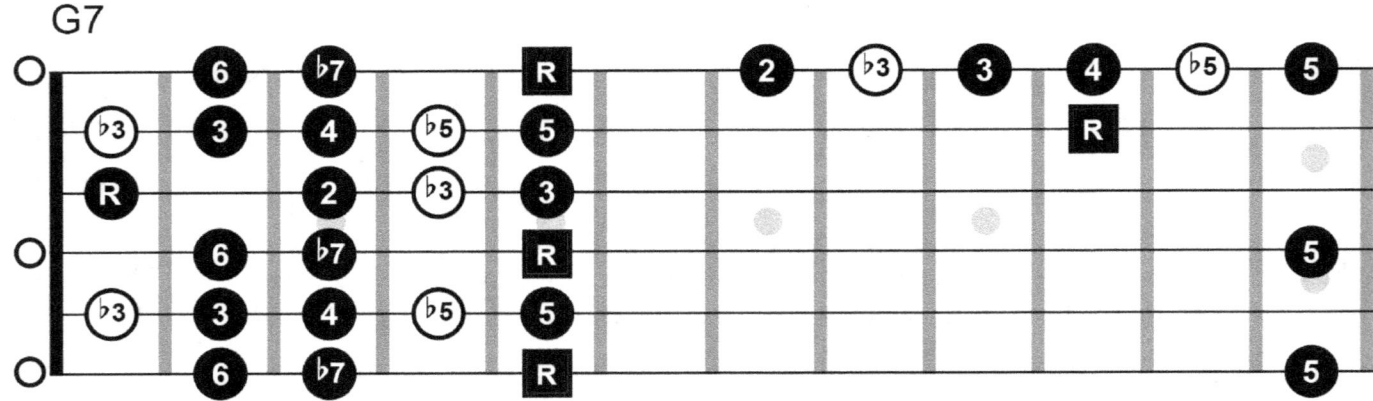

Now here are some open string licks for the V chord (A7) in open D tuning. The root note is on the second string and these licks focus their melodies around that point.

Example 10o:

Again, explore this idea on your own to develop a personal language. Below I've mapped out the "home" position of A Major – this time on the 7th and 5th frets – and added the available notes in the open position. Once again, the white notes are tension notes that should be resolved to the black chord tones.

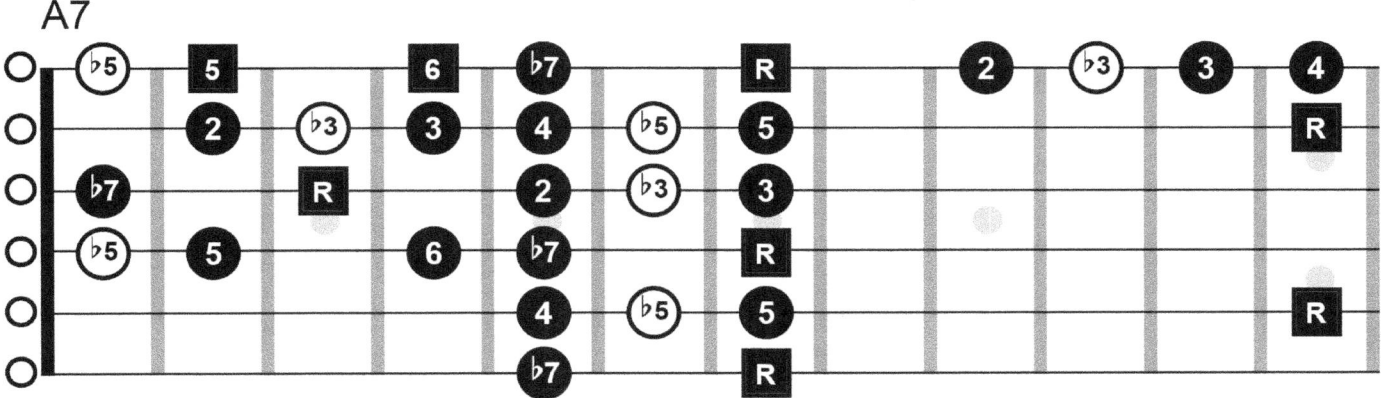

Even though we covered the layout of the best notes to use on D Major earlier, I've included them all on the following diagram so that all the diagrams are in one place.

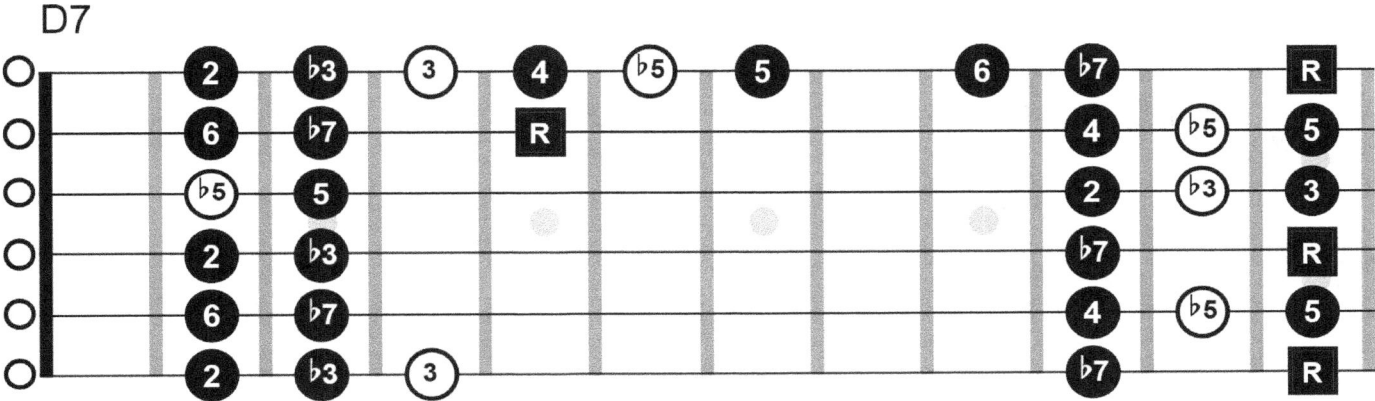

These positions will be exploited fully in the solos chapter at the end of the book, so get familiar with them now as you'll need them soon!

It's important you understand that whether you're in open D or open G tuning, the I chord will always be formed from the open strings, the IV chord will always be played at the 5th fret, and the V chord will always be played at the 7th fret.

To show you what I mean, let's look at how this works in open G tuning. The I, IV and V chords in the key of G are G Major, C Major and D Major respectively.

Example 10p:

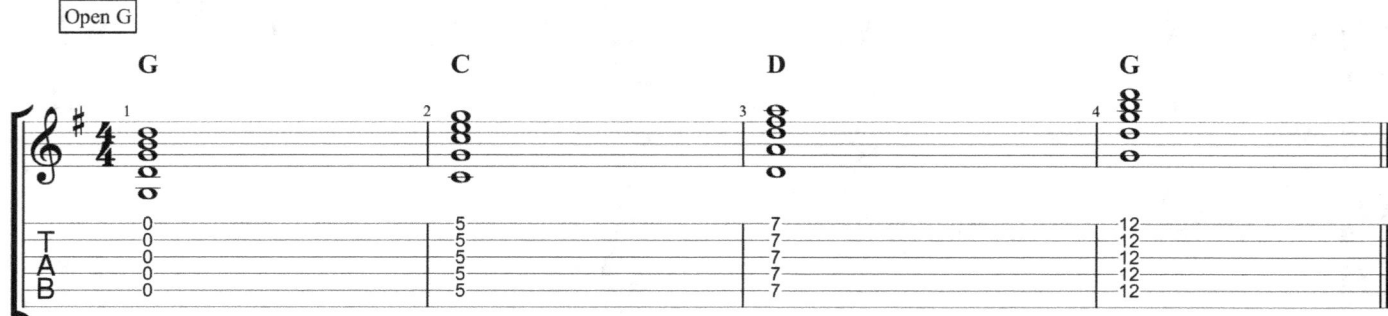

We can explore this further by examining a 12-bar blues idea that outlines the chord changes by shifting between the open, 5th and 7th frets.

Example 10q illustrates a riff-based idea around the all-important open position.

Example 10q:

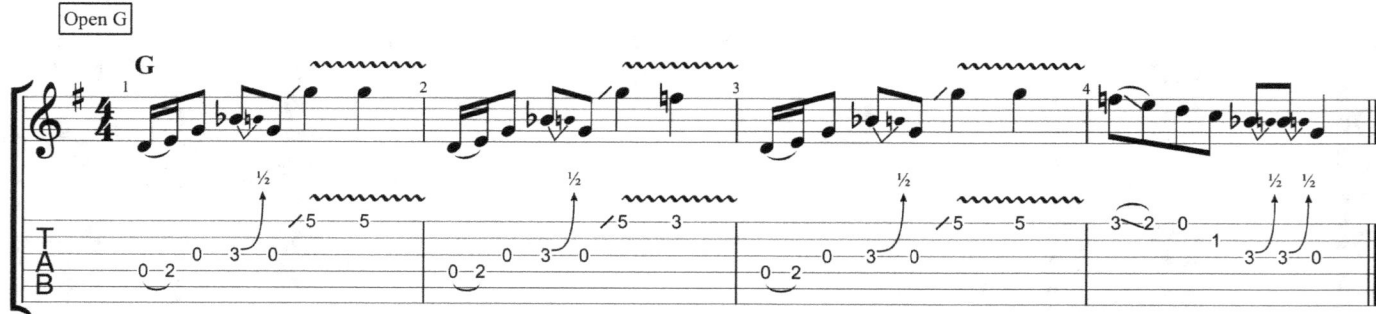

Example 10r begins by targeting the IV chord (C) on the 5th fret, then plays a lick based heavily around this position before moving back down to the open position to outline the chord change back to G.

Example 10r:

73

The V chord, D Major is played at the 7th fret. The following example targets "home" again with a barre chord shape on beat one, then decorates it with a riff using the box pattern you're familiar with by now.

The final four bars move down through the V, IV and I chords before returning to the V chord (this is called a *turnaround*). Notice how the changes are clearly outlined by moving the home position on each chord.

Example 10s:

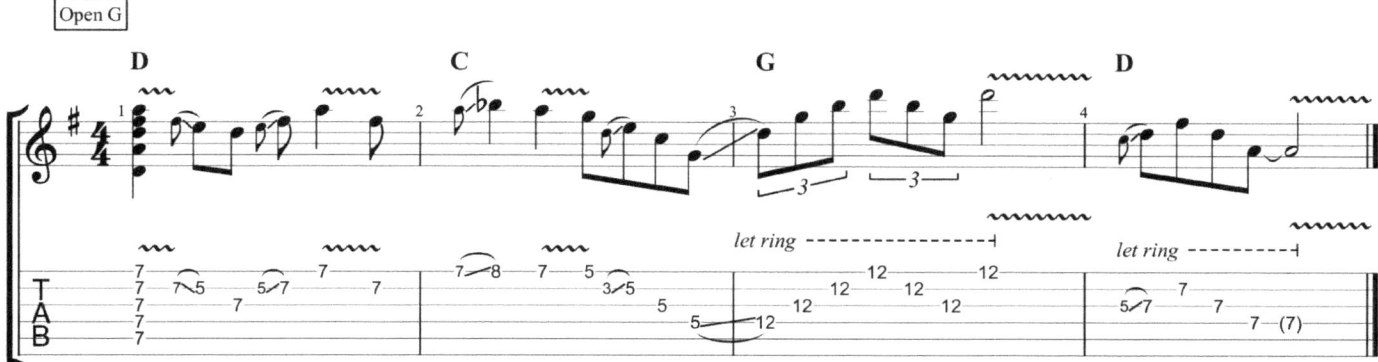

Go back over this section slowly, and really pay attention to these "home" positions. This is an integral part of learning to change chords fluently when playing slide. Once you get your head around the idea that playing slide often means treating a barred fret as "home", you'll take to learning licks and patterns much faster.

Chapter Eleven – Fretting Notes Using Fingers

The Delta blues style goes beyond just playing notes with the slide. You also need to become comfortable playing notes with your spare fingers, whilst wearing the slide.

I wear my slide on my pinkie finger as it fits my particular style of playing best, but you can use it on the ring finger too. Experiment with what's most comfortable for you, and work through the examples in this chapter to find the best way to execute them.

One of the most common blues riffs is easily executed with just one finger in the open position in either open D or open G tuning.

Use the index finger to play the fretted note in the first example, while wearing the slide on your chosen finger. This can be played either straight or with a shuffle feel.

You'll see in the tablature below that there is no way to know whether the fretted note is played with your finger or with the slide. Unfortunately, this is one of the drawbacks of music notation. Sometimes you just have to use some common sense and your ears to figure out which notes are fretted with the fingers and which are fretted with the slide.

Example 11a:

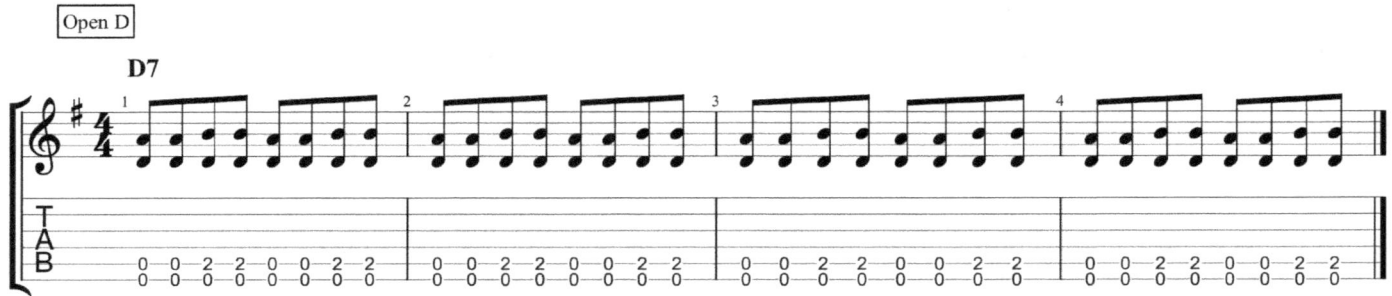

This example begins with the same blues riff, then moves up the neck to play a melody with the slide.

Example 11b:

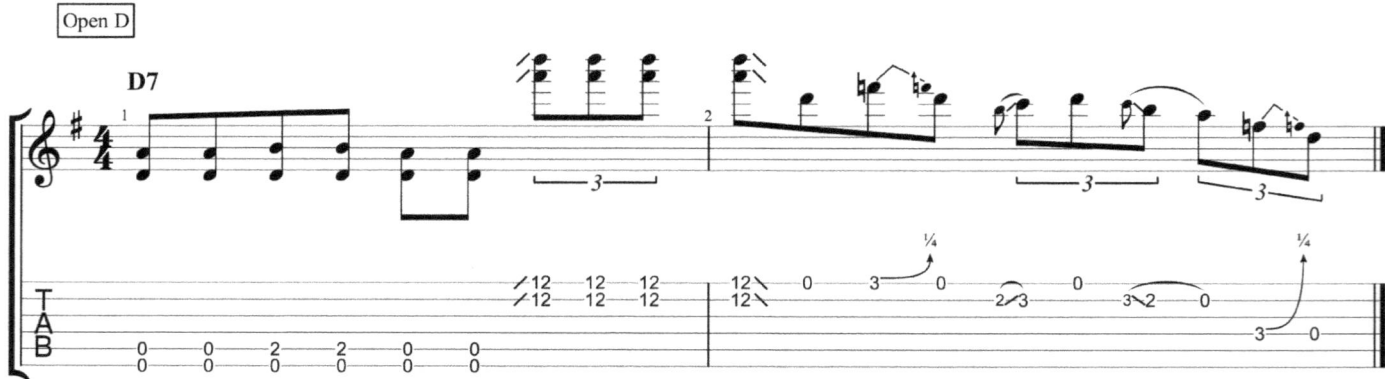

Still in open D tuning, let's try that riff on a G Major chord. The following example does not use a slide, but you should still be wearing it!

Example 11c:

An easy note to add to the open D riff is the C at the 3rd fret on the fifth string. The C is the b7 of D and creates a bluesy D7 sound.

Example 11d:

A similar idea adds some movement between the I (D) and IV (G) chords. Play the D riff for three bars and the D7 sound in bar four. This helps pull the chord progression to the G chord in bar five.

Example 11e:

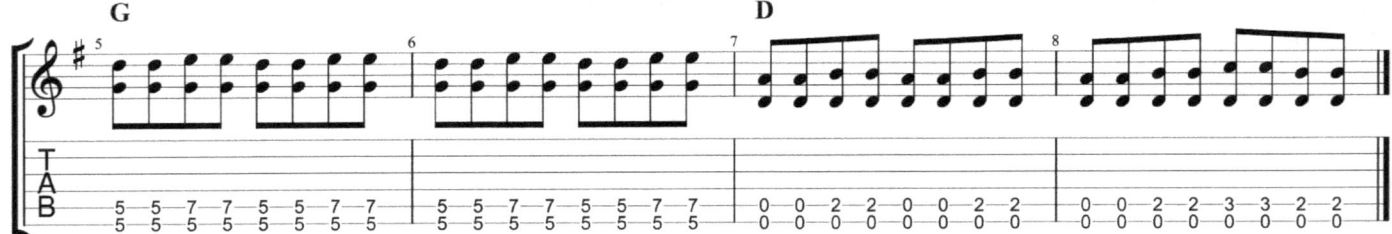

Let's add the V chord (A) using the same pattern at the 7th fret to complete the blues pattern.

Example 11f:

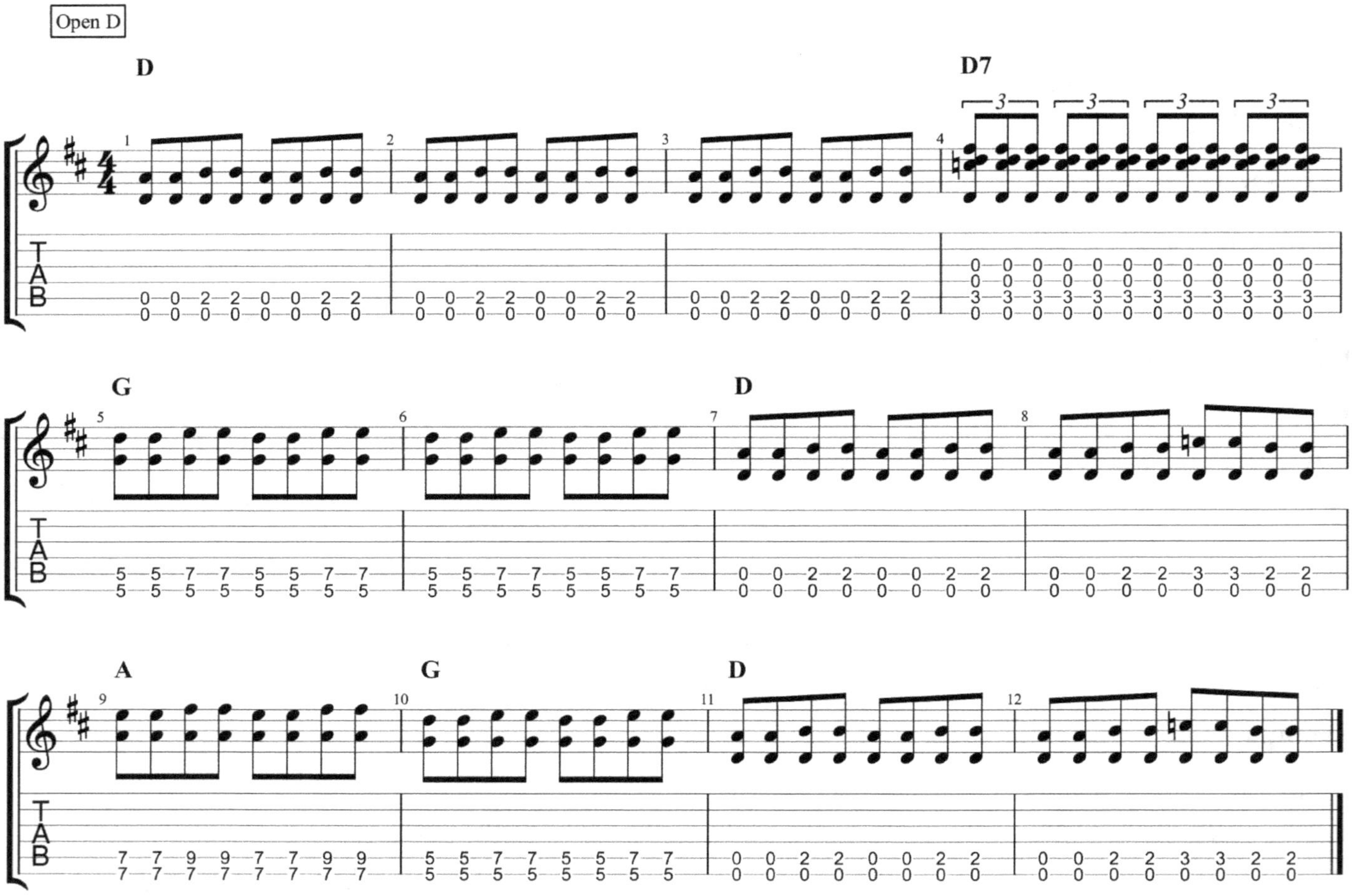

There are many ways to decorate these basic riffs to outline the sound of the blues. Here's another voicing that can be used in place of the IV (G) chord in bars five and six.

This voicing is much harder to play as it requires the use of three fingers. This is one where the slide being on the pinky will come in handy!

77

Example 11g:

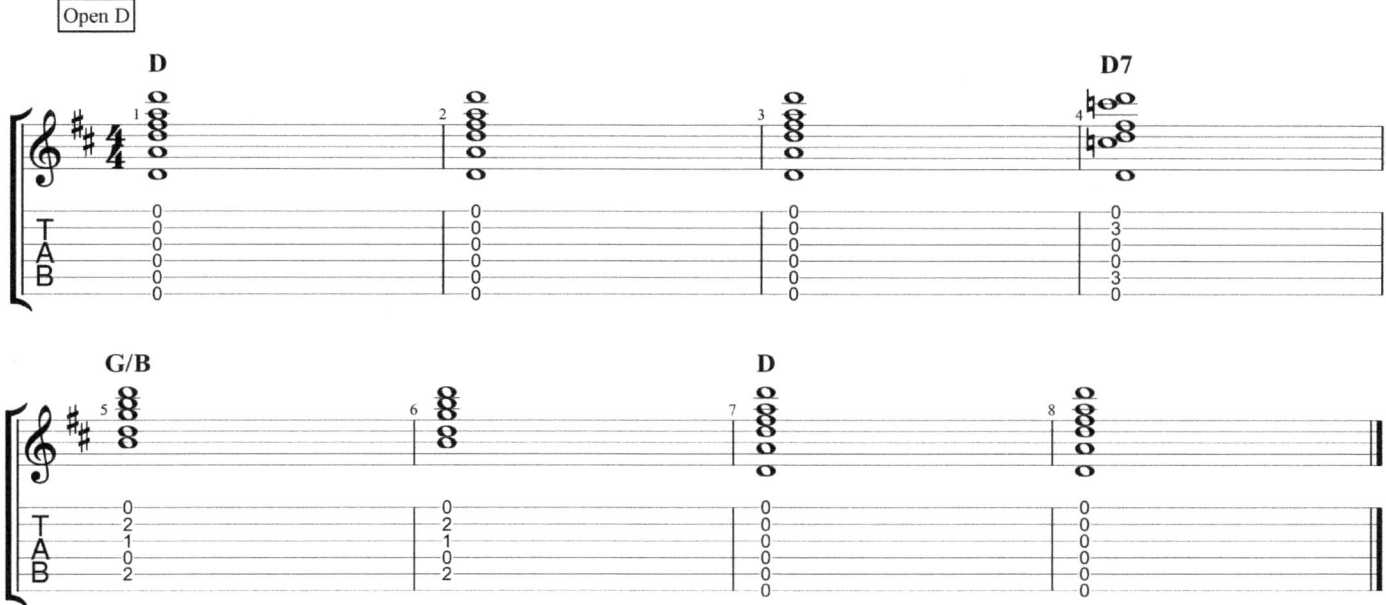

Here's a three-finger voicing that can be used to play the V chord (A Major) in open D tuning. Remember, you should still be wearing your slide!

Example 11h:

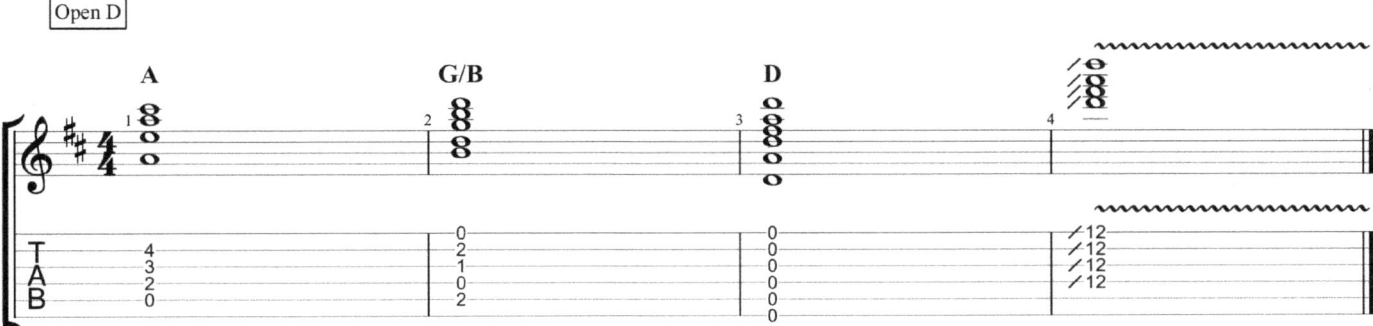

We can use the spare fretting fingers to play single notes that punctuate open position riffs, as this *Death Letter Blues*-inspired riff demonstrates.

Example 11i:

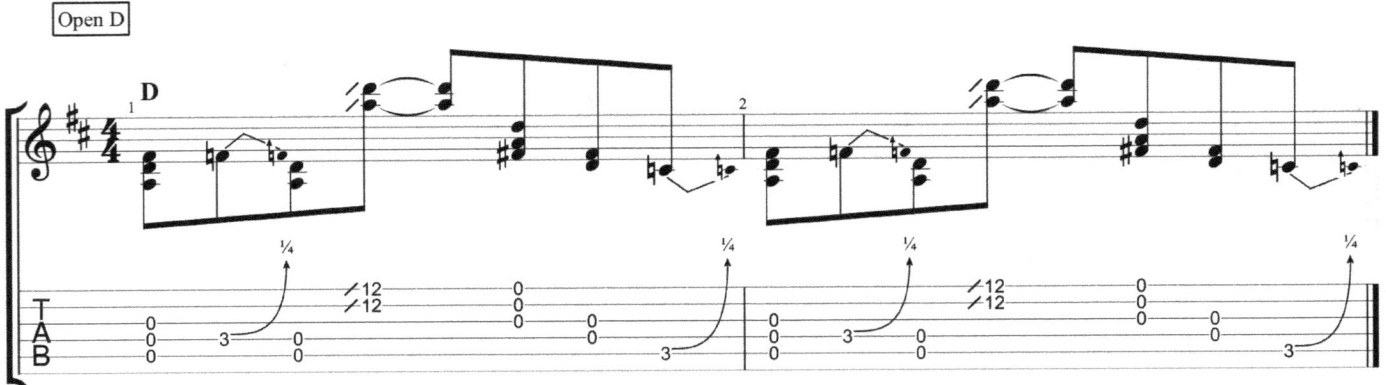

We can also use fretted notes to play a stereotypical blues turnaround, as demonstrated in the following *Crossroads*-inspired lick.

Use the first finger of the fretting hand to move downwards chromatically on the fifth string, before shifting up to the V chord (A) on the 7th fret with the slide.

Example 11j:

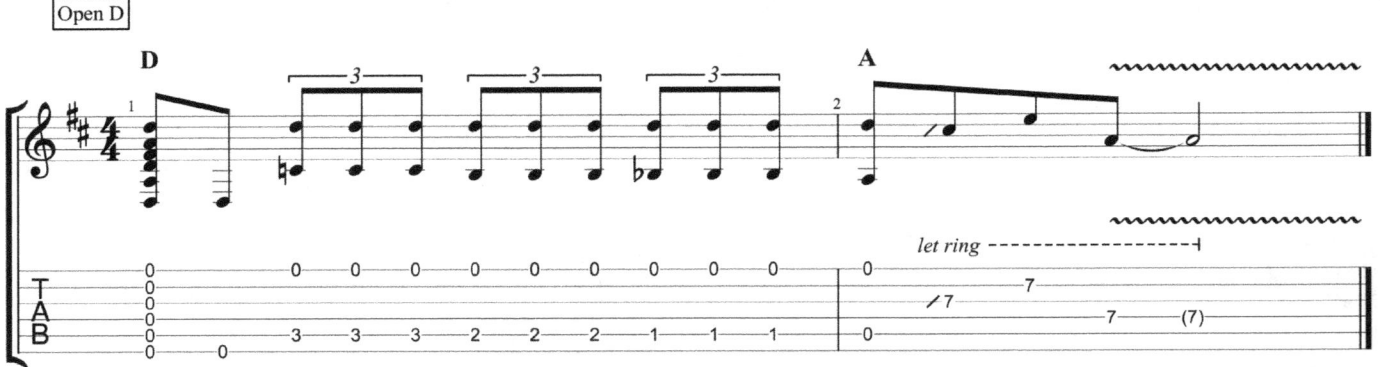

The next example has a similar pattern, but mixes it up by adding the second string to the triplet part and adding descending quarter notes in the bass part. Turnarounds like this were very common in the playing of Robert Johnson.

Example 11k:

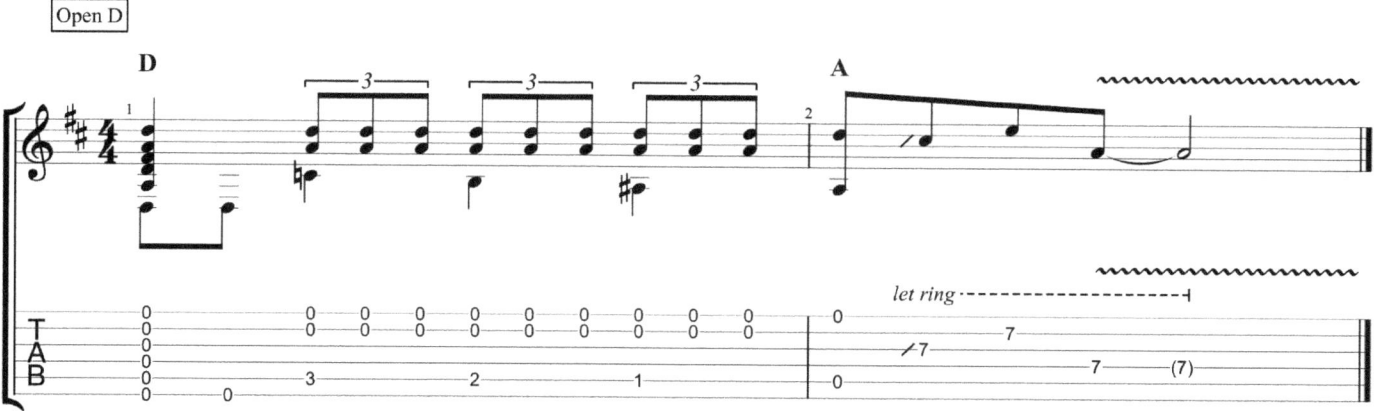

Depending on the tuning you're in, this same pattern can be exploited elsewhere. In open D, both the fifth and second strings are tuned to A, so the descending bass note that was played on the fifth string could be moved over to the second string for an alternative approach.

Example 11l:

Double-stops are also a nice way to add some variety to your playing. They sound great when you add in the slide for fills.

To execute these 6th intervals, you must use the index and middle fingers of the fretting hand while keeping the slide out of the way.

Example 11m:

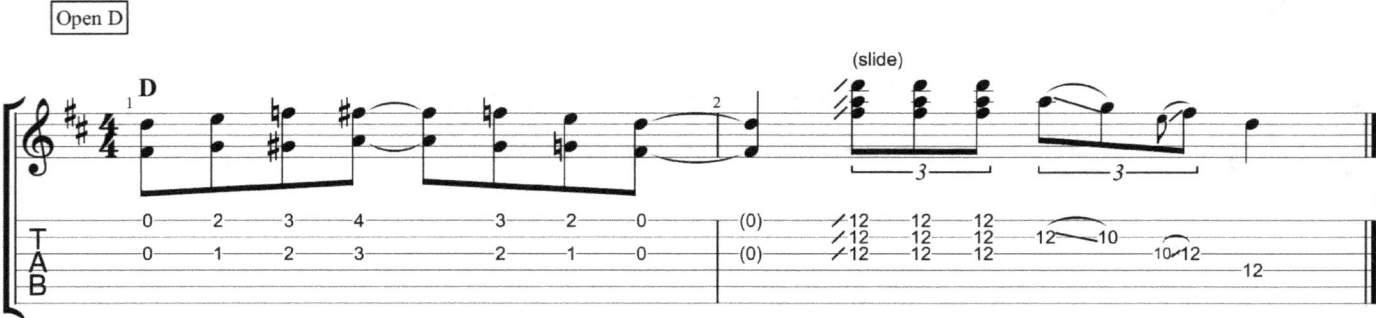

This idea can also be adapted to help you play more interesting turnaround licks, this time with descending 6ths on the third and fifth strings.

Example 11n:

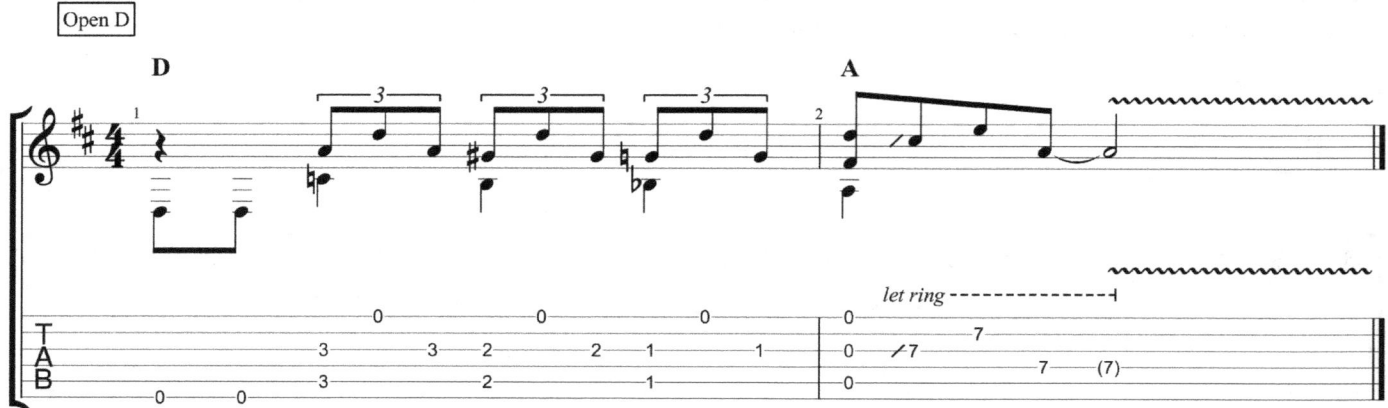

Playing these 6th intervals can be tricky, because the note patterns change as you move up the neck. Octaves are an easier option for the aspiring slide player. As the first and fourth strings are tuned to D, and the second and fifth strings are tuned to A, playing two notes on the same fret on these strings allows you to play an octave easily.

Example 11k showcases these patterns on both strings. As with the previous example, use the first and second finger to fret them.

Example 11o:

You can also play octaves between the fourth and sixth strings. Play the following lick to master the string changes while playing octaves.

Example 11p:

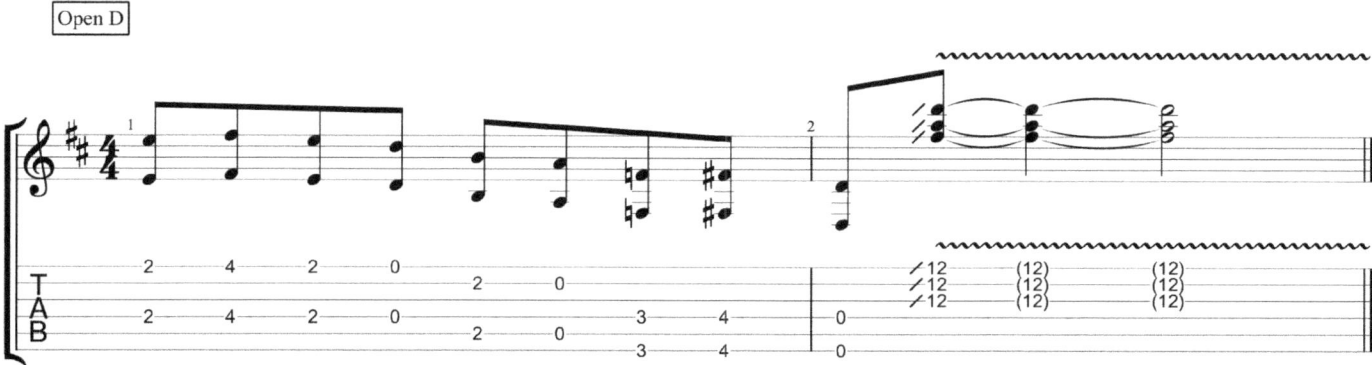

One final use of the fingers is to play single note melodies with techniques like hammer-ons and pull-offs. While it's possible to play these with a slide, fretting these notes normally will always give you accurate intonation and help you play cleaner notes, as playing them with the slide can cause adjacent strings to sound.

The following lick sounds a little cleaner when hammering onto the 2nd fret with the index finger of the fretting hand, rather than the slide. The slide is then used to play a bluesy bend on the fourth string.

Example 11q:

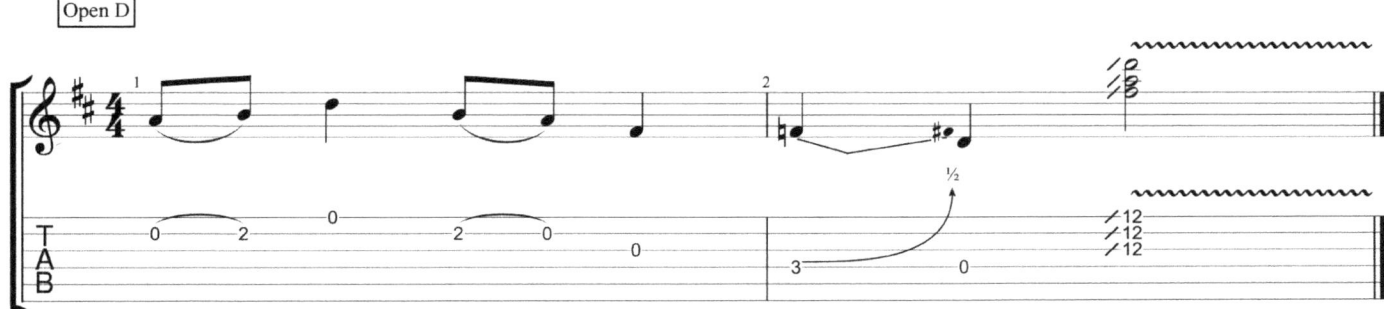

There really is no end to the possibilities here and they go way beyond the scope of a book focused on Delta blues slide playing. Playing slide blues is about the slide becoming an extension of your body. A big part of that is learning to use the fingers independently while wearing the slide.

It's worthwhile grabbing any resources on playing fingerstyle blues and learning to play the licks and phrases in your chosen tuning while wearing the slide. Developing this level of dexterity is an excellent use of your time as you'll to make the slide contribute to, rather than hinder, your blues vocabulary.

Chapter Twelve – Solo Blues

With all the basic Delta techniques understood, there's no better way to practise fluency than by learning a full solo.

I've composed this tune in open G, so you can see just how similar these tunings are. While open D can be a lot of fun, having the I chord sounding so low can be a drag. Open G brings a nice change of pace as the I chord is now a 4th higher and you have the notes in the box pattern available below the chord.

Here's a full neck diagram of the notes in open G tuning showing their relationship to the tonic G Major chord. This map combine the notes of the G Mixolydian mode (G A B C D E F) and the G Blues scale (G Bb C Db D F), to create a hybrid blues scale consisting of the intervals R 2 b3 3 4 b5 5 6 b7.

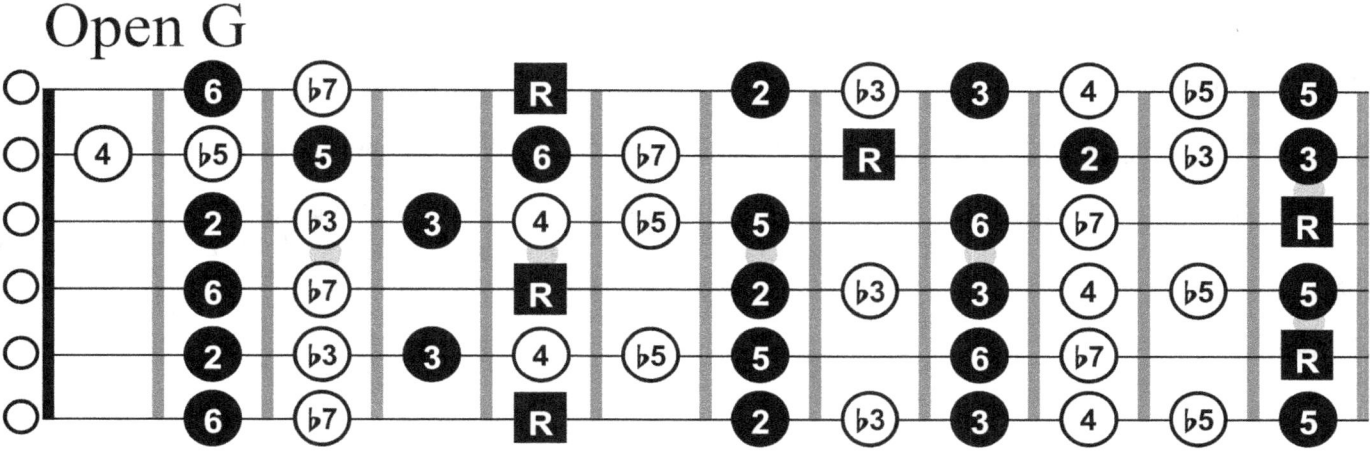

While this diagram contains a lot of notes, remember that most of your playing will be based around the "home" position of G Major on the 12th fret, and the line of notes below that on the 10th fret. The other notes provide colour or tension to create more interesting melodies.

Notes such as the b3 and b5 should be used as passing notes and resolve to stronger ones. In the following piece, you'll gain most mileage out of focusing on the G Major Pentatonic scale (1 2 3 5 6).

Open G - G Major Pentatonic

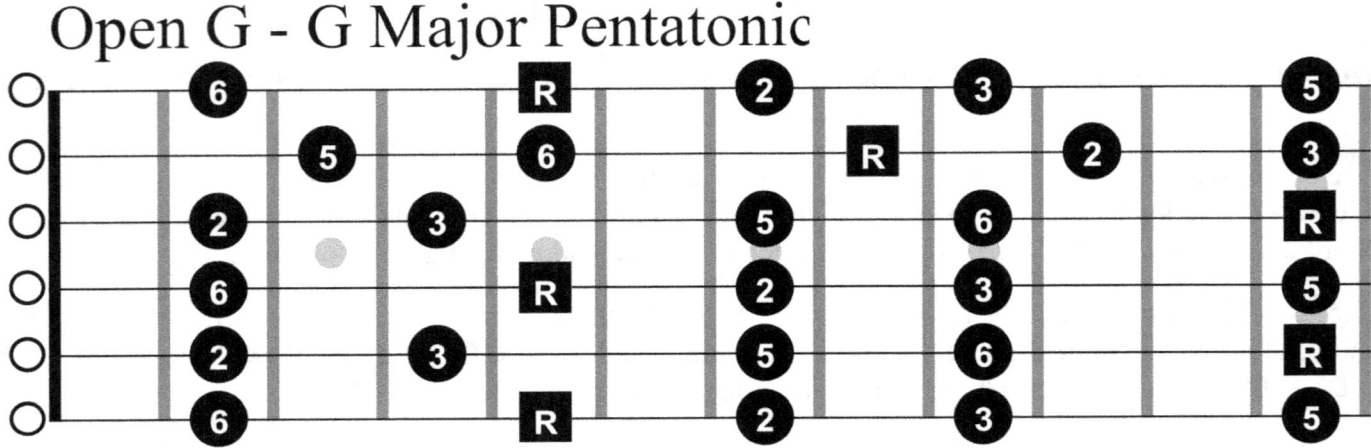

Blues Solo Breakdown

Learn the following sections individually before joining them together into one complete piece.

The first four bars all outline a G Major chord using a barre at the 12th fret and the first lick acts as an introduction to the twelve-bar form. To make things bluesy, move the double stop slides in bar three really slowly.

Example 12a:

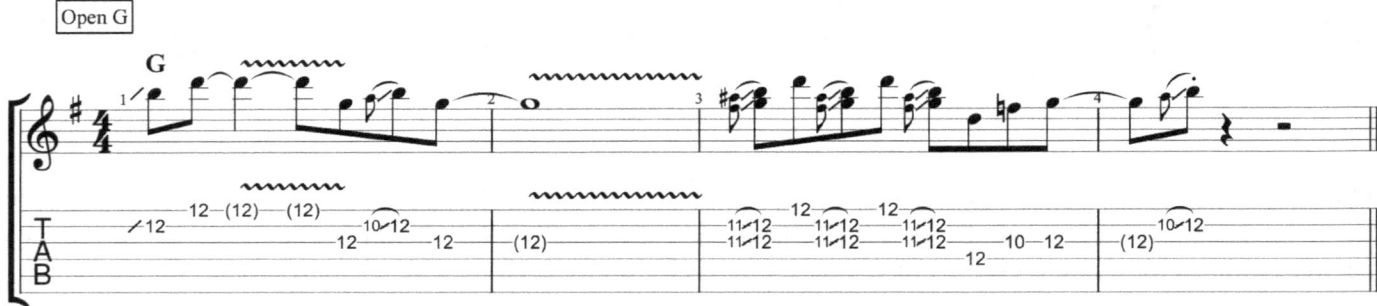

The next four bars complete the introduction by hitting the V chord (D Major), then playing a classic turnaround to get you into the song.

In the first two bars, use your finger to play the 1st fret on the second string, and hammer from the open fourth string to the 2nd fret.

The turnaround lick can be tricky to play, as it requires fingers to fret notes while the top and bottom notes move in different directions. After playing the open G Major chord in bar three, the notes on the fourth string descend chromatically from the 3rd fret, while the notes on the second string ascend chromatically from the open string.

Example 12b:

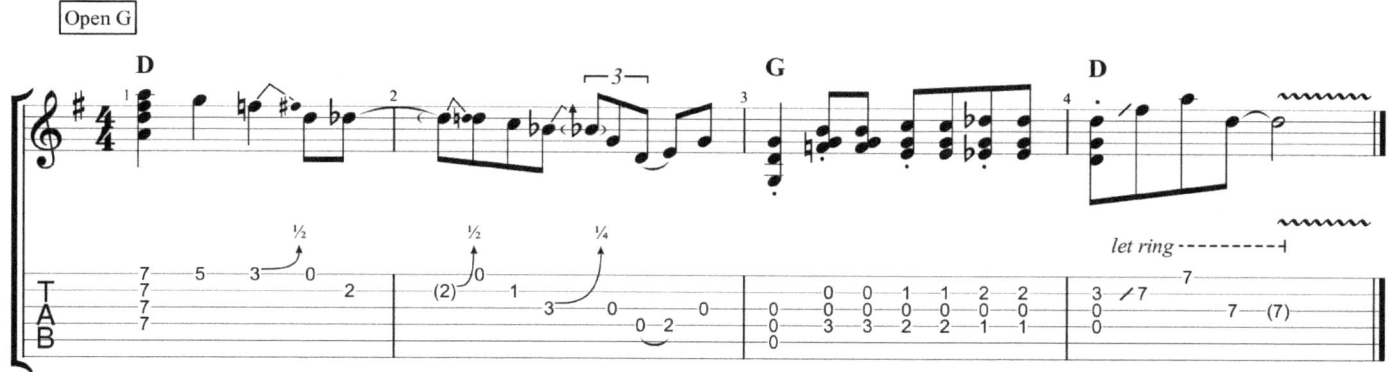

The next riff forms a repeating figure that defines the first chorus and will take some patience to perfect. The slide on the sixth string and the open double stops are ideally played with a thumb pick, while the other notes are played with the fingers.

The notes with downward stems indicate that the bass notes should be played with the thumb. The up stems should be played with the fingers.

Learn this idea extremely slowly until it feels effortless, because a real Delta blues player would be able sing while playing a guitar part such as this.

Example 12c:

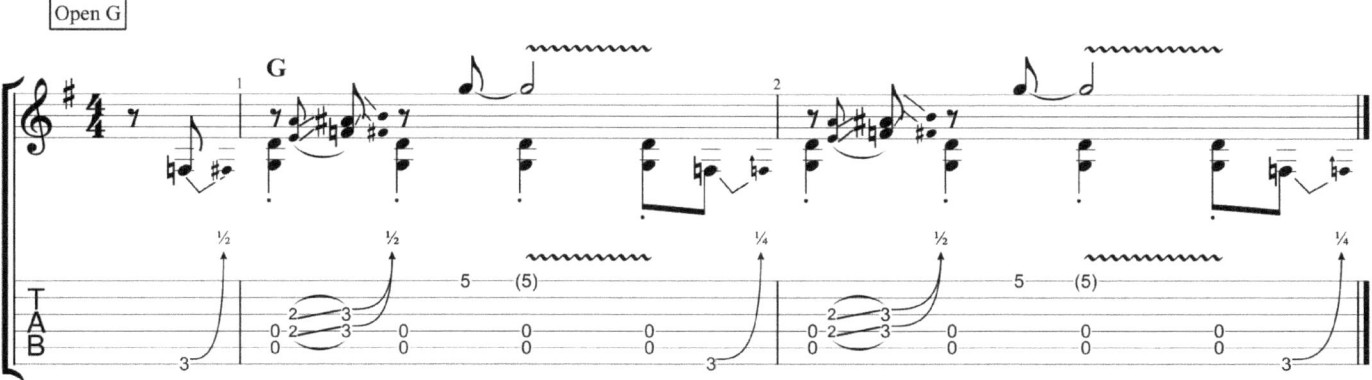

The following two bars continue the same feel with a repeating double stop played by the thumb, while altering the melody a little with a slide up to the 12th fret.

The final barre here can be tricky, as you need to let the open strings ring while playing the double-stop with the slide *and* applying vibrato. The final chord hints at an F Major triad over a G bass which creates a G7 sound.

Example 12d:

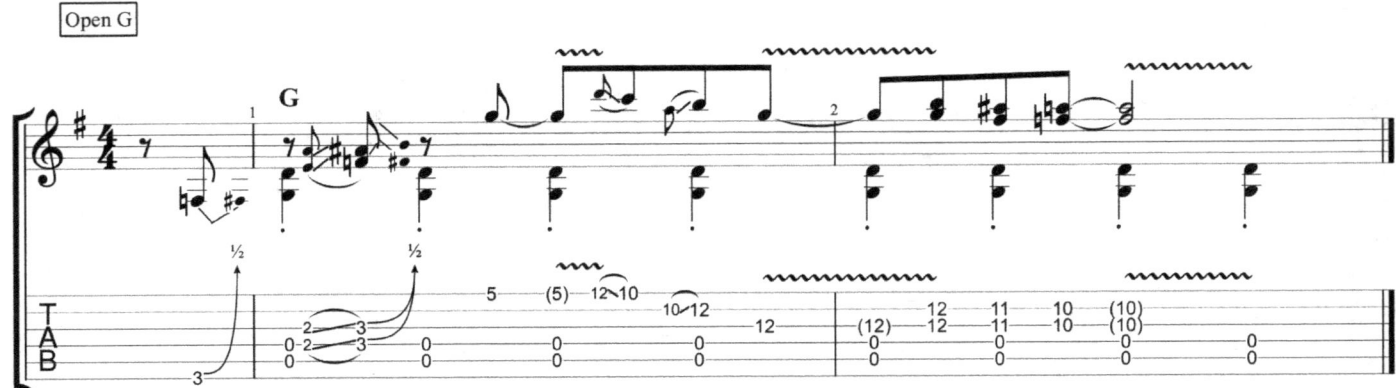

While you might expect the next two bars to rest on the IV (C Major), you'll find a slight variation in the progression, where the C Major chord is shifted up to Eb Major in the second bar. This creates a bluesy tension that pulls the progression back to the I chord.

The notes in beat 3 of the first bar should be fretted while the 4th beat is played with the slide.

When the song moves back to the G chord, use the thumb to pound away on the double-stop and keep the groove.

Example 12e:

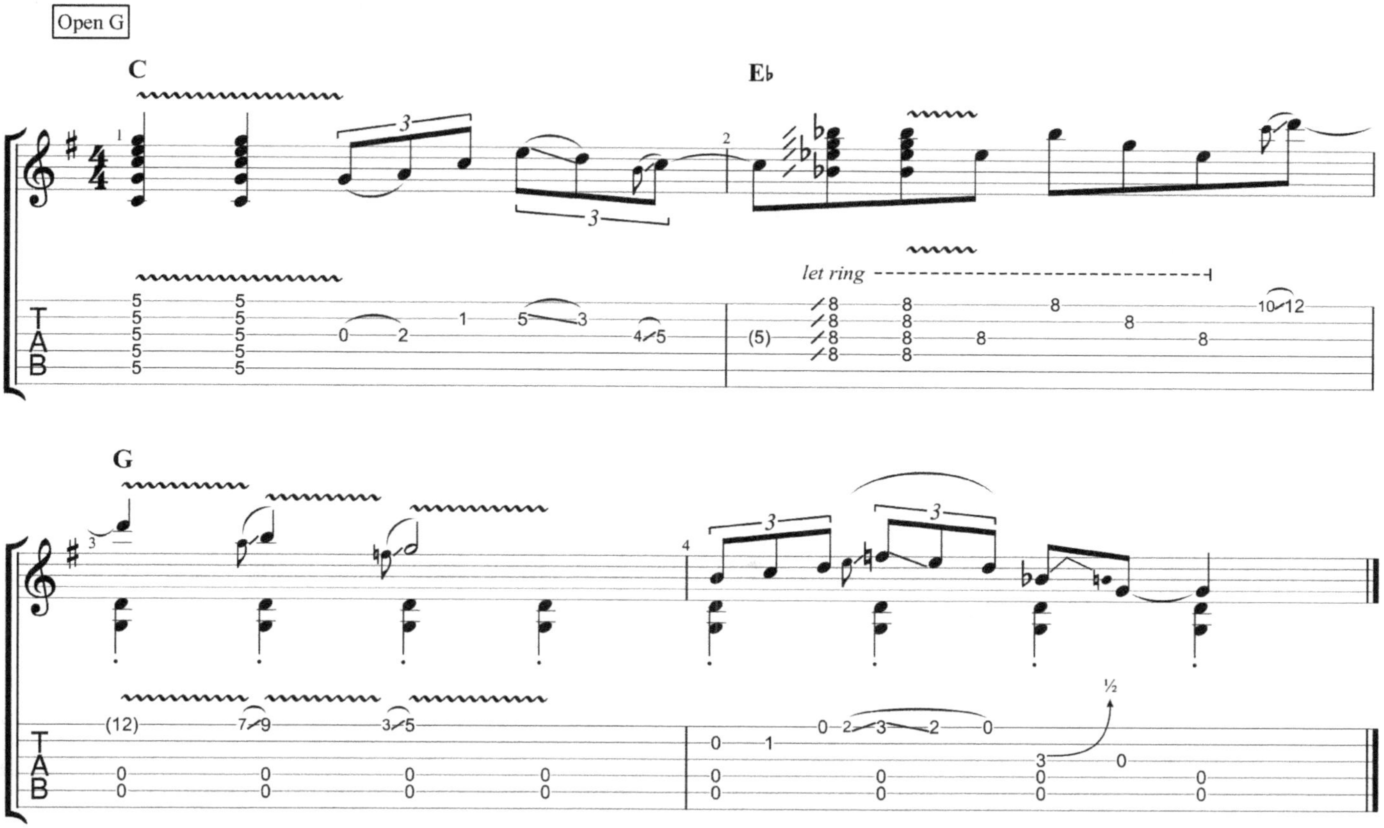

Playing over the V chord (D Major) is achieved by moving to the 7th fret where a melody in octaves on the first and fourth strings decorate the chord.

We then move down a tone to the 5th fret to outline the IV chord (C Major), before ending on a turnaround lick which is played without the slide. The slide is used for the final chord at the 7th fret.

Example 12f:

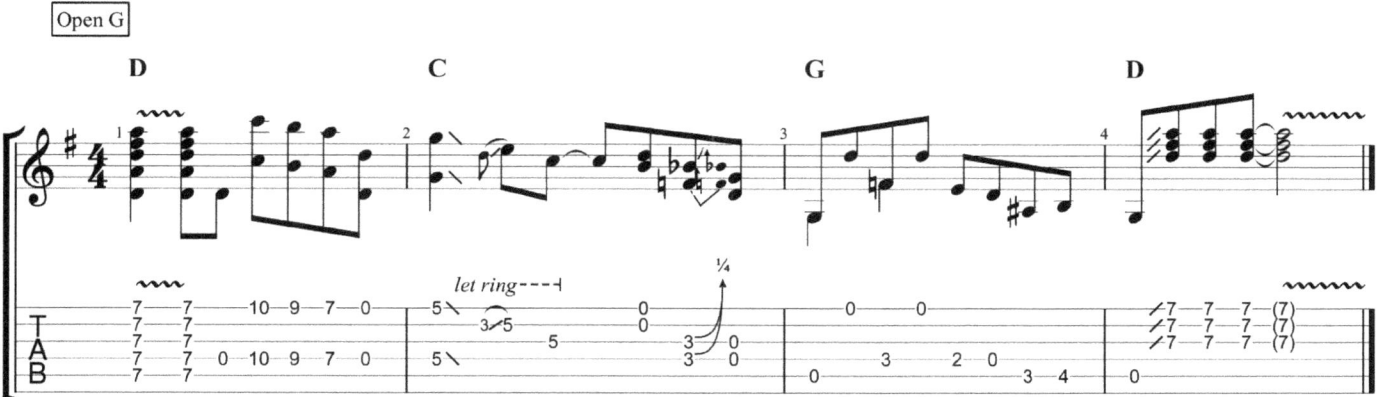

On the second time through the progression, things are mixed up a bit with an open position riff which you should fret with your fingers, and added melodies with the slide for variation. All the double-stops are fretted with the finger and the single note melodies are played with the slide.

Example 12g:

On the IV chord (C Major) the fretted riff moves up to the 5th fret, which requires you to hold a two-fret barre with the first finger and to play the 7th fret with an additional finger. (As I place the slide on my pinkie finger, I'm using my ring finger, but any available finger will work).

The slide is again used to add single note melodies, offset against the riff.

Example 12h:

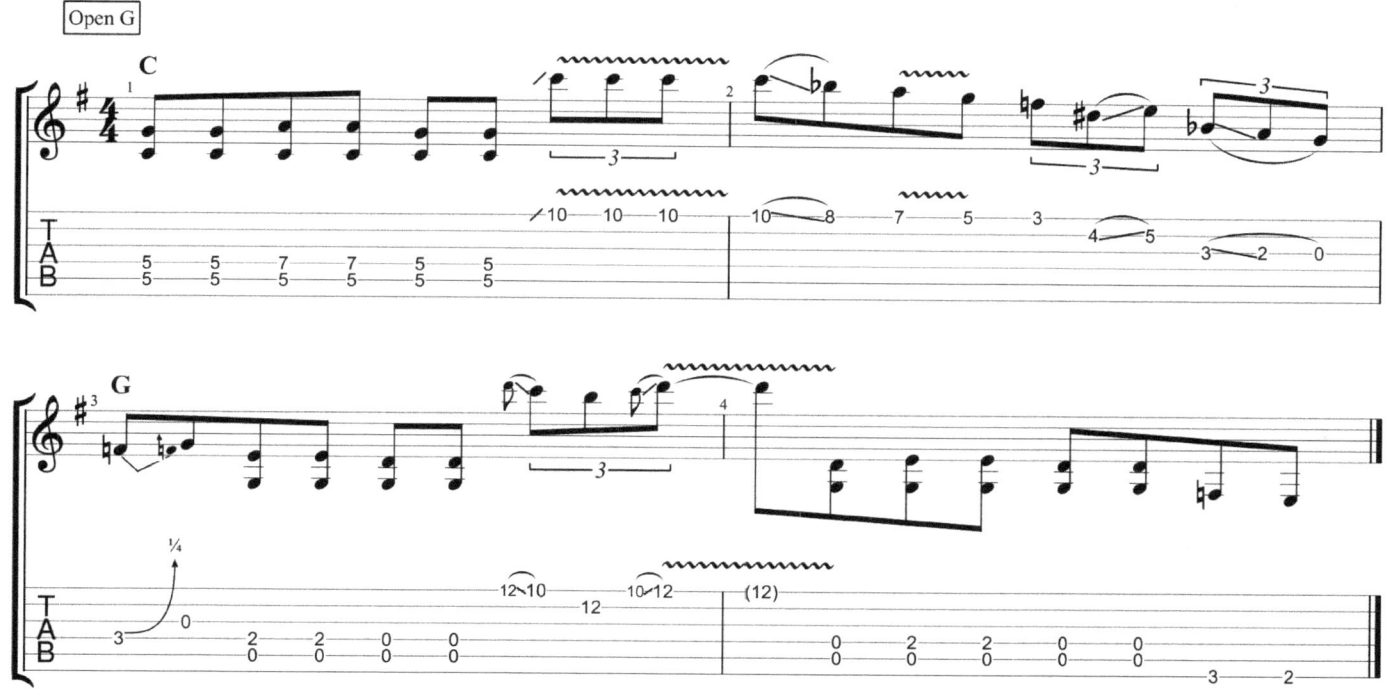

The final part of this solo continues with the theme of fretted chords and single note melodies played with the slide.

To outline the D Major chord, an open position C Major chord has been moved up two frets. This still gives us the D and F# notes, but with an open G string added, and results in a more colourful Dadd11 chord.

The solo ends with the same turnaround idea from the introduction, which now resolves to the I chord (G Major) at the 12th fret. Ending on the I chord like this gives the feeling that the music has come to an end.

Example 12i:

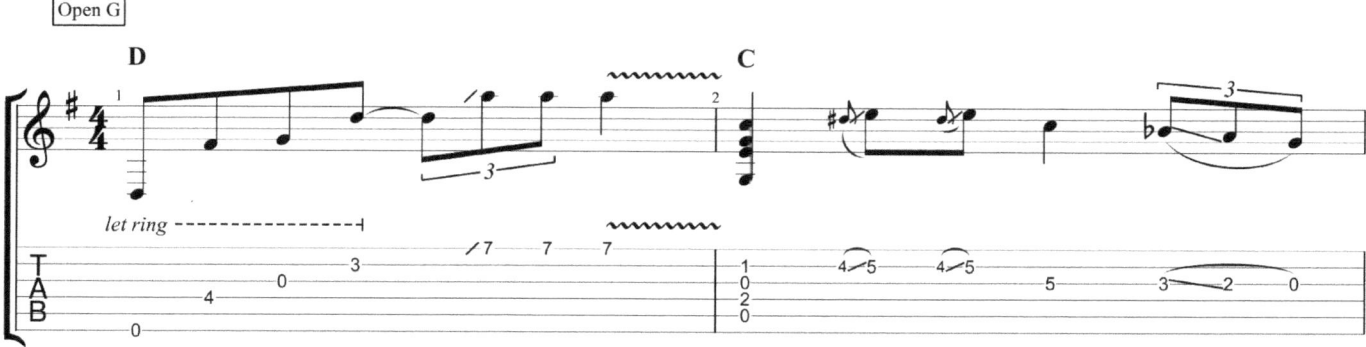

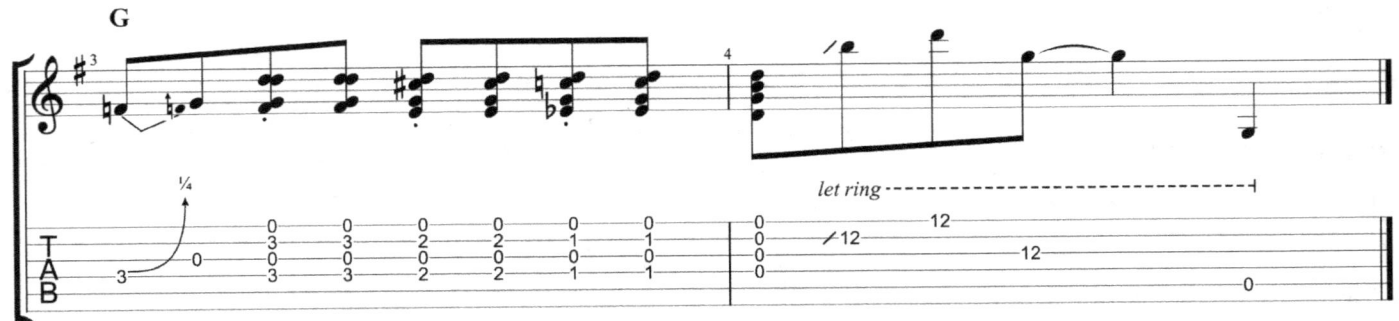

Once you have this entire piece under your fingers, you'll have a feel for how to play a twelve-bar blues in the Delta style. There's a fixed chord progression that's being followed, and as long as you know where you are in the chord progression you will be able to play some great music.

With the structure of the blues in mind, you could pick absolutely any lick from this book and use it in place of the licks that have been played in blues the tune above.

Nothing is set in stone. Delta slide guitar is about expressing yourself, so experiment and substitute the licks and lines you like the sound of into the tune. Write your own solos and discover the musical voice you have inside you.

Chapter Thirteen – Blues Rag

At the birth of the slide guitar movement was the *Guitar Rag*. Similar in style to the twelve-bar blues, the rag is a common chord progression used in early blues music. This tune includes a country-style thumb picked alternating bass line, so pay attention to the directions of the note stems so you know what should be played with the thumb, and what should be picked with the fingers.

For "Blues Rag", I've composed two full choruses of the progression and added an extra eight bars to end. The song is presented here one section at a time, but when you're comfortable with each section, you should play it as one complete piece as heard on the audio download.

While the twelve-bar blues in the previous chapter only included the I, IV and V chords, the ragtime progression also adds in the II chord (E) for some additional movement and shows an early jazz influence.

The first eight bars of the progression are predominantly based around the tonic chord of D, though there's a quick move to the V chord (A) in bar six, which creates a little movement without impacting the melody.

Throughout the first four bars, play the hammer-on with the first finger, then switch to the slide for the sustained notes on the first string.

When the chord moves to A Major in bar six, the octaves are fretted with the first and second fingers before using the slide on the 3rd fret bend in bar seven.

The most important part of the song is always the melody, so play the higher notes a little louder than the thumb part so they ring out clearly.

Example 13a:

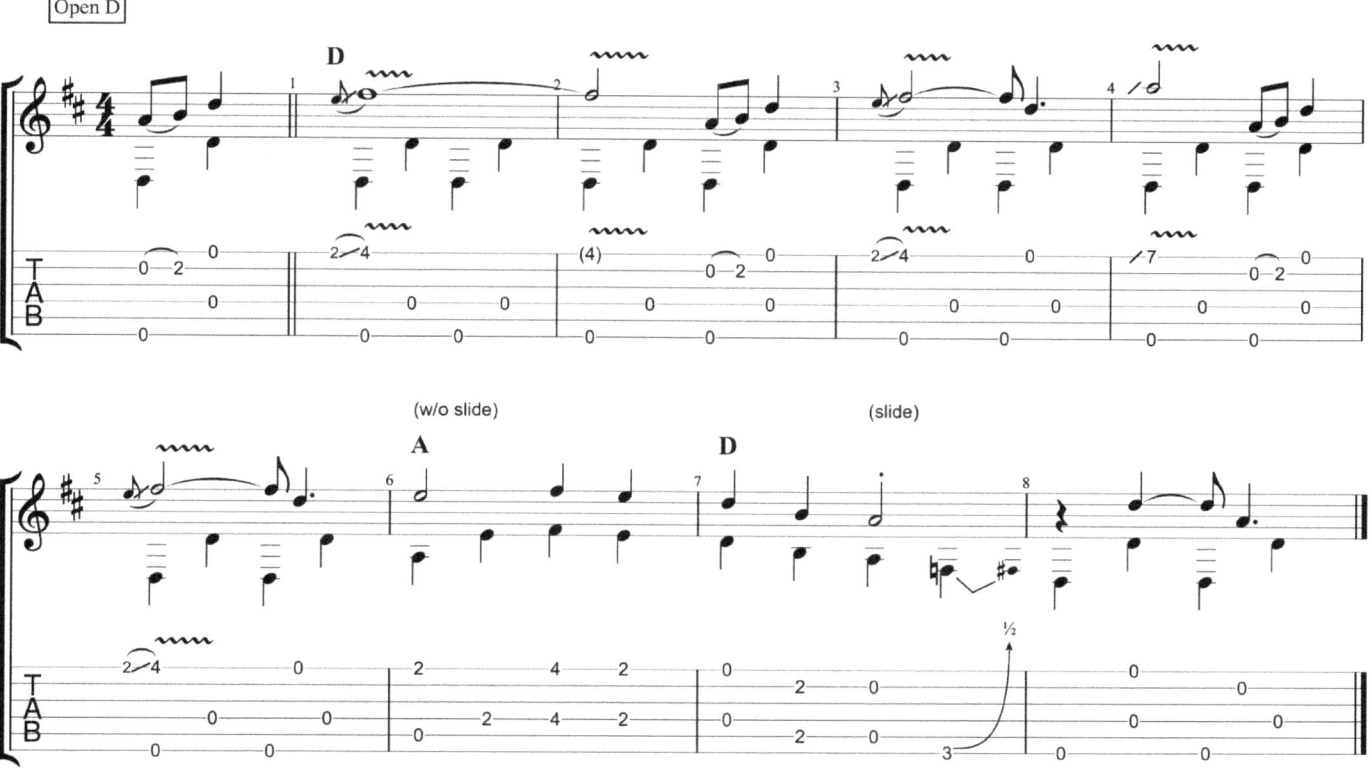

Before tackling the next section as a complete part, it's worth getting to grips with the chord movement.

For this entire section, the slide barres across all six strings as it moves from chord to chord. The chord progression is G Major, D Major, E Major, A Major (IV I II V). The most authentic way to play this is to let the notes ring out and add a soft vibrato to help with the intonation.

Practise the isolated bassline before moving on.

Example 13b:

Playing the driving bass part means you can't really move the slide to play the melody, so all the melody notes need to fall under the slide.

When the chord changes to the open D, the slide is suddenly free to add a little more melody on the first string.

At the end of the progression the slide moves down from the 7th to the 6th fret on the final beat. This melody links back to the G Major chord at the 5th fret on the repeat.

Example 13c:

The next part of the melody is similar to the previous section, this time moving from E Major to A Major, then up to D Major in the final four bars.

This is a pleasing resolution as the melody can continue up the neck while the bass part moves down to the open strings.

Example 13d:

In essence, that's all there is to the tune, but that's the beauty of an uncomplicated song – it's possible to endlessly explore the tune and create variations that can be added to develop the music.

Here's a more challenging version of the first eight bars of the piece.

Example 13e:

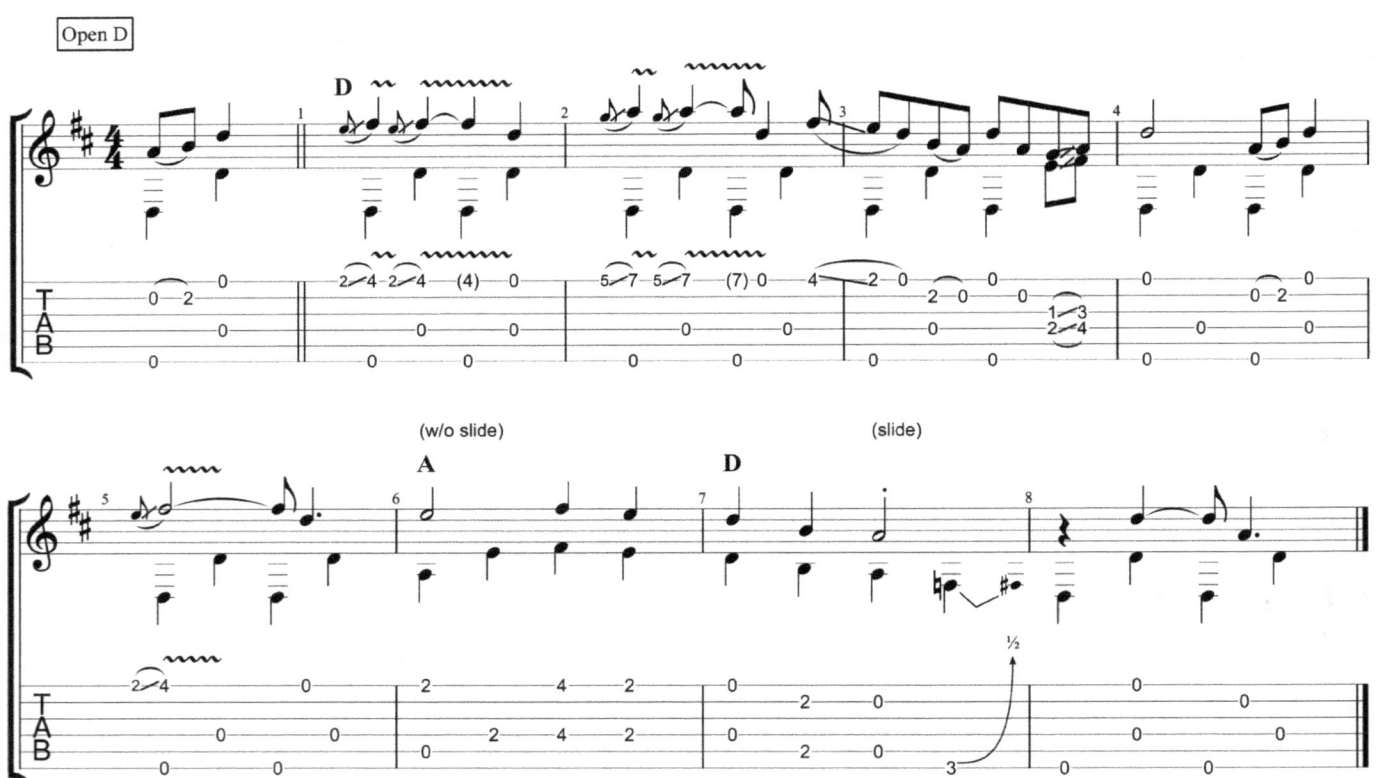

Here's a more embellished version of the following section, this time with an open position lick in the third bar, and a slide into the E chord in the fifth bar.

You could play absolutely any lick in bar three; it's about adding something interesting to guide the listener into the D chord. Everything else is under the slide.

Example 13f:

Here's a much trickier lick on the D chord in the next section. The lick begins with the slide, but then plays three notes fretted with the fingers before playing the open strings and sliding up to the 12th fret. It will take time to get that to feel natural, but it's a perfect example of what can be achieved using the slide and fingers together.

Example 13g:

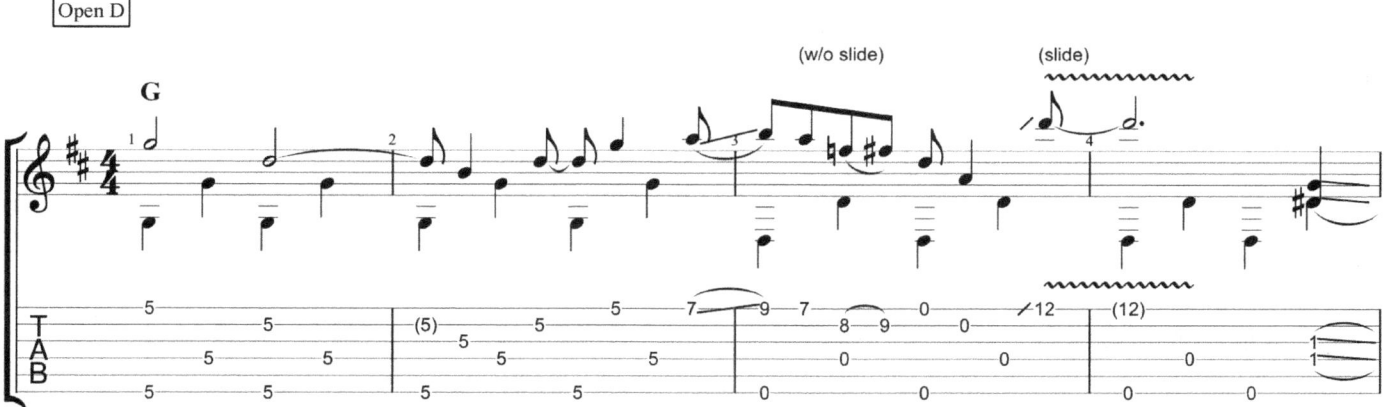

After two passes through the whole form, I've ended the performance with a final run through the first eight bars, with a slight variation on the melody. Gradually slow the piece down as you come to an end for a feeling of completion. Listen to the audio to hear how this should sound.

Example 13h:

Progressing from here is just a case of listening, copying and experimenting.

Listen to as many recordings and videos as you can find of people playing this song form (however, not the Merle Travis *Cannonball Rag* which often comes up when searching!)

The more comfortable you are with the style, the more fluent you'll become adding your own licks and phrases to the music. Take every opportunity to put your own stamp on the tune, express yourself and play the music that you want to hear.

Good luck!

Conclusion

You should now be well on your way to having a solid understanding of the wild world of Delta blues slide playing.

However, as with any book like this, you're not at the end of the journey. In fact, you've just begun and there's still a long path to walk before you'll feel right at home in this genre. The fascinating thing about this style of playing is just how hard it is to imitate authentically. The people who played this music really didn't know much about music theory, so it's a style that is learnt more by *listening* and *doing*.

You only need to listen to a few Son House or Bukka White recordings to hear that this is a genre that can be simple and complex at the same time. Usually this comes to individual style. Each player had their own approach to hitting the strings. Some Delta bluesmen were precise fingerstyle players, while others were wild and percussive. Son House was so aggressive he would treat his guitar like a drum. Bukka White would flail his arm from bridge to nut when strumming. There's something to be said for the dynamic rage these legends were capable of, even if they were less concerned with things like structure and harmony!

The twelve-bar form was far from established at this period in time. The chords tended to follow the vocal wherever it led. It's not uncommon to hear someone sit on the I chord for ten bars, then go to the IV chord for three bars, then back to the I. The key is listening. Listen, listen, then listen some more. The most effective way to learn to speak a language is to hear it in context.

You have to hear this music to really understand it, otherwise you'll stand out like a sore thumb among the purists. Thankfully, most of this music is from the '20s and '30s and is easy to find online on sites like YouTube or Spotify. You'll pick up CDs for pennies and the charity shops are full of them. There's no excuse for hiding from it, even if it's just a cheap compilation CD (a rarity in 2018!)

To get you started, here are some recommendations of artists and albums to listen to. Most of the names here all predate the traditional album format, so many will be compilations of singles they released in their time. Don't be worried, it's all above board!

- Sylvester Weaver – Complete Recorded Works in Chronological Order Volume 1
- Robert Johnson – The Complete Recordings
- Son House – Son House Library of Congress Recordings 1941 – 1942
- Bukka White – High Fever Blues: The Complete 1930 – 1940 Recordings
- Blind Willie Johnson – The Spiritual Blues
- Blind Willie McTell – King Of The Serpent Blues
- Tampa Red – You Can't Get That Stuff No More
- Charley Patton – The Definitive Charley Patton
- Blind Boy Fuller – Get Your Yas Yas Out
- Leadbelly – The Very Best of Leadbelly
- Elmore James – The Sky Is Crying

- Muddy Waters – The Chess Singles Collection
- Lightnin' Hopkins – Dirty House Blues

When you've got the sound deep in your soul, it's all about experimentation. There's rarely anything so complicated that it can't be worked out with a little exploration. The longer you play, the more of a connection you'll develop between your fingers and your ears, and then you'll really be cooking!

If all else fails, you can always head on down to the crossroads and make a deal…

Good luck!

Levi

SLIDE GUITAR SOLOING TECHNIQUES

Discover the Techniques and Secrets of Modern Slide Guitar Playing

LEVI CLAY

FUNDAMENTAL CHANGES

Chapter One: An Introduction To Slide Playing

Playing slide is one of the few techniques that can change your approach to the guitar at such a fundamental level that it almost becomes a new instrument.

For over 100 years, players of stringed instruments have experimented with items like medicine/beer bottles, copper pipes, knives and more to press on the string and act as a "movable fret". This gives the player near infinite expressive possibilities as they slide between pitches and capture microtonal detail like that of the human voice, rather than the fret-by-fret steps of regular guitar playing.

Finding popularity with the import of the "slack-key" guitar to Hawaii (Spanish guitars that were tuned to open chords and played with a bar), slide guitar found prominence in the blues playing of the Mississippi Delta, with guitarists like Bukka White, Sylvester Weaver, Son House and Robert Johnson taking the style across America and beyond.

This early style of slide blues predated guitar amplifiers, and is an important introduction to the style, often played on beat up old acoustic or resonator guitars with a high action. I covered this style in detail in my book *Delta Blues Slide Guitar*, so check it out if you want an authentic trip down the Delta.

This book examines slide playing in a landscape of loud amplifiers and effects, where slide guitar became a technique that could take the spotlight and captivate audiences.

Electric slide guitar developed an early audience due to players like Elmore James and Muddy Waters, but really took off in the 1960s, coinciding with the British blues boom. Bands like The Rolling Stones, Fleetwood Mac and Led Zeppelin all wore their American blues influences on their sleeve. American rock groups were also featuring slide guitar more prominently, with Duane Allman, Garry Rossington of Lynyrd Skynyrd, Johnny Winter, Ry Cooder and many others all establishing slide as a staple sound of the electric guitar.

Slide playing has been a great tool to bring rootsy blues influences to any genre and can be heard in diverse styles, from Zakk Wylde's work with Ozzy Osbourne to Slash's emotive solos with Guns n Roses, to Joe Perry's work with Aerosmith.

Other important slide guitar work includes the gospel and jazz stylings of Derek Trucks, Sonny Landreth, Jack White of the White Stripes, and Dan Auerbach of the Black Keys. One of my favourite players is Joey Landreth, who fluidly combines American jazz and soul influences with modern blues songwriting. He's proof that slide is a style that continues to evolve. There are also guitarists who go out of their way to emulate slide guitar on a fretted guitar, with players like Jimmy Herring and Michael Lee Firkins being renowned experts.

It's important to point out that slide guitar isn't a "science" in the same way that classical guitar is. It doesn't have centuries of pedagogy surrounding it. Slide guitar is unorthodox at its core. In some ways, this book is a direct contradiction to the ethos of playing slide! Slide guitar has an aural and personal tradition, so while I'm going to teach you everything I know about slide guitar in this book, remember that I learnt it with my ears and eyes.

That said, I can confidently say that learning slide guitar will make you a better, more lyrical, and more expressive guitar player – with or without the slide in your hand. This book will help guide your journey and give you a good head start, but never stop listening to real slide music. Never stop experimenting and never stop learning!

Choosing a slide

Deciding what kind of slide to use and which finger to wear it on is a big decision.

I don't recommend that you wear the slide on the index finger, but the middle, ring, and pinky fingers are all viable candidates. Each finger has its own set of pros and cons, so I suggest you try it on each finger and see which you find most comfortable.

I learned with the slide on my ring finger *ala* Derek Trucks, but then found myself switching to the middle finger like Brett Garsed. In the last couple of years, I've developed a lot of vocabulary with the pinky finger and I'm now able to switch between fingers, depending on how I want to play. The point is, nothing is set in stone – once you understand the technique required to play slide guitar, you'll be able to relearn with the slide on a different finger quite quickly.

Another tricky aspect of slide choice is the diameter. This will depend on the size of your hands, which finger you wear it on and how you like the slide to feel on the finger. I like quite a loose-fitting slide on the ring finger, but something a little tighter on the pinky, so I have various slides. It's important to give different slides a try and not to write the technique off as uncomfortable, when it may be a case of not having found a slide that's comfortable yet.

The final thing to consider is the slide's material. The most popular materials are brass and glass, but you'll also find slides made from copper, ceramic, nickel and more if you shop around. Each material sounds slightly different, but the biggest difference to a beginner is normally the weight. I like to use a thick glass slide (although I'm also fond of brass as it's a little heavier and creates some aggressive high frequency string noise, which is great with an overdriven tone!)

If you're shopping online, I can personally recommend The Rock Slide company in the USA who make an awesome selection of slides with various modern twists like ball ends and tapered interiors for your playing comfort.

Guitar Choice and Setup

Where electric slide guitar differs greatly from early Delta slide is the range of notes that can be played. As a soloist, you'll play all over the neck, so an instrument with good upper fret access is preferred.

The Gibson SG can't really be topped as an instrument for slide guitar. It features two wonderful, high-output humbuckers, and the two cutaways allow the neck to join the body right up at the 21st fret to give unrivalled access to the upper range of the guitar.

Of course, there are no rules. Duane Allman was a die-hard Les Paul player, yet I can't think of a more cumbersome instrument to play slide on!

I recorded the audio for this book using two Telecasters. One was made by Suhr with a mini humbucker in the neck and a vintage Telecaster bridge pickup. The other was a Fender Telecaster with Joe Barden's Danny Gatton pickups.

The most important area for consideration is the *setup* of your instrument.

Setup covers factors like how high your strings are above the frets (known as the *action*), and how much bow there is in the guitar neck (known as *neck relief*). Action is extremely important when you begin playing slide guitar, as the strings need to be high enough above the frets that they don't push the strings down onto the actual fret.

Modern electric guitars ship with a medium-to-low action, but they can be setup for slide easily, usually by adjusting some screws at the bridge (though this will vary depending on your specific model). If you're not sure, pop into your local music shop and ask if someone is able to help. If you have a bit of a budget, you can pay their resident guitar technician to set your guitar up for slide.

Once you've got a feel for playing side on a well set-up instrument, you shouldn't have a problem applying the techniques in this book to any guitar. I play slide on many different guitars, including my Vigier which has one of the lowest actions I've ever seen.

The last thing to consider is the strings. While playing fretted guitar with lighter strings such as .009s is fine, slightly heavier strings can help with slide technique, so consider bumping up to .011s.

Getting the Tone

Now that you've chosen a slide and what guitar to play, it's time to think about your tone. While tone is always a personal choice, there are some things you can do to ensure you always create a good one!

The early electric slide players took advantage of the ability to naturally overdrive a tube amplifier. This happens when you push an amp beyond its normal operating volume and the cone reaches the end of its bevel. When the cone hits the end of its movement range, it stops suddenly and the normal sine curve of the sound wave begins to clip to create a nice overdriven tone. This overdrive creates a natural compression that softens off the peaks of the louder notes and evens out your dynamics.

Playing slide guitar without overdrive is certainly possible, but you will have to work a lot harder. A compressor pedal will help you get more out of your slide playing and can add more attack and sustain to your sound.

Aside from natural amplifier overdrive, there are many overdrive and distortion pedals that can help you get more mileage from your amp. These pedals add gain to simulate natural overdrive and smooth out your tone with natural compression. Experimentation is key: most guitarists own several overdrive pedals as we're constantly for searching for ways to create the sound we hear in our heads.

However, always remember that slide player extraordinaire Derek Trucks still goes straight from his guitar to his amp (where he might add a touch of reverb). So maybe there is some truth to the "tone in the fingers" rumours!

While it's possible to play slide guitar with a pick, most great players use only their fingers. One reason for this is that it makes muting the un-played strings easier and I highly recommend this approach.

Finally, and I cannot stress this enough, *slide guitar transcends notation*.

You may be the most competent reader in the world, but music notation was not designed with the nuances of slide in mind. It's near impossible to indicate accurate representations of notes being in (or out of) tune, and it's impossible to show clearly just how long a slide between two notes might take.

For that reason, I've gone out of my way to make sure that every audio example in this book is pristine. Download the audio now and use your ears to hear the nuances that can't be described in the tablature. Listen carefully to each example and focus on turning the notes on the page into the sound you hear on the recordings.

With all that technical stuff out of the way, let's get playing slide guitar!

Get the Audio

The audio files for this book are available to download for free from **www.fundamental-changes.com.** The link is in the top right-hand corner. Simply select this book title from the drop-down menu and follow the instructions to get the audio.

We recommend that you download the files directly to your computer, not to your tablet, and extract them there before adding them to your media library. You can then put them on your tablet, iPod or burn them to CD. On the download page there is a help PDF and we also provide technical support via the contact form.

For over 350 Free Guitar Lessons with Videos Check out:

www.fundamental-changes.com

Over 10,000 fans on Facebook: **FundamentalChangesInGuitar**

Instagram: **FundamentalChanges**

Chapter Two: Getting in Tune

My last book bounced between the Open D and Open G tunings commonly used for Delta Blues rhythm guitar, but due the soloing oriented nature of this book, I'll begin by focusing on Open E tuning, then adapt the concepts to standard tuning later.

Open tunings (tuning the open strings of the guitar to a chord) are popular for slide guitar because the slide can be used a bit like a capo. It's useful to be able to strum with the slide touching the strings above a fret and play a chord that will always sound good. When soloing in an open tuning, you're also able to let strings ring slightly and it won't sound too bad. This usually isn't an option in standard tuning.

I've also chosen to teach in Open E as it's closely related to standard tuning, and is the tuning of choice for players like Elmore James, Duane Allman and Derek Trucks.

One frustrating aspect of relying on open tunings, however, is that you often don't know how to use a slide when playing a regularly tuned guitar, so in this book I'll teach you to apply everything you learn to standard tuning too.

First then, what is Open E tuning and how do we tune our guitar to it?

Open E means tuning the open strings of the guitar to the notes of an open E major chord (E G# B).

A quick way to do this is to look at an open E chord and tune the open strings *up* to the fretted notes in the chord.

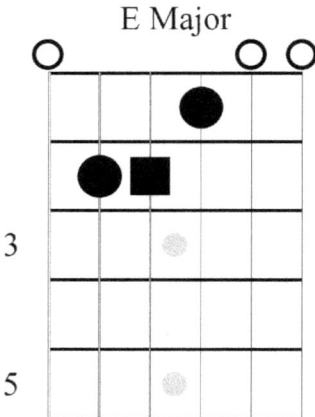

To retune the open strings so that they contain the fretted notes of the E Major chord, we must:

Tune the A string up a tone (whole step).

Tune the D string up a tone (whole step).

Tune the G string up a semitone (half step).

From low to high, the guitar should be tuned E B E G# B E. It's that easy to tune your guitar to Open E!

This first example shows me playing an open E chord in standard tuning.

Example 2a

Now here's me playing the open strings with my guitar tuned to Open E. You can hear that it sounds identical.

Example 2b

We could stop there and just start playing licks, but I want to equip you with the tools to understand music at a deeper level and teach you another way to think about open tunings. Then you will be able to use them without having to think about shapes.

An E major chord contains the notes E, G# and B, so if you tune your strings to these notes, you'll be in open E tuning. However, the notes don't need to be in that order, so please don't run off and tune your guitar E G# B E G# B!

In standard tuning the notes of the strings are E A D G B E. Knowing this helps us to quickly adjust these notes to create the open E tuning (E B E G# B E).

The low E string is already tuned to the root note of the chord.

The A string can be tuned up a tone to B.

The D string can be tuned up a tone to E.

The G string can be tuned up a semi-tone to G#.

The B string is already in an E major chord.

The high E string is already in an E major chord.

Knowing this, instantly gives you a better understanding of how other open tunings work. For example, if you know that a G major chord contains the notes G, B and D, then you could quickly create Open G tuning:

The low E string can be tuned down a tone to D.

The A string can be tuned down a tone to G.

The D string is already in a G chord.

The G string is already in a G chord.

The B string is already in a G chord.

The high E string can be tuned down a tone to D.

Another tuning you may come across is Open A. Knowing that an A major chord contains the notes A, C#, and E…

The low E string is already in the A chord.

The A string is already in the A chord.

The D string can be tuned up a tone to E.

The G string can be tuned up a tone to A.

The B string can be tuned up a tone to C#.

The high E string is already in the A chord.

I interviewed Joey Landreth recently, and when I asked about his tuning he talked for a bit and then nonchalantly said, "So it's just a root, 5, root, 3, 5, root tuning."

I had to stop him and draw attention to this. It confirmed to me that high level players are necessarily aware of the key they are tuned to when they play. Joey was thinking in terms of intervals rather than notes. We know that the E major chord contains E (root), G# (3rd), and B (5th), so our open E tuning of E B E G# B E could be described as R 5 R 3 5 R.

This may feel like more information than you need to know at this stage, but as you progress through this book, returning occasionally to this chapter will help you master open tunings in no time at all.

Before learning to use the slide, I want to show you some exercises that highlight the benefits of Open E tuning. As the open strings are tuned to an E major chord, if you hold a barre across the first fret, none of the intervals will change – you will be playing a major chord a semitone higher i.e. F major.

It's therefore easy to play a I IV V progression in E major by playing the open strings and barring at the 5th and 7th frets. The 12th fret is an octave higher than the open position, so this is another way to play an E major chord.

Example 2c

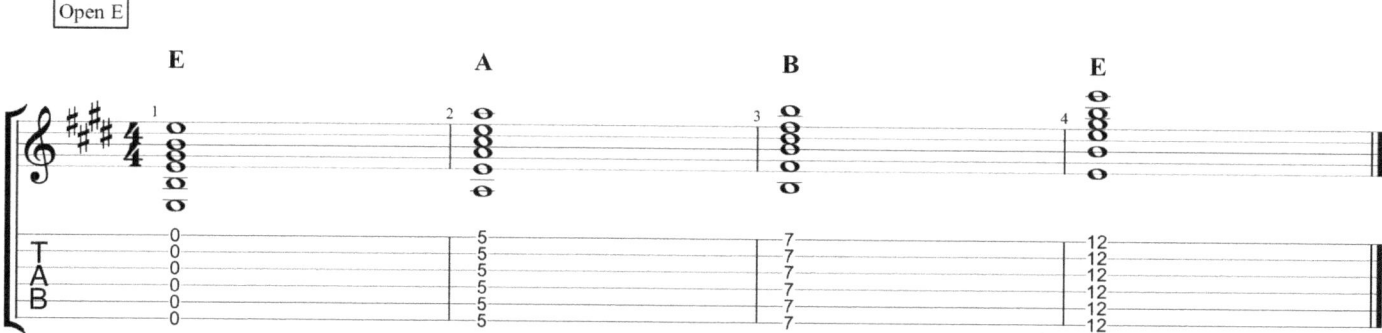

You don't even need to play all six strings. Here's the same I, IV, V, I chord progression using just the top four strings.

Example 2d

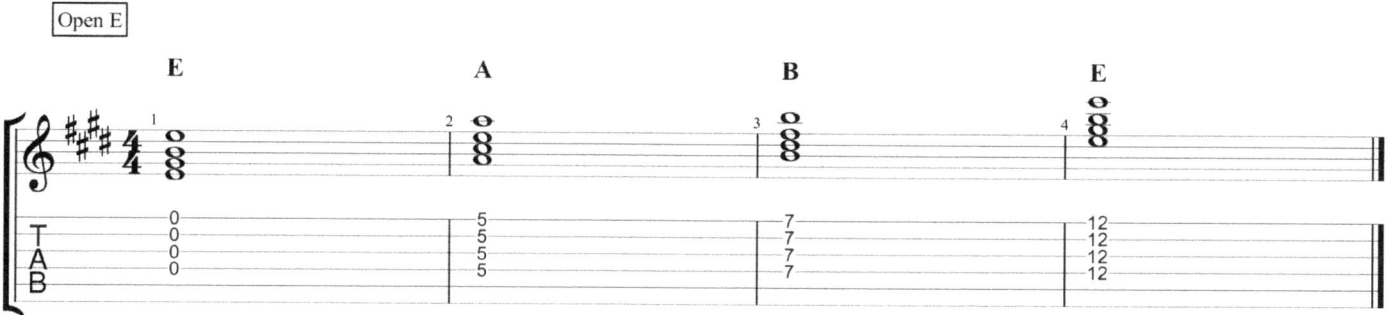

Here's a simple open E riff similar to Derek Trucks' groove on the song *Made Up Mind*. This doesn't use a slide, but gives you a good idea about how to form a riff with the open tuning.

Example 2e

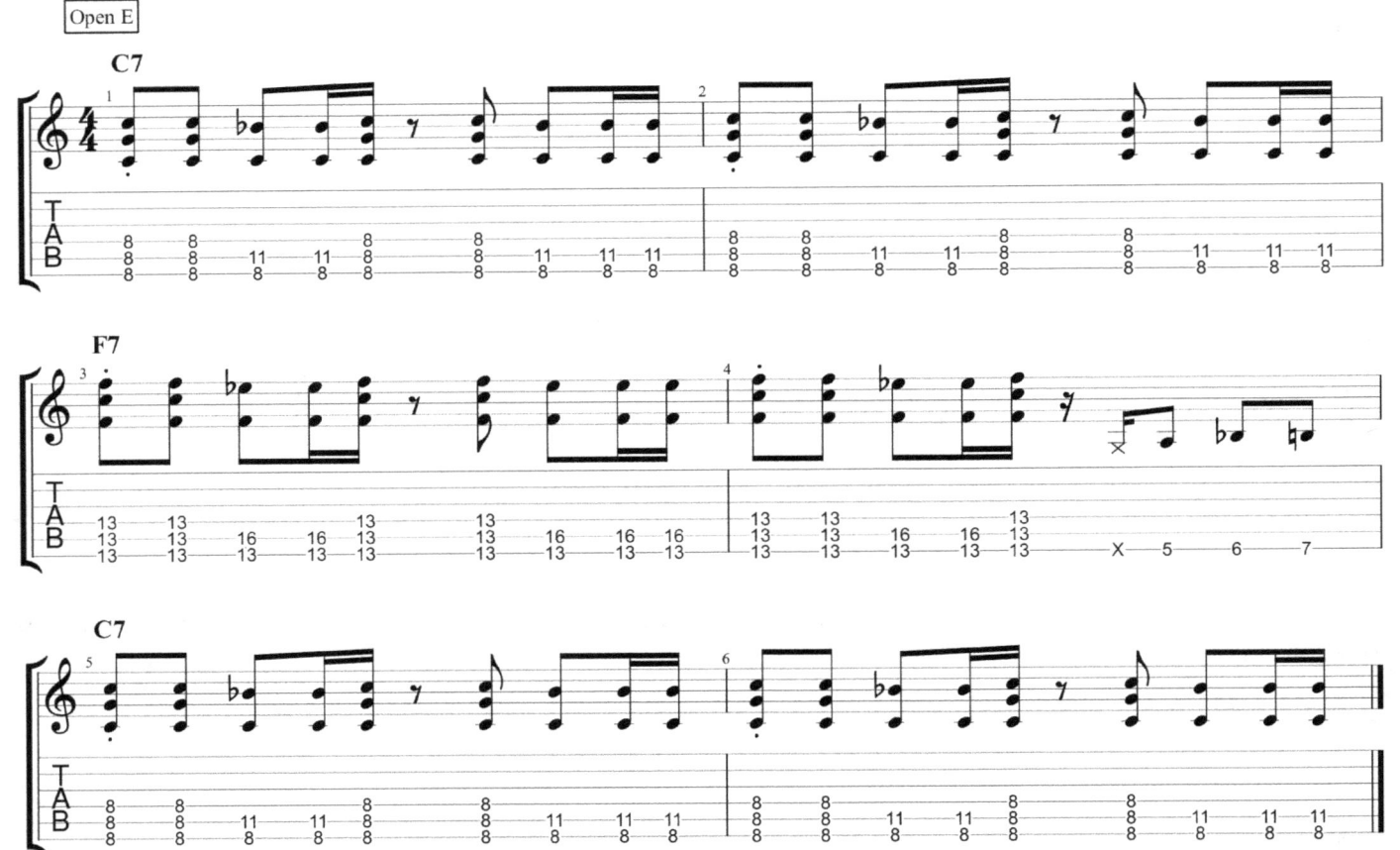

Before moving on, practise moving your standard tuned guitar to Open E and back again. The ability to confidently tune your guitar should not be overlooked.

Chapter Three: An Introduction to Using the Slide

The most important part of playing slide guitar is understanding how the slide works, so that you can play using the minimum required effort and create the cleanest, most reliable sound.

The slide functions like a movable fret. To really understand that, it's worth thinking about how stringed instruments work and what a fret actually does.

On a fretless instrument like a double bass, the string vibrates when it is plucked. When you press a finger down on a string and it makes contact with the fingerboard, you reduce the vibrating length of the string so it vibrates at a higher frequency to create a higher pitch.

Unfortunately, on a double bass or violin, you can place your finger absolutely anywhere on the string to create near infinite, microtonal pitch options. This makes playing fretless instruments tricky as your fingering has to be perfect to get the correct intonation.

On a fretted guitar, pressing the string down anywhere between the 2nd and 3rd fret will push the string down so that it makes contact with the 3rd fret. This makes playing in tune much easier. However, a slide makes contact with the string from above, so you have to be very accurate if you want the note to be perfectly in tune.

It's important to realise that the slide doesn't press the string down so that it comes into contact with the frets. This means that you must develop a feel for how much pressure is required to create a strong note, without pushing so hard that the slide touches the frets.

The first exercise I want you to practise doesn't require any notation. Simply play the open strings and *lightly* place the slide on the strings directly over a fret and keep strumming. At first, the pressure will be so light that you won't create a decent note, but as you gradually increase pressure with the slide, the note will begin to sound cleanly.

It's important to spend time getting a feel for the minimum pressure required to create a strong note without pressing the strings into the fret. This takes time and is something that will improve naturally as you progress through the book.

Intonation is the other aspect of using the slide that requires careful attention.

Intonation refers to the tuning of a note. Because the slide can fret the string at any point, it's easy to place the slide inaccurately and play a note that's out of tune.

In the next example, I play the open strings and place the slide precisely over the 12th fret. Next, I play the open strings again and place the slide midway between the 11th and 12th frets. Listen carefully to the recording and notice how the open chord sounds like an E major, and the second sounds flat.

Example 3a

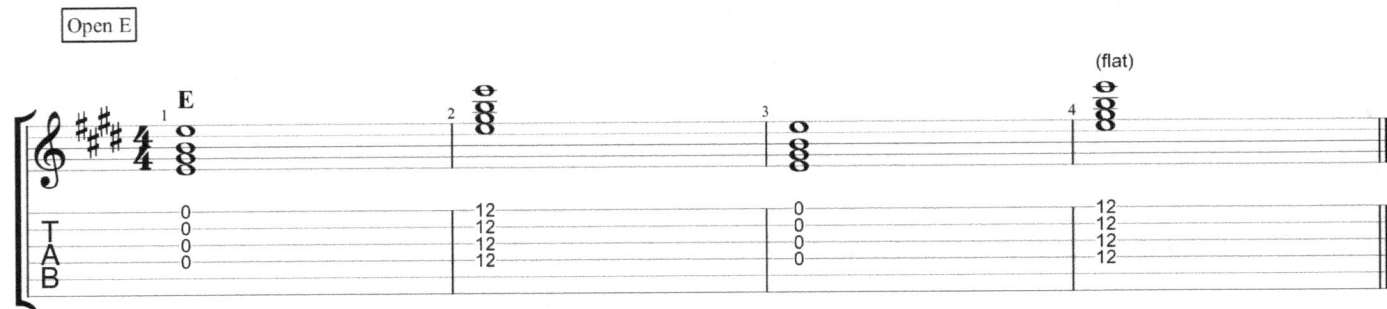

When playing slide, your goal is to place the slide as close to where the fret would make contact with the string as possible.

Here's an exercise that features notes of the E major pentatonic scale (E, F#, G#, B, C#) played against an alternating open E string.

Play the open E twice, then the F# at the 2nd fret, then the open E twice, followed by the G# at the 4th fret, and so on. Keep the fretted note as accurate as possible and don't add vibrato. Vibrato covers a multitude of sins, so focus on getting the notes perfect. You'll learn to add vibrato later.

Example 3b

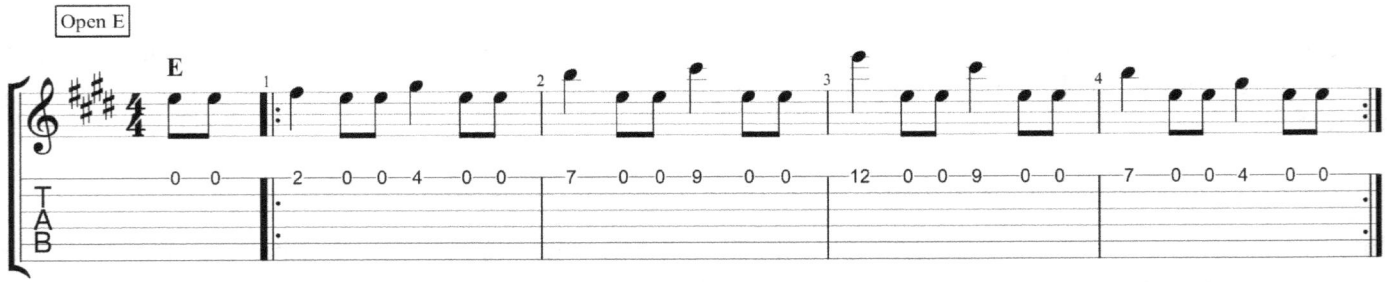

Regardless of which finger you wear the slide on, you must rest the remaining fingers on the strings behind the slide (between the slide and nut) to dampen the strings and prevent any unwanted vibrations. This is why the slide is not worn on the index finger.

Let's learn how the slide can create smooth transitions from one pitch to another with a *glissando* (smooth slide between notes). Sliding with a bottleneck requires you to maintain an even pressure on the string as you move, because reducing the contact with the string will kill the note.

Place the slide on all the strings at the 2nd fret, strum the guitar and slowly slide up the neck to the 12th fret. The focus here is on maintaining the note. Move the whole arm horizontally – don't try turning the wrist or moving the fingers, and don't squeeze with the thumb on the back of the neck.

Example 3c

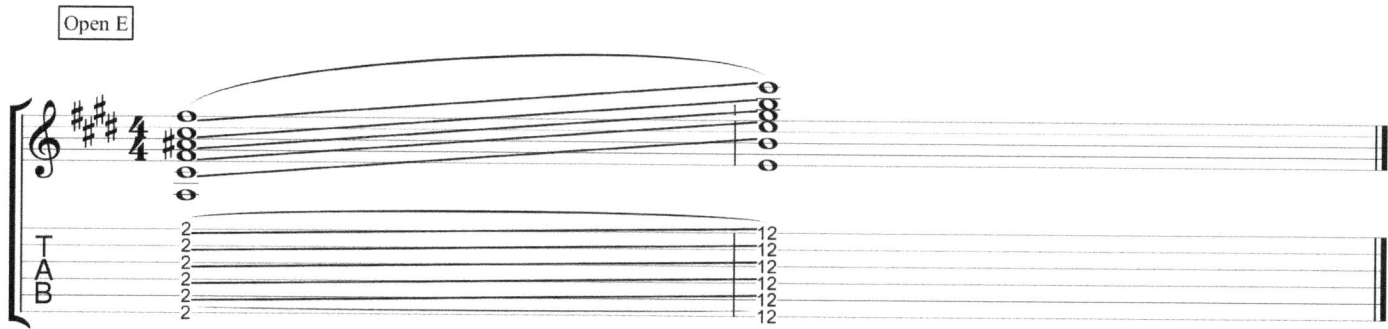

The same exercise can be played on a single string too. Here's the same idea applied to just the high E string.

Example 3d

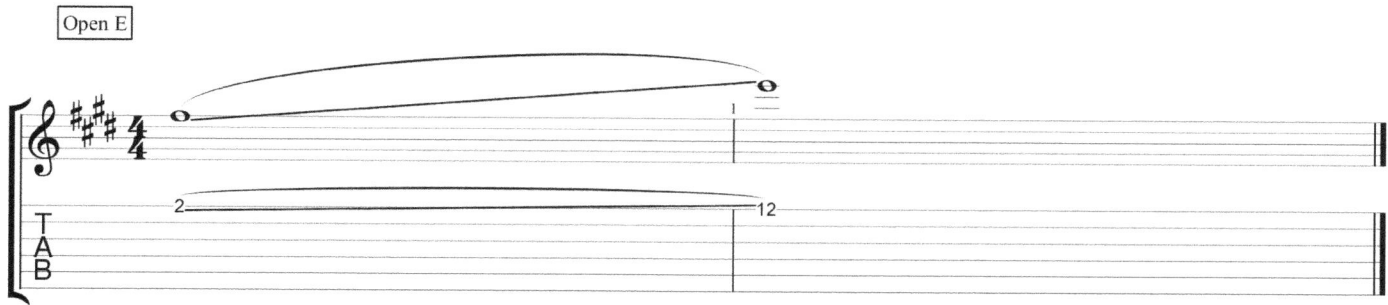

Now play it on the third string.

Example 3e

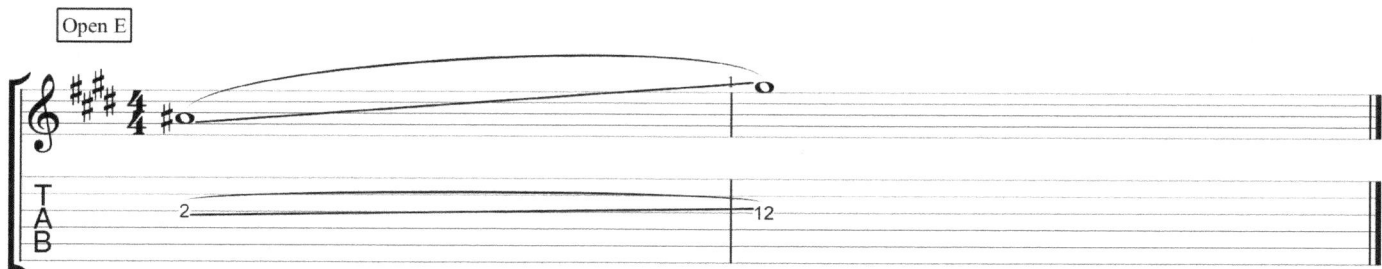

With this motion under control, try Example 3f. Notice that there's no fixed place to slide from – it depends on how fast you plan on sliding, and how you want to the note to sound. As a guide, aim for around two or three frets below the target note.

Example 3f

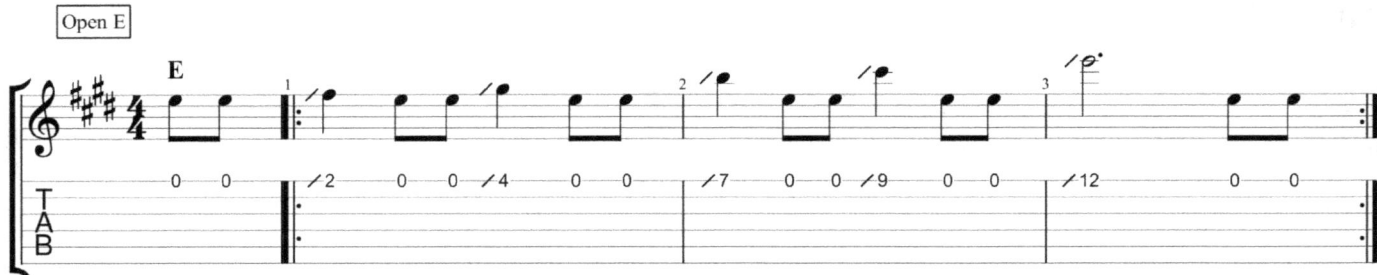

Reverse the exercise and slide into the fretted notes from above.

Example 3g

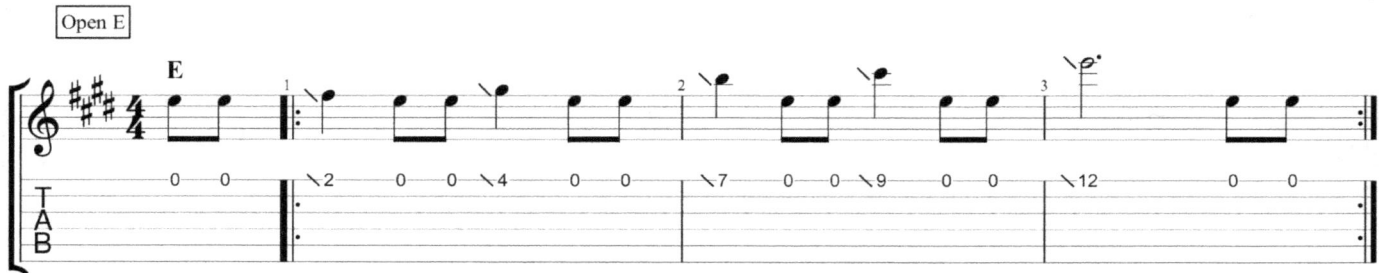

The previous two exercises feature the same notes but with different *articulations*.

These "indiscriminate" slides are great for effect, but there's much more to playing slide guitar than that!

Let's use the E major pentatonic scale on the high E string, but this time slide between defined pitches.

Play the E at the 12th fret and slide down to the 9th fret and pluck it twice. Pick once more and then slide down to the 7th fret and pick this note two more times, and so on.

Example 3h

This idea can be applied to the ascending the scale too.

Example 3i

Now combine the ascending and descending versions of the exercise for something more lick-like.

Example 3j

Finally, combine the slides in both directions to make a more musical phrase.

Pick the 12th fret, move down to the 9th, then descend to the 7th. Next, ascend from the 7th to the 9th before descending from the 9th to the 4th and repeat this pattern.

Example 3k

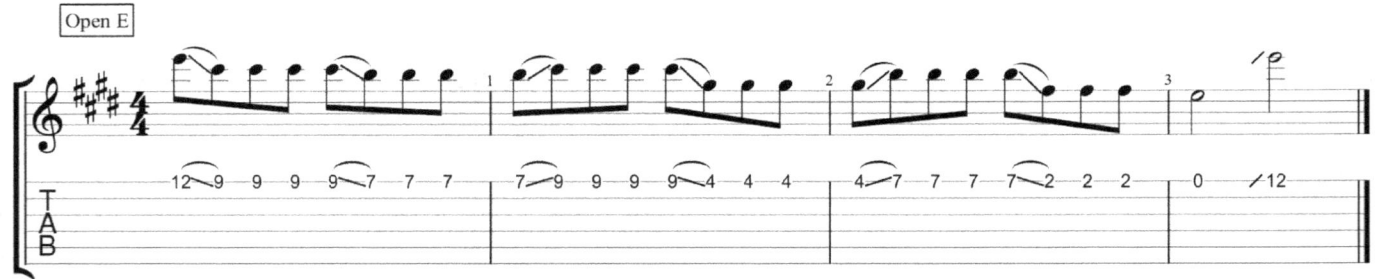

A useful exercise to help develop your intonation and technique is to slide into a note then, without repicking, drop down in pitch and slide back into the note. This can be repeated as many times as you like, or until you lose sustain.

Example 3l

It is possible to play a hammer-on with a slide, although it's a tricky technique. Slide hammer-ons are executed in the same way as you would play them with a finger, but as the slide sounds the note when you make contact with the string, it's important not to hammer on too hard and make contact with the fret.

In this example, alternate between picking the open E string and hammering on to notes of the E major pentatonic scale.

Example 3m

So far, all of the exercises have been played on the high E string, but we can play any of these ideas on other strings too.

Here's Example 3k played on the second (B) string, meaning the lick now uses the B major pentatonic scale (B, C#, D#, F#, G#).

Example 3n

Here's the same idea again, but this time played on the third (G#) string to create a lick in the key of G# (or Ab).

Example 3o

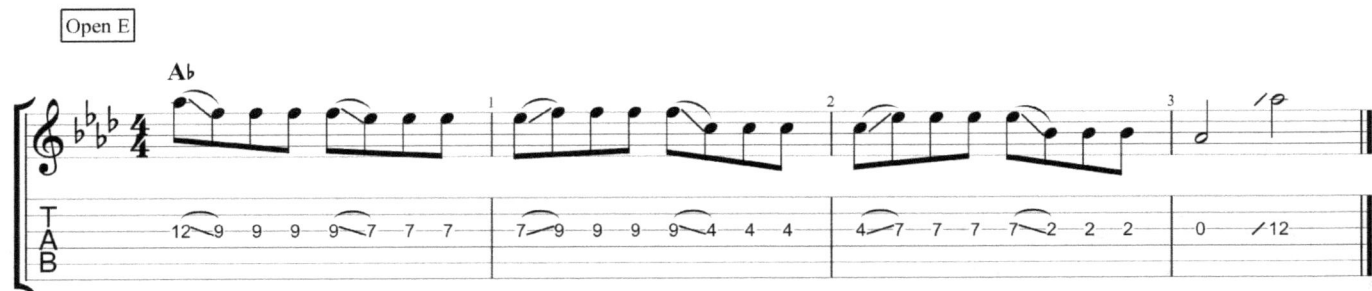

Another important technique is the use of *micro slides*. These are more akin to the quarter step bends or *blues curls* you often hear on a fretted guitar.

Play the 3rd fret and then move the slide ever so slightly sharp, much in the same way you'd bend the string on a fretted guitar. Getting these to sound right is an important part of nailing the bluesy sound of slide guitar.

Example 3p

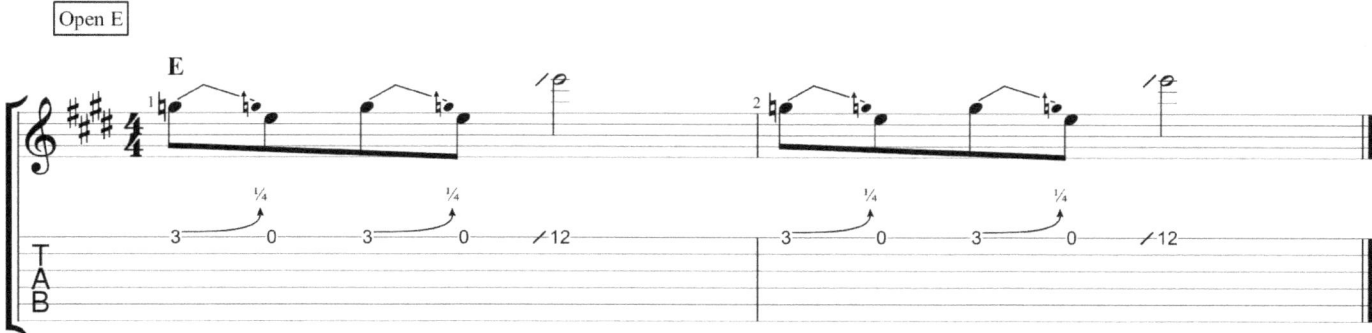

With the ability to play notes accurately and the sliding mechanics under your fingers, the next thing to learn is how *vibrato* is created with the slide.

Vibrato is the technique of producing rapid changes in pitch, and creates a more expressive, melodic sound. Unfortunately, on an unfretted instrument, vibrato is sometimes used to help mask inaccurate intonation. That's why we should learn to play a pitch perfectly before adding vibrato.

Vibrato with a slide is created by combining multiple tiny slides that remain close to the intended pitch. It's a deeply personal subject – a player's vibrato is like a signature or fingerprint. Some players have a wide, fast vibrato, while some prefer a narrow, slow vibrato. There are so many variables that it's best if I show you the basic concepts surrounding the technique and you can find the sound that you prefer.

In notation and tablature, there's only one symbol for vibrato, but to help you understand it a little more I've created some graphical representations of the "sound" of different types of vibrato. It's really important to listen carefully to each audio recording of the following examples and compare what you're hearing to the images below. More important still is to copy the ones you like the most!

The first concept to understand is "intended pitch". As the name suggests, this describes the perfectly in-tune note that you are targeting. This pitch is indicated in the diagrams by a horizontal line.

The wavy line that intersects the intended pitch represents the vibrato applied to the note. When written above the intended pitch, the slide is moving sharp of the intended note. When it's below the intended pitch, the note is being played flat.

On a fretted guitar, the only way to create vibrato is by bending the string, so vibrato only ever *raises* the intended pitch of the note.

Example 3q

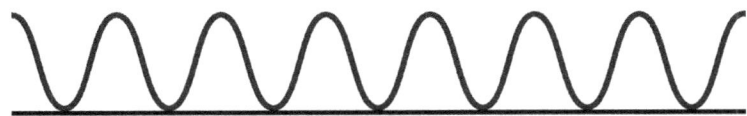

When we use a slide to apply vibrato *below* the intended pitch, it sounds just as jarring.

Example 3r

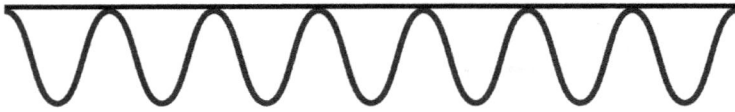

Vibrato that moves both above and below the intended pitch certainly sounds more musical.

Example 3s

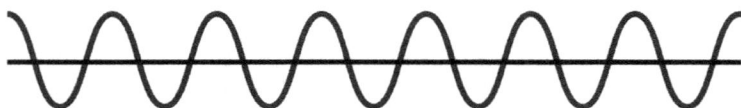

However, you don't need to achieve a vibrato as even as this. I like to go further below the intended pitch than I do above it. It's hard to record something like this perfectly, because it's not a science – it's a feel thing – and is subjective, based on what appeals to your ears.

Example 3t

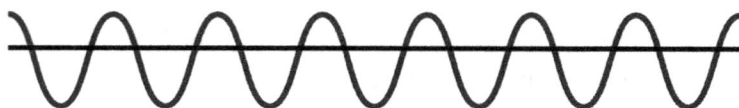

Another important aspect to consider is the *speed* of your vibrato.

It's possible to have an extremely slow vibrato.

Example 3u

Or one that's extremely fast

Example 3v

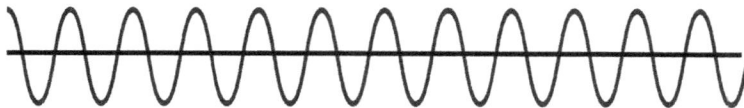

You could even mix up your speeds, perhaps beginning slow and gradually increasing speed.

Example 3w

Then there's the *width* of your vibrato: how far you move from the intended pitch. This could be subtle with a thin vibrato.

Example 3x

Or wide enough to drive a truck through!

Example 3y

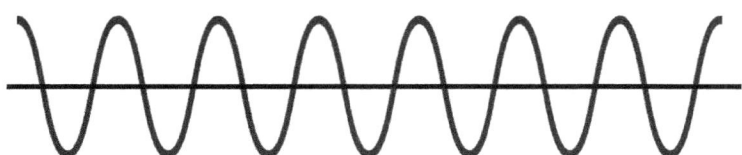

I encourage you to take a break from reading now and listen to some of your favourite slide players. Try to describe their vibrato styles and compare them. How are they different? What do you like? What don't you like?

It may seem odd to talk about vibrato in so much detail so early on, but it really is one of the most defining characteristics of any melody played on the guitar, whether it is with a slide or not.

Now that you understand how the slide works and how vibrato can be applied, spend some time getting comfortable with the technique before moving on to the next chapter. In Chapter Four we'll learn some expressive phrasing exercises.

Chapter Four: Single String Exercises

We'll get to examples across multiple strings later in the book, but one of the most unique aspects of slide guitar is the transition between notes – which lends itself to playing up and down the strings rather than across them. For this reason, it's worth exploring vocabulary that uses just one string as a way of improving our slide control. This will also help you learn various scales you can use when improvising.

The first scale worth exploring is the trusty minor pentatonic scale, which in E contains the notes E, G, A, B and D.

If you learn this scale as a set of intervals rather than notes, it will allow you to use it in any key. Instead of E, G, A, B and D, it is easier in the long run to think of this scale as Root, b3, 4, 5, b7.

This isn't a book on music theory, so if these terms are completely new to you, I'd recommend checking out one of Fundamental Changes' theory books. They will help you to brush up on the inner workings of music. Here, we are only worrying about playing!

Before getting into the examples, it's worth mentioning the muting techniques required to play these ideas cleanly and authentically.

As mentioned earlier, you should be using the fingers behind the slide to mute the string, but attention needs to be given to the strings in front of the slide.

As all of these examples feature just one string, it will serve you well to keep the strings you're not playing quiet.

If you're using a pick, this can be tricky as you'll need to experiment with some careful palm muting. This is the main reason I recommended fingerstyle technique for slide guitar – you can rest the side of the thumb on the lower strings, and use the fingers you're not plucking with to mute higher strings.

If, for example, I'm picking the high E string, my thumb will rest on the second, third, fourth, fifth and sixth strings, allowing me to strike the first string as aggressively as I like with the index finger.

If I'm playing the third string, my thumb will rest on the fourth, fifth and sixth strings, while my middle and ring fingers will rest on the second and first strings respectively, allowing me to strike the third string with my index finger.

This will take time and experimentation, but I can't stress enough how important this is in the long run.

The first example lays out the notes of the E minor pentatonic scale on the high E string, and as this book is focused on electric guitar, it's assumed you won't have any problem going above the 12th fret (though just how far will depend on the guitar you're using!)

Example 4a

Here's that same scale, but played on the B string, still beginning on the E root note, but now at the 5th fret. You'll notice that the distance between notes is the same as in the last example, you're just starting in a different place.

Example 4b

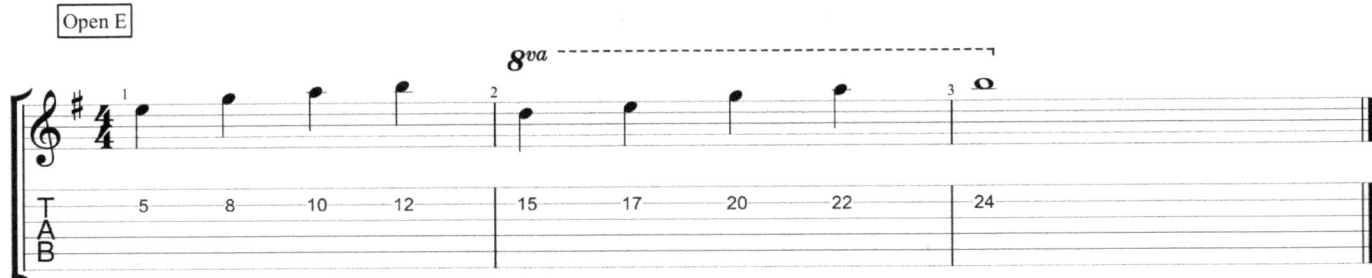

Here's the same E minor pentatonic scale, but on the G# string. Now the E root note is found at the 8th fret, but again, from there the pattern is the same.

Example 4c

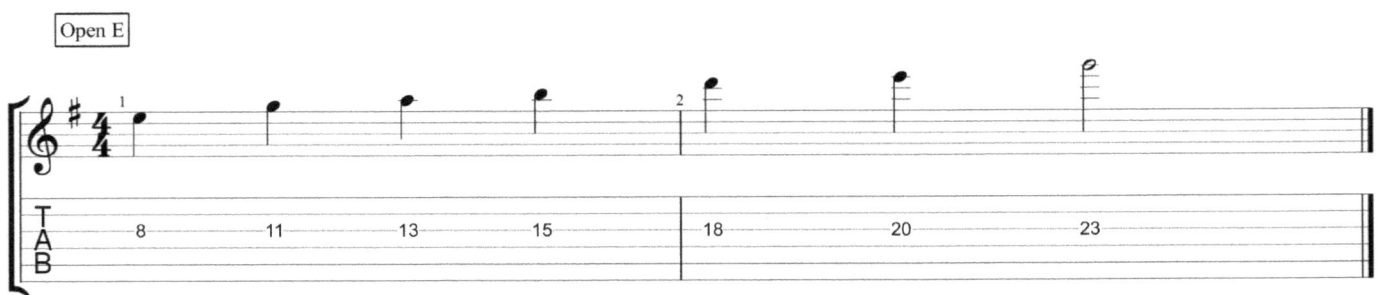

With the larger scale out of the way, I find it best to really dig into smaller fragments of the scale and make music, so we'll begin with the root and b3.

When playing the root of a chord/scale, the b3 will always be three frets higher.

Notice that in the following examples, I always tend to bend that b3 a little sharp. This helps to give it that blues vibe.

Example 4d

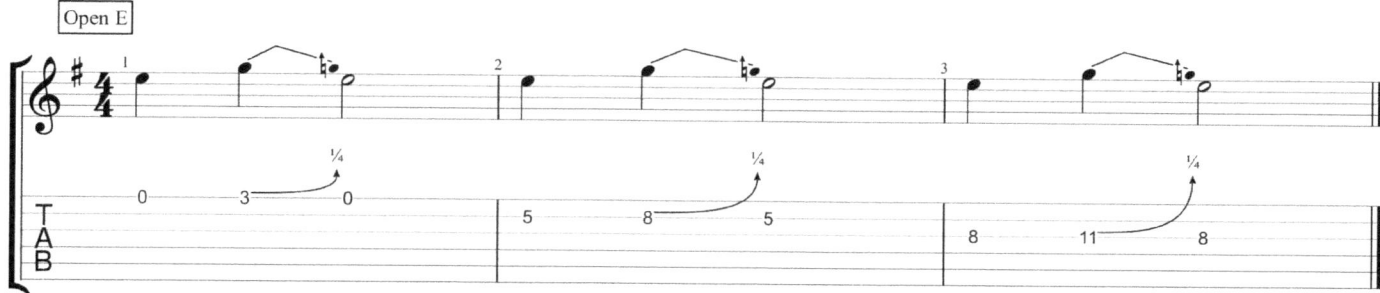

Two frets below the root note you'll always find the b7. This is a great note found in both minor 7 chords and dominant 7 chords, so perfect for blues, rock and jazz.

Obviously, you won't be able to do this on an open string, but anywhere you can find a root and can move two frets below, this will work.

Example 4e

Now you've learned two strong notes around the root note, here's a simple phrase using just those three notes, with the root note at the 5th fret of the B string

Example 4f

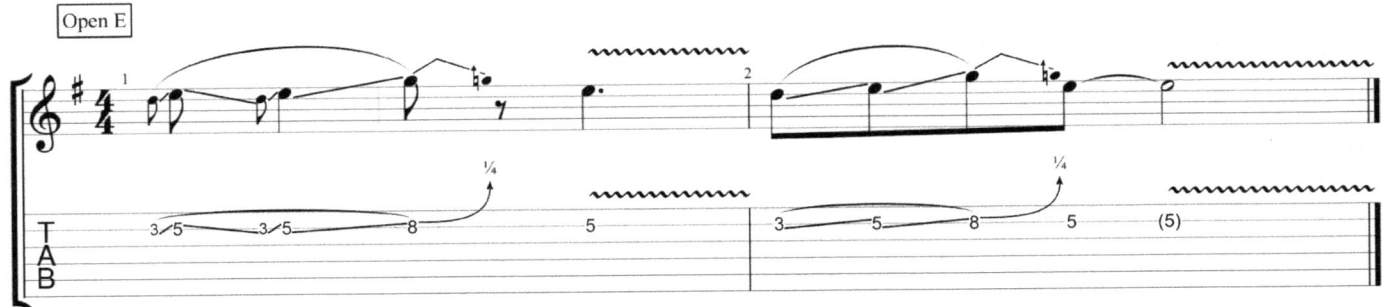

Here's that same idea, but an octave higher, on the high E string at the 12th fret.

Example 4g

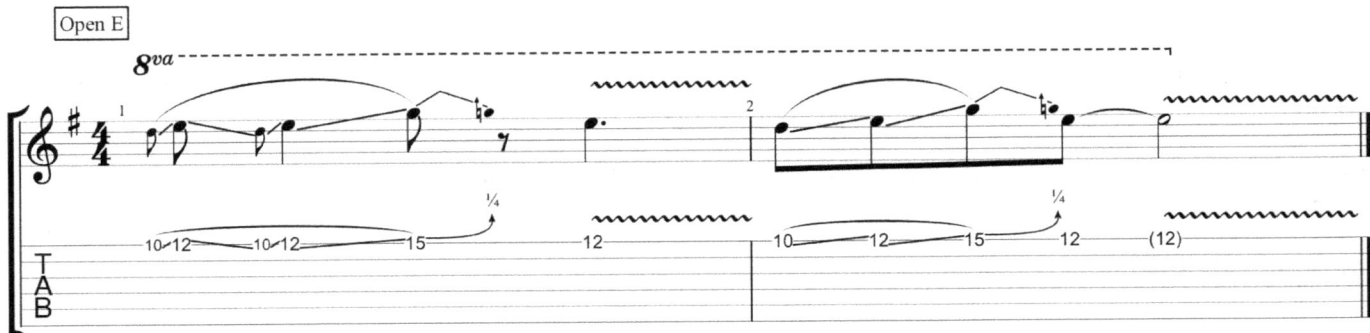

Here's the same thing, but now down on the fifth string.

Example 4h

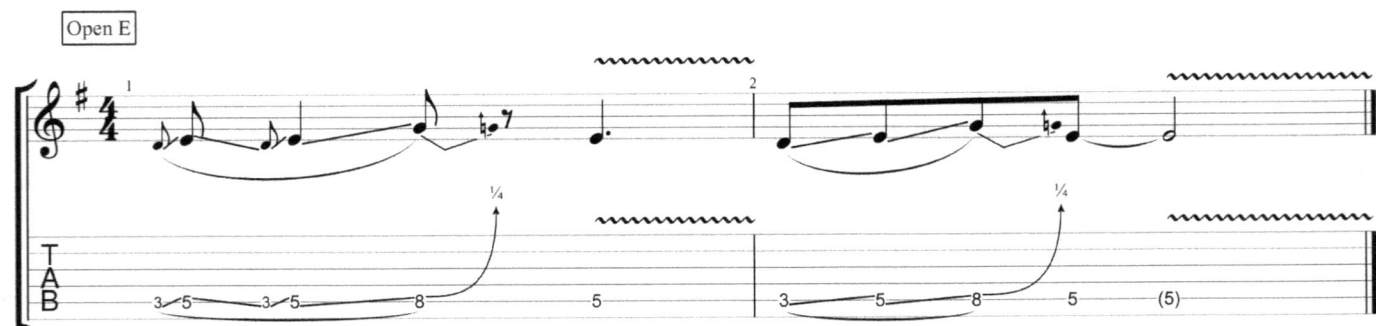

With that simple phase out the way, here something a little longer. This one features slides between multiple notes without repicking them, so take it slowly at first until you can make these transitions without losing the note.

To mix things up a little, this time you're in C, at the 8th fret of the high E string. Once you have these patterns down, it's easy to move them to any key. Before moving on, take this lick and play it in several keys on different strings.

Example 4i

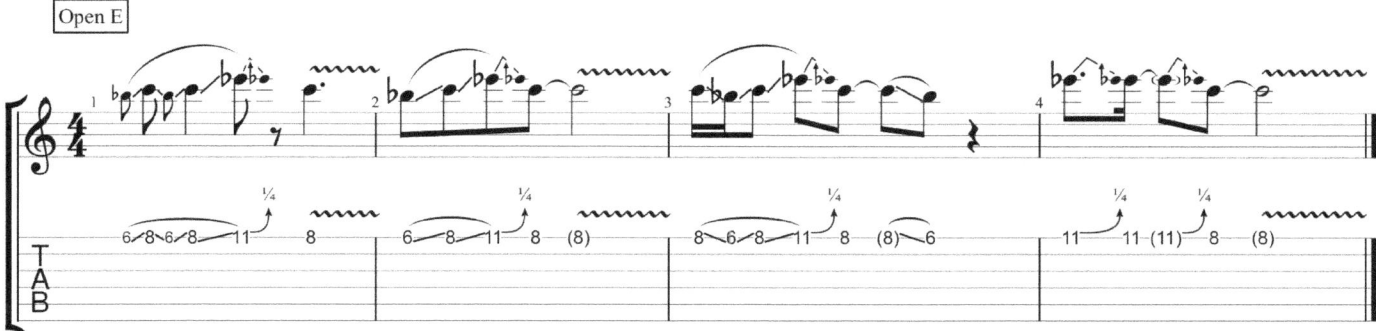

A tone higher than the b3rd is the 4th, and when you are here you can slide up a further tone for the 5th.

Here's a musical phrase beginning on the root, but moving up to that 5th, seven frets higher. This is played in two different octaves, on the same string twelve frets higher.

Example 4j

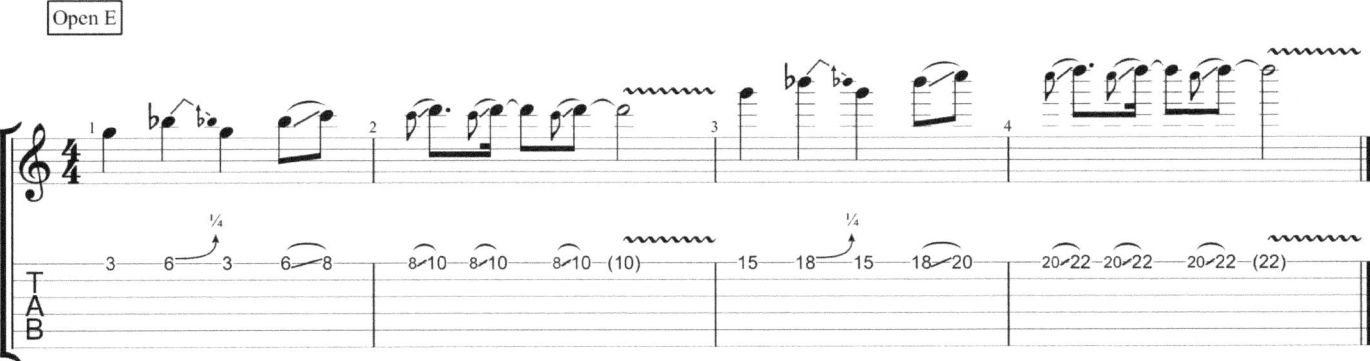

You'll have noticed that the last lick wasn't in E, it was in G. Again, using intervals means you're able to transpose these ideas quickly to any key without needing to know the names of the notes in a G minor pentatonic scale.

To highlight this, here's another lick in G, but this time adding the b5th (a semitone below the 5th) into the equation for a bluesy sound. There's no need to know the note as Db, as long as you know what it sounds like, and where it is in relation to that root note!

Example 4k

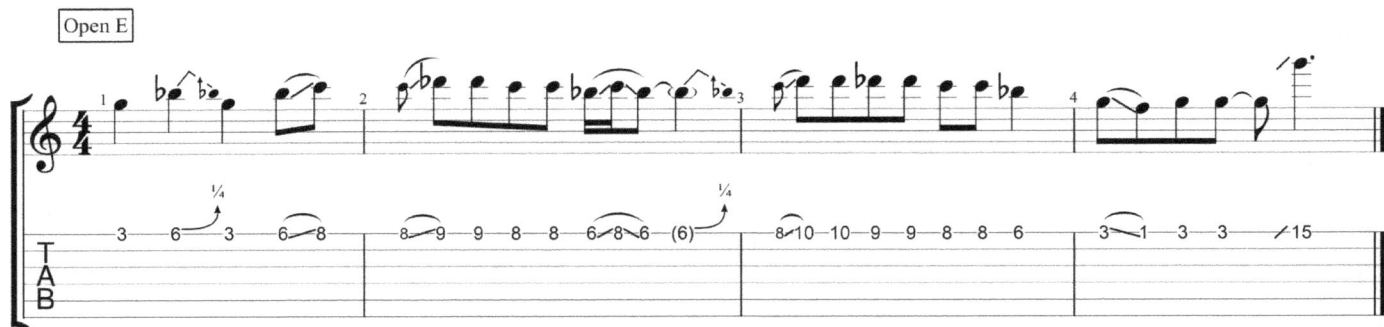

When on the 5th, you can slide up a further three frets and you'll be on the b7th.

Here's a great lick that begins on the 5th and slides up to the b7th. From there you use the b5th before sliding up to the root note an octave above.

Note the vibrato here and how fast I slide between notes. Some sound best played fast, but others are really expressive if you take your time.

Example 4l

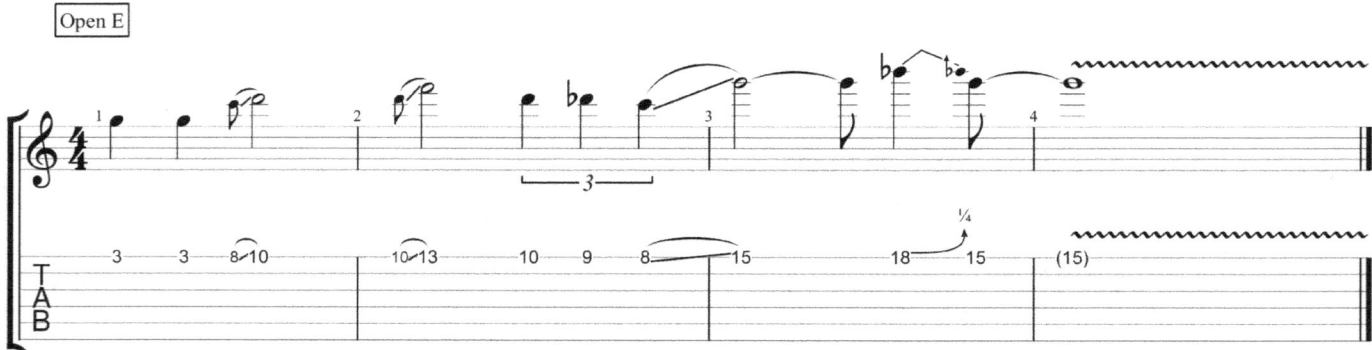

With all of these little fragments under your belt, here's an idea in C that begins on the 8th fret of the high E string, ending an octave higher at the 20th fret. This may feel high up, but when you listen to Duane Allman's classic slide solo on Layla you quickly realize that slide players can play pretty high up.

Example 4m

With those essential minor sounds out of the way, it's time to move on to the major pentatonic scale.

E major pentatonic contains the notes E, F#, G#, B, and C#, or the Root, 2, 3, 5 and 6.

Here's the full scale, first on the high E string, then beginning at the 5th fret of the B string.

Example 4n

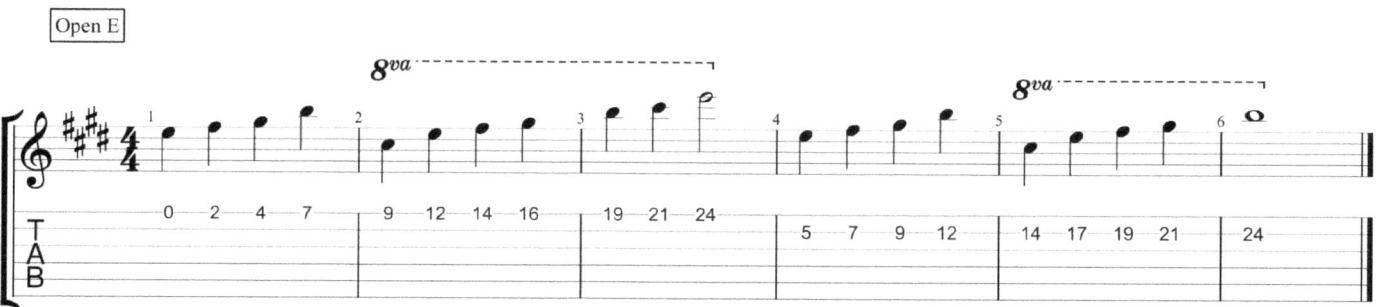

Now let's begin learning the scale in smaller fragments. Here's the root note, followed by the 2nd and 3rd, then a lick using them both in a musical context.

Example 4o

Three frets below the root is the 6th. This note has a really sweet sound that I associate with gospel and soul music. To mix things up, I've played this in B, around the 12th fret of the B string. This means the 6th is found at the 9th fret.

Example 4p

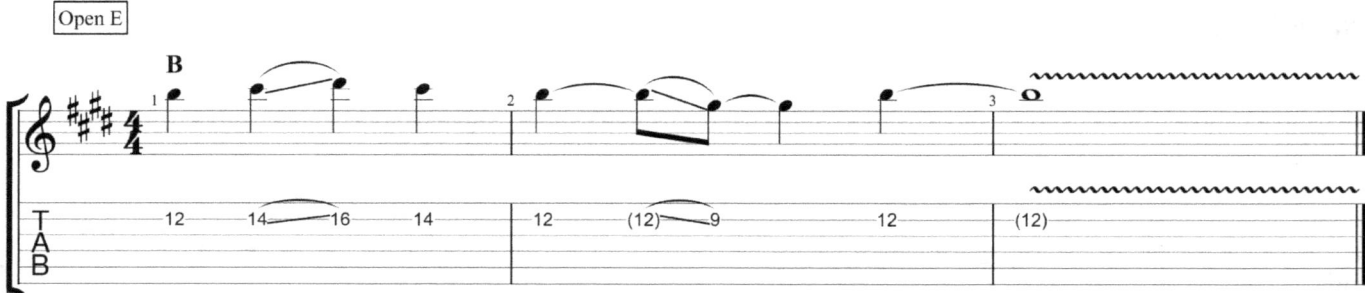

You should already know where the 5th is and the 6th can be found a tone above it. There are literally limitless ways to use this, but here's a lick that I play often.

Example 4q

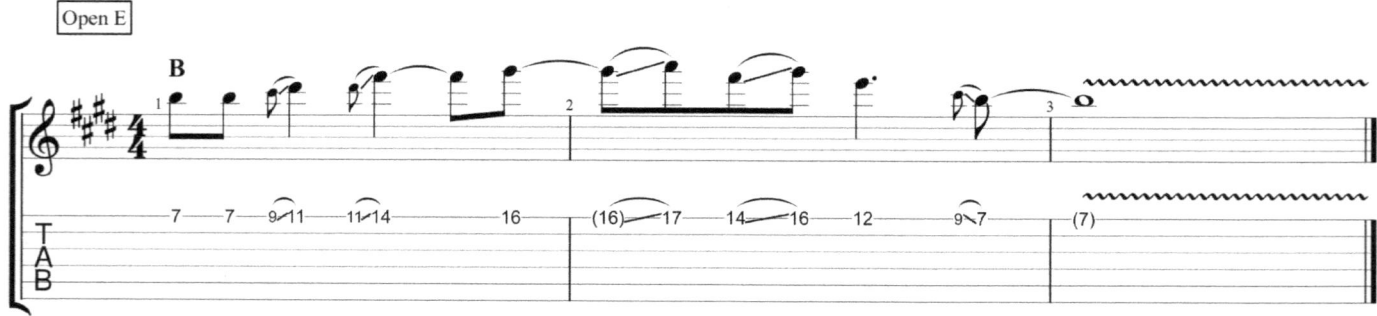

Now you have the notes of both the blues scale (R, b3, 4, b5, 5, b7) and the major pentatonic (R, 2, 3, 5, 6), you have the tools to start painting your own sounds. I love the sound of the minor pentatonic scale, but I find the b7 is quite dark in sound, whereas the 6th from the major pentatonic has a much sweeter quality.

It's possible to create a hybrid of these two scales, R, b3, 4, 5, 6. I've heard this called many things, from the "minor 6 pentatonic" to "Dorian pentatonic", and even the "Robben Ford pentatonic", but to me it's just tweaking the notes of one scale to give it the feel I want.

Here's a lick played using just the notes of the minor pentatonic scale

Example 4r

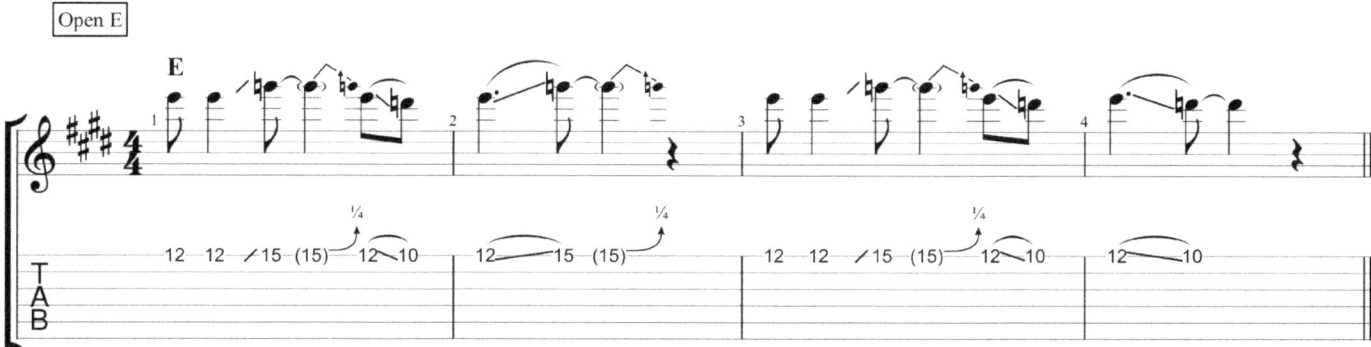

Now, here's the same lick, but with the b7 switched out for the 6th. Notice how it instantly takes on a completely different, funkier vibe.

Example 4s

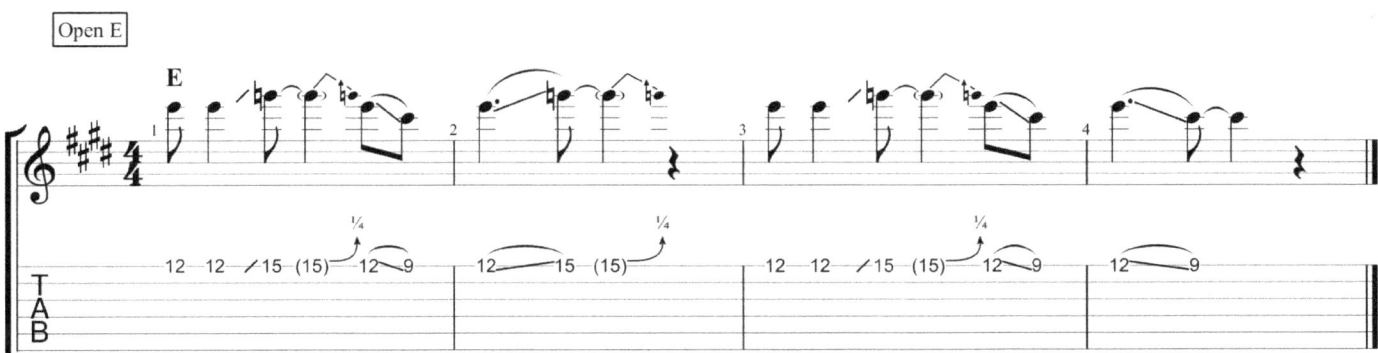

Here's another lick using the same intervals, but this time played in a lower register, using the fourth (E) string.

Example 4t

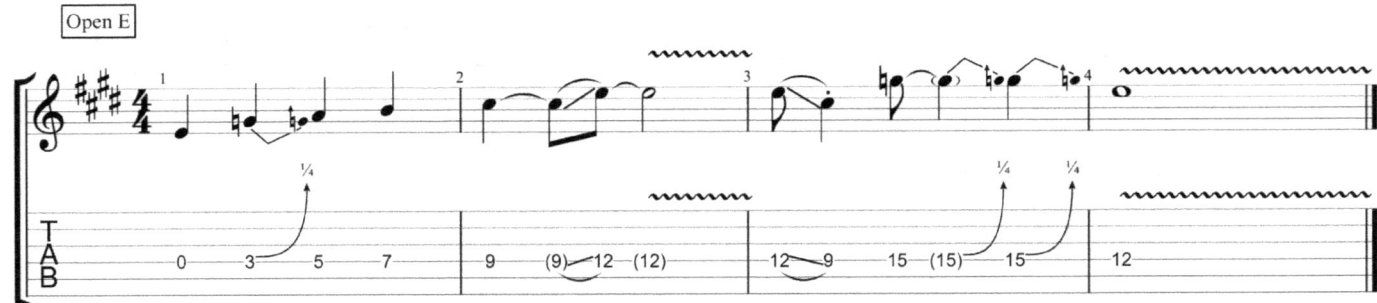

Another scale worth working on is the trusty major scale. In E, that's E, F#, G#, A, B, C# and D#. Or Root, 2, 3, 4, 5, 6 and 7.

If you've been paying attention, you'll probably have noticed that you know six of these seven notes. The only one that needs addressing is the 7th (D#).

As the scale on a single string shows, the 7th is found a semitone below the root note.

Example 4u

This scale can sound a bit "nursery rhyme", but it's an essential sound to have under your belt as its parent chord (the major 7 chord) does come up in jazzier music.

Here's an example of a jazz lick (THE lick!) adapted for slide guitar on one string.

Example 4v

Here's another major scale idea which you'll notice ends on the 24th fret. Don't worry if your guitar doesn't have a 24th fret, your slide IS the fret, so you can put it wherever you want. It's hard to get up this high (unless you're playing an SG of course!) but if you have access, the sky is the limit. You can select the bridge pickup and slide right up to where fret 30 would be if you're seeking a range that will drive dogs wild!

Example 4w

As mentioned in the introduction, a lot of the early slide influences came from Hawaii, but one of the more exotic influences some slide players explore is the world of Indian classical music.

This is a subject that could easily warrant its own book (or series!), but in short, Indian classical music uses collections of notes called "ragas" (or sometimes *raagas*) which don't readily translate to Western music theory. Each collection of notes is considered to have the ability to colour the mind in a certain way, and tends to be used in specific circumstances, such as the time of day.

It's an extremely deep subject, but one that Derek Trucks has explored for many years and he has used this influence from time to time in his compositions.

Here's an attempt to translate the Raga Yaman to slide guitar. In its basic form it looks like the Lydian mode.

Example 4x

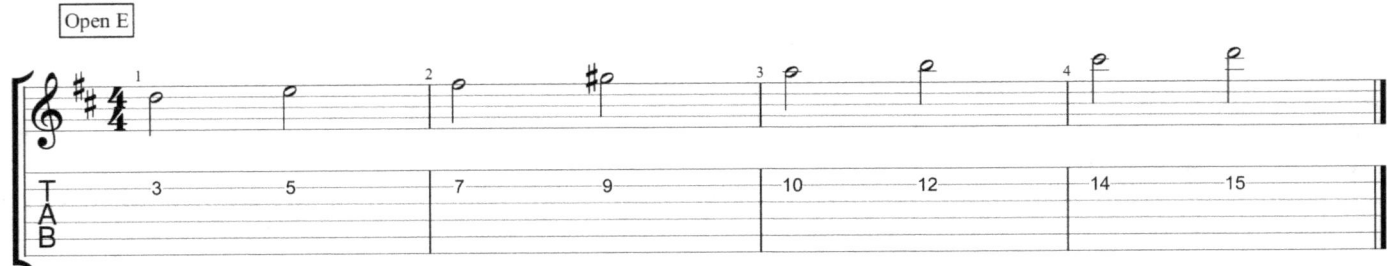

And here's a lick using this raga.

Example 4y

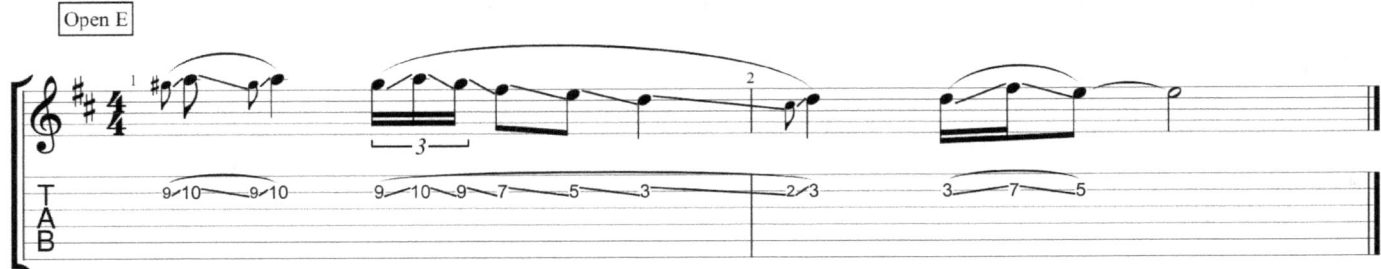

Finally, here's an example adapted from the Derek Trucks band piece, *Maki Madni* from 2002's *Joyful Noise* album.

One could attempt to analyse this in relation to Western music theory, but this would miss the point as this style of music cannot be boiled down to a formula.

Example 4z

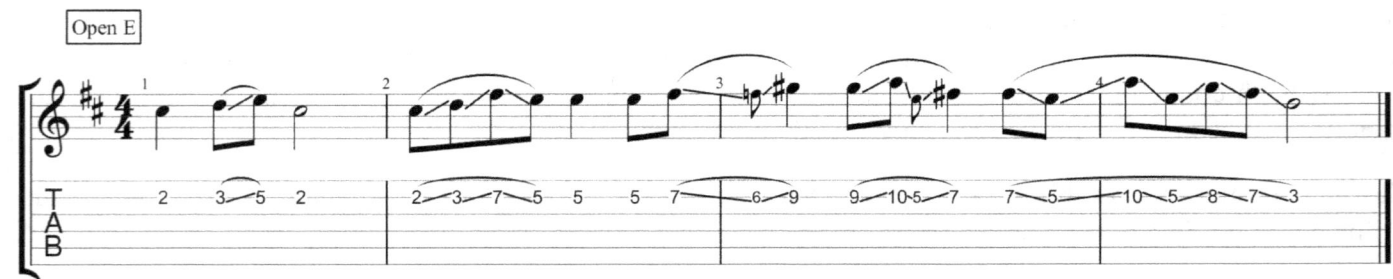

With these single string ideas under your belt, I'd recommend you get used to playing different scales on each string as a way to practise your muting technique and attack. As I said at the beginning of this chapter, much of your slide vocabulary will exploit this single string style of playing, so it's something you should feel at home with before moving onto string crossing.

Chapter Five: Single String Solo

Now you have some simple, single string vocabulary under your fingers, I want you to see just how much music you can make already. If you can make a solo sound cool with limited single string vocabulary, just imagine what you can do when you add more strings into the equation!

Before launching into the solo, let's discuss the chords and how we're going to play them in Open E tuning.

The chord sequence is a simple diatonic progression with a bluesy soul vibe in the key of C Major. There are many ways to play these chords in Open E tuning and we'll look at some more voicings later, but for now here's a simple way to voice them.

Use your picking hand fingers for these chords as this will allow you to create incredible dynamic range. If you play rhythm guitar through a loud amp, but play as soft as a whisper, you can build up in volume with the band.

Example 5a

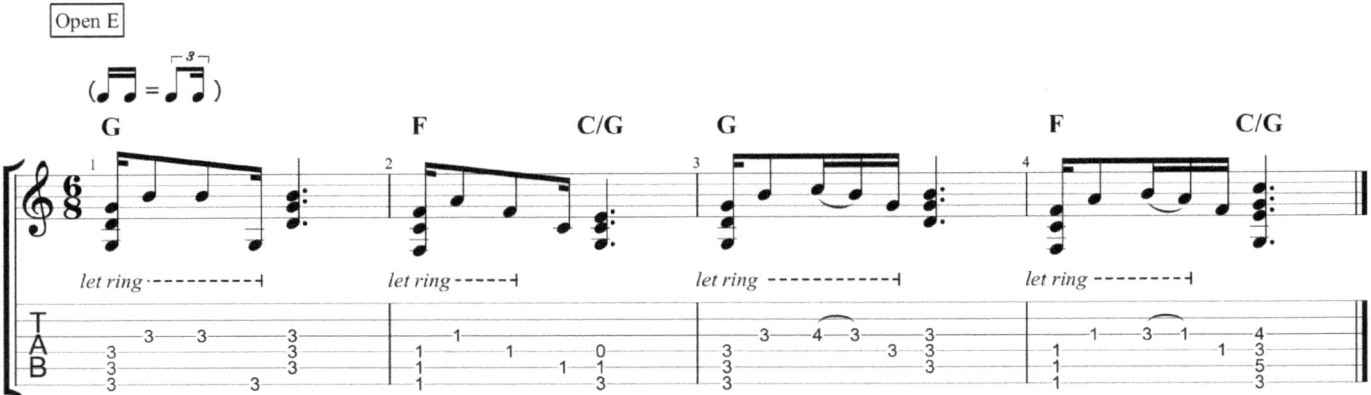

The first lick stays on the fourth string and uses notes of the C major scale.

Listen carefully to the recording, as the nuance in the rhythm is a big part of what the slide brings to the style.

Example 5b

Example 5c has a similar feel to the pervious idea, but is now moved over to the second string.

The final Bb comes from the G minor pentatonic scale, and bending it slightly sharp gives it a wonderful aggressive blues rock vibe.

Example 5c

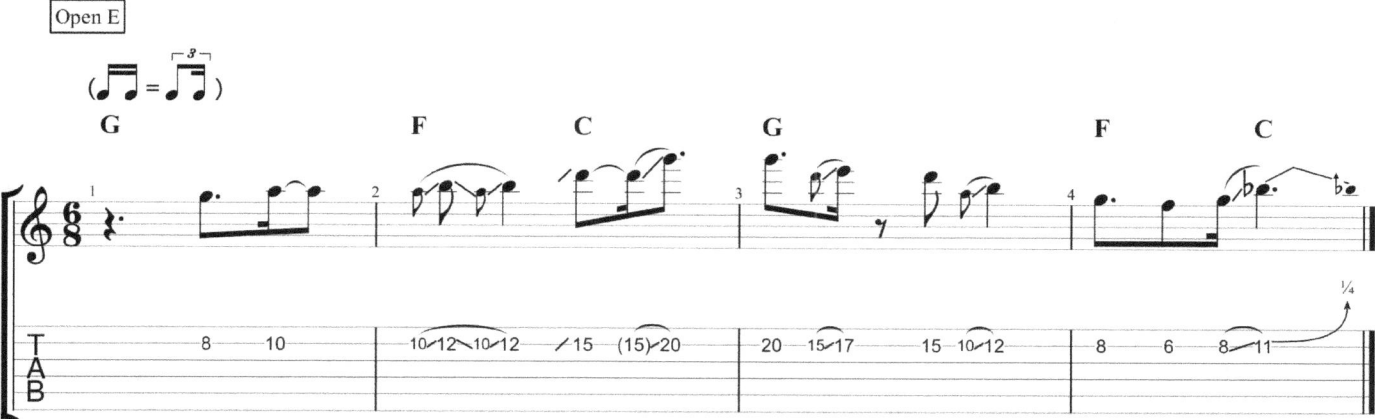

The next example moves to the high E string and covers a massive 20-fret span! It's important to learn the lick in small sections and look at where you're aiming *to slide to*, rather than where you are.

Example 5d

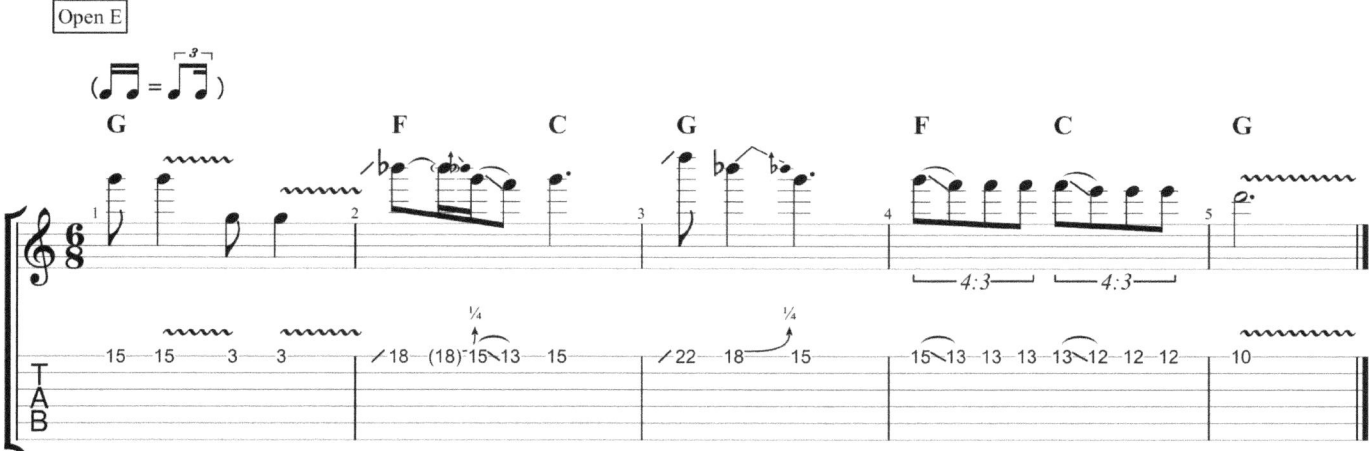

The final example focuses on simple major scale melodies that complement the chords. It's is about playing strong melodies, rather than showing off.

On the final note, gradually increase the width of your vibrato as you re-pick it. This is a great way to reach a climax in a solo.

Example 5e

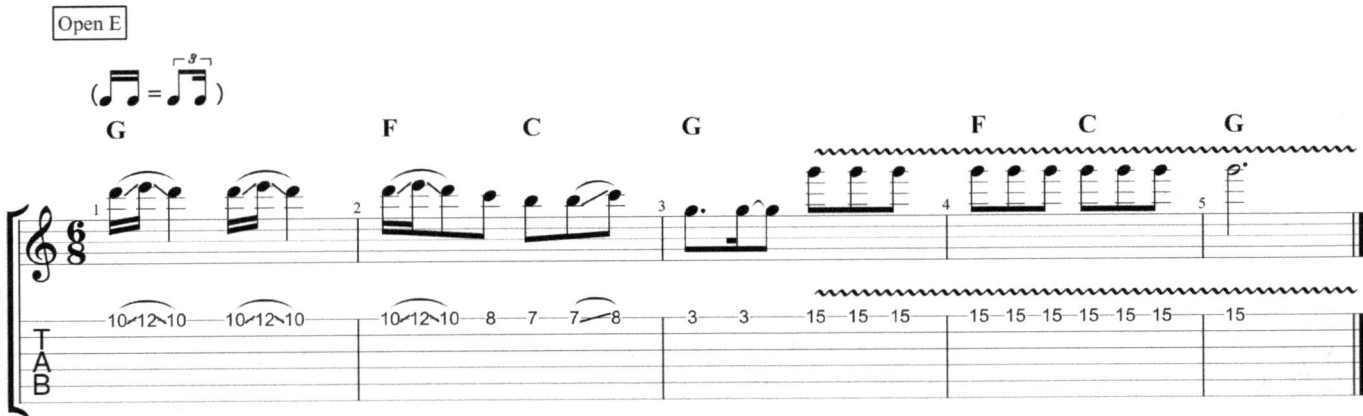

Creating solos like this is rewarding as you're able to use the slide to make something exciting and musical, despite the potential limitation of playing on single strings. If you can develop great vocabulary on single strings like this, you'll only improve your musicality and options when playing on multiple strings.

Chapter Six: Changing Strings

Now you're starting to get your slide skills under control and you have some musical vocabulary under your belt, it's time to expand your vocabulary with some licks that use multiple strings.

The toughest aspect of changing strings when playing slide guitar is stopping unwanted string noise. This won't always be necessary, but it's much better to develop the skills and not need them, than need them and not have them.

The first example features an E major chord at the 12th fret. As all of the notes are in the chord, it really doesn't matter too much if the notes ring into each other a bit.

Example 6a

This same idea can be played again, but without having the notes ring into each other. In order to execute this, begin by muting strings 6-2 with the thumb and striking the first string with the index finger.

As you switch to the second string, the hand moves over so that the thumb mutes strings 6-4, with the middle finger muting the first string. This leaves the index finger free to pluck the second string.

For the third string, the thumb moves over again, while the index and ring fingers mute the first and second strings. As with the previous strings, the index finger is now free to pluck the third string.

Continue this idea across the neck and focus on having as little note-bleed as possible.

Example 6b

Here's another idea that covers multiple strings using 1/4 notes, so you can focus on your muting technique. Listen to the recording and use that as a benchmark for how clean this should sound.

Example 6c

Another common string crossing mechanic slide players employ is alternating between adjacent strings.

This will often be played a little bit faster, which makes using the index finger to pluck both strings problematic.

In order to build this one up, use the index finger to pluck the higher note, and the thumb to pluck the lower note. When plucking the high string, the thumb mutes the lower strings, and as soon as you pick the low note, the index or middle finger touches the high string to mute it. This has the added benefit of the finger now being placed ready to re-pick the note and continue the pattern.

Example 6d

Example 6e uses the same mechanics, but applied to a musical phrase. It's unlikely this will be perfectly clean, but the goal isn't to be robotic, just to clean things up enough to sound like you're in control.

Example 6e

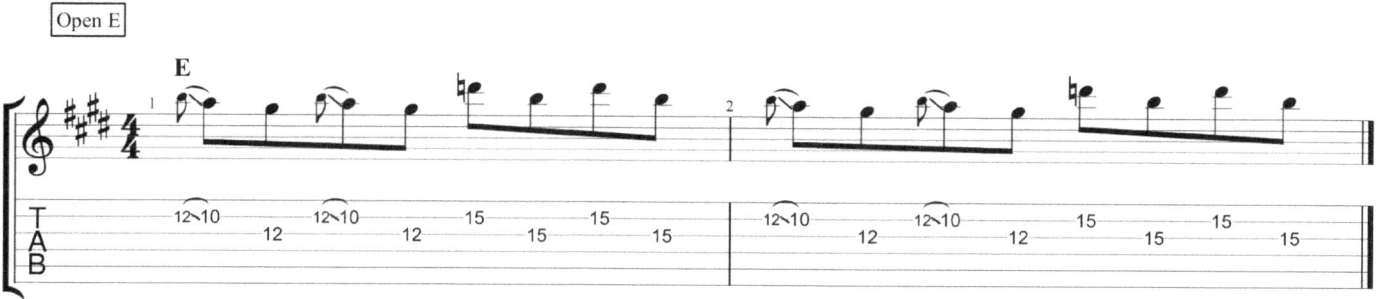

With those two mechanics covered, let's look at the first box pattern you need to know in Open E. In fact, this one could be just about all you need!

Back in Chapter Two, I mentioned the interval structure of our Open E tuning. With our single string scales nailed, and due attention paid to the various intervals in different scales, this tuning analysis should make a little more sense now.

As a refresher, Open E tuning (E, B, E, G#, B, E) can be described as R, 5, R, 3, 5, R.

The first pattern to learn is formed by taking this barre form and adding notes a tone below. This is purely about "geometry" rather than it being a true "scale". Looking at the following diagram, you should be able to tell that none of these notes are "bad" notes. Each of them is found in either the major or minor pentatonic scale.

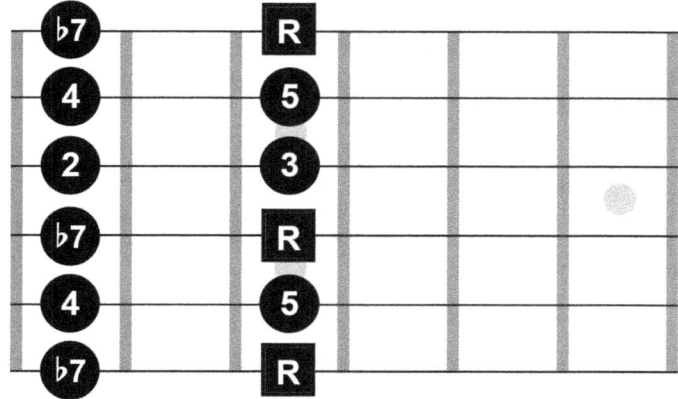

Begin by practising this pattern ascending and descending. The focus here is not having any of the notes ring into each other.

Example 6f

Here's the same idea, but now sliding between notes.

Example 6g

My approach is to think of the 12th fret as "home" and the notes two frets lower as adding "colour" for melodic interest. I will drop down to the 10th fret when playing, but it's unlikely I'll stay there for long, because none of these notes sound as strong as the chord tones at the 12th fret.

As an example, here's a lick that moves down from the 12th to the 10th fret on the second string (taking you away from home), then shifts back from the 10th to the 12th fret on the third string (taking you back home), before playing the root note on the fourth string.

Listen carefully to the audio, because it's almost impossible to capture the nuance of a lick like this in notation and tablature. To my ears, it sounds best when you slide slowly between those first notes, rather than the quicker slide that the notation would suggest! However, experiment with both because you're likely to find a setting in which each will work.

Example 6h

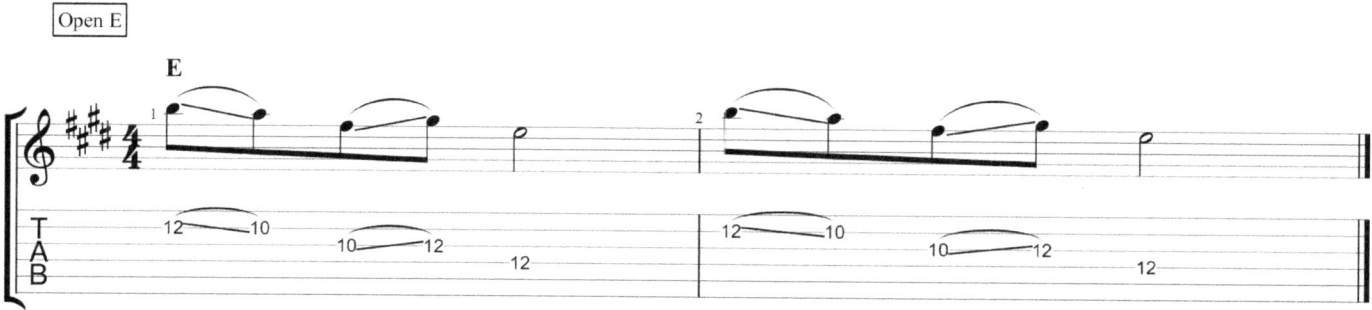

Here's another lick in the same area, but now moving more quickly between the second and third strings. Here you'll slide quickly down from the 12th to the 10th fret, then pick the third string at the 12th fret without any noticeable slide to it. This will take time to master, but it's one of the most played clichés in slide guitar.

On the repeat, you'll notice that after playing the root note on the first string, I slide up to the same note on the second string. This is the single string improvisation influence coming in.

Example 6i

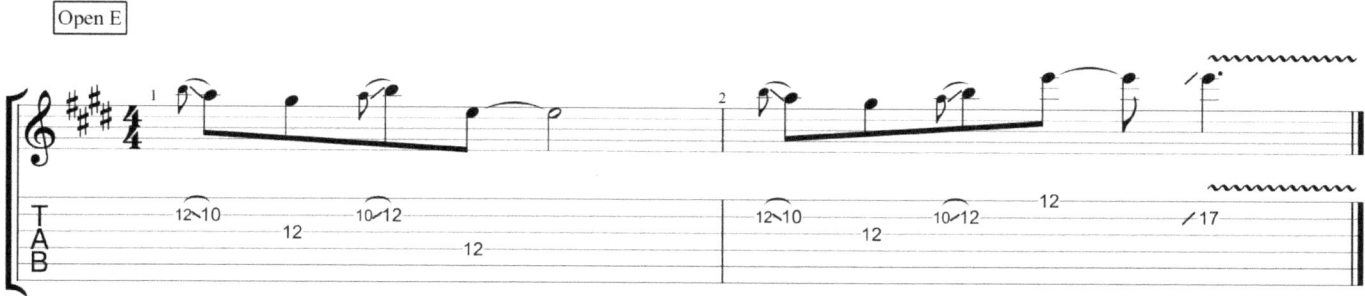

Here's that same string crossing idea with the switch to the root note on the second string at the end. This time I expand the idea a little with some single string minor pentatonic improvisation around the root note.

Example 6j

To demonstrate the viability of this approach, here's the same idea, but now in C. This is as simple as moving your "home" barre position down to the 8th fret, instead of the 12th. The notes have changed, but the intervals are exactly the same!

The only drawback is that by moving down four frets, some of the notes on the lower positions in E won't work, but that's not a problem… just play something else around that home position!

Example 6k

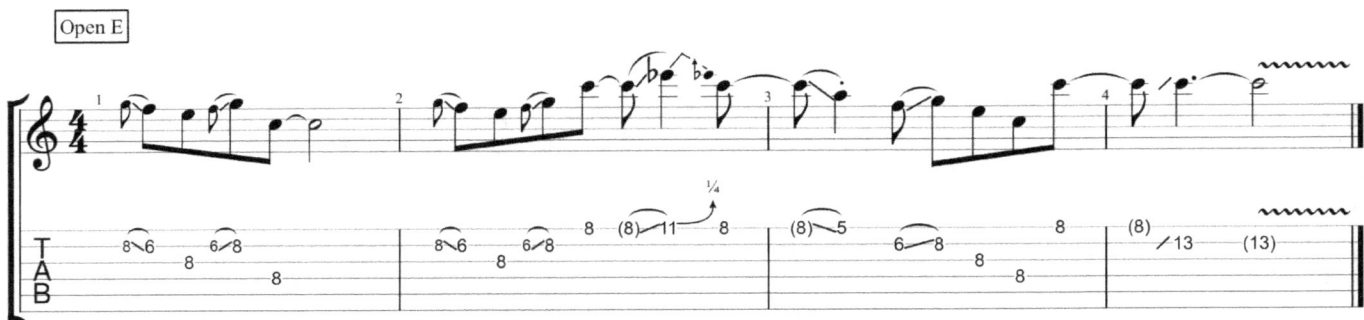

Another way to enhance this shape is to add notes three frets higher than the home position. Look at the diagram and you'll see that the intervals this creates are notes that keep the minor flavour, so they will work fine.

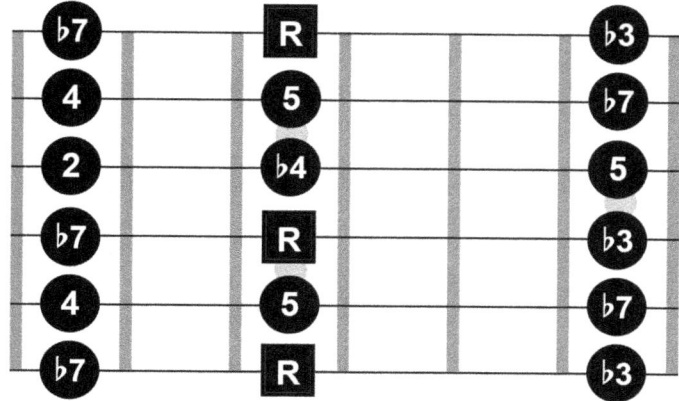

A common idea you'll see using this shape is moving up three frets on the second and third strings for some bluesy tension, before going back down to the position covered in the last examples to bring it home.

Example 6l

As with Example 6k, it's possible to move this pattern to anywhere it might be needed. Here's the last lick, but now moved to C at the 8th fret area.

Example 6m

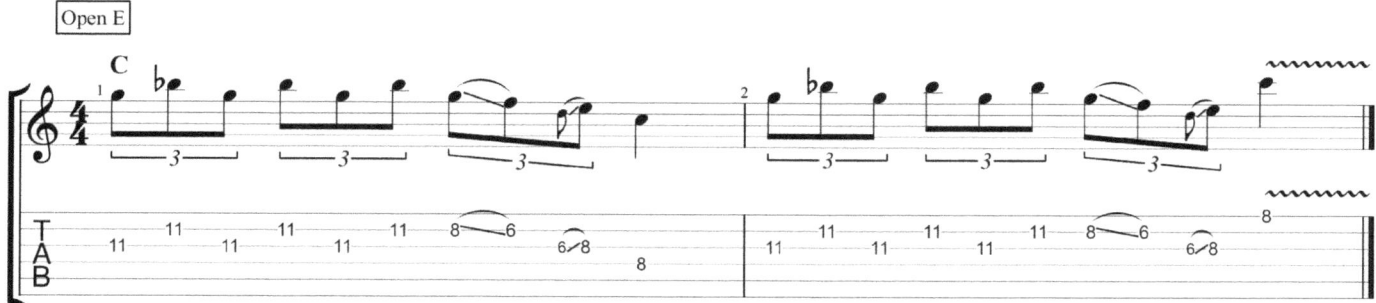

We've gone into some depth analysing these shapes, but it's worth remembering that what we're learning is a "pattern" rather than anything more intellectual. Players from Elmore James to Bonnie Raitt use this kind of pattern to play entire blues solos. There's more than enough here to give you an authentic blues vocabulary without having to worry too much about playing the right notes over the chord. As long as you come "home", it's going to sound good.

To demonstrate this, here's a full twelve-bar blues solo using nothing but the shape we've looked at so far – both the previous pattern and the single string scales.

Example 6n

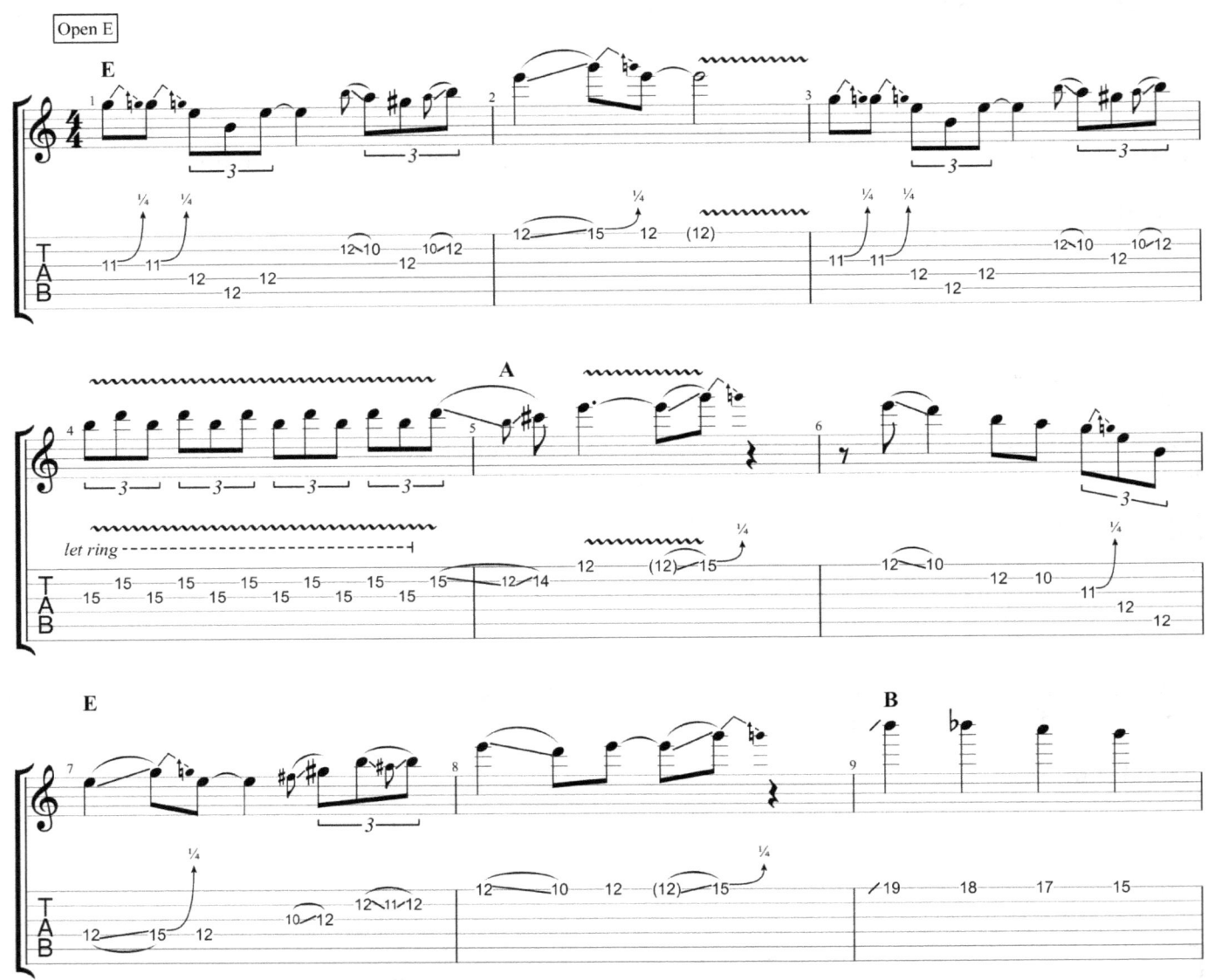

The next logical step with this pattern is to fill in some of the blanks using chromatic passing tones. These are usually applied a fret below your home position. You can see from the diagram, however, that the intervals created are a little more questionable.

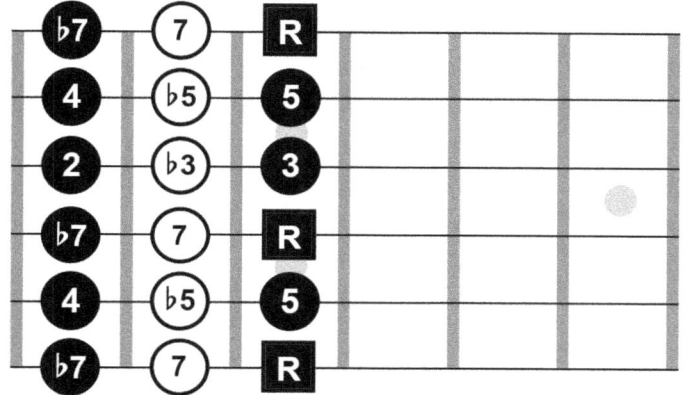

Despite that, the focus should be on the home position, with the other notes used to create tension before returning home.

Here's a simple lick that doesn't use these passing tones. It doesn't sound bad, but it's a bit by the numbers.

Example 60

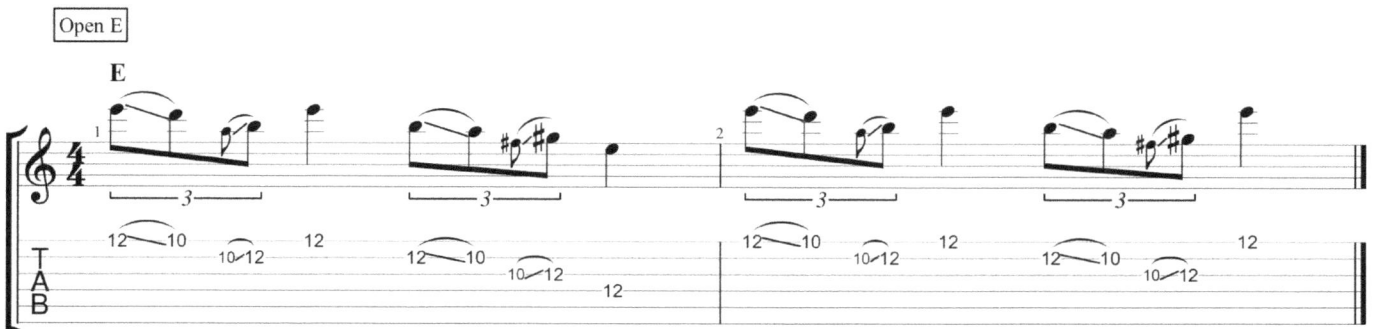

Now here is the same idea, but instead of using the 10th fret each time, sometimes I'm using the 11th. Pay attention when you play these notes and listen to how much tension they add to a lick.

Example 6p

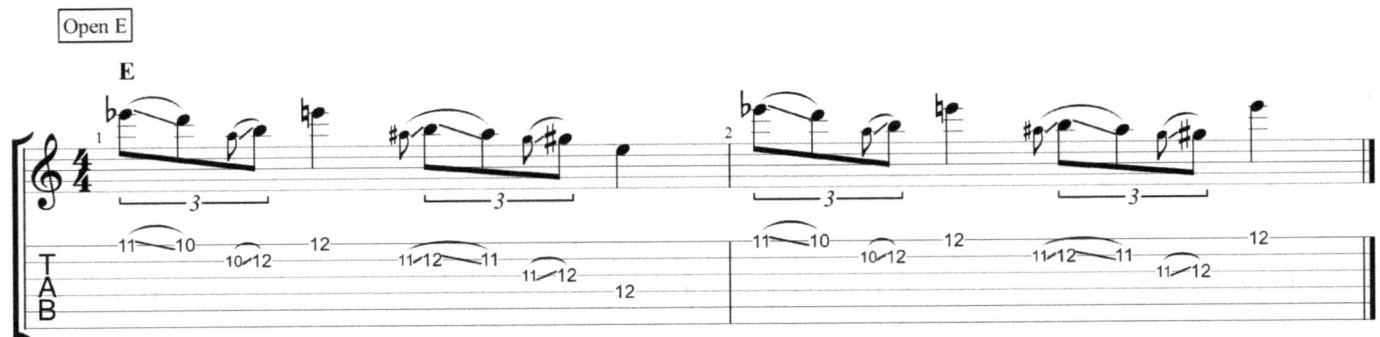

I can't stress this enough: if we could wind back the clock and talk to someone like Duane Allman in his prime, I don't think for a second that he'd talk to us about scales and chords. It was all about the music. But when you start to get the music under your fingers, learning some scales will become more worthwhile, as you'll have a much better idea of how to use them.

Chapter Seven: Slide Guitar Scales

Now you can change strings easily, it's time to learn full scales in a single position. This section will develop your technique and refine your skills as you become 100% accurate with your fretting and eliminate excess string noise. You'll naturally develop this ability, because unwanted notes ringing out will destroy the sound of the scale.

The following scales will enable you to play much more music than the blues. If you want play traditional gospel, soul, and jazz progressions it's essential to know the following melodic scales.

The minor pentatonic scale is the basis of countless blues and rock improvisers' vocabulary, so it's essential that any versatile slide player has this scale nailed. It can be played in the following way using Open E tuning.

Notice the articulation and how I move between notes. This isn't the only way to play this scale, but the phrasing is loose and melodic and takes advantage of the nuances of slide playing.

You'll notice there are three notes on the fifth string. This isn't ideal for easy fingering, as you're probably used to playing two-note-per-string shapes, but unfortunately that's the nature of Open E tuning and staying in one position is often impossible if we are to play every note in the scale.

Example 7a

E Minor Pentatonic

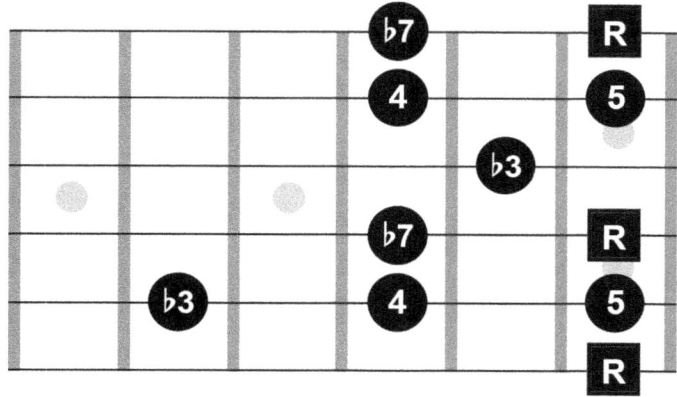

When playing licks with this pattern you'll quickly get used to bending the b3rd a little sharp and applying some of the phrasing ideas from the previous chapter.

Example 7b

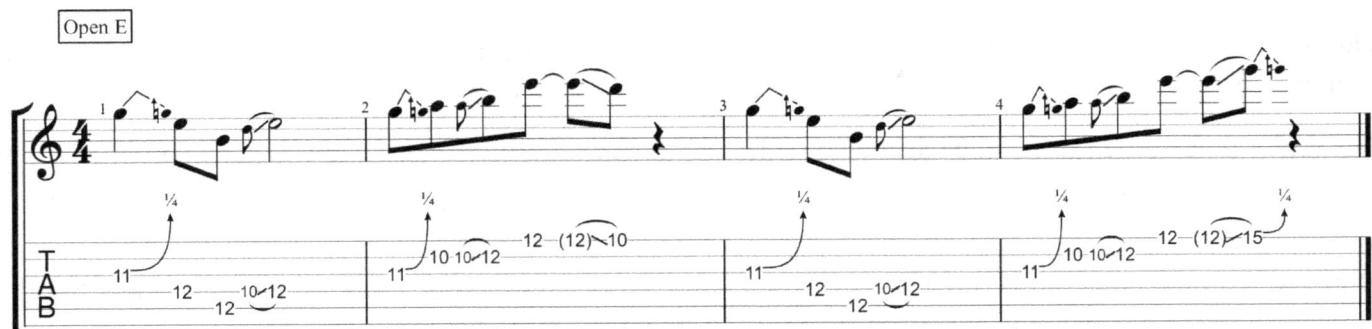

As the guitar is tuned to a major chord and this is a minor scale that fits a *minor* chord, the first position of the minor pentatonic isn't available in the same way as it is with open tuning. This means that playing a barre with the slide at your home position is now off limits, because that would form a major chord. This is a challenge of open tunings and we'll look at how to surmount it in later chapters.

Another common scale which is a slight variation on the minor pentatonic scale is the blues scale.

The blues scale is the same as the minor pentatonic scale with an added b5th. Pay attention to how that b5 sounds, and how it instantly gives the scale a darker, bluesy vibe.

Example 7c

E Blues

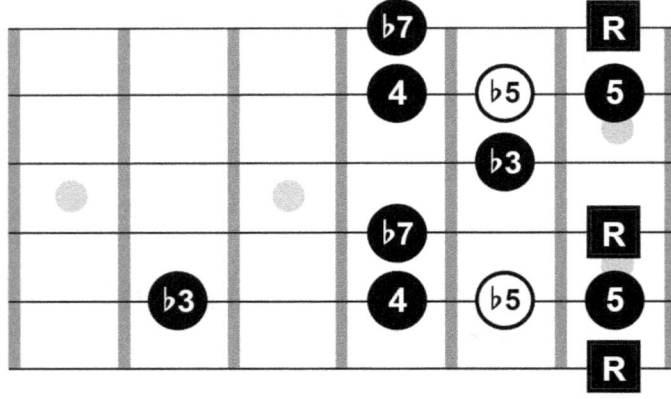

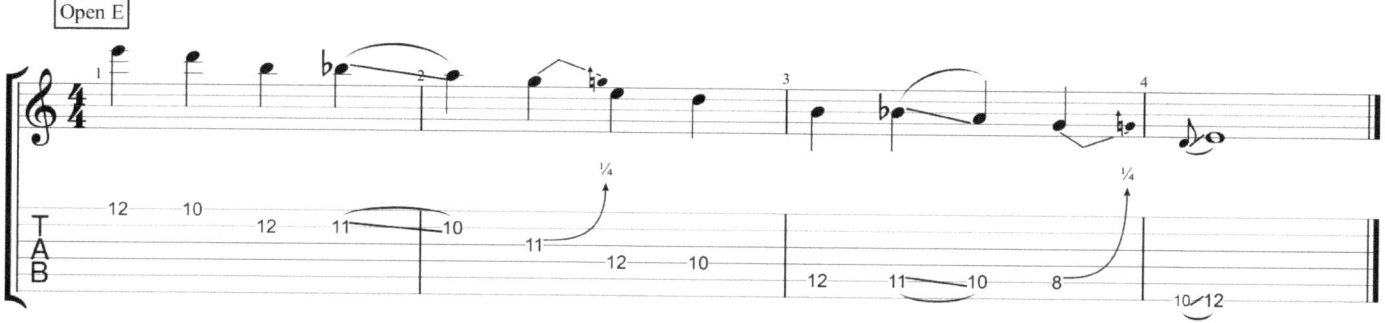

Here's a lick using the blues scale. Lines like this require a little more consideration than the geometric shapes from the last chapter, but the reward is well worth it.

Example 7d

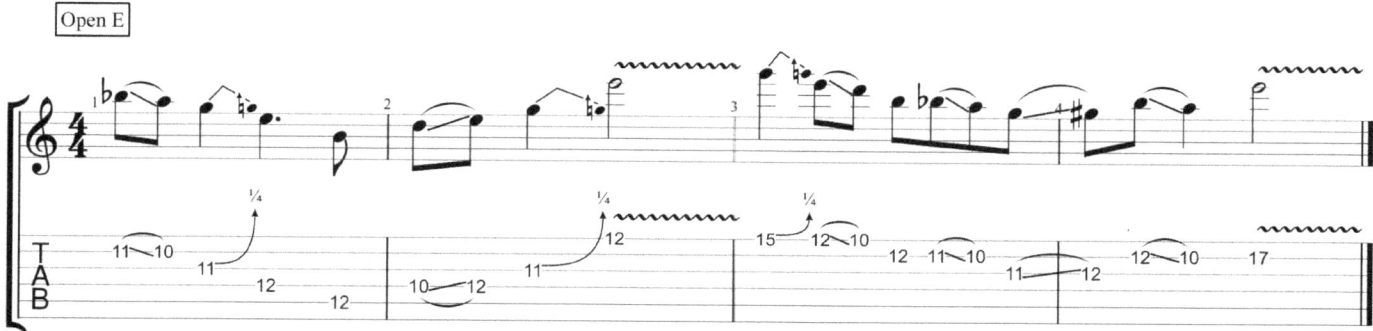

Next up is the major scale. This is the parent scale from which all Western music is built, so while it may not be the most usable scale right now, it will prepare you for learning other scales and modes.

E Major

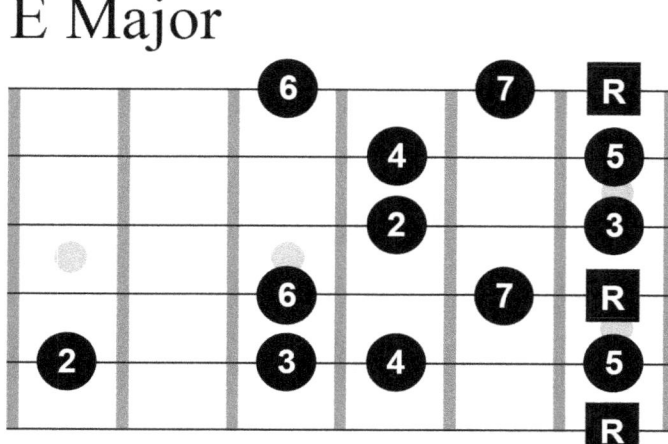

As with the previous scales, this one can be a bit tough to play cleanly in one position. If you compare playing the major scale in one position to playing it on a single string, you'll have a good idea of why slide players tend to play up and down strings, rather than across them.

Playing the major scale in one position with a slide is a great way to practise your muting technique though, especially as you build speed.

Example 7e

Here's the scale used to play something a little more musical.

Example 7f

A scale you're more likely to use in blues and rock soloing is the Mixolydian mode.

This mode consists of the major scale with a b7 and has the formula 1 2 3 4 5 6 b7.

Example 7g

E Mixolydian Mode

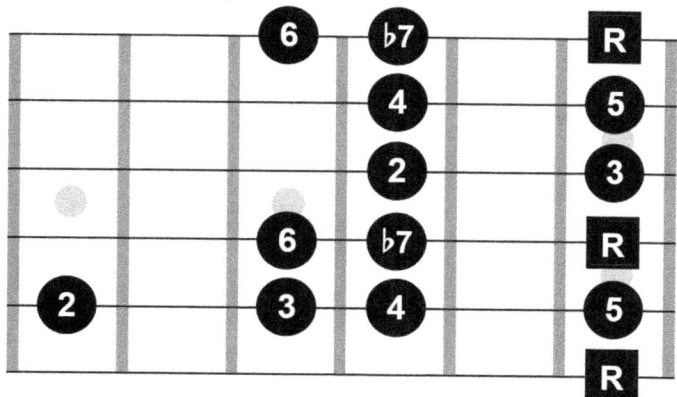

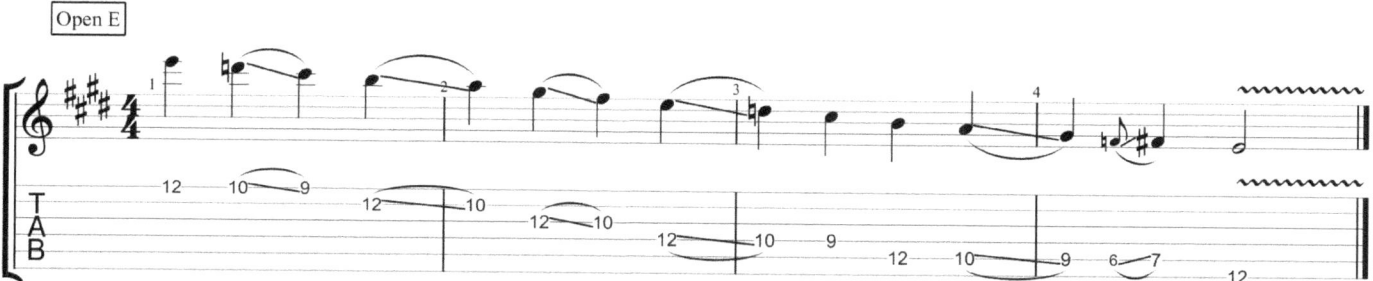

A bluesy way to play the Mixolydian mode is to approach each 3rd from a semitone below. This "minor 3rd to major 3rd" sound is a huge part of authentic blues playing.

Here's a lick that uses the notes of the Mixolydian mode with the added b3.

Example 7h

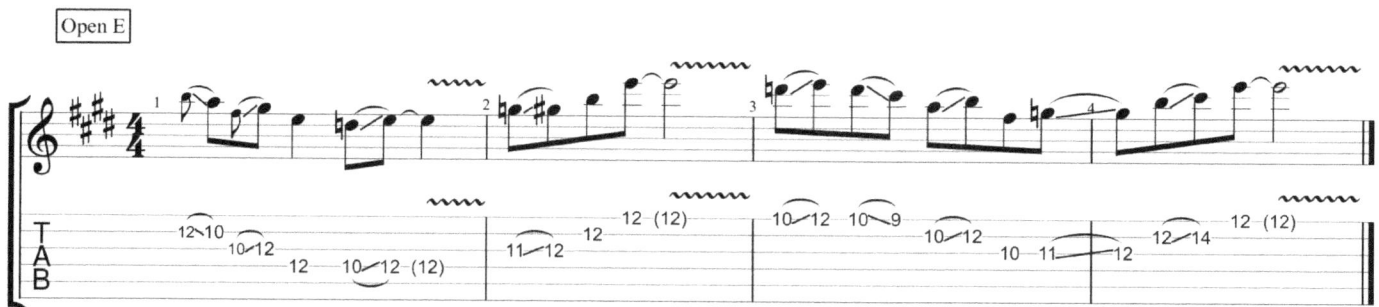

Here's that same lick, but moved up to the 15th fret, resulting in a key change from E to G.

Example 7i

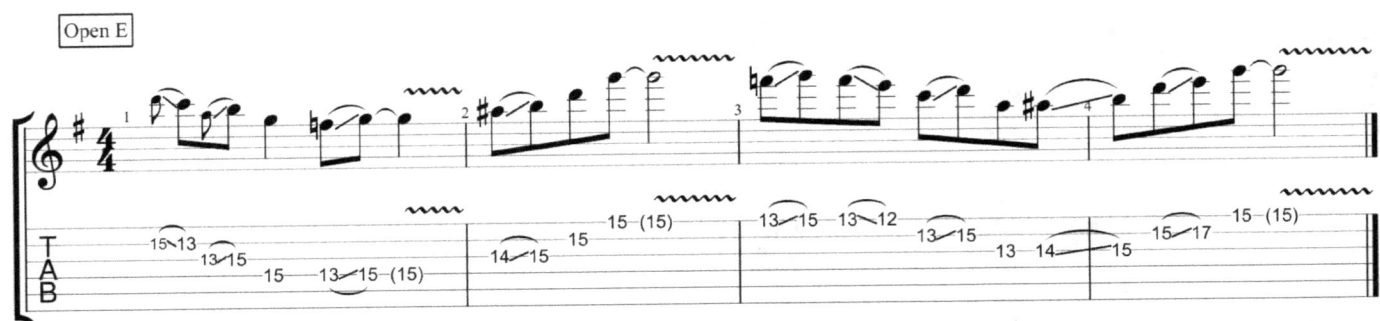

Chapter Eight: Chord Inversions

One big appeal of open tunings is that playing a major chord with the slide is extremely easy. By moving the slide to different frets, it functions as a barre and any major chord can be played by simply strumming all the strings

However, while playing these simple barred chords is extremely easy, playing major chords in other areas of the neck become much trickier. Most slide players understand that this challenge is part of the territory and rely on three *inversions* of the major barre chord that are relatively easy to play. This can unlock the rest of the neck.

As the word suggests, an inversion is where you take a chord and turn it on its head.

An E Major triad (1 3 5) contains the notes E, G# and B. The root (E) is the lowest pitched note, so this is called the *root position chord*.

In an inversion, a different note from the chord is played as the lowest pitch. For example, if you move the note E to the top of the chord and a G# is played in the bass, the chord voicing becomes G# B E. This is still an E major chord as it contains the correct three notes, but the 3rd (G#) is now the bass note. This is a *first inversion chord*.

By moving the G# to the top of the chord and placing the B in the bass, we get B E G#. This is still an E major chord, but it is now in *second inversion*.

Let's look at how to play these three inversions on the guitar. Learn them without a slide to begin with and we'll learn them with a slide later.

The following diagram shows the three inversions played along the neck on the second, third and fourth strings. The root position chord is played at the 12th fret, the first inversion is played at the 4th, and the second inversion is played at the 7th. I've shown the triads in black and white alternately, so you can see each one more clearly.

E Major

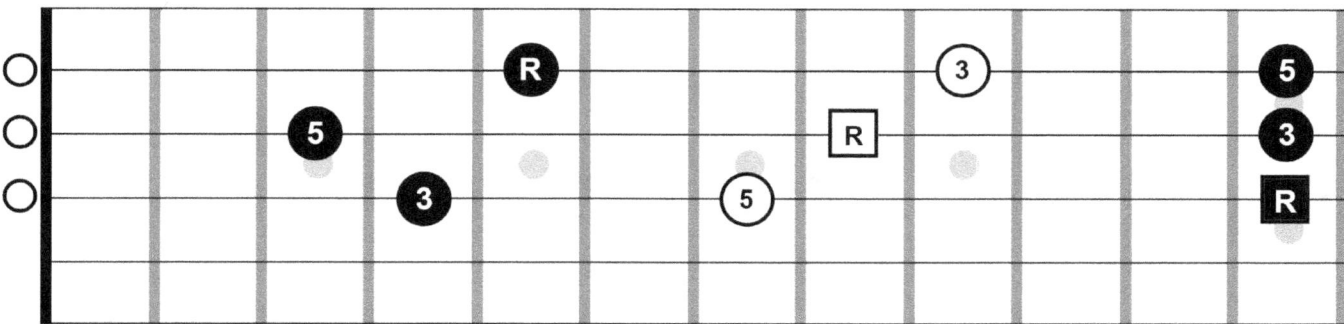

Play through these inversions ascending and descending on the middle strings.

Example 8a

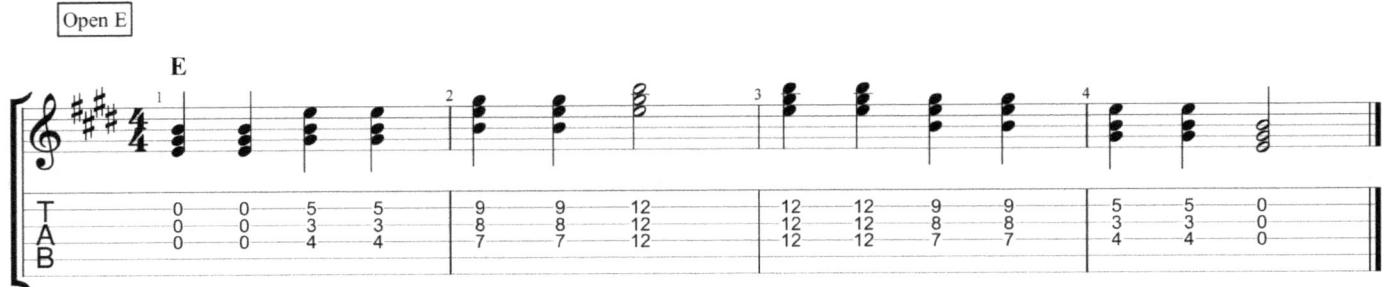

These three shapes allow you to play *any* major chord in *any* inversion. If you want to play an A major chord, the "straight" shape can be found at the 5th fret, then each inversion will move up the neck as they did for the E chord.

Example 8b

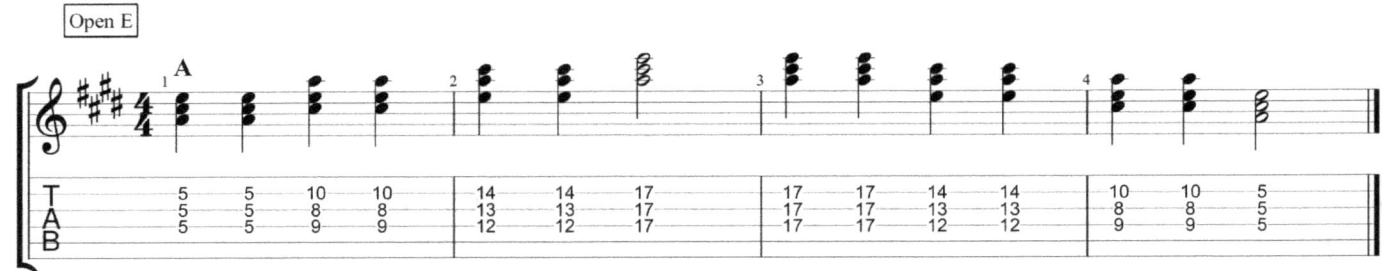

The same is true of a B major chord.

Example 8c

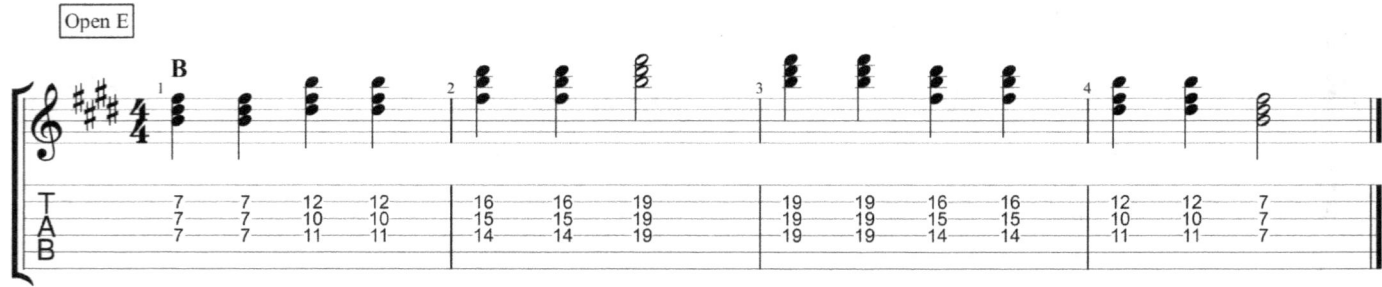

Link these three triads one after the other to form a chord sequence of E A B E in each position before moving on to the next area of the neck.

Example 8d

A handy feature of this tuning is that we can move the note on the fourth string over to the first string and play a different voicing of the same chord. This is another way to invert the chords without having to move up and down the neck.

Example 8e

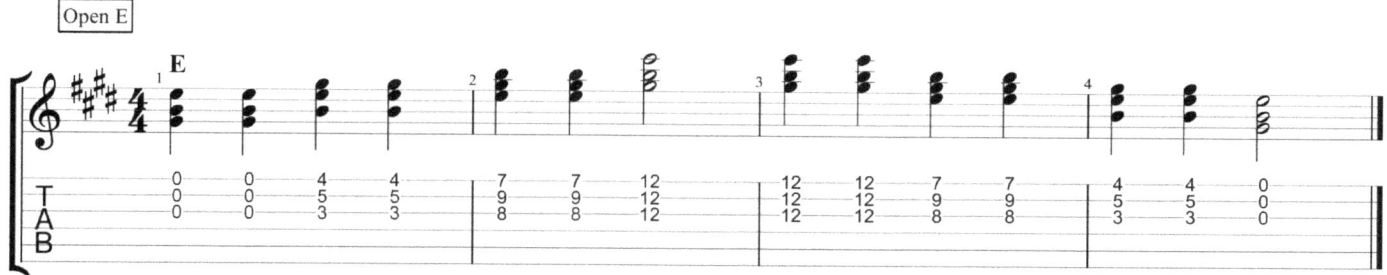

It's also possible to move each shape down a string set onto the third to fifth strings.

Example 8f

With these chords under your belt, you now have three basic "master positions" for major chords in any open tuning.

E Major

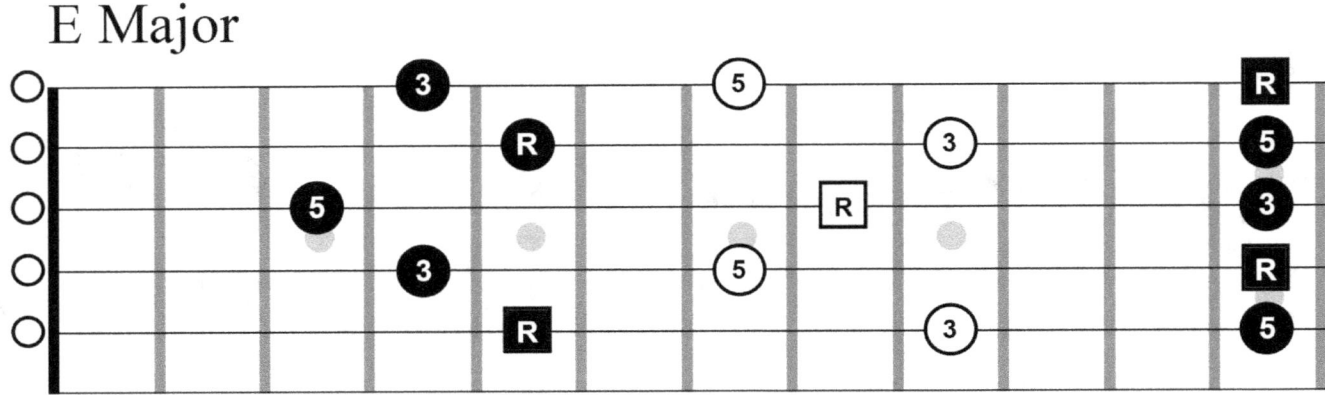

These patterns can be played across the strings like this.

Example 8g

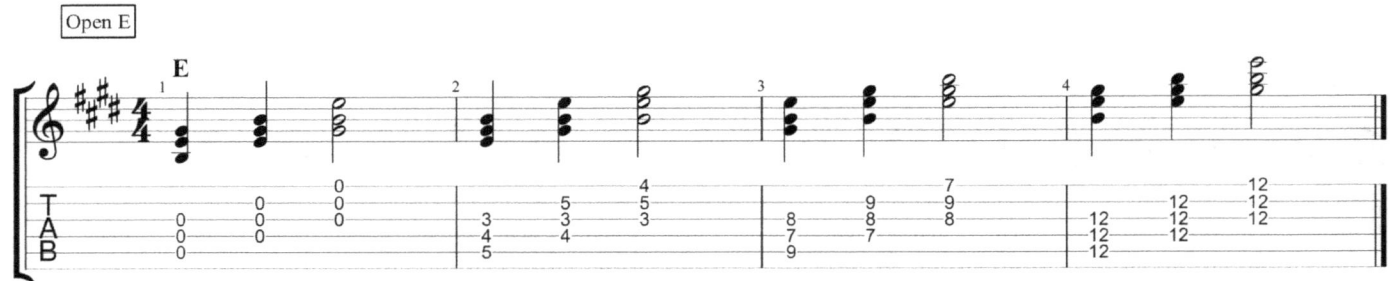

Now we understand the "geometry" of the open tuned guitar, how can we go about extracting music from these shapes and integrate them into your playing?

In chapters six and seven we learnt licks and scales around the "home" position (the one where the chord is played with the straight slide). This chapter will apply these concepts to the other two positions and give you a solid grasp of how to move between them in a musical way.

This next exercise moves from the root (straight barre) position to the next inversion of the chord and then adds an arpeggio fragment around it. You may wish to experiment with which finger you wear the slide on, but the important part to focus on is the melody. Try to visualise the chord while you play the melody.

Example 8h

Here's the same idea played an octave higher.

Example 8i

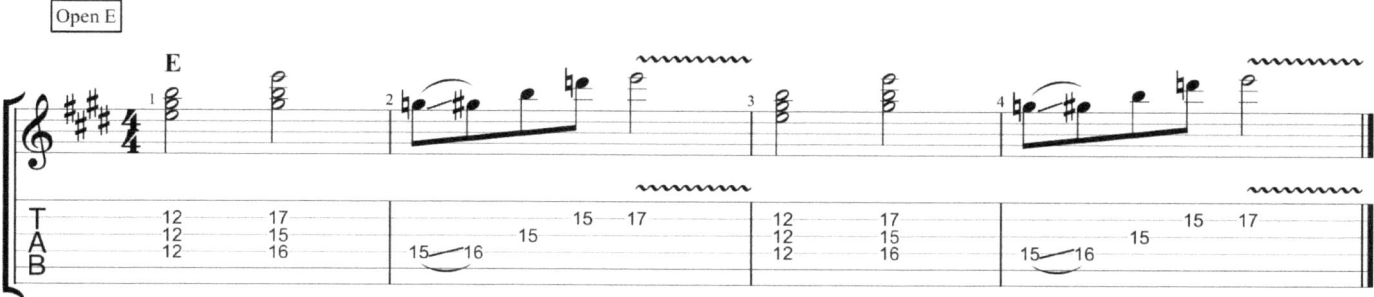

This idea can be played in any key. Here it is played on a C major chord. Try moving these ideas to different keys and playing them over the moving chords of a twelve-bar blues.

Example 8j

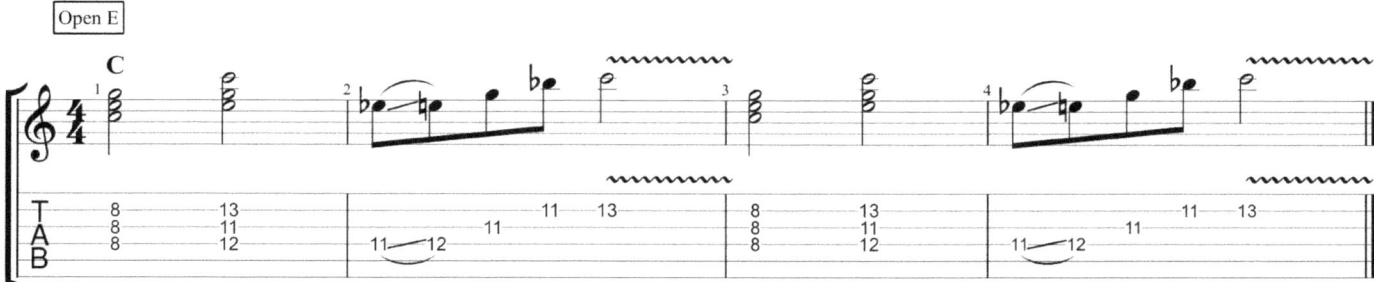

Here's a lick in C that uses the two positions. Begin by playing the chord at the 8th fret, then move up the neck for the single note melody with the triad fragment. To finish, I use a single string approach by sliding up three frets from the root to the b3.

Example 8k

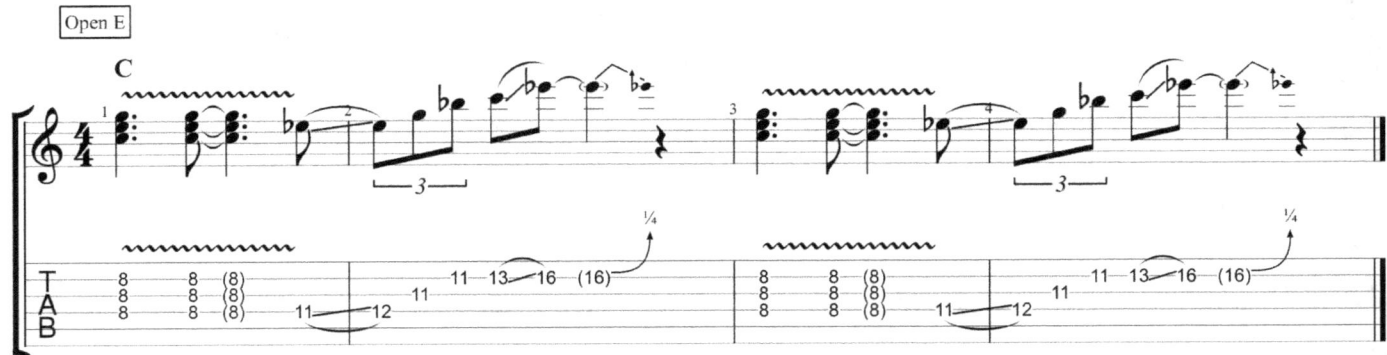

Again, in the key of C, the next lick begins with a melodic fragment around the barre position before shifting up to the next triad via a slide on the second string.

Example 8l

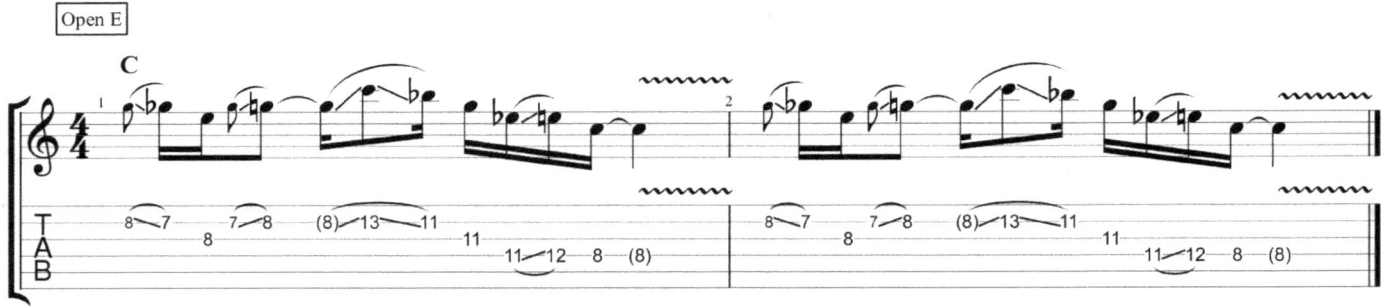

When you're comfortable with the triad position on the second to fourth strings, start adding more melodic notes around it. Here are two more notes added on the high E string that move down to the barre position.

Example 8m

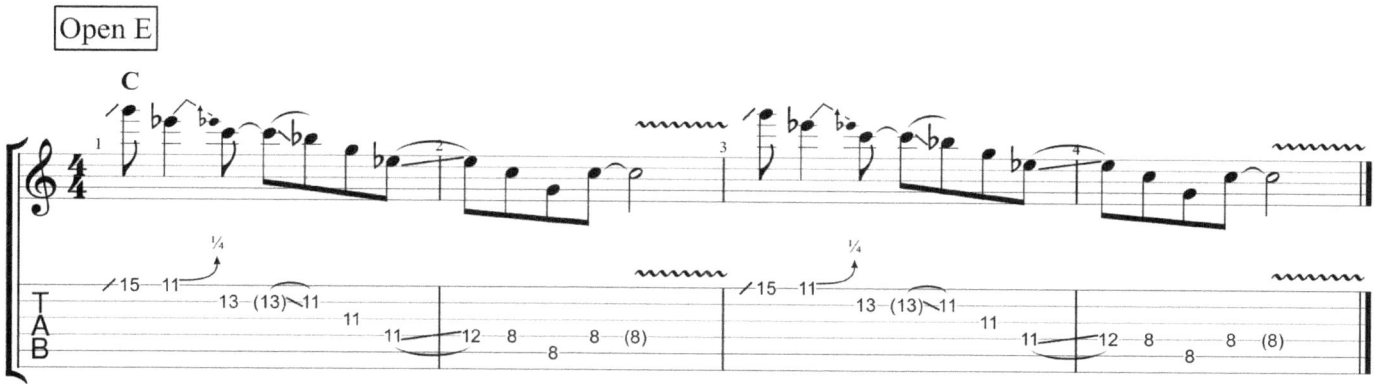

You should be able to transition between these positions on any string group. Here's a lick that moves down from the first inversion to the barre position on the third string.

Listen to the audio and pay attention to how I take advantage of the barre position by allowing the notes to ring out when playing in this location. Muting is important in other positions, but here any extra notes will be contained in the chord.

Example 8n

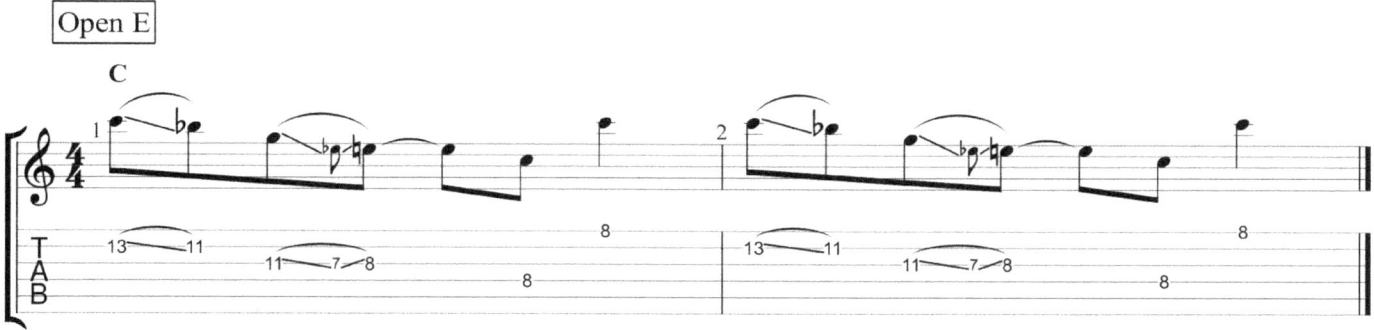

It's possible to expand the first inversion triad position to open up your sonic palette a little.

The fragment in the previous lick added a b7 degree note to the triad, giving it a distinctly dominant quality. It's also easy to add the 6th degree too in this position to create a major pentatonic flavour.

The following example switches to the key of G and plays the same shape from before. On the repeat we swap the darker b7 note (played on the second string) for the 6th (played on the third string)

Example 8o

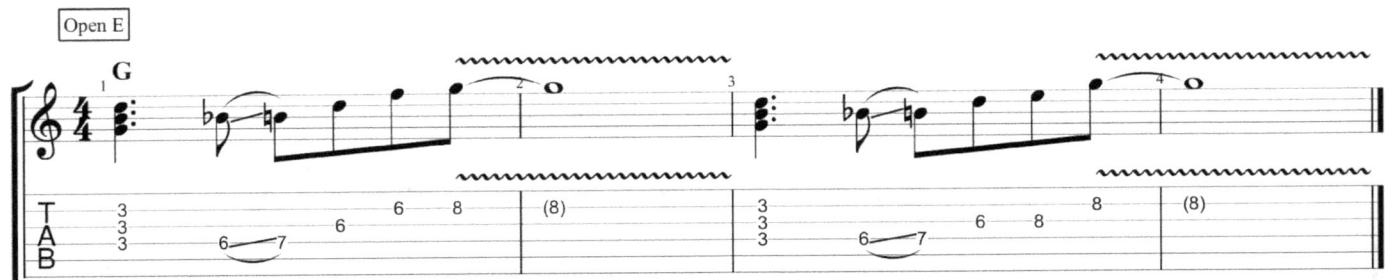

The following lick demonstrates how using both the 6th and b7th brings you closer to a bluesy Mixolydian sound. The secret to learning and internalising a lick like this is understanding how it connects back to the home position (the 3rd fret in this instance, as this idea is played in the key of G), even when it's not actually played.

Example 8p

The final example moves quickly between the 6th and 8th frets and is difficult to do cleanly. However, the noise created by switching between frets quickly gives you an authentic slide guitar sound.

Example 8q

With the first inversion position under our fingers, it's time to move on to the second inversion position.

The following G major example begins in the home position and moves up through the inversions before decorating the second inversion position with a single-note melody. The shape presented here again uses the 6th of the scale to create a strong G Major Pentatonic sound.

The lick ends by shifting up to the 15th fret and returning back to the home position.

Example 8r

To explore this position further, I have used the fragment from the last example and ended the phrase in a more musical way, firstly by moving down to the root note, then by moving up to the root at the 20th fret on the repeat.

Example 8s

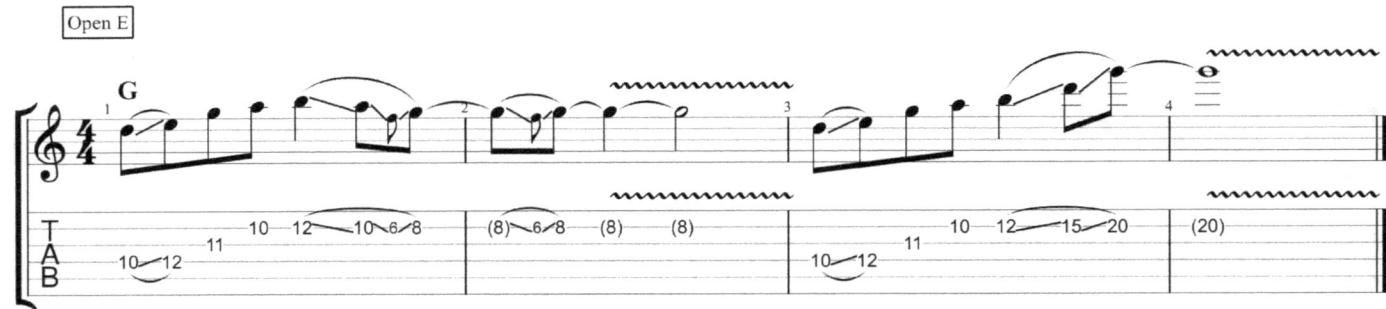

Here's a similar lick that changes the 6th (E) on the fourth string to a b7th (F) on the third. Getting a feel for how these subtle differences in note choice alter the sound so dramatically is the secret to learning to play the music you hear in your head.

Example 8t

The next example is another lick in this same position that explores more strings. Learn to focus on the smaller triad in the centre of the position and visualise the melody notes around it, so you're able to access this sound in any key.

Example 8u

Now you have some vocabulary around each of the three inversions, the rest of this chapter will focus on melodic ideas that move horizontally between each inversion.

The first example begins in the barre position at the 3rd fret before moving up to the first inversion. At the end of the first bar, shift up to the 11th fret and bend it up to the 12th fret, which is in the second inversion position. The line ends by ascending again to the 15th fret, bringing you back to the home position.

Example 8v

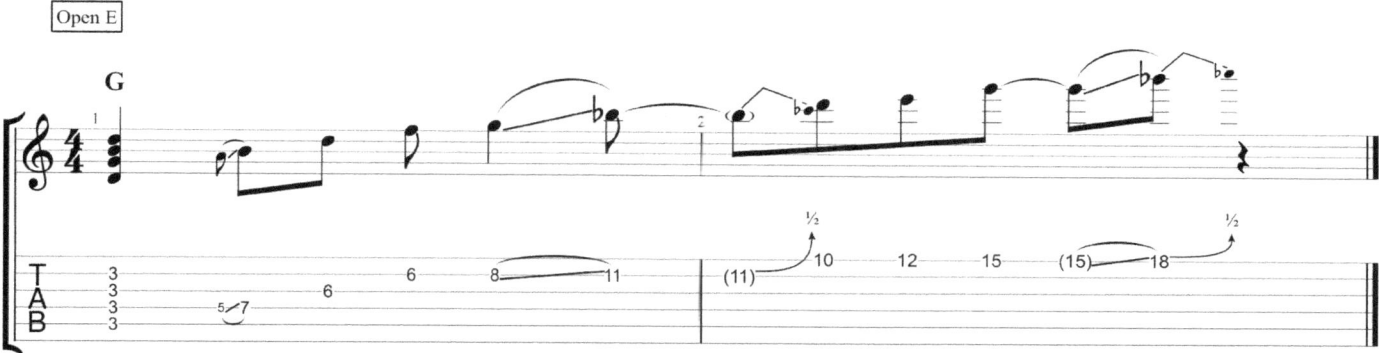

Another excellent way to consolidate your fretboard knowledge is to take a short musical phrase (motif) and play it in each of the three positions. This approach creates a certain cohesiveness that gives the listener something structured to latch onto.

Example 8w

Example 8x takes the motif approach through the root and first inversions, before shifting up the neck with some soulful single-string slides. These can be unbelievably lyrical when played right – just listen to AJ Ghent!

Example 8x

To conclude this chapter, I've written a full twelve bar solo piece with a soulful blues vibe.

The most effective way to create the vibe of a solo slide guitar blues is to outline the chord changes. A twelve-bar blues in G contains the chords G major, C major and D major, so they need to be emphasised.

The first two bars of the solo begin on a G major chord and contain all three chord inversions along with some expressive single-string lines built from the G Minor Pentatonic scale. This phrase is repeated an octave higher in bars three and four.

When the chord changes to C major, I move to the first inversion pattern in bar five and shift down to the root (straight) barre position.

In bar seven we return to the G major chord where I use a first inversion pattern.

For the D major and C major chords in bars nine and ten, I use the root position barre chord again. You don't have to do something clever to sound great.

The final two bars outline a G major chord by moving up the neck, and a D chord by descending. There's nothing fancy here, just outlining the chord tones and using the patterns in the chapter to help guide us to the best notes.

Example 8y

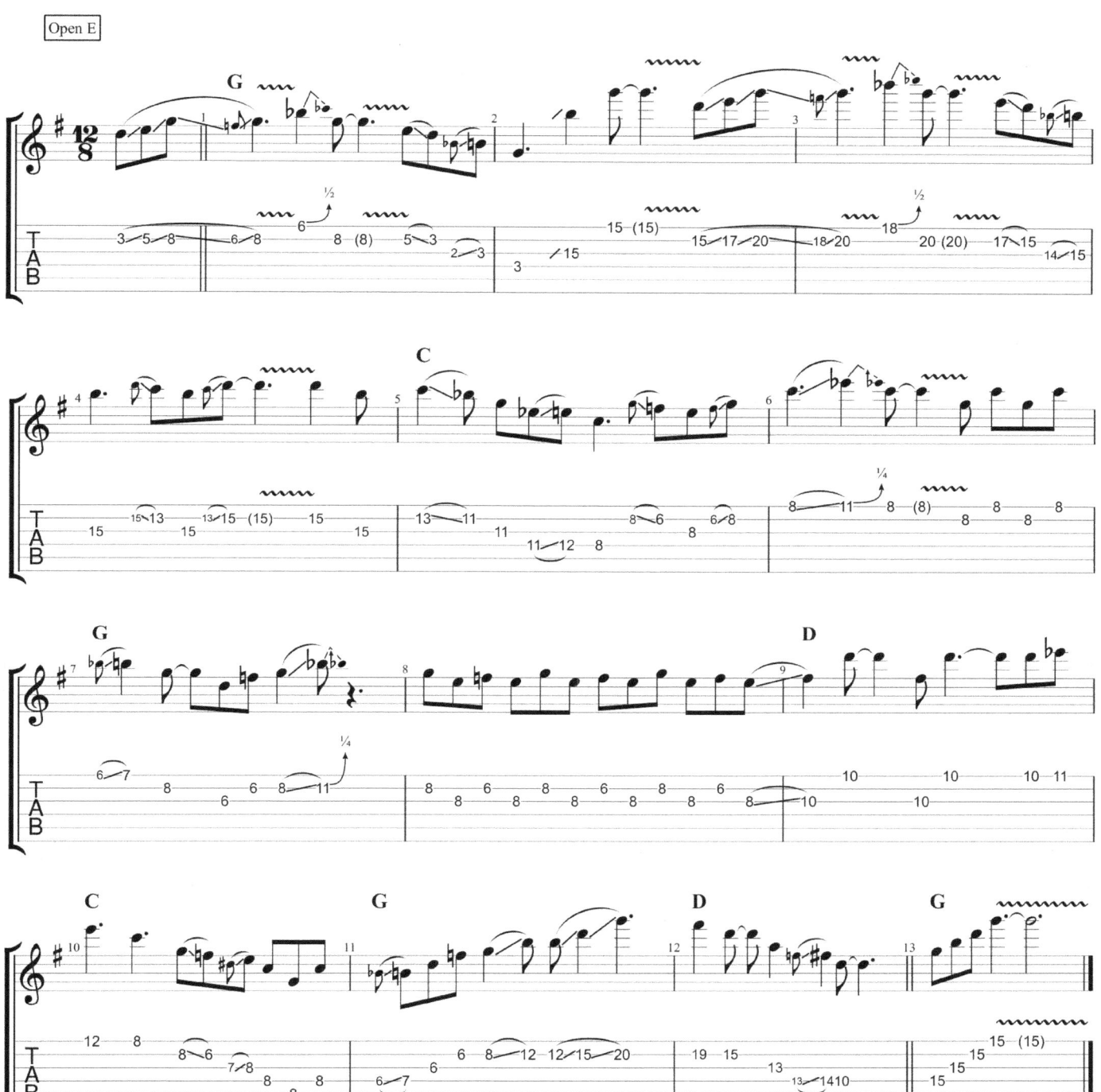

Chapter Nine: Advanced Techniques

It's probably safe to say that by now, you're beginning to get a decent grasp on slide guitar playing and its vocabulary.

This chapter focuses on some more advanced techniques that will take your slide guitar playing from "clinical" to "authentic". These examples will take some time to master, but with each practice session you will get better and more musical.

The first, and probably most important, technique to learn is the rake.

When you listen to the great slide players, they rarely play only the note they want you to hear, and will often precede it with a rake through some muted strings before hitting the target pitch. Non-slide players like Stevie Ray Vaughan do this with the pick, but most slide players will do this with the fingers of the picking hand. Whether you use fingers or a pick, you will be able to add some punch and aggression to your melodies.

Example 9a shows a simple melody played as cleanly as possible.

Example 9a

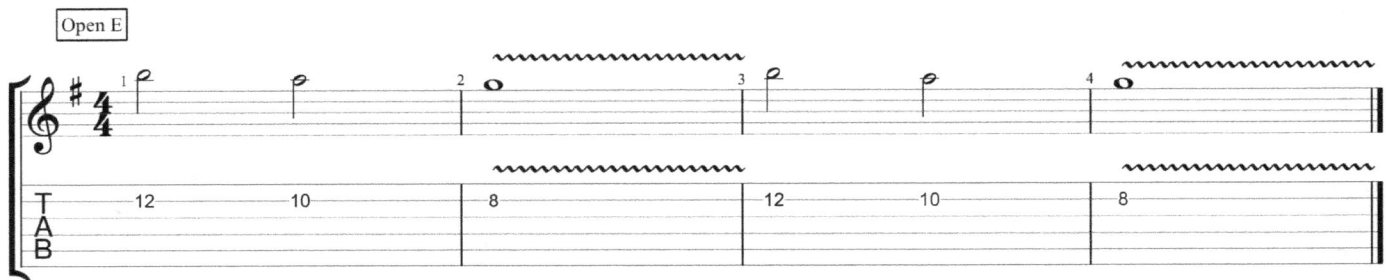

Example 9b contains the same melody, but this time adds rakes into each note. There is no universal way to notate a rake, so I've shown it in two different ways. In the first two bars I've used grace notes, and in the second two I've used brush arrows on the muted notes. These sound identical, they're just included here to help you know what to expect if you see any music written for slide guitar.

Listen to Example 9a and Example 9b and notice how different they are before learning the examples.

Example 9b

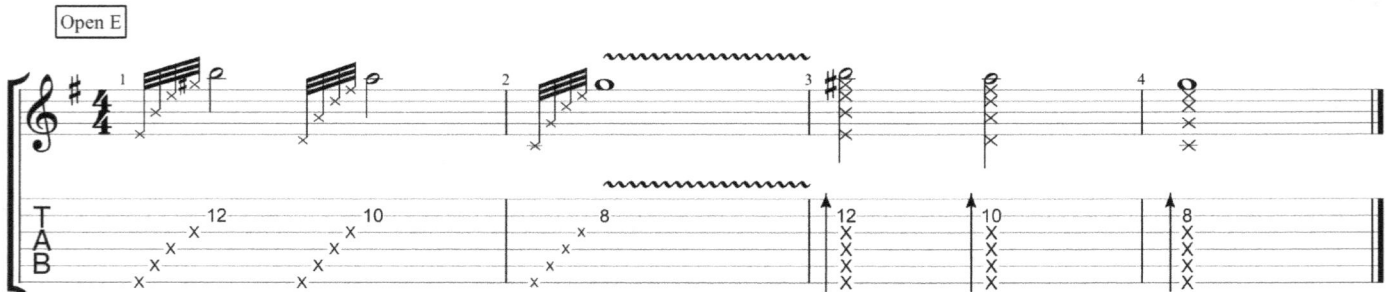

Teaching this technique is a nightmare because it's not an exact science and the results will vary depending on how you play.

The problem comes from the slide itself. If the slide is touching the string when you pick a note, you will always create a sound – there is no way to mute notes with your fretting hand as you would normally.

As I use the fingers of my picking hand instead of a pick when I play slide, I rest the fleshy part of my palm on the strings (just over the bridge pickup) and use the thumb to rake down through the low strings, pushing it firmly through the sixth, fifth and fourth strings and coming to rest on the third string as I pluck the second string with my finger.

If you were to play it slowly and in time (which goes against the whole idea but will help you to understand the mechanics) it would look like example 9c. As your finger plucks the second string, the thumb should be resting on (and muting) the third string, just as if it were ready to pluck it.

Example 9c

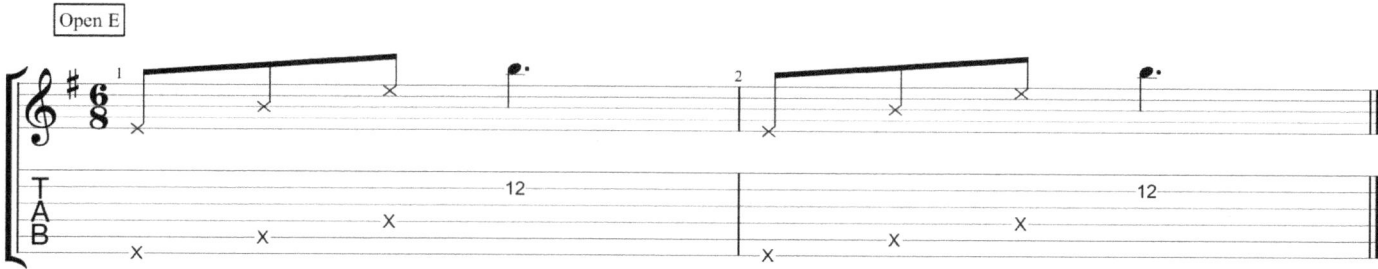

When this technique starts to feel comfortable, you can use it almost anywhere. Here's an example of it being used to slide into notes, with the rake occurring as the slide moves up the neck. I've used the arrow marking to indicate the rakes, but in most transcriptions, this type of articulation is often omitted and left to the discretion of the player. Listen carefully to the audio and try to match my phrasing.

Example 9d

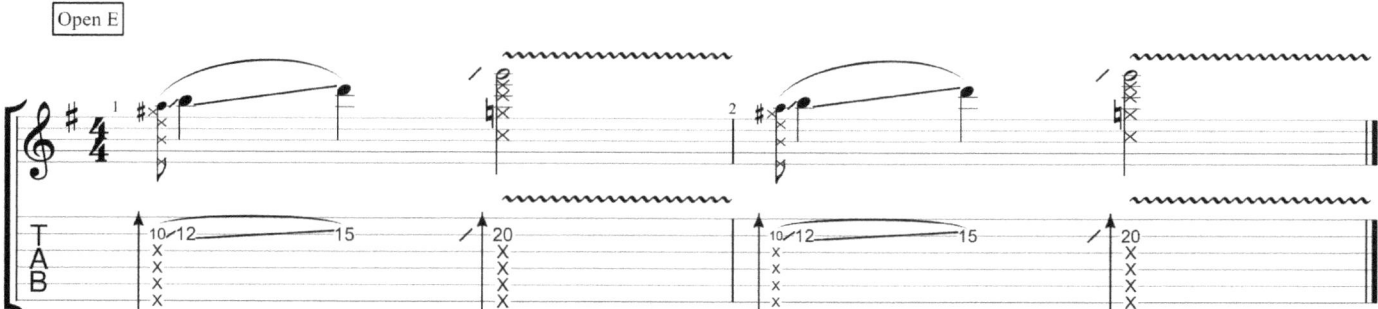

You may have noticed in the audio examples for earlier chapters that this technique is something I use all the time. When you've mastered the rake it's hard to stop using it to add snap to a melody note!

Here's another raked idea, but this time I haven't notated any of the rakes, so listen to the audio track to see where I add them.

Example 9e

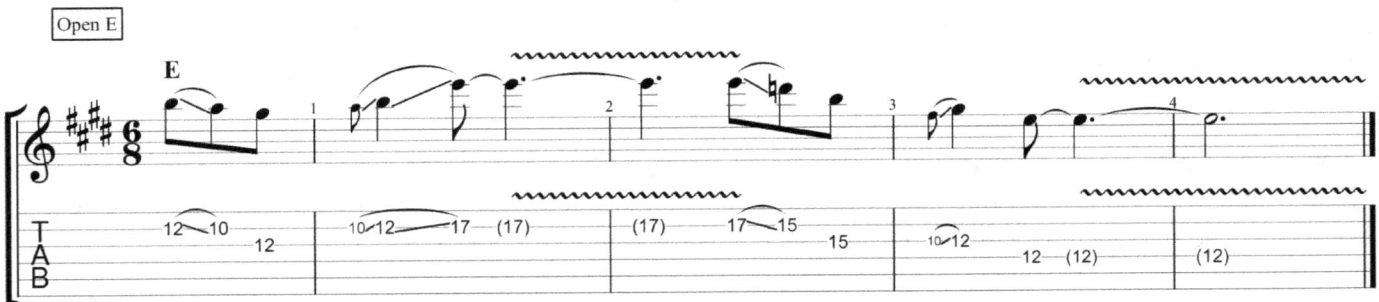

Another technique that may seem simple but is tough to execute cleanly with a slide is playing octaves.

In our Open E tuning there's an octave between the first and fourth strings (that are both tuned to E), the second and fifth strings (both tuned to B), and the fourth and sixth strings (both tuned to E). This means that you can play the same fret on these string pairs and add a note one octave below the melody. This is a lovely way to thicken up the texture and tone of your music.

This sounds easy, but it is tricky with a slide because you'll likely to get some sympathetic resonance from the strings between the ones you're trying to play. This resonance can be quite ugly and get in the way of your melody.

As with most things in slide guitar playing, the answer to this problem lies in good muting, but this is one of the trickiest muting techniques you're likely to come across.

In the following example, pluck the fourth string with the thumb and place the index finger of the picking hand across the second and third strings to keep them silent. Then use either the middle or ring finger to pluck the first string.

Example 9f

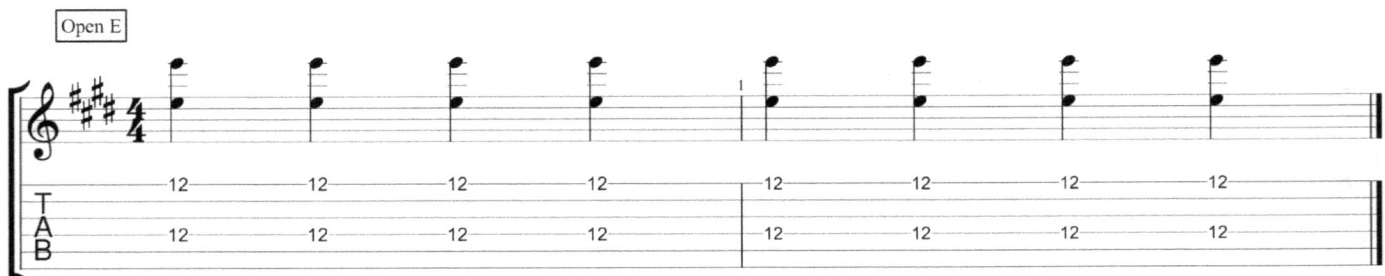

With this mechanic mastered, you can now play anything from your single string vocabulary with an added note one octave below the melody.

Here's a lick using the notes of the E Minor Pentatonic scale.

Example 9g

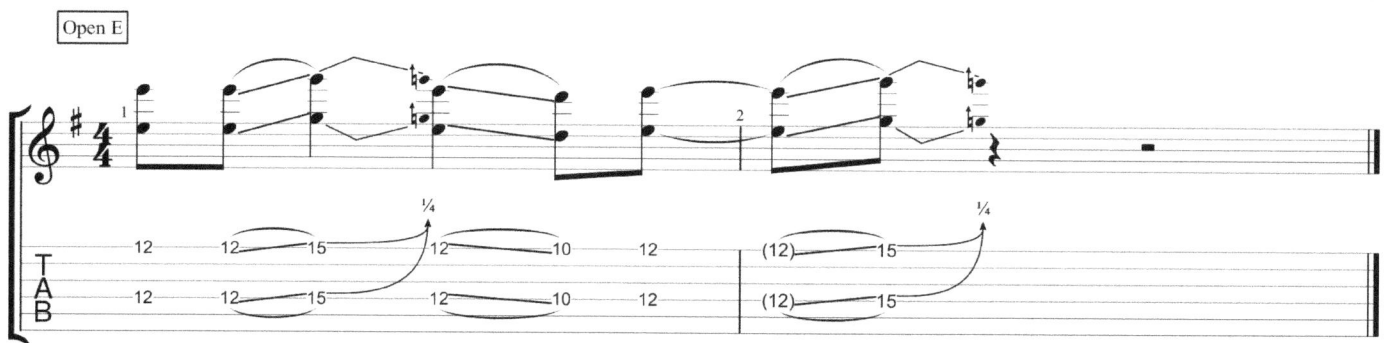

As you'd expect, it's important to practise moving this technique across string sets. It requires careful attention as the distance between the paired strings gets smaller towards the bass strings.

Learn the following example slowly and ensure you mute the middle strings cleanly with the index finger.

Example 9h

When you have got this string-crossing mechanic under your belt, you will be able to freely play octave licks across string groups with ease.

In the next example I play a lick as a single-string idea, then repeat it in octaves.

Example 9i

One unorthodox technique involves angling the slide so you're able to play two notes on different frets. This is something you might see Australian guitar whizz Brett Garsed use in standard tuning to create the illusion of playing in an open tuning.

This example is almost impossible if you wear the slide on any finger other than the second (middle).

Begin by playing the first double-stop with a straight slide, then begin turning the slide to play the two notes on different frets as you ascend the neck.

Example 9j

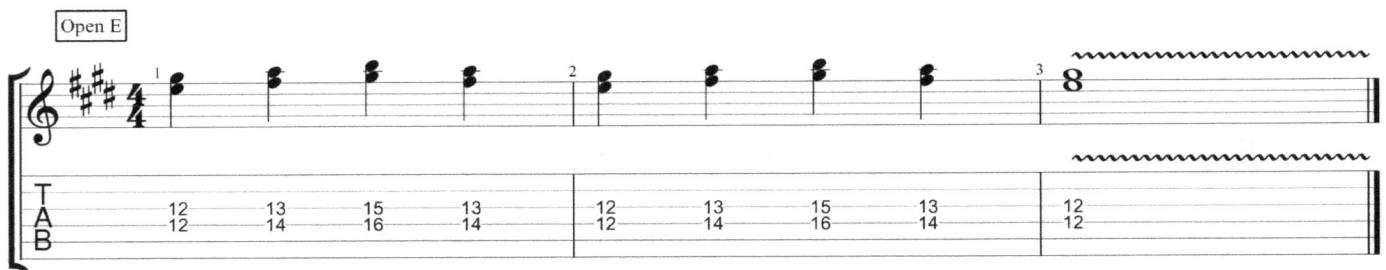

This technique can also be used to play single note ideas, as the following lick demonstrates.

Example 9k

This is a technique you're more likely to use in standard tuning rather than open tunings, but I felt it was worth mentioning, as once you have it mastered it opens a lot of creative doors as a slide musician.

One of the flashiest techniques I've ever seen on slide guitar involves playing artificial harmonics.

An artificial harmonic is created by fretting a note, placing the tip of the index finger (of your fretting hand) on the string twelve frets higher and plucking the string with another finger (in my case, the ring finger). This results in a note sounding an octave higher than the original fretted pitch.

Example 9l

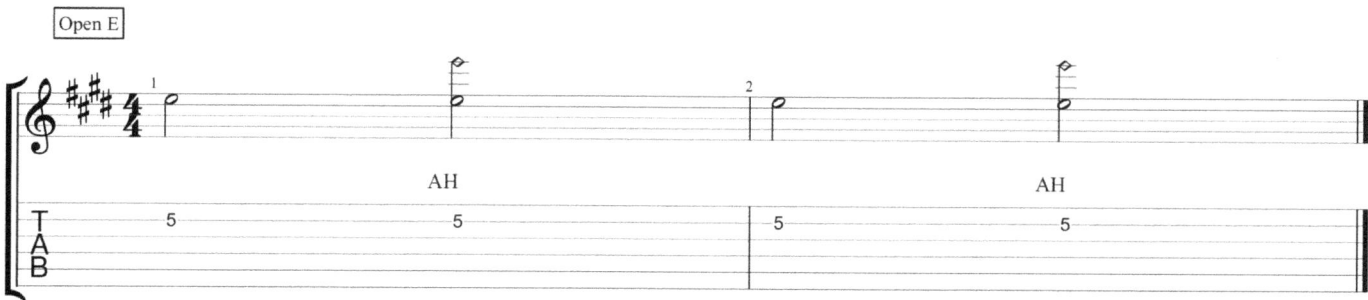

The unique aspect of these harmonics is that once the harmonic note is ringing, you can slide it up or down the neck.

In the next example, play the artificial harmonic then shift the slide up to the 17th fret while keeping in contact with the string. This will create a screaming harmonic an octave higher than the 17th fret (E note).

Example 9m

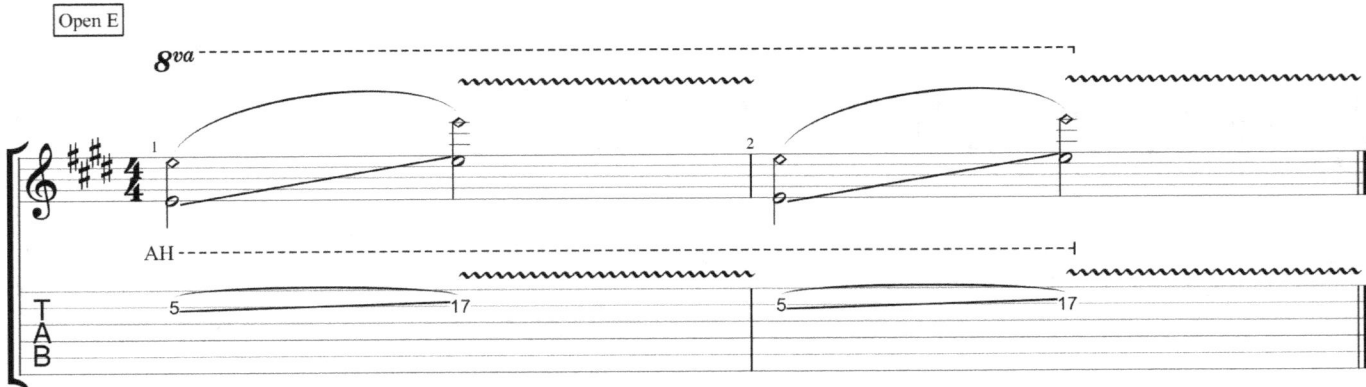

These harmonics can be played in the middle of licks to create fluid position shifts and grab your audience's attention with these unique sounds.

The following is a lick in E that begins around the first inversion position. It then shifts up an octave before resolving to the barre position at the 12th fret. Notice that after sliding the harmonic up to the 17th fret, I slide back down to the 14th. These harmonics can be treated like any normal note and will sustain as long as the string vibrates.

Example 9n

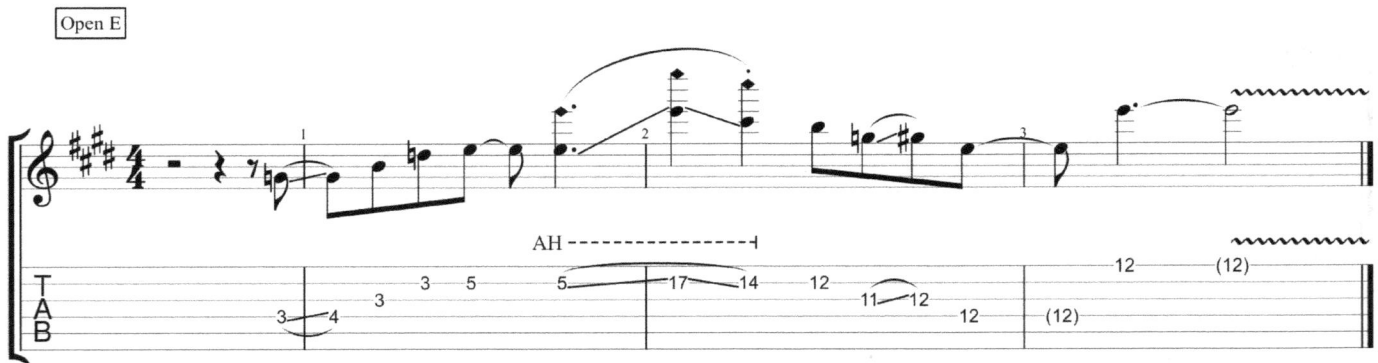

This final harmonic lick begins with a riff in E and adds a small chord played in harmonics that slides up to the 12th fret to form a beautiful E major chord played in harmonics.

Example 9o

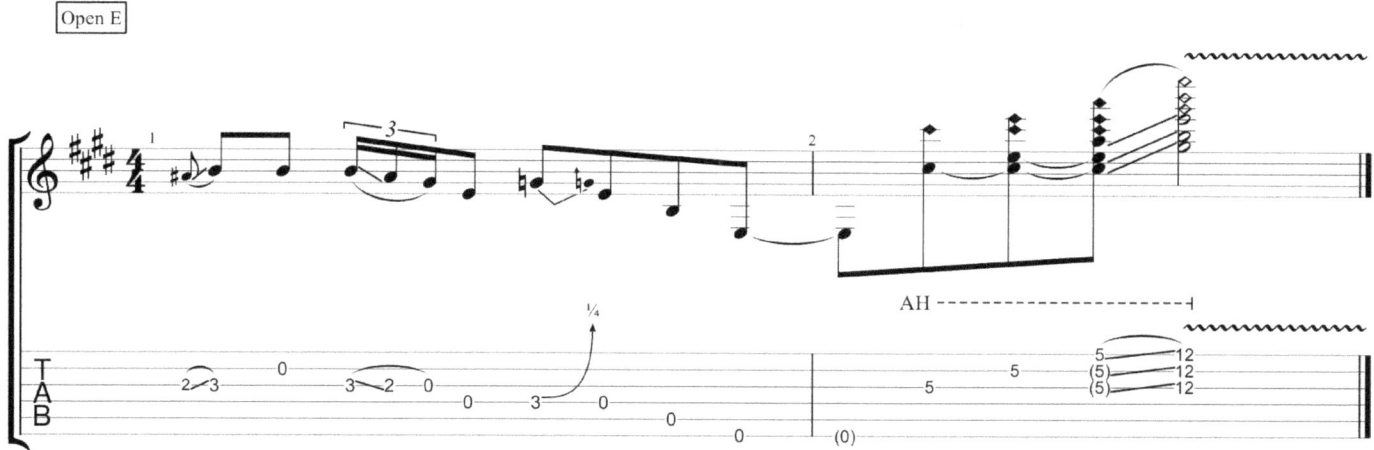

This next example will teach you a technique that Sonny Landreth often uses, which involves picking the strings between the slide and the nut. This creates a haunting resonant sound and is perfect for adding atmosphere to a chord. Don't forget to lift up the fingers you use to mute behind the slide!

He's the same lick as shown in Example 9o with the pick behind the slide added in bar three.

Example 9p

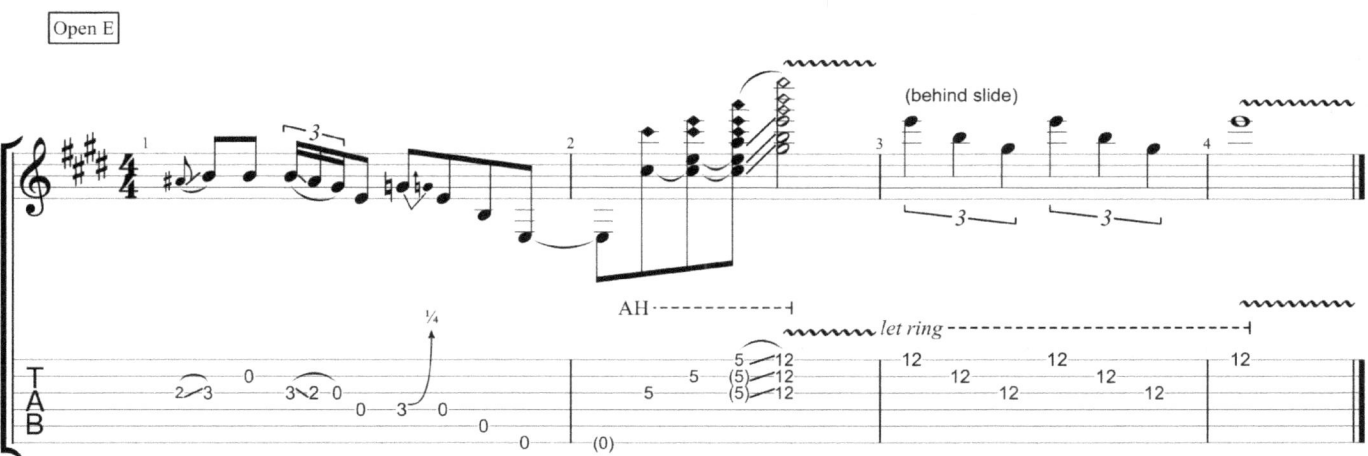

The most versatile advanced technique to learn is how to use the fretting hand fingers to play notes behind the slide. This technique is easier with the slide on the pinky, but can be done with the slide placed on other fingers too.

The idea is that when the slide is on the strings, it acts like a fret, but if you use a finger to press down the string behind the slide, the string stops touching the slide and the fretted note will sound. This allows you to play chords and melodies that would be impossible to play with the slide on its own.

As I've mentioned several times already, slide guitar came about hundreds of years after conventional notation was standardised, and traditional notation is often unable to convey the musical techniques we use with the slide. Fretting behind the slide is an extreme example of this limitation as it's such an unorthodox technique. In the following examples, I have uses brackets to show the notes that are fretted *behind the slide*. In traditional notation, these would normally represent ghost notes, but I felt this was the clearest option in the context of this book.

In the following example, place the slide over the 12th fret and strum the lowest three strings twice. Then, use the index finger of the fretting hand to fret the 10th fret on the fourth string, as indicated by the bracket.

Example 9q

With practice, this technique will allow you to play additional fretted notes with some real speed, as the next example shows.

As you're now able to fret notes behind the slide, the slide itself can remain at the 12th fret while the index finger frets and releases the 10th fret note.

Example 9r

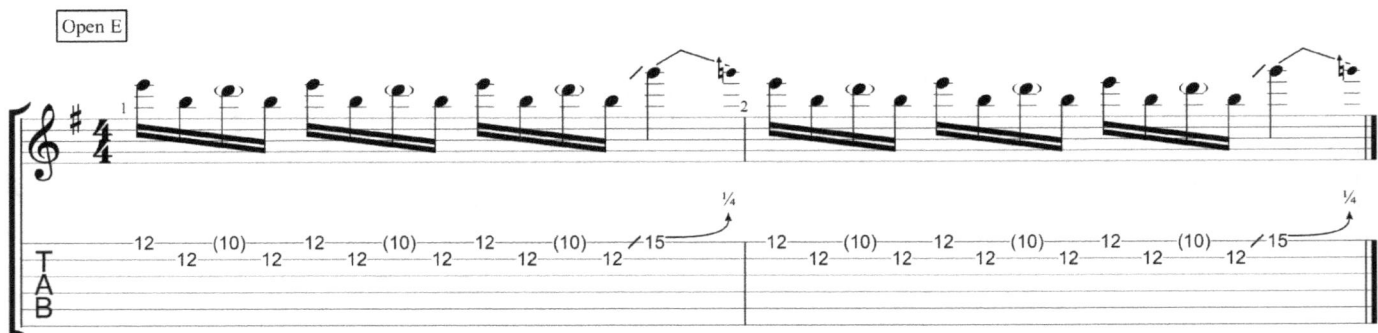

Here's the same mechanic, but moved down a set of strings. Playing something like this without fretting behind the slide would be extremely problematic or even impossible!

175

Example 9s

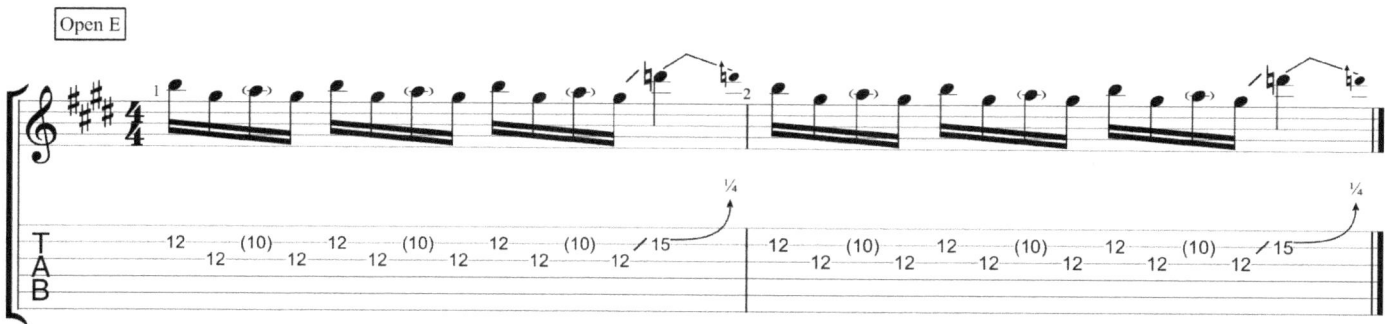

In the next example I use both the middle and index fingers to fret two notes behind the slide to create a cool little E Minor Pentatonic run. Try playing this without fretting behind the slide and see how difficult it is. While fretting behind the slide may feel odd at first, mastering the technique is much easier than trying to play without it!

Example 9t

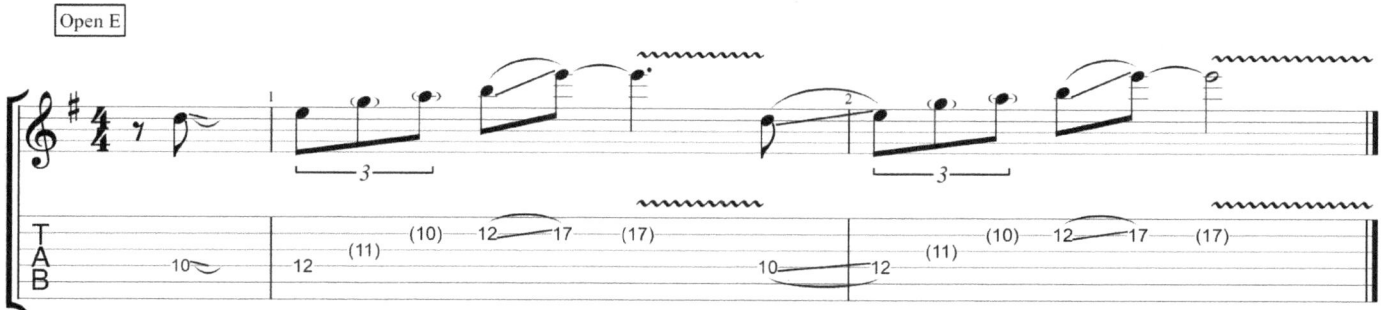

The next lick develops the previous idea by playing behind the slide in the first inversion area at the end of the lick. As the fretboard is a little cramped up here, I use my middle finger to play the 15th fret.

Example 9u

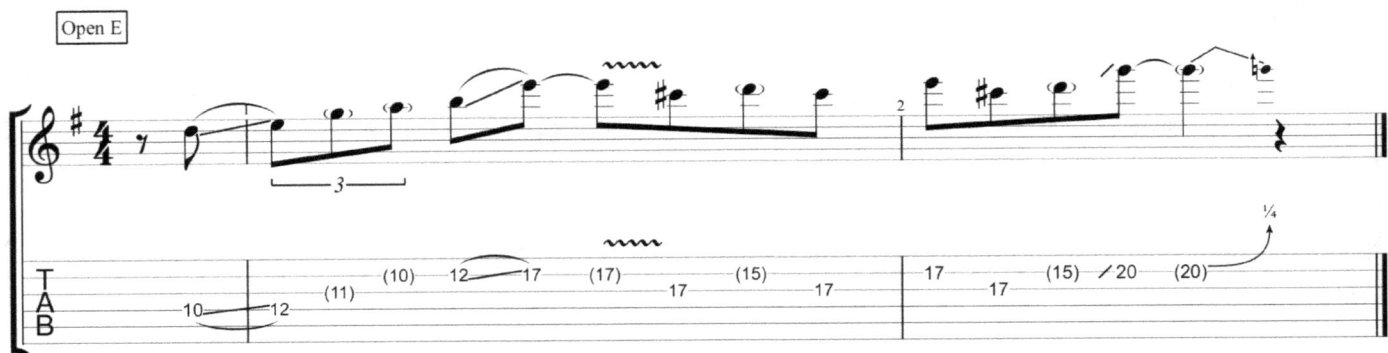

A similar idea is to play the same fragment around the second inversion pattern.

Example 9v

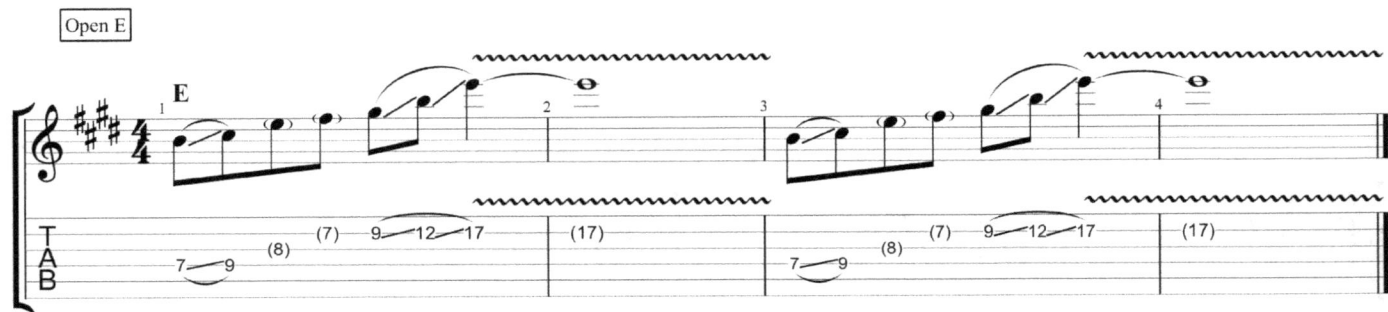

You should be able to tell by now that mastering this technique and integrating it into your playing is as simple as taking each of the triad inversion positions and seeing how you can use the notes behind the slide to facilitate fast, fluid lines.

Here's another lick around the second inversion position that adds some b7s to create a bluesy, dominant 7 sound.

Example 9w

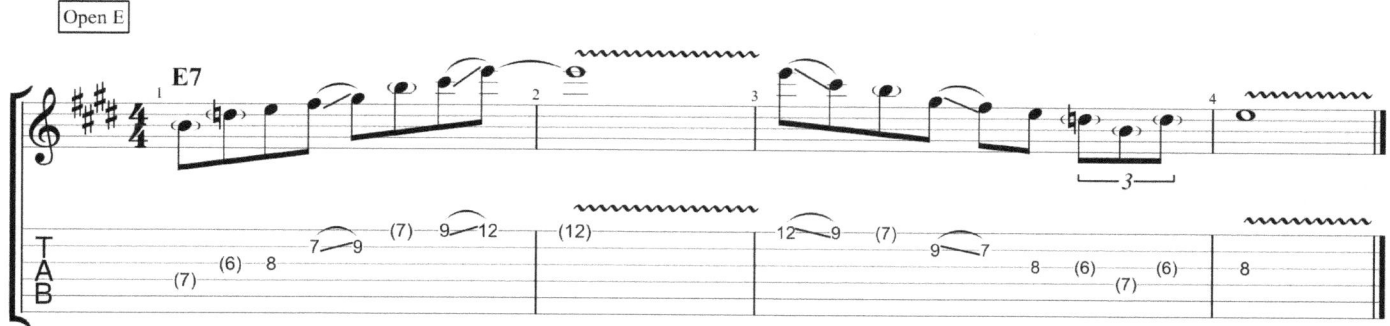

You can get extremely in-depth with this technique and even add hammer-ons between multiple notes behind the slide. I've demonstrated this as shown in the following tricky E Minor scale idea. At first this will be difficult, but over time you'll find the approach quite elegant as the slide stays at the 12th fret for the first half of the lick before moving up to the 15th fret.

Example 9x

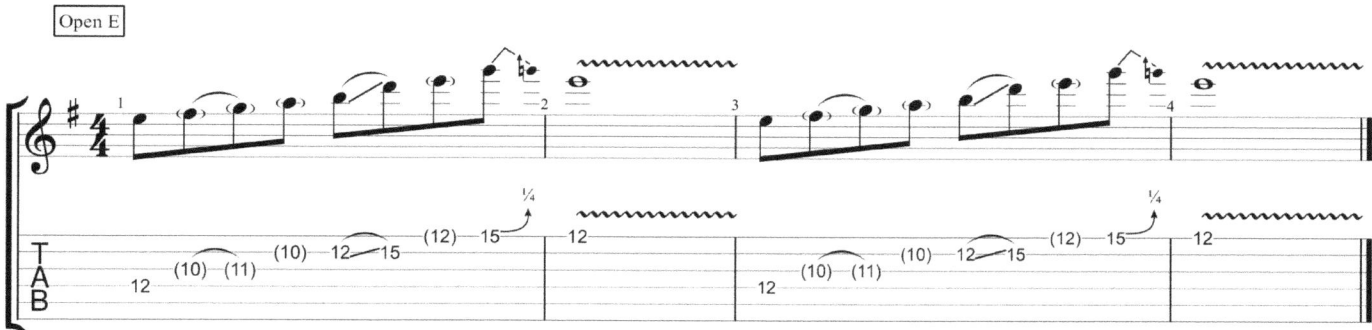

The next lick covers a full twelve-fret span on the neck and uses notes played behind the slide to facilitate position shifts and speed. Take it slowly and make sure you keep an eye out for notes in brackets and fret them behind the slide!

Example 9y

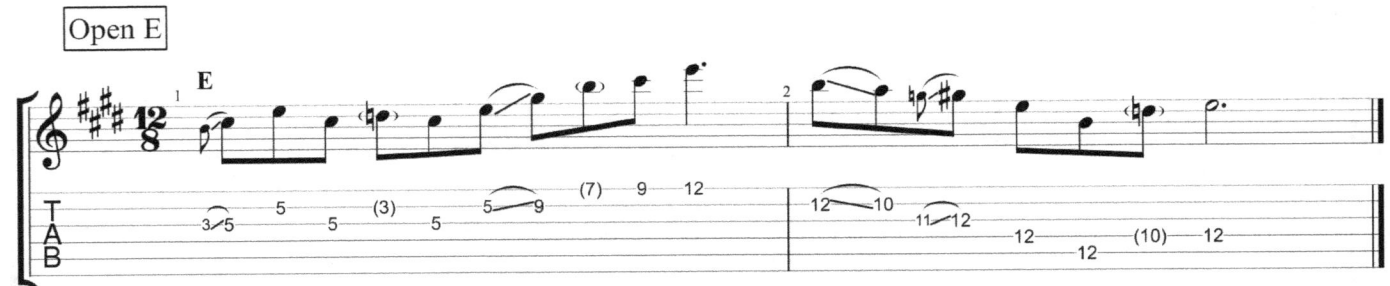

The collection of techniques in this chapter serves as a solid starting point for your slide guitar creativity, so make as much music with them as you can.

In the next chapter, you will learn a full blues-rock solo in open E tuning, before we explore how to play slide in standard E tuning.

Chapter Ten: Open E Solo

Now you're armed with a full toolkit of slide guitar techniques, the most valuable use of your practice time is to develop strong musical vocabulary while playing real music. To that end, I've composed a solo for you to play with a full band backing track. You can use it as both as a vehicle to practise the concepts covered and as a tool to develop your own ideas and style.

Before learning the lead guitar part, it's important to understand the basic part, especially here, as this is a great example of fretting behind the slide to help create a riff.

The chord progression is a slight variation on a twelve-bar blues in E, with the only change being a move to the bVII7 (D7) chord after the V chord in bar nine, instead of the more traditional IV (A) chord.

Here's the riff idea played around an E chord at the 12th fret. Again, I use brackets in the tab to indicate notes that are fretted *behind* the slide. Unfortunately, the nature of tab is that notes that are rhythmically tied are *also* shown in brackets. This is certainly not ideal, but a quick analysis of the notation helps to distinguish between which notes are tied and which are played behind the slide. The 10th fret notes are played behind the slide, but that pesky 12th fret note with vibrato on beat 3 is played normally with the slide!

Example 10a

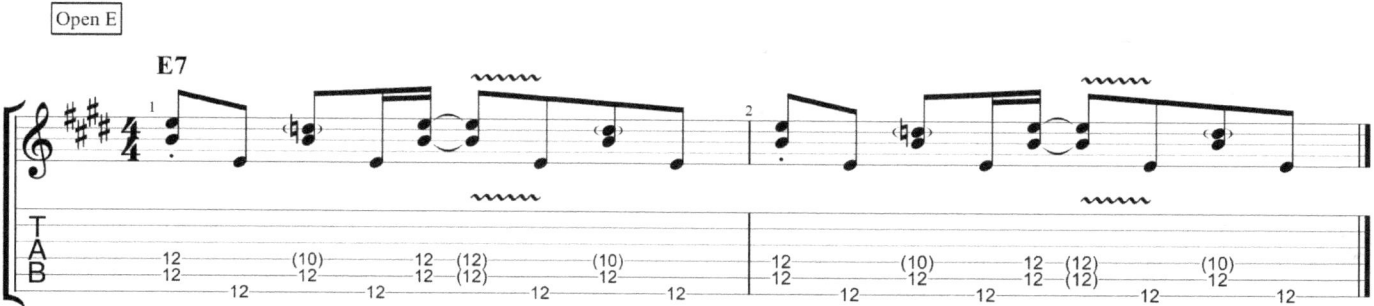

With that first riff under your fingers, here's the full progression. It's simply a case of taking the riff and moving it down to the 5th fret in bar five to outline an A major chord, the moving to the 7th fret to outline the B major chord, and so on…

Example 10b

Now on to the solo!

The first lick of the solo exploits a single-string pattern around an E major triad in three positions. I've spiced this up with some rakes and repeating slides into notes. Listen to the audio for the phrasing.

Example 10c

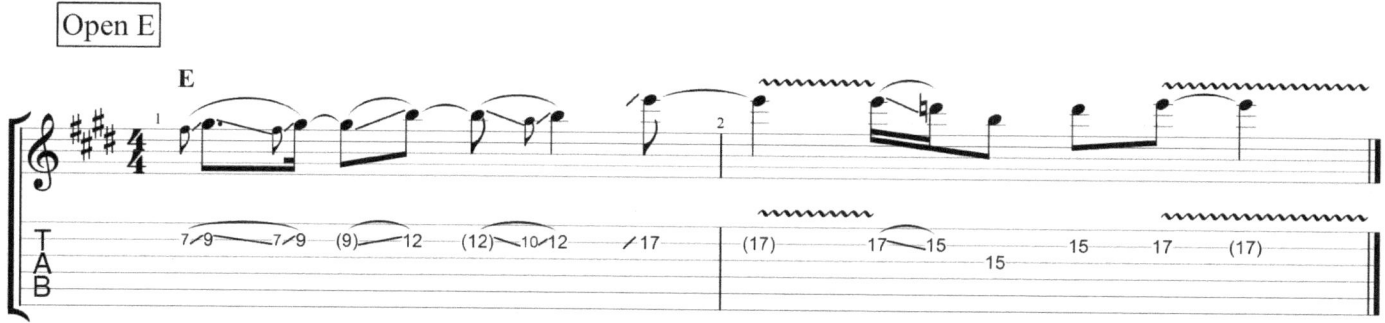

The next lick uses the same basic idea, but instead of sliding up to the note E, it ascends to D (the b7) to create an E7 chord sound. The line finishes with a slide cliché around the 12th fret barre position.

Example 10d

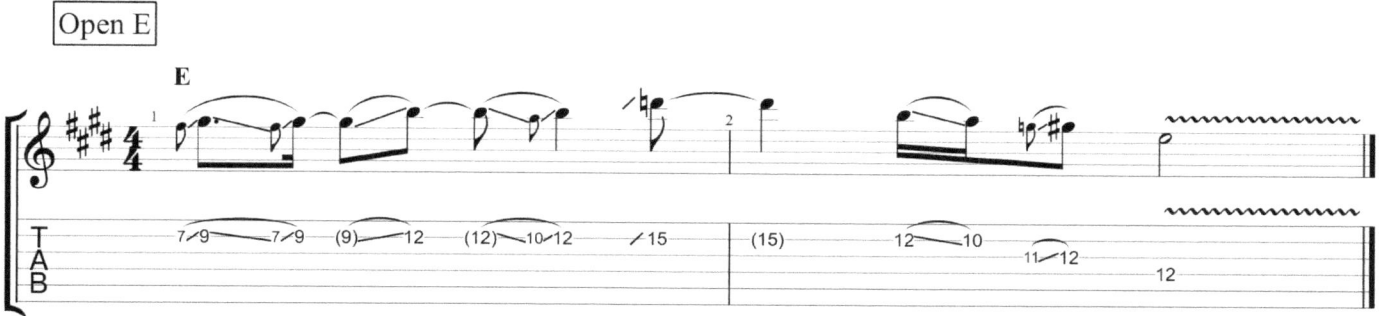

As the chord changes to A major, your perspective needs to change to address it. As I finished the previous phrase at the 12th fret, it makes sense to stay close to that area and use the first inversion of the A major triad. This contains its lowest note at the 9th fret, so it's a great way to transition into the A major chord.

After ascending the triad, there's a phrase on the second string which descends the neck to the A major barre position at the 5th fret.

Example 10e

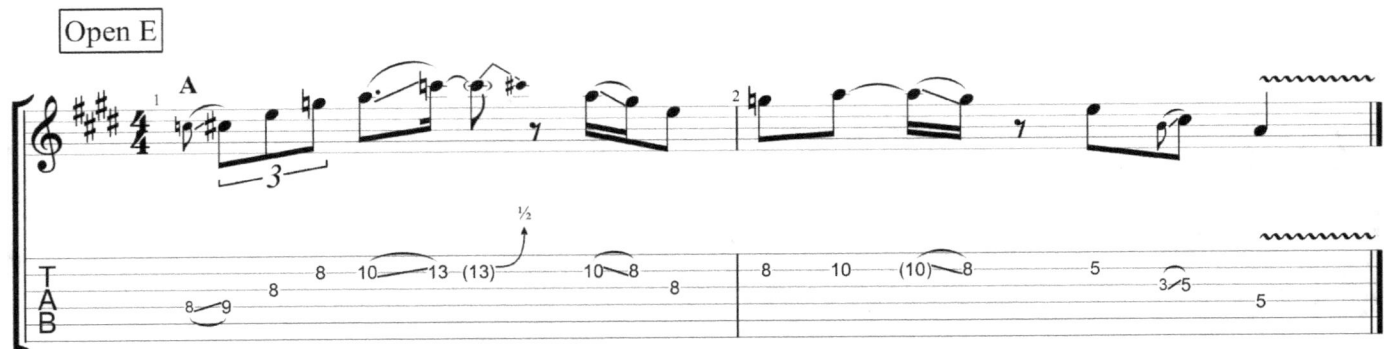

When the backing returns to the E major chord, I play a tricky little line that ascends from the 3rd fret, all the way to the 20th. This is a perfect example of how slide guitar players generally move horizontally. Sliding between notes is the most expressive approach you have at your disposal, so take your time mastering this line and make sure that all your notes are in tune.

Example 10f

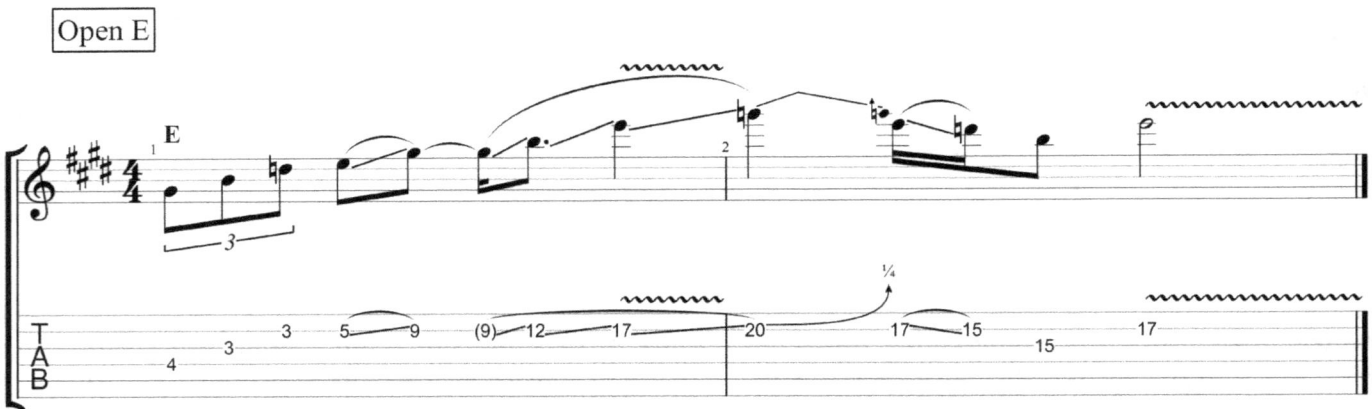

The next lick moves from the B7 to the D7 chord, and in order to play something that sounds articulate, I stick closely to the chords. The first bar descends through the second inversion position of B major, while the next bar descends through the first inversion position of D major.

Seeing chord positions like this, and being able to use them to outline whatever chord changes are thrown at you, is great practice and will help to develop your musical versatility.

Example 10g

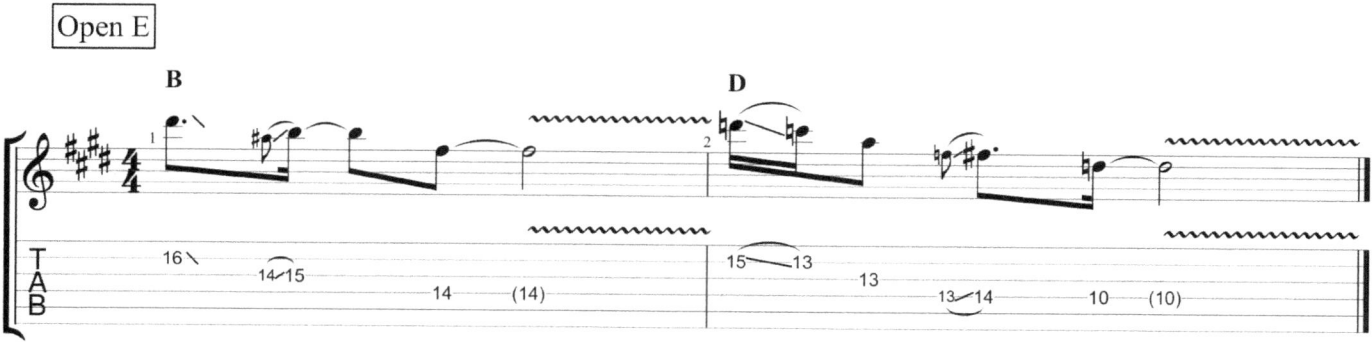

The end of the first chorus introduces some rapid fretting behind the slide. This sounds complicated, but the slide stays at the 12th fret and the index finger plays the 10th fret as you alternate between the first and second strings.

Example 10h

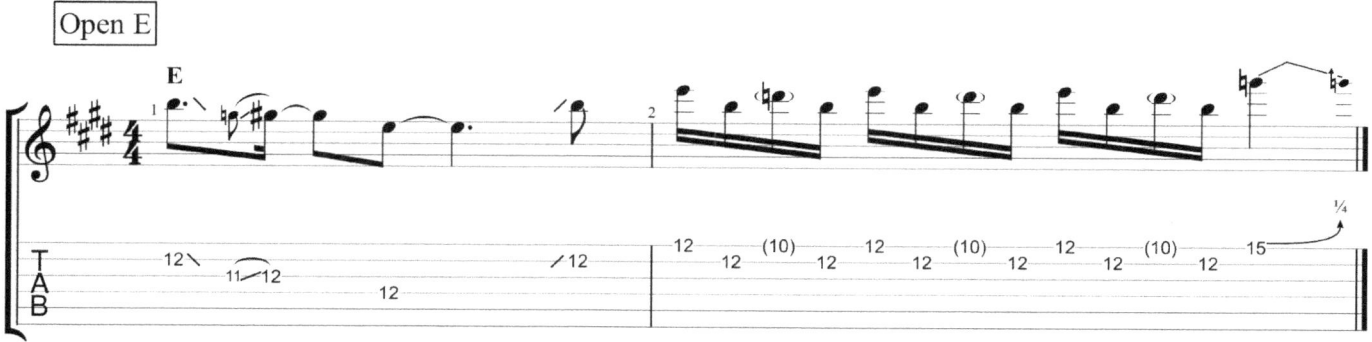

Example 10i is the start of the second chorus. To step things up a bit, I've moved over to the high E string to access a higher note range. Aside from that, it's similar to the theme in the first chorus which helps to tie the full piece together.

Example 10i

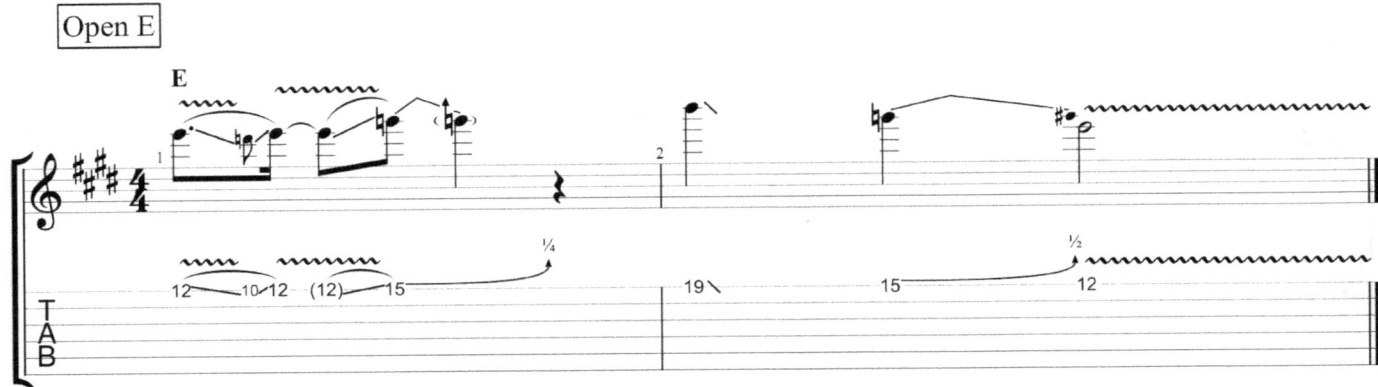

The following lick begins by repeating the previous phrase, then switches to a tricky 1/16th note run in E Minor Pentatonic, using fretting behind the slide to add notes outside of the barre position.

Example 10j

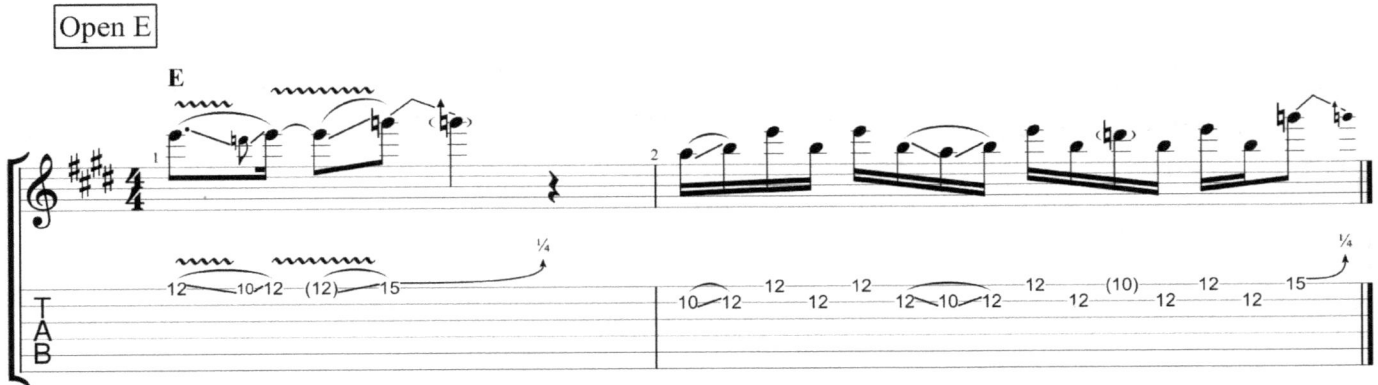

From here, the chord progression moves to A major. I play the root note at the 17th fret of the high E string, then descend to the 12th fret area which contains the second inversion shape.

The second bar is an excellent example of how to use notes fretted behind the slide in different positions to facilitate smooth scalar playing. This would be tricky to pull off with the slide alone.

Example 10k

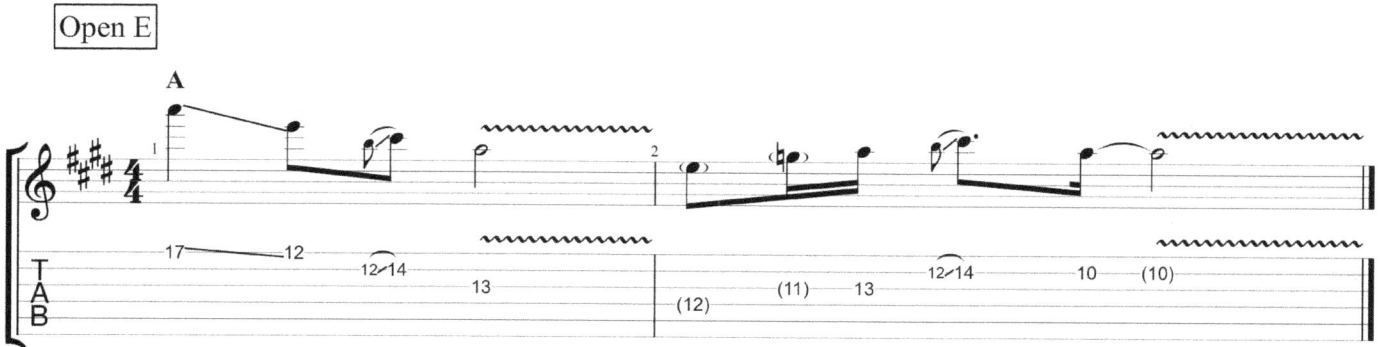

As the chord moves back to E major, your perspective must move to the first inversion pattern at the 5th fret.

In the second bar I introduce another advanced slide guitar technique. Hammer from the open B string onto the third fret with the index finger. This combination of fretted open position and slide notes is a trademark of high-level slide players.

Example 10l

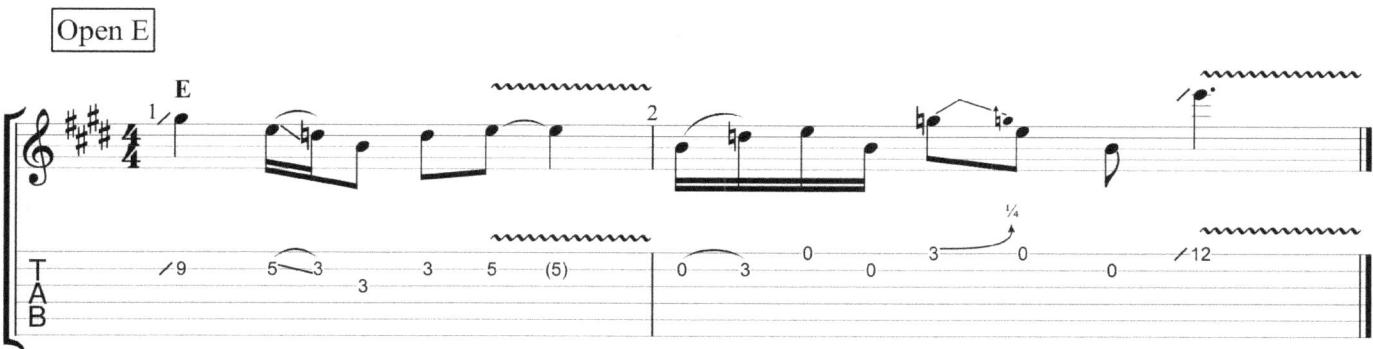

As with the previous chorus, outlining the B major and D major chords is easy to do if you stick closely to the chord tones. I play the notes of the B major chord (B, D, F#) on the high E string, then explore the barre position (10th fret) on the D chord.

Example 10m

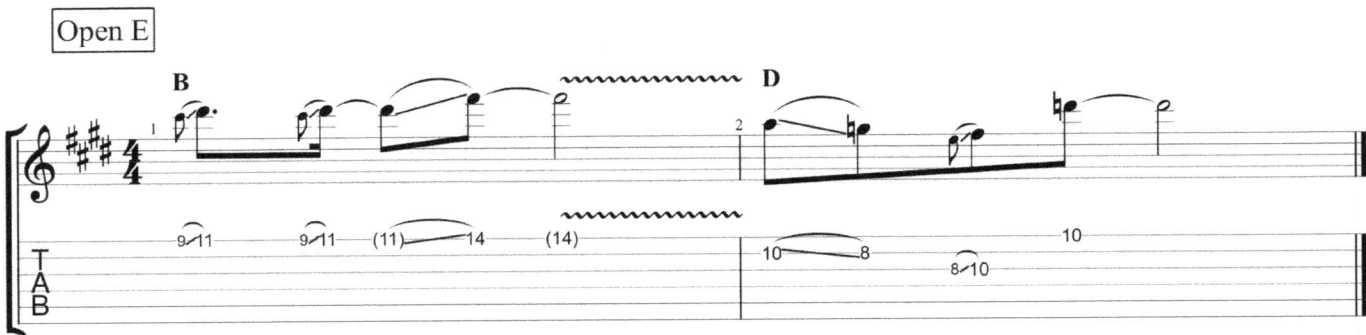

The final lick in this solo will test your technique as you move around the neck and add rapid notes fretted behind the slide. If you study the notes here, there's nothing more than the E Minor Pentatonic scale, but the speed and accuracy may cause problems!

Example 10n

When you have got the solo under your fingers, spend some time experimenting over the backing track with the ideas covered earlier in the book, along with some of your own musical inventions. Remember, you picked this up book because you wanted to master slide guitar, not to play like me!

Find your own voice, and you'll find your own audience.

Chapter Eleven: Standard Tuning

Now you've developed the skills to play slide guitar in Open E tuning, it's time to return to standard tuning and learn to deal with its pitfalls and advantages.

The secret to mastering slide in standard tuning is to find the strengths of open tunings and exploit their parallels in standard tuning. Then use advanced techniques make melodic playing easier.

In Open E tuning, the barre position is extremely easy to play around, but the two inversions present more of a challenge. We used things like fretting behind the slide to make those positions more manageable. Using these kinds of advanced techniques can make playing slide in standard tuning a real possibility.

Here's a simple lick in open E tuning built around the 12th fret barre position.

Example 11a

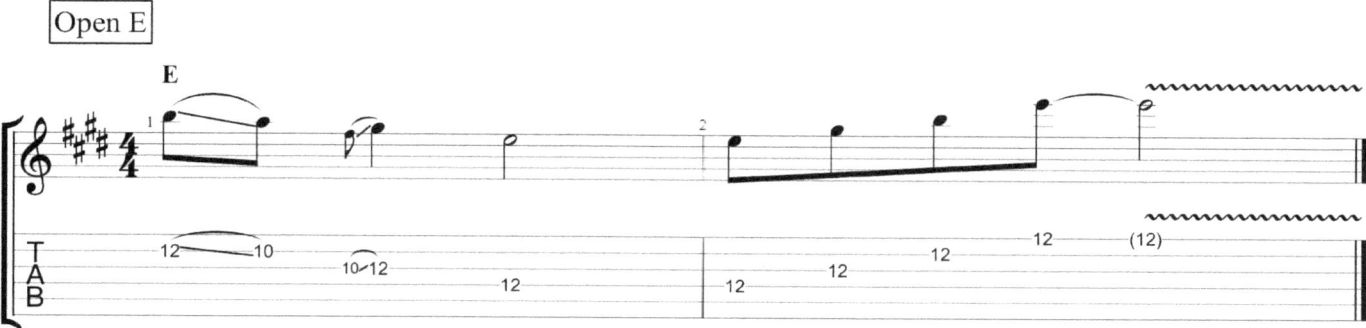

Here's the same lick, but now played in standard tuning (note the standard tuning marking in the top left).

You'll notice that the first bar is hard to play… but the second bar is impossible if you want to let it ring out as you would in Open E tuning.

Example 11b

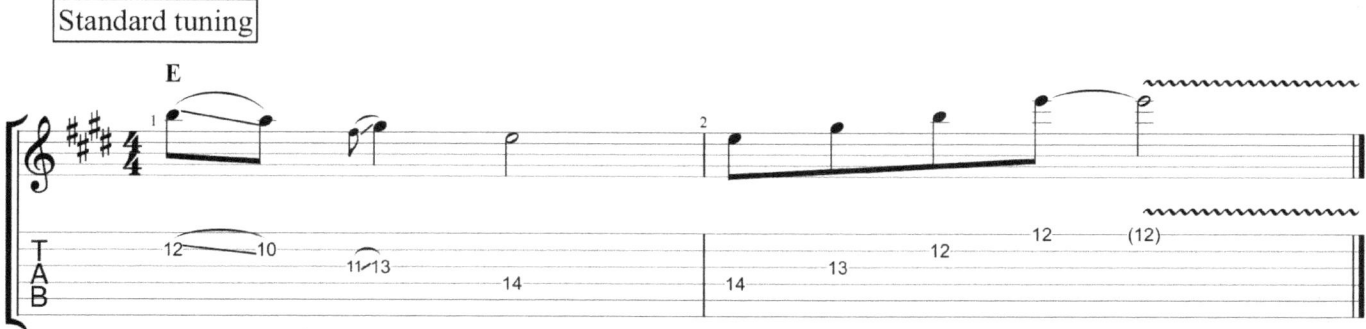

So, root position is hard to play in standard tuning with a slide, but what about the other positions?

The next example demonstrates the three inversions of the triad played on the D, G and B strings, and you will notice that there is a triad position in standard tuning that can be barred with a single finger. In standard tuning this is the source of many slide licks, as it allows you to access some of that open tuned charm.

Example 11c

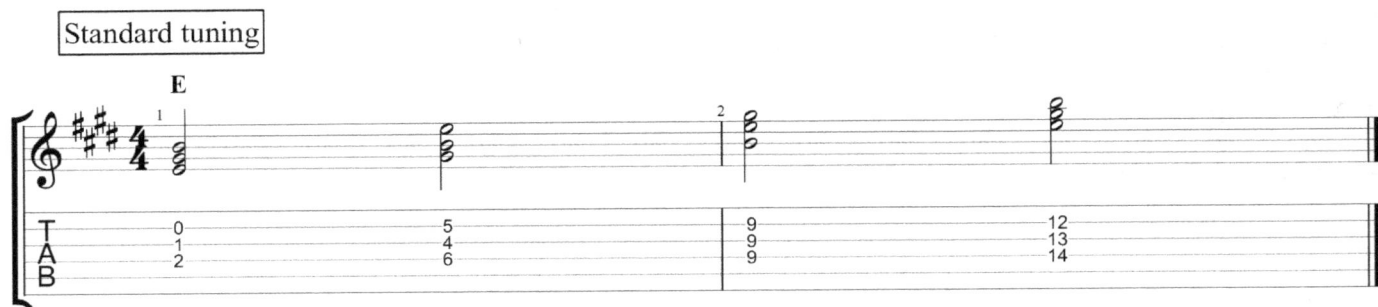

I'm not going go into too much depth here, but I would advise you to learn to visualise each of the above triad positions as part of a larger CAGED barre position.

In the next example I play the larger barre chord form of each chord, then isolate the smaller three note-chunk within this form. This will help you reconcile the chord fragments with what you probably already know about barre chords.

These three major triads are taken from the E, C and A shapes of the CAGED system.

Example 11d

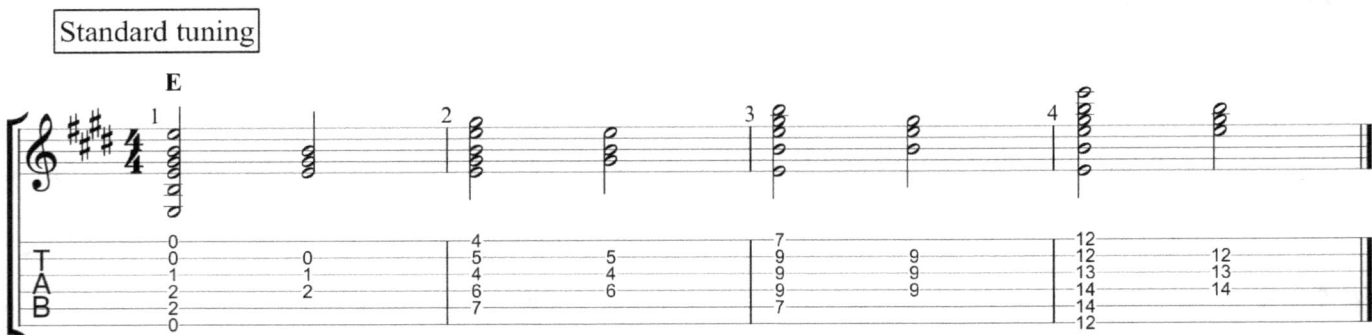

As you can see, none of these positions lend themselves to barring playing across all six strings with the slide, so no matter where you are, you always need to play accurately and use good muting to make sure no unwanted strings ring out.

I could spend an entire book talking about fretboard visualization, but our focus is slide guitar, and I want to stay on topic!

The first thing to point out is that single string soloing works in the same way as it does in Open E tuning. All the scale and interval patterns are the same along each string – all that changes is that some root notes are located in a different place.

Here's a pattern we used in Open E tuning, but played in standard tuning. As the second (B) string is unchanged in both tunings, it will sound identical whichever tuning you use.

Example 11e

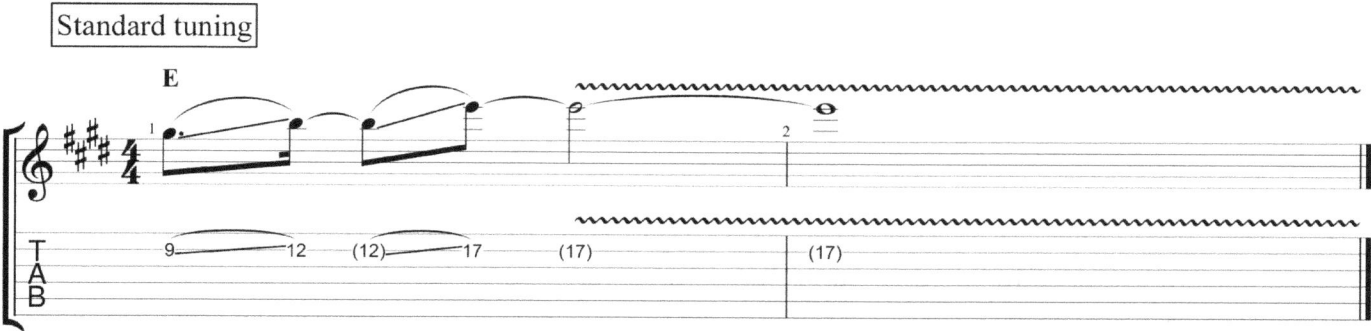

Ideas like the previous example will always work on any string, but they will have different pitches depending on the tuning of the guitar

In standard tuning, we often need to be bit more versatile with our approach to playing and wearing the slide on the little finger makes it possible to fret "normal" notes and later introduce the slide for melodic lines.

Here are three bars of a country rock pattern in E major followed by the slide lick from Example 11e in bar four. This is a great way to practise integrating the slide with normally fretted notes, and also teaches you to play guitar while wearing a slide, even if you're not using it.

Example 11f

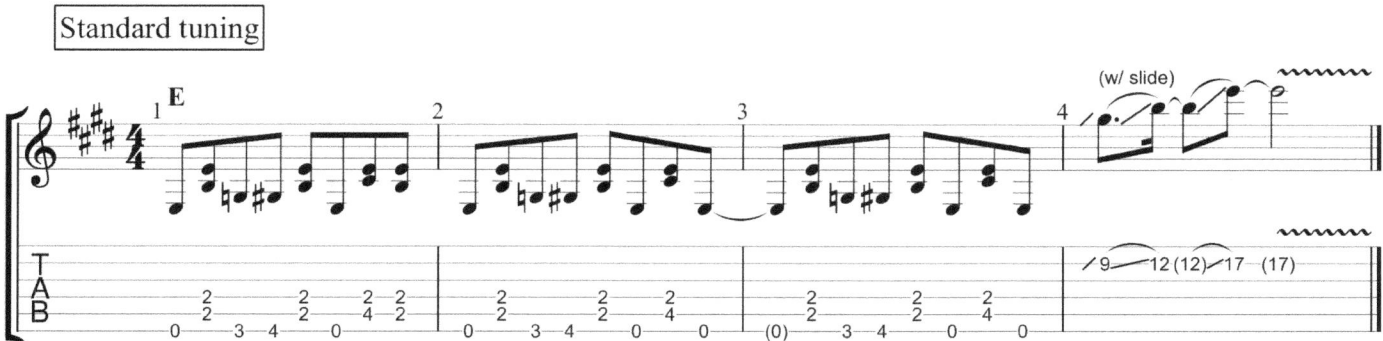

The most important thing to learn in standard tuning slide playing is how to change strings cleanly and keep un-played strings well muted. Let's learn this technique using the small barre shape triad as it is the simplest shape to begin with.

Example 11g

Here's another lick around that position that ends on the root note at the 12th fret. You could call this root an *exit note* – a possible place to end a lick. Learning where these notes are located near the triad inversions is a great way to know you'll always finish with a strong note in your phrase.

Example 11h

Of course, you can play these licks in any key if you can visualise the chord form you're basing the idea around.

Here's the same lick played in A major. First play the open A major chord, then play the lick around the same shape an octave higher.

Example 11i

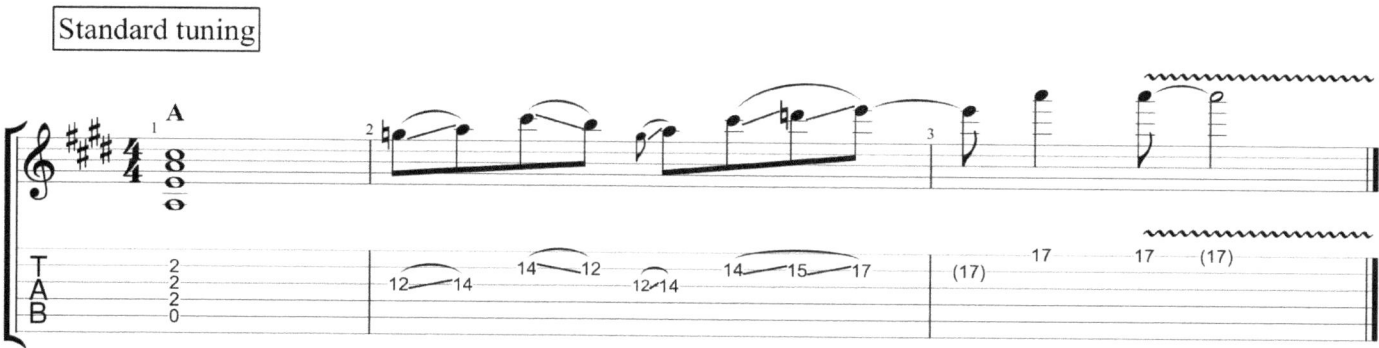

Here are some 1/16th note slides, still around that position of A major.

Example 11j

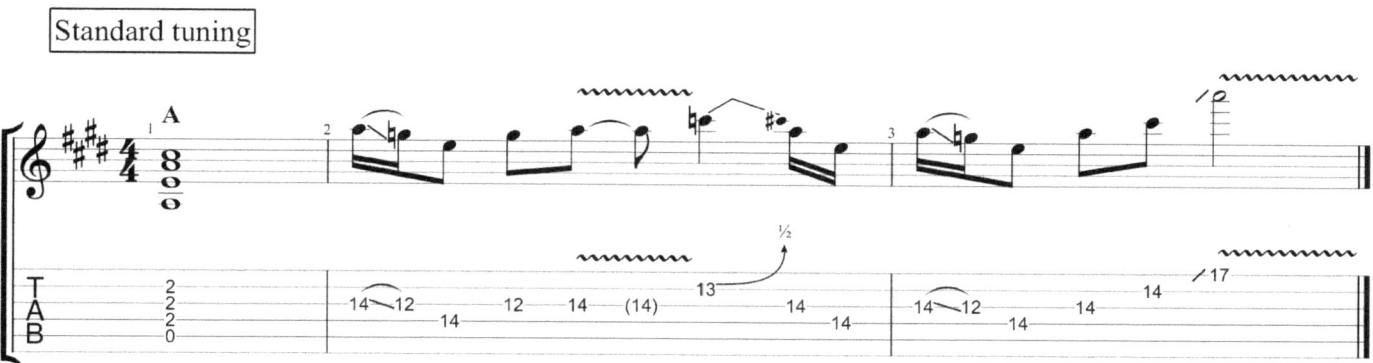

This shape can be used to finish any standard tuned slide lick, as shown in the following A major example.

The lick begins by outlining A major on the high E string and then moves across the strings around the E major barre position before shifting up to the same A major barre form at the 14th fret.

Example 11k

You don't need to play the full position to use this idea to end a phrase, as demonstrated by this predominantly single string lick in A.

Example 11l

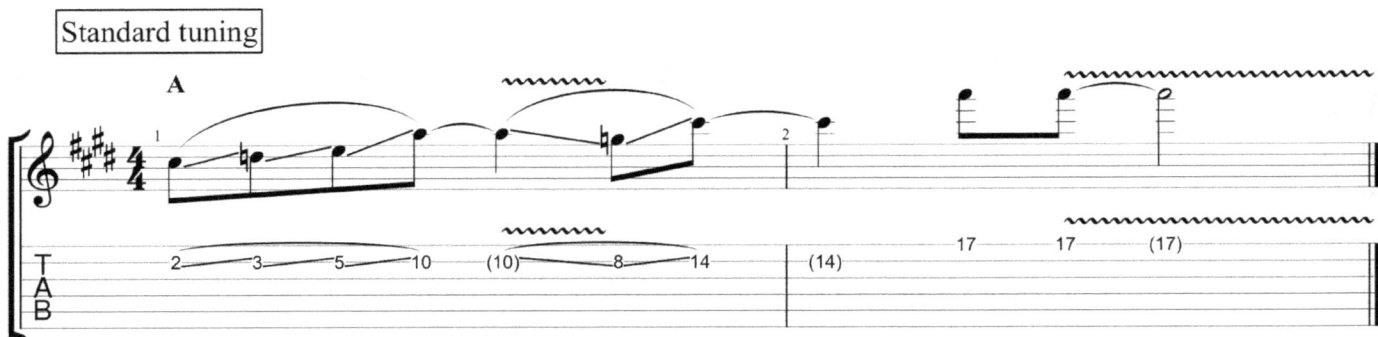

Here's one final A major idea that combines some tricky string changing mechanics with single string playing. This juxtaposition of approaches is a good way to see which aspects of slide you enjoy most and can exploit further.

Example 11m

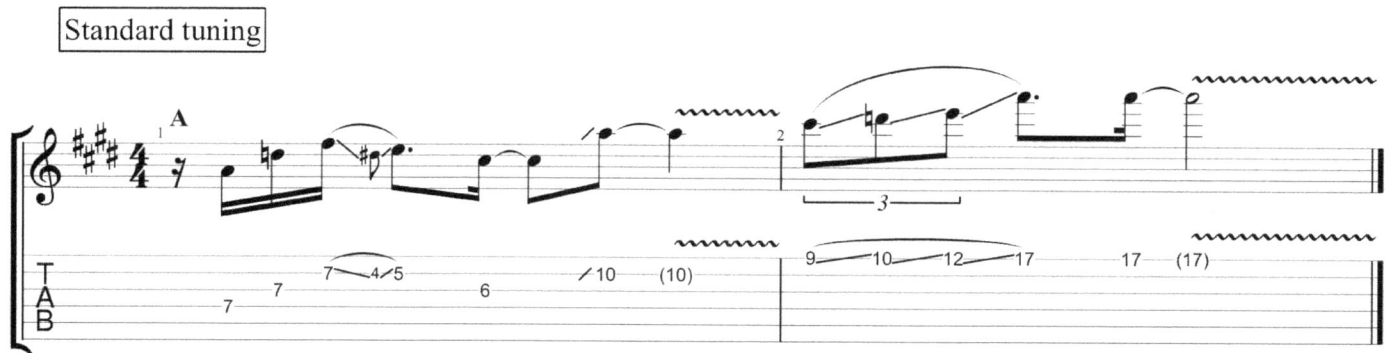

Now you understand how licks work in standard tuning, let's look at some exercises that will help you focus on developing a clean muting technique.

The next two examples consist of an A major triad played from low to high. Each example takes a different melodic path as it ascends. There are countless ways to do this, and each presents its own muting hurdles to overcome.

Example 11n

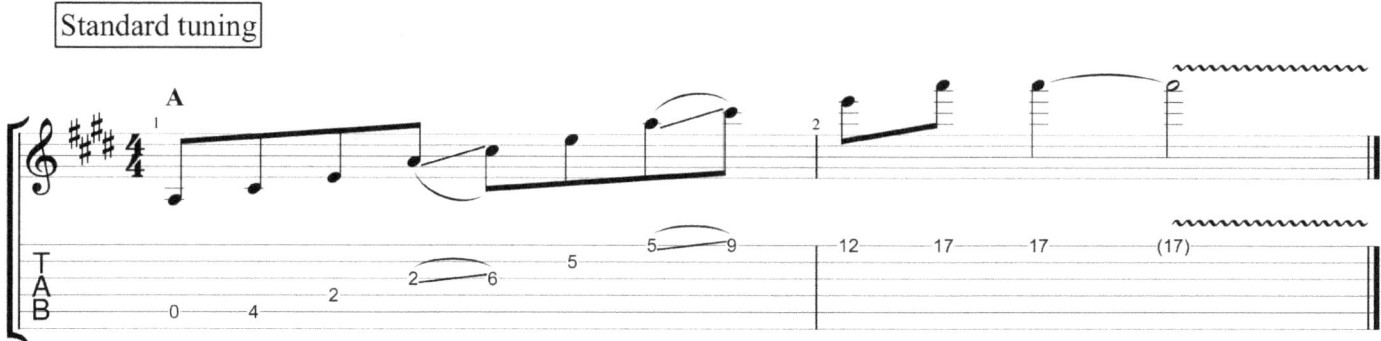

Example 11o

The previous examples highlight some important benefits of standard tuning, and, assuming you have some proficiency in the tuning already, and can introduce slide technique cleanly, you'll be unstoppable!

Before moving on to the final solo, I want to teach you a collection of minor pentatonic licks to show you how I develop my own slide guitar phrasing. First, learn these without the slide, then introduce it when you have the line memorised. This way you're just adding slide phrasing to lines you already know.

Example 11p

Example 11q

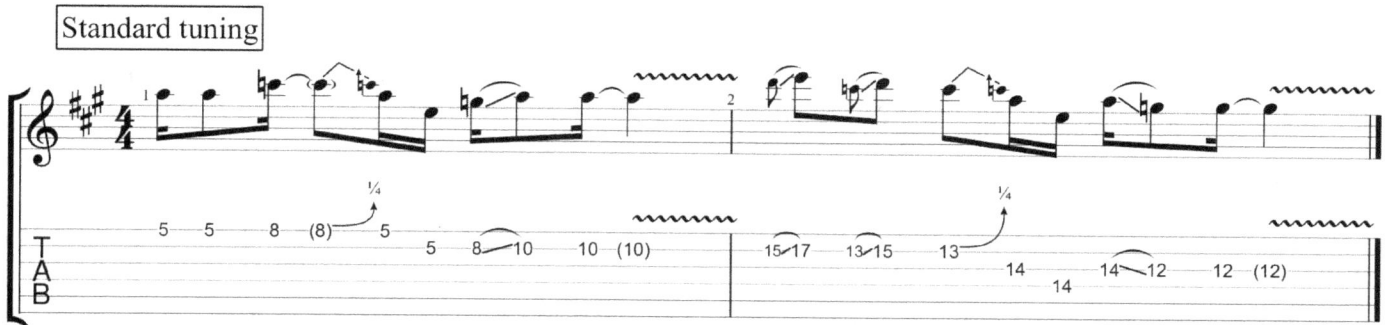

The final line requires some quick shifting on the second and third strings. This requires careful attention to your intonation and good muting technique, so the 9th fret on the B string doesn't ring when you play the 9th fret on the G string.

Example 11r

After working through the book to this point, you're fully prepared to become a fantastic slide player. Moving forward musically is now about developing your vocabulary and technique, and becoming free to express yourself fluently through improvisation.

If you're determined to play slide in standard tuning, I suggest that you go back to the start of the book and work your way through each of the Open E examples, then develop them to work in standard tuning. This will take time, but using techniques like fretting behind the slide will give you some useful creative options.

All that's left now is the final chapter: a full slide guitar solo in standard tuning! So, take a breath, then move on when you're ready.

Chapter Twelve: Standard Tuning Solo

Keeping in line with the roots of this book, the final solo is played on a traditional twelve-bar blues in A – the kind you're likely to find at any blues jam night.

Step one is to learn the rhythm guitar riff. It's a little flashier than using just simple chords, but it can be played with the slide kept on the little finger.

The secret to mastering a track like this is understanding how each melodic idea fits around the underlying chord. The first riff fits around an open A chord and in bar five, when the chord changes to D, the same basic idea shifts over to an open D chord.

In bar eight I play an open E chord and add some descending 6ths on the A and G strings.

Bar nine features a rich Dadd11 chord, which is formed from a D triad on the low strings and an open G sustained over the top.

Example 12a

198

Now to the solo!

The first lick begins with some minor pentatonic phrases and descends to outline an A7 chord by targeting the note C#, the 3rd of the chord.

Example 12b

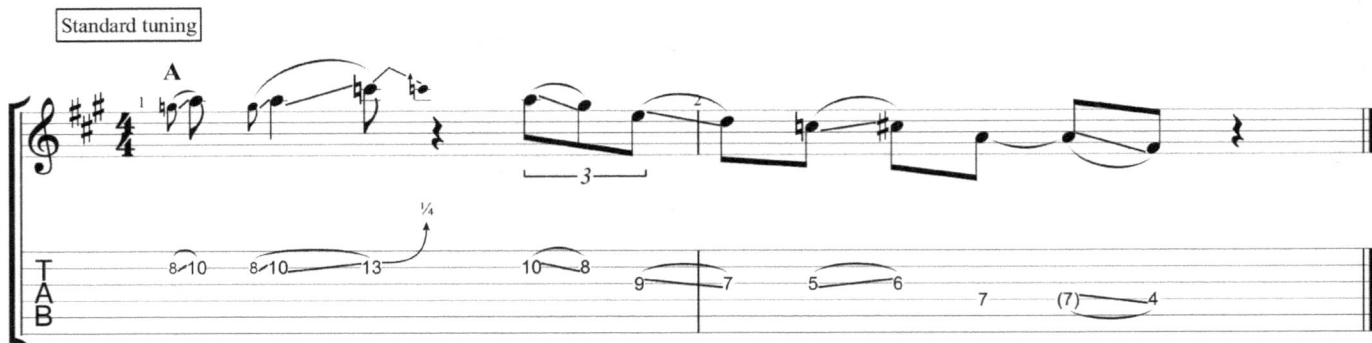

The second lick draws a little more from the A Major Pentatonic scale that's still played in the root position triad.

Example 12c

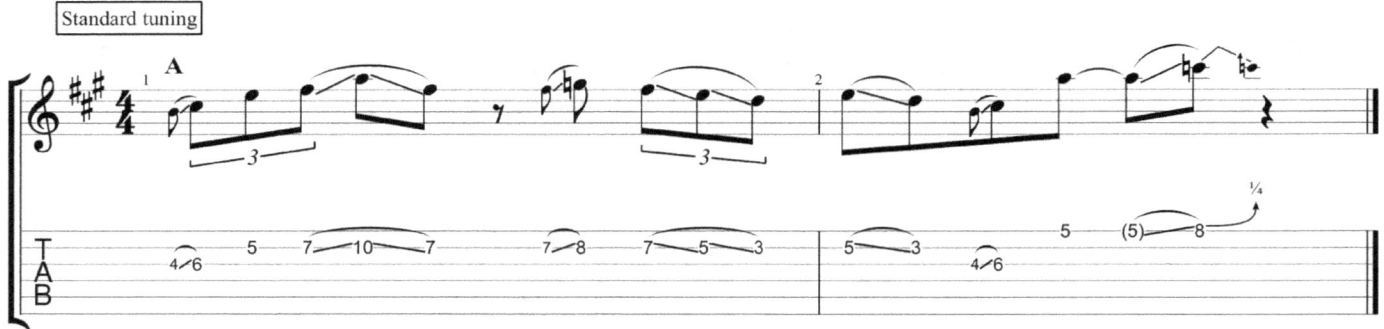

As the chord changes to D, our perspective changes again to target notes around the chord. This begins by landing on an F# (the 3rd), then ascending to a D triad on the second string. When I reach the root note at the 15th fret, I draw from the D Minor Pentatonic scale.

Example 12d

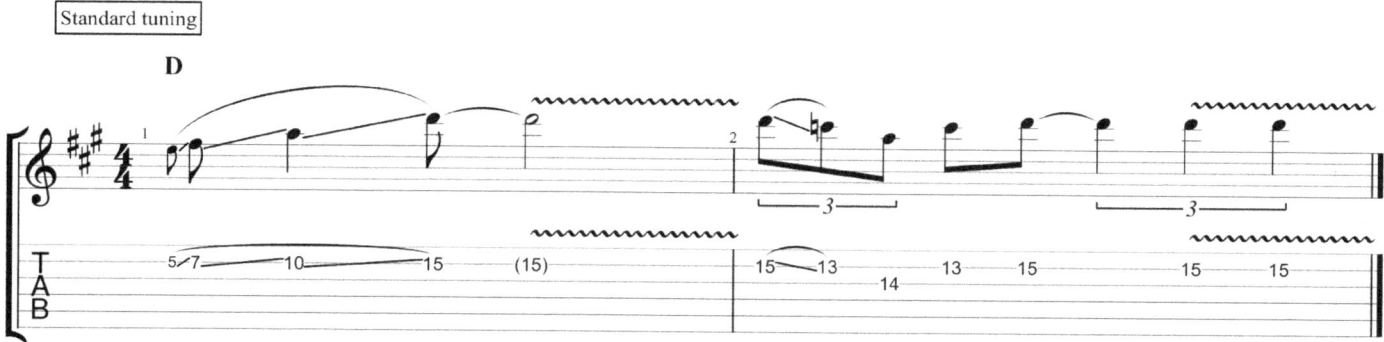

After two bars of D major, the chord returns to A major. Again, I land on the 3rd (C#) in the second inversion triad position.

Example 12e

On the first E major, I target the 3rd (G#) and root (E), then shift up to land on the 3rd (F#) of the D chord before descending through the D Mixolydian mode on the way back to the tonic A major chord.

Example 12f

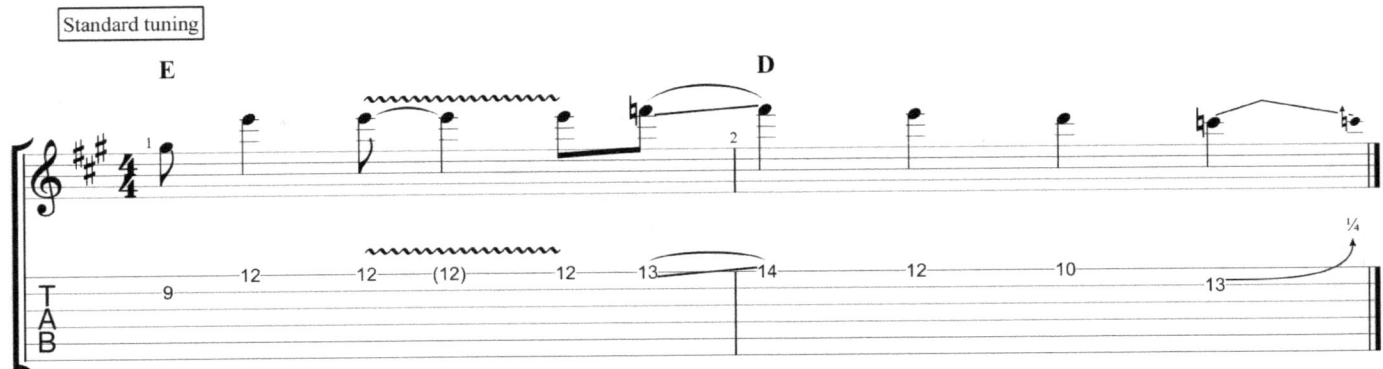

The final lick in the first chorus moves from A major to E major – first by descending the notes of A Mixolydian, then outlining an E major chord as the chord changes.

Note how many times I land on the 3rd as the chord changes. It's not a rule, but it's an effective tool to give your soloing a touch of sophistication.

Example 12g

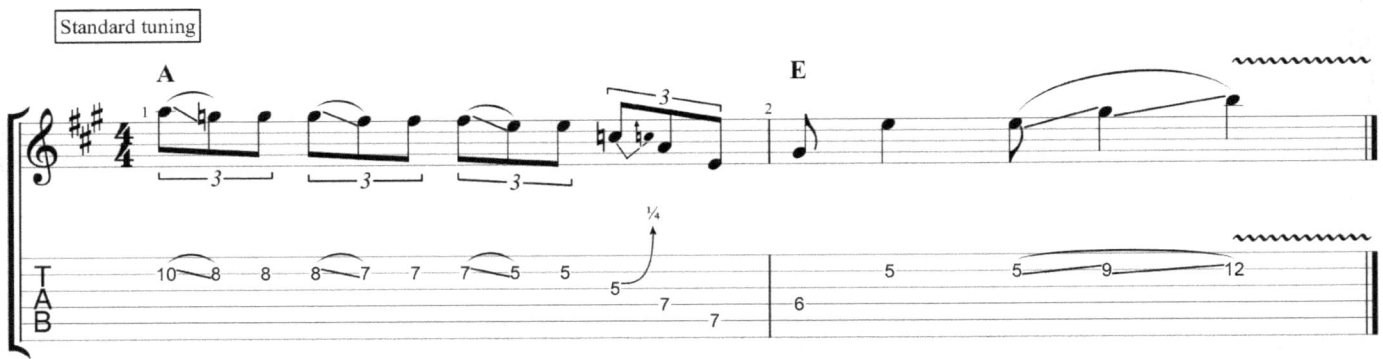

The second chorus is a little more advanced, with some behind the slide fretting to help imitate open tuning. Keeping the slide on your little (pinkie) finger is easiest, but you can get by with it on the ring finger.

The chorus begins high up on the neck using notes of the A Minor Pentatonic scale. Beginning a chorus with a strong, repeatable melody is the best way to craft a solo your listeners will remember.

Example 12h

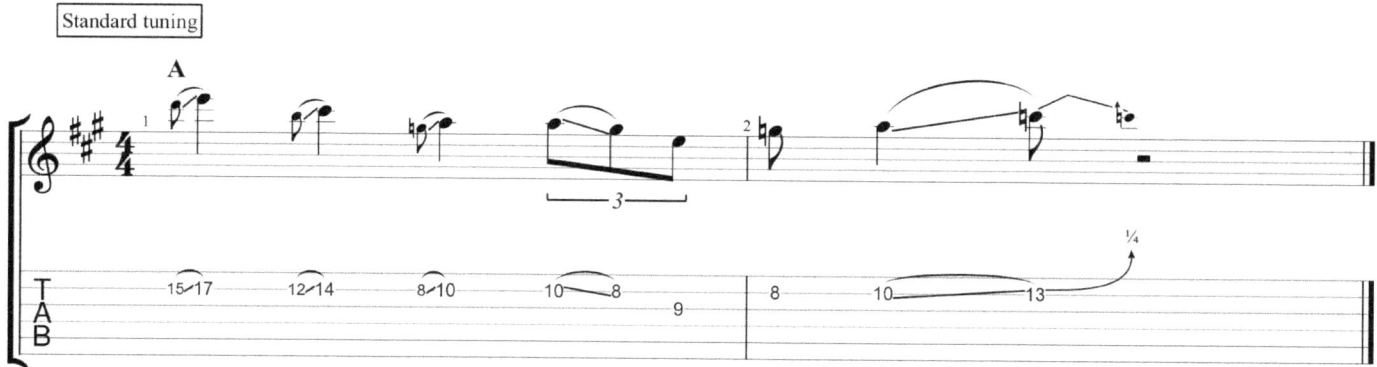

The next line begins with the same phrase as before, then shifts to a complicated lick in the second bar. Slide from the 8th fret down to the 7th and keep the slide here as you descend the D Major triad, then fret the two notes behind the slide to form an A major triad.

Example 12i

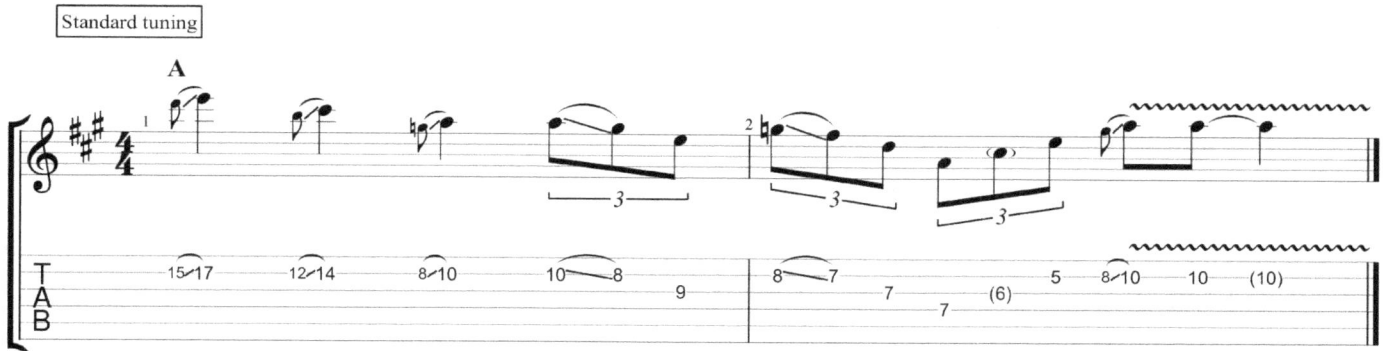

On the D Major chord, I use the same fretting behind the slide pattern. This pattern is a great one to master in standard tuning as it gives you the ability to play a root position major chord and let it ring out as it would in open E tuning.

The second bar ascends the neck with notes from the minor pentatonic scale, and by targeting the 3rd (F#) of the D chord.

Example 12j

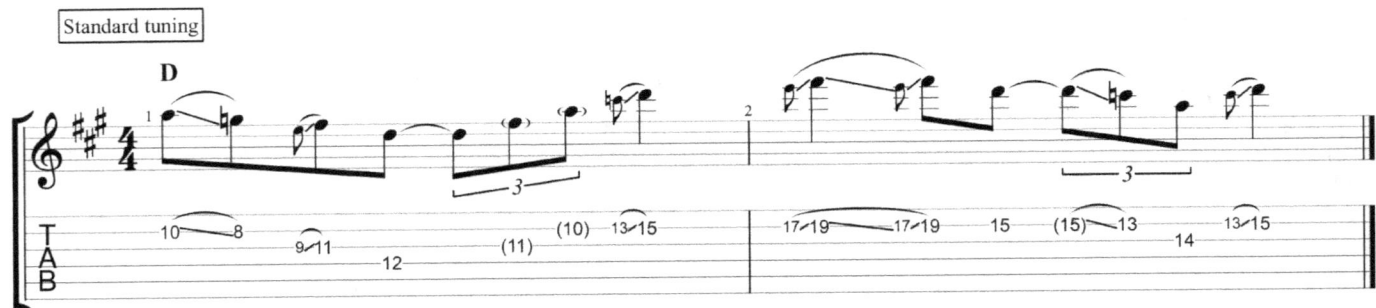

When moving back to A major, I switch to a combination of an A Major chord and an A Minor Pentatonic scale. The 3rd (C#) is played to begin the phrase before switching to root position of A Minor Pentatonic as the lick progresses.

Example 12k

Over the E major chord I play an E7 arpeggio (E, G#, B, D) idea, then transition into the D major chord with another fretting behind the slide lick. It's important to practise making this transition fluid to articulately outline the chord changes.

Example 12l

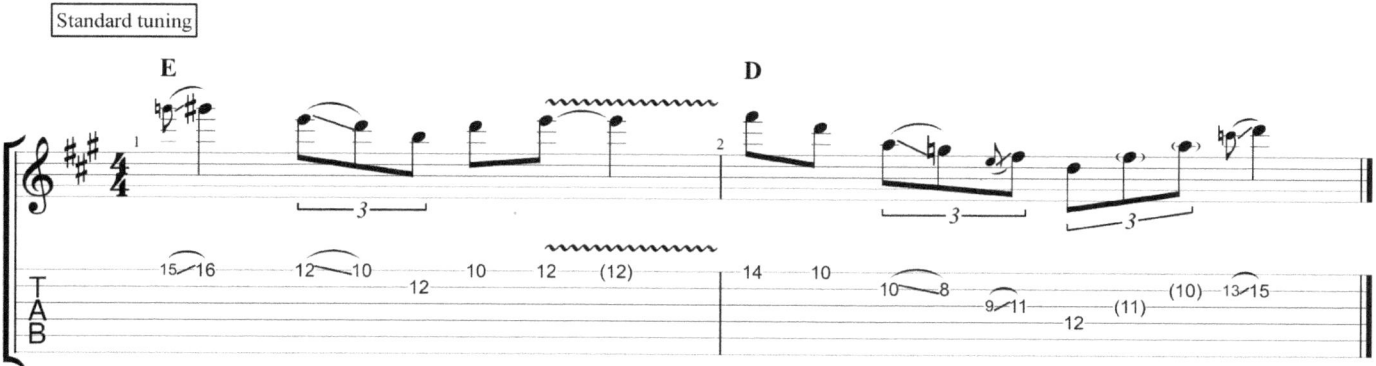

The final lick combines some challenging triplet ideas with fluid fretting behind the slide (8th fret, B string) to let the double-stops ring into each other and create the illusion of an open tuning.

Apply light vibrato to the descending E major triad in the final bar before resolving to the A root note to finish.

Example 12m

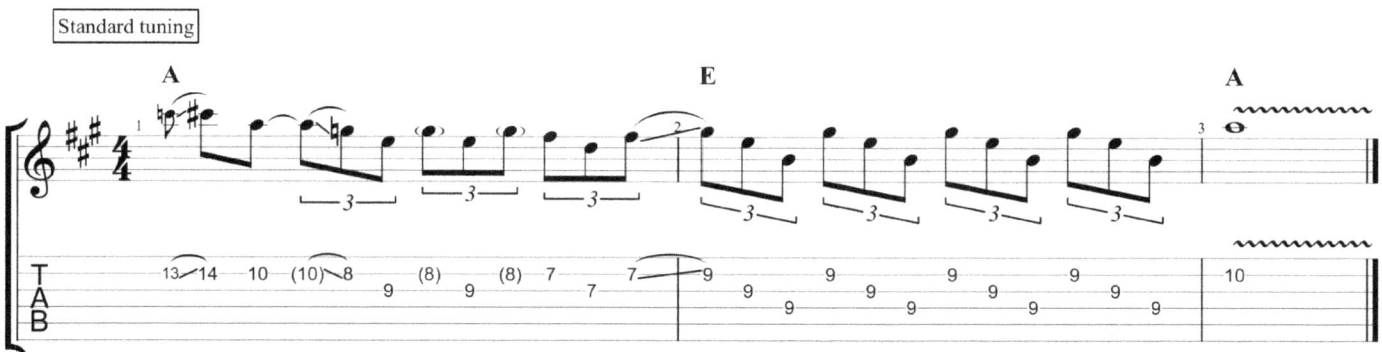

And that's it! Playing this solo cleanly and in full isn't simple, so don't rush ahead – learn each lick slowly. Master each one fully before stitching them together over a longer period of time.

There's no rush and going faster than you need to will only create tension and stress in your playing. Every note needs to be effortless and musical, so it's not like you're just repeating a collection of notes you've memorised.

Keep working at it. Every day is a step closer to your goal, and you will get there in your own time. Just don't give up!

Conclusion

Don't think for one second that the final page of this book is the end of your journey.

You've now been given the skills you need to play slide guitar, but never forget that music is a language. Even though you've learned to speak, there's still a lifetime of vocabulary and expression to learn, adapt and master.

Music can't be learned in a vacuum, that's why I've made a point of encouraging you to listen to the recorded audio for each of these examples. You need to hear as much slide playing as you can and learn to imitate how it sounds, rather than how you imagine it sounds.

It's imperative that you listen to as much great playing as you can, make a note of the bits you love, and then try and copy these sounds to understand the language of the professionals.

The following is a listening list of my favourite recordings that feature prominent slide guitar playing. Some are slide playing from start to finish, others only include a few moments.

Expose yourself to this music. Listen to it regularly and internalise the ideas.

At Fillmore East (1971) – The Allman Brothers Band

The Sky Is Crying: The History of Elmore James (1993) – Elmore James

Layla and Other Assorted Love Songs (1970) – Derek and the Dominos

Sail On (1969) – Muddy Waters

Nick of Time (1989) – Bonnie Raitt

Ry Cooder (1970) – Ry Cooder

Big Sky (2002) – Brett Garsed

From the Reach (2008) – Sonny Landreth

Shout! (2013) – Gov't Mule

Joyful Noise (2002) - The Derek Trucks Band

Let it Lie (2013) – The Bros Landreth

Made Up Mind (2013) – Tedeschi Trucks Band

Beyond It All (2006) – Allen Hinds

The Neo blues Project (2018) – AJ Ghent [pronounced "j-ent"]

What better way is there to end a book on slide guitar than with these words from one of the fathers of the style?

> "There are many different forms of communication, but music is absolutely the purest one."
>
> –Duane Allman

"In The Style Of…"

100 SLIDE LICKS FOR BLUES GUITAR

Master 100 Slide Guitar Licks in the Style of the World's 20 Greatest Blues Players

LEVI CLAY

FUNDAMENTAL CHANGES

Introduction

For over 100 years, adventurous guitar players around the world have taken to using various objects – metal pipes, bottle necks, even medicine bottles – as movable frets on their instruments.

Originating from the "slack-key guitar" style of Hawaii, and the African-imported slave music/blues of mainland USA, slide guitar has evolved dramatically over a century. So much so, that sometimes it's incredible to think that the branch you're on stemmed from the same tree as another slide player.

In part this is due to the relatively uncommon use of the slide among guitar players. That's not to say it's not practiced by many people, but compared to other guitar playing tools – like the capo or pedals – it surprises me how many guitarists I meet around the world who have never even held a slide, let alone practiced with one. The result is that guitarists who base their playing around the slide have a much easier job of creating a style unique to them, instead of following the same path as millions of others.

For those new to this style, I'd encourage you to get a grasp of the content in my two previous Fundamental Changes books, *Delta Blues Slide Guitar* and *Slide Guitar Soloing Techniques*. These books will teach you everything you need to know about what a slide is, how it works, and all the associated techniques.

This book is aimed at the intermediate player who wants to explore the style of various well-known slide guitar players, expand their musical horizons, and begin to develop their own musical vocabulary.

Those who have read my *100 Licks For Country Guitar* book will know that I'm a firm believer in the importance of *vocabulary*. Music is a language comprised of words, not letters. Knowing the blues scale but never having heard the blues would lead me to conclude you probably can't play the blues. Blues is a language made from well-established phrases and progressions. It's what makes the genre relatable. Of course, you should add your own twist to things, but if you don't tip your hat to tradition, you'll just sound out of place. I liken it to Allan Holdsworth playing on an Albert King record, or Chet Atkins sitting in with Zakk Wylde. Without taking anything away from these incredible players, they would be out of place simply because they speak different musical languages. Just knowing the alphabet won't get you by as an Englishman in El Salvador!

This book consists of 100 licks from 20 great slide players. The licks will give you an idea of what each player is about, but more importantly will arm you with some great vocabulary you can use in your playing. You won't just learn licks, however, you'll learn about the artists behind them, making you a master of both the style and the history.

Here are a few important things to consider before you continue.

Slide choice

There are numerous slides on the market, made from various materials. Where possible, I've tried to use something close to what the artist in question would have used. When the choice was left up to me, I opted for one of my Star Singer Slides (that beautiful, eye catching slide on the cover!). These are wonderful ceramic slides, hand made in Glastonbury, here in the UK. Each one has a unique crackle finish and they have the kind of weight I look for in a slide.

Tunings

The nature of slide guitar – using a straight bar to play the strings – lends itself to open tunings. While not all slide guitarists play in open tunings, the majority do. Different players, however, prefer different tunings, so pay attention to the description of each lick and make sure you're in the correct tuning before attempting it!

Setup and tone

This leads to the subject of setup and tone. Each of these artists sound very different (I'll give you tone pointers in each chapter), but one consistent theme that will help you play these licks easier and make them sound good is having a good setup on your guitar.

This isn't a book on setting up guitars, but here are a few pointers to help with slide playing.

Having a high enough action (vertical height of the strings from the frets), a straighter neck (achievable with truss rod adjustments) and maybe a slightly taller nut will all contribute to your ability to play slide well. If this is an area you're unfamiliar with, take your guitar to a professional and have them set it up for you.

I'd also recommend a string gauge that lends itself well to detuning. A set of 11-52s from Ernie Ball (the Burly Slinky set – they come in a red pack!) is a great place to start.

Finally, on the page that follows is the important "Get the Audio" information. A lot of effort went into recording every single lick for your study, so don't forget to spend time carefully listening to the audio, as well as studying the musical examples. One of the incredible things about slide guitar is that it doesn't lend itself well to the conventional western system of notation or tab. There's no effective way to illustrate the microtonal options slide provides, so listen to the recordings and do your absolute best to imitate them carefully!

Good luck!

Levi

Get the Audio

The audio files for this book are available to download for free from **www.fundamental-changes.com.** The link is in the top right-hand corner. Simply select this book title from the drop-down menu and follow the instructions to get the audio.

We recommend that you download the files directly to your computer, not to your tablet, and extract them there before adding them to your media library. You can then put them on your tablet, iPod or burn them to CD. On the download page there is a help PDF and we also provide technical support via the contact form.

For over 350 Free Guitar Lessons with Videos Check out:

www.fundamental-changes.com

Over 11,000 fans on Facebook: **FundamentalChangesInGuitar**

Tag us for a share on Instagram: **FundamentalChanges**

Chapter One – Duane Allman

Many would consider Duane Allman to be the perfect place to begin when learning slide guitar. He's a player who influenced a generation in the short 4-year period in which he was recording. Few people could have had such an incredible impact in such a short space of time, and this is testament to Duane's incredible musical vision.

Born in 1946 in Nashville, his family moved to Daytona Beach in 1957. Duane picked up an interest in guitar in 1960 when his brother, Gregg, purchased a Teisco Silvertone from Sears. The guitar caused fights, and this was solved when Duane got his own Silvertone after wrecking his motorcycle (a tragic case of foreshadowing). Music really brought the two together and they played in numerous bands before making it big.

Interestingly, both brothers were left-handed, but learned to play right-handed – probably due to the scarcity of left-handed guitars in the '60s. Some would argue that having one's dominant hand in control of the slide could give you significant benefit when playing, but this isn't an argument I'd make – just try playing slide left handed!

Duane picked up slide in 1968, using a glass Coricidin pill bottle to imitate the slide playing of Jesse Ed Davis and Ry Cooder on the Taj Mahal cut of *Statesboro Blues*. Duane was a natural and his use of the slide would quickly become a defining part of his sound.

Outside of his own bands, Duane started to become popular on the session scene where he added a touch of rock to R&B and soul records, recording with names like Clarence Carter, Aretha Franklin and Wilson Pickett. It was his legendary cut on Pickett's cover of *Hey Jude* that brought him attention from record execs and peers alike, landing him a role next to Eric Clapton on the seminal Derek and the Dominos album, *Layla and Other Assorted Love Songs*.

The defining period of Duane's career was the formation of the Allman Brothers Band, alongside his brother Gregg on piano/vocals and Dickey Betts on second guitar. The group showed promise with their 1969 release, *The Allman Brothers Band*, which they followed up in 1970 with *Idlewild South*. While neither album was a commercial success, their live performances carried good word of mouth, and the collaboration between Duane and Eric Clapton was enough to see 1971's live album, *At Fillmore East*, chart in days. The album went on to reach number 13 on the Billboard charts, going gold that year, and eventually going on to achieve platinum status in 1992.

Despite having a career spanning half a century, Duane's tenure with the band was short lived. He was killed in a motorcycle crash in Macon, Georgia, in October 1971. While the band would continue and grow (featuring stints of over a decade with both Derek Trucks and Warren Haynes – two other slide masters found in this book), Duane's musical fingerprint served as the DNA for the band and influenced countless guitarist the world over.

When it comes to sound, Duane was well known for his stunning Gibson Les Pauls –both a '57 Goldtop, a '59 Standard Cherry Sunburst and, towards the end of his career, a Tobacco burst nicknamed "Hot Lanta" which he acquired from Billy Gibbons of ZZ Top. He was also known to play Stratocasters from time to time, and a '61 Gibson SG for some slide work (probably due to the incredible upper fret access provided by the design of the guitar).

Amp-wise, he was fond of a 1969 Marshall Super Bass – one of the iconic "plexi" models Marshall made during this period. While he owned a Dalla Arbiter Fuzz Face pedal, he would more often than not just run straight into the amp and play loud.

Duane was most well known for using open E tuning (E, B, E, G#, B, E), though there are examples of him playing slide in open A (E, A, E, A, C#, E), and standard tuning

Finally, there's the slide. He continued to use a medicine bottle, like the one he'd first picked up, and wore this on his ring finger. While these glass bottles are no longer produced, many companies offer replicas, such as the Planet Waves Glass Bottle Slide.

Now, onto the licks!

When it comes to playing slide, Duane takes full advantage of the barred position that open E tuning provides and bases a good 80% of his playing around this.

When playing rock in E, combining the notes on the 12th fret with those on the 10th fret gives you enough potential vocabulary to learn hundreds of classic licks. See the diagram below.

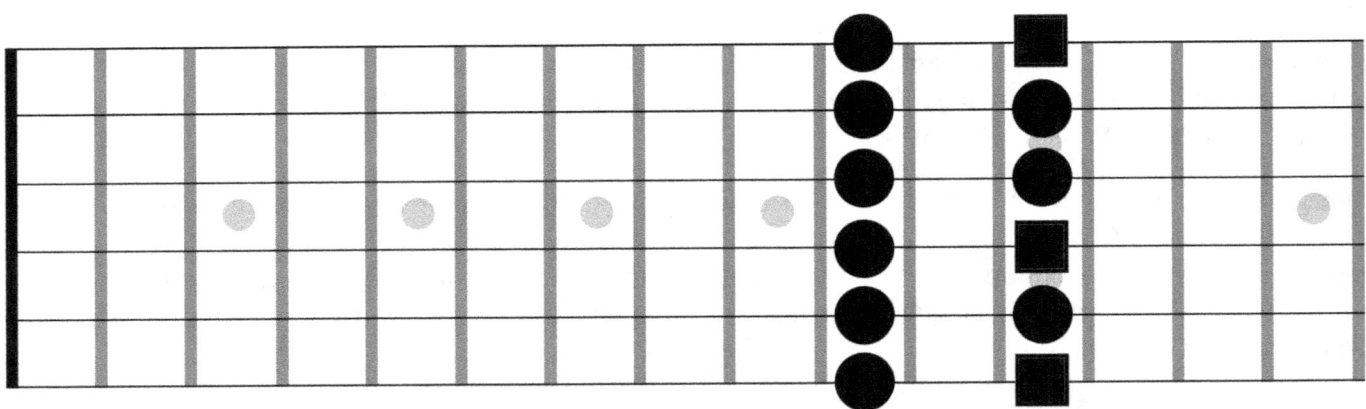

As an example, here's a lick similar to something Duane played on *Trouble No More*.

Beginning with a slide up to the root note (E) on the 12th fret, notice that all the notes are located on the 10th, or 12th fret. Think of the 12th fret as "home" and the 10th fret as notes for melodic embellishment you can use before going home.

Listen carefully to the audio for this lick as standard notation can't capture details such as how slow a slide is from one note to another. I've tried to include as much detail as possible (like the 11th fret bluesy notes that slide up into the 12th), but nothing will be quite like the recording.

Example 1a

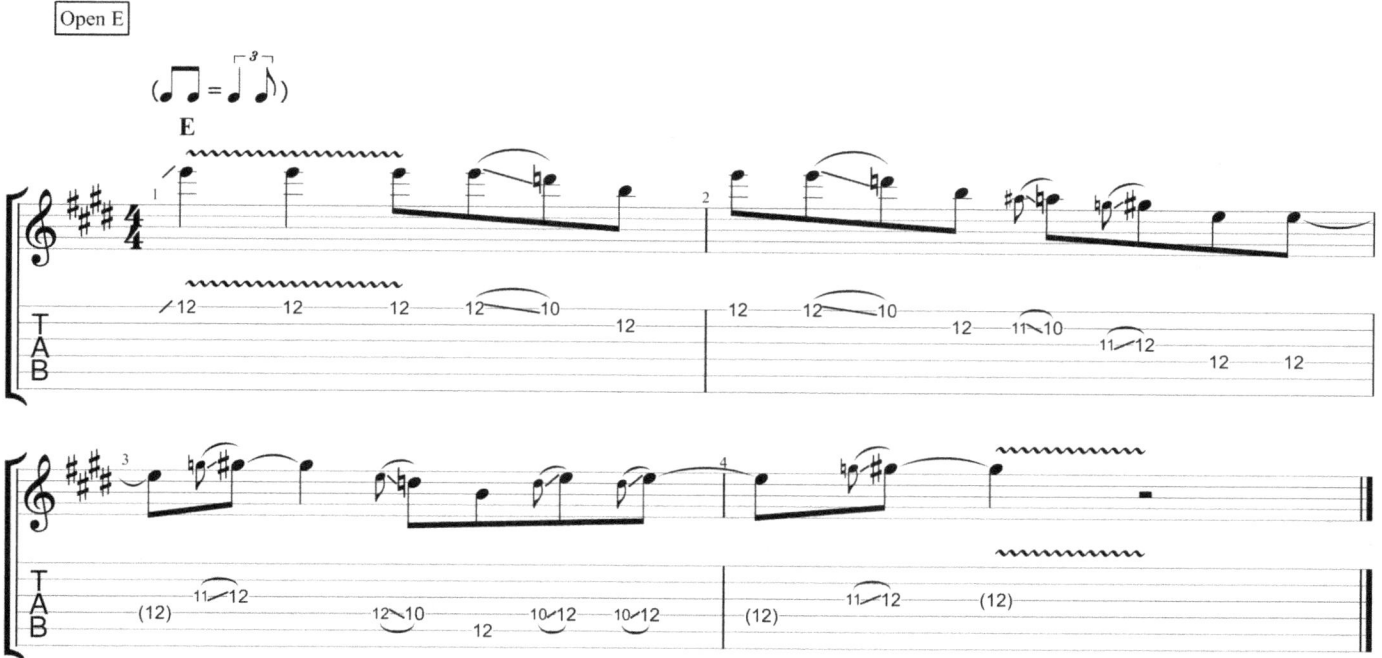

The second example continues with this idea, but now higher up the neck as the underlying chord is a D. Home is now all the way up at the 22nd fret!

After playing a simple melody for two bars, I come down to that same root note (D) on the second string, 15th fret, and play a similar idea to the first two bars, but now an octave lower.

This lick should remind you of Duane's stellar playing alongside Eric Clapton on the Derek and the Dominos classic, *Layla*.

Example 1b

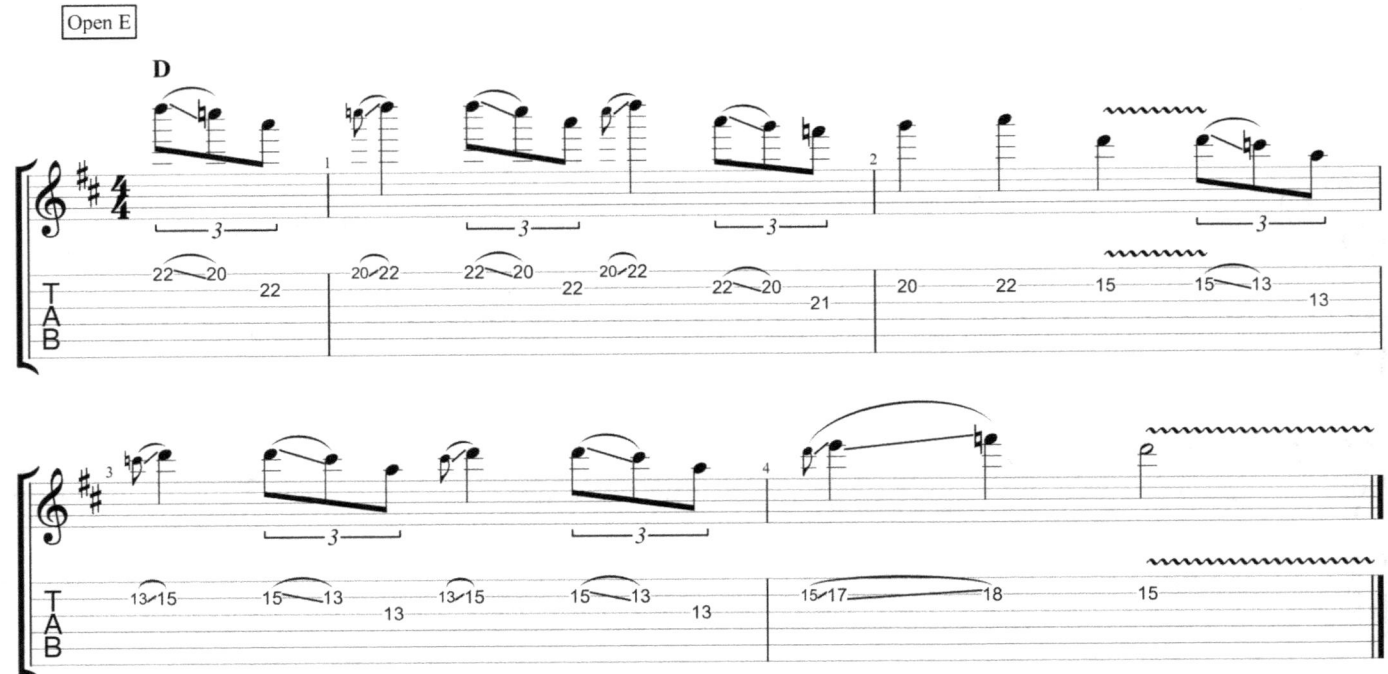

The next lick might remind you of *Statesboro Blues*. This example really milks the bluesy b3 (F) on the 9th fret of the third string. In the notation I've written *bends* rather than *slides* to indicate that the notes are slowly pushed up, as opposed to quickly slid.

The second part of the lick shift up three frets higher than the "home" position on the second and third strings. This highlights the 5th (A) and b7th (C) of the underlying D chord – which is perfect when you want to emphasise the D Minor Pentatonic (D, F, G, A, C) sound that's so prominent in rock music.

Example 1c

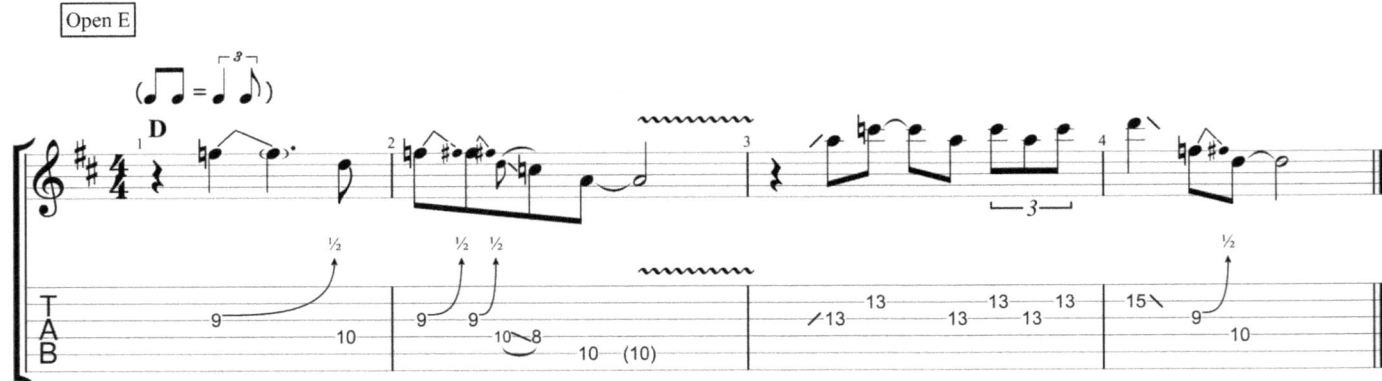

The final two examples move away from the overplayed minor sound and are based on chord progressions in E Major.

The first of these alternates between E Major and A Major – chords I and IV in the key of E Major – so the notes of the E Major scale (E, F#, G#, A, B, C#, D#) are going to work well here.

Example 1d begins with a slide into the home position at the 12th fret and continues with a repeating triplet. Care needs to be taken over the sudden shift up to the 17th fret to play a simple melody in the second bar.

The second half of the lick is played over the A Major chord. While the notes of E major are still in use, because the chord is A Major, the new home position is at the 17th fret.

Example 1d

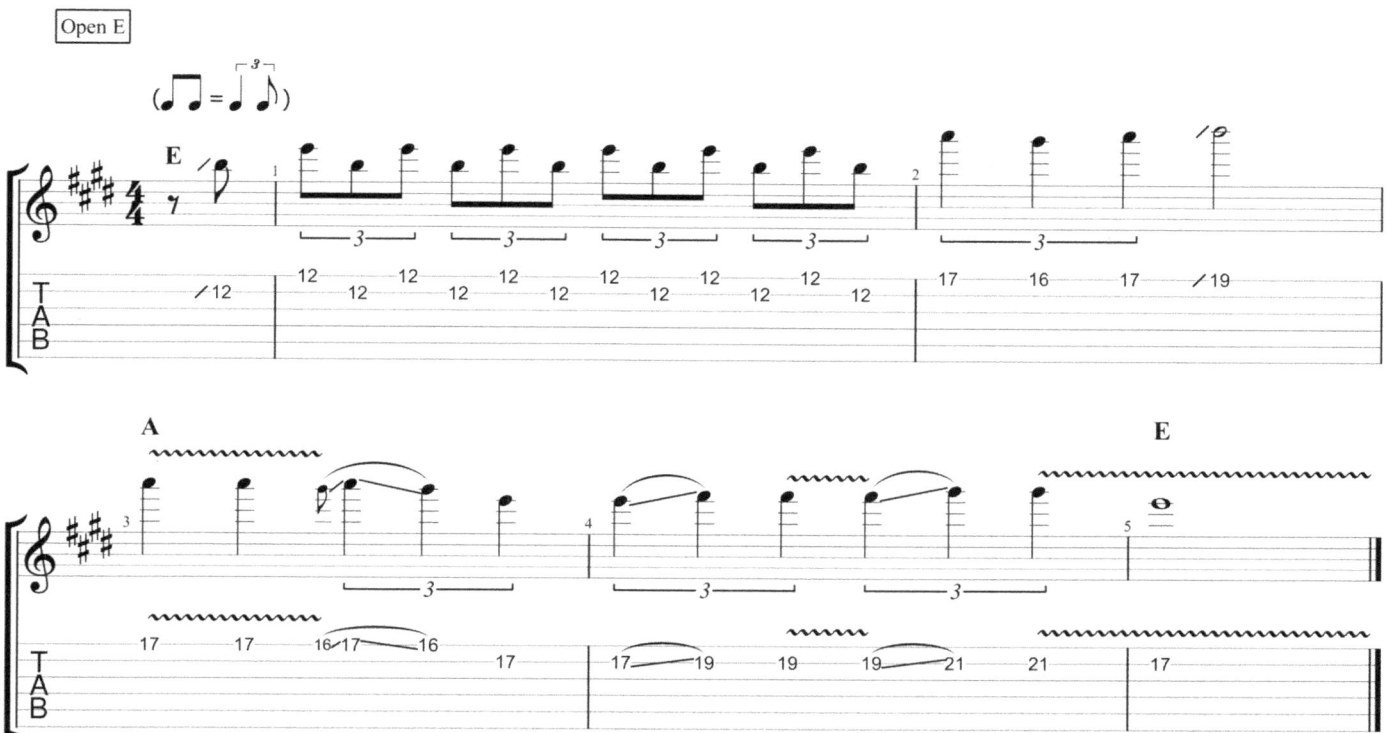

The final example takes inspiration from the Allman Brothers classic, *Melissa*. The chords move between E Major, F#m11 and E/G#. This can be seen as a simple I to ii progression in E Major, with G# added to the bass to keep some interesting movement.

The notes used here are largely found in an E Major triad (E, G#, B) but with the addition of slides from below and a killer slide up to the 17th fret towards the end.

Example 1e

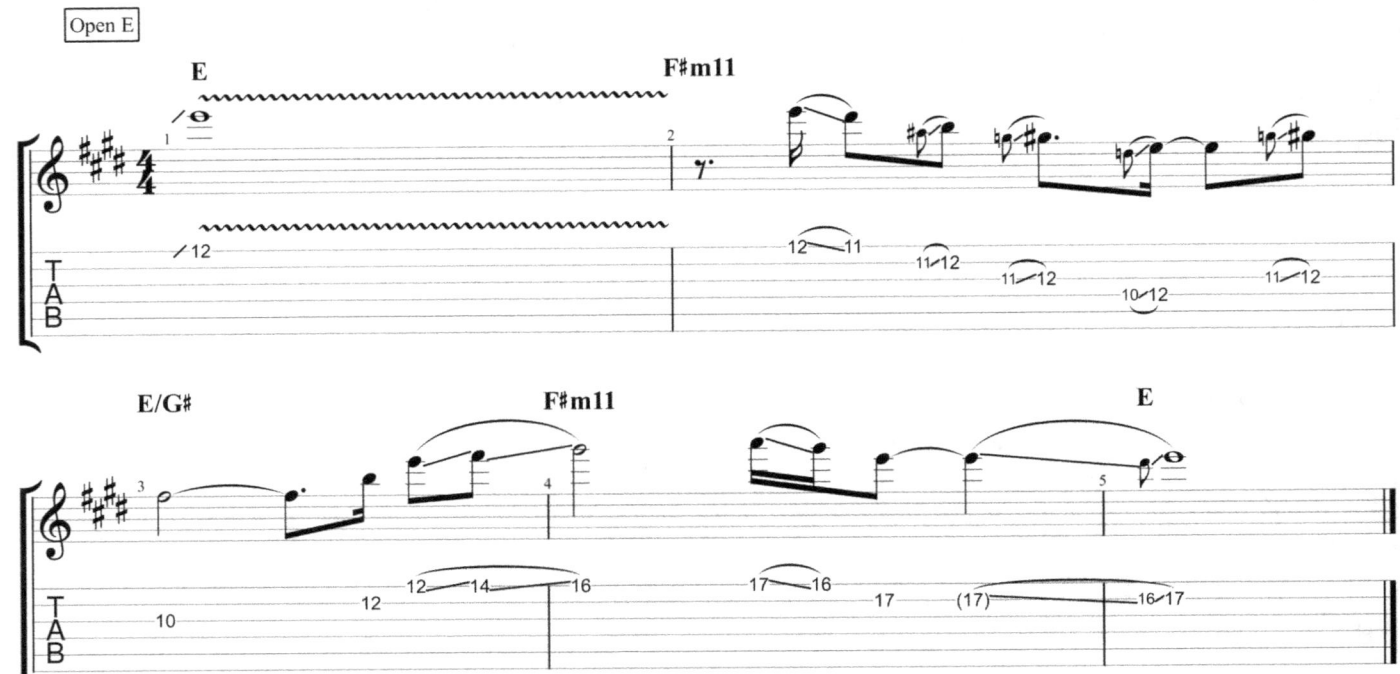

As you can see from just the short examples in this chapter, Duane's style is instantly accessible to almost any slide player, no matter how new the technique is. Listen to his music and be inspired by how willing he is to just experiment and look for melodies. He's not the most advanced player, but there's a reason he's one of the most influential.

Chapter Two – Ry Cooder

Although he's not one of the household names in this book, there can be little argument that Ry Cooder is one of the players most widely heard and respected by his peers.

Born in LA in 1947, Cooder is one of those artists who claims to have started playing guitar at such a young age that it's hard to believe, first picking up the instrument at just three years old! By the age of eight, he was reasonably adept on his instrument and decided to take things seriously.

While still in high school, he got the opportunity to play banjo with bluegrass legends Bill Monroe and Doc Watson in a thrown-together outfit, when Monroe's proper band found themselves stranded after a bus breakdown. While this didn't turn into a dream gig touring the country, it was a sign that music could be a serious option for Cooder.

At 17, Cooder was part of the original lineup for the band Rising Sons. While they didn't achieve success, the group became well known when Cooder and singer Taj Mahal found cult followings in later years.

After Rising Sons, Cooder went on to join Captain Beefheart and his Magic Band, recording guitar on 1967's *Safe as Milk*. But despite the promise this project had, the eccentricities of singer Don Van Vliet didn't gel with Cooder's musical ethos and he left suddenly in the same month the album came out.

From here Cooder turned his hand to session work and releasing his own music. To say his session career was a success would be an understatement. With over a thousand credits as guitarist on AllMusic, it's fair to say Cooder was a go-to name for anyone requiring authentic slide guitar.

As a session player Ry worked with The Rolling Stones, Van Morrison, The Monkees, The Beach Boys, The Everly Brothers, The Doobie Brothers, James Taylor, Eric Clapton and many more.

Outside of his session playing, his work as a composer for his own albums and film soundtracks is equally impressive and extensive. He has produced 17 solo albums spanning nearly 50 years and 17 film soundtracks (including the iconic guitar romp, *Crossroads*). If you're looking for a place to start, nowhere makes more sense than 1970's *The Slide Area*.

As a player, Ry hops genres like most guitarists hop notes. You'll find everything from authentic blues to folk, Gospel, pop, Tex-Mex, calypso, Hawaiian and Cuban sounds on his records. He's extremely hard to pin down to one style, which makes presenting just five licks in his style tricky! In fact, if you manage to get some of his slide licks down, you could still spend a lifetime working on his fluid fingerstyle approach to rhythm.

When it comes to gear, Ry has used a lot over the years, but he's best known for his two Strats. The first is a '67 Daphne Blue, which has undergone many mods, eventually settling on a Guytone pickup in the neck and a custom-built steel guitar pickup in the bridge. His main guitar is his iconic "Coodercaster", built from a Buddy Holly replacement body and a custom-made neck. This was eventually fitted with a Valco steel guitar pickup in the bridge (with base plate) and a cheap Teisco pickup in the neck.

Ry plays in several tunings, but most commonly open G (D, G, D, G, B, D) for rhythm guitar, and open D (D, A, D, F#, A, D) for lead. He often uses flatwound strings (10–50) on the blue Strat, and D'Addario Jazz Light 12-52 strings on the Coodercaster.

As a session player who lived through the '80s, Ry's amp choice varied greatly depending on the era. He has used everything from a custom-made Dumble amp, to rack systems that would rival the Starship Enterprise. The same is true of effects: if it existed, there's a chance Ry tried it!

In terms of slides, Ry is most commonly seen with a glass bottleneck-style slide, which he wears on his pinky finger.

Now, onto the licks!

Before looking at some lead guitar work, it makes sense to examine Ry's incredible rhythm work. Much like Eddie Van Halen, who is thought of as one of the all-time great rock soloists, Ry is best known for his unrivalled slide playing. In reality, however, his right hand work is just as impressive and considerably more subtle. Just one of Ry's albums will provide enough for a lifetime of learning before you even pick up the slide. Check out the rhythm guitar on a song like *On a Monday* or the intro to *The Very Thing That Makes You Rich (Makes Me Poor)*.

Example 2a is played in open G tuning and arranged so that the notes ring out to hold that G Major chord sound in the ear.

Wearing the slide on the pinky finger makes fretting the first chord easy. This is followed by a pull-off to the open strings, then a slide up to the 5th fret on the first string.

Note that the hammer-on to the 2nd fret, fourth string, can be played with either the slide or a finger. Other than that, you're using the slide for all single-note runs.

Example 2a

The next example explores the possibilities of open G further by introducing the low string, using the slide to play barred chords at the 3rd, 5th and 12th frets.

You'll notice that the final bar contains the same ending as the last idea. Clichés become clichés for a reason – they sound great, so you keep using them!

Example 2b

When it comes to Ry's lead work, you're looking at the very pinnacle of what slide guitar is about. It's the sound you hear in your head when someone says, "Slide guitar…"

Here's a lick played on an up-tempo blues in Bb. I've kept this in open G and played around the 3rd fret, though Ry may play something like this by placing a capo on the 3rd fret, allowing him to use open strings.

The important detail here is how you slide between the notes. You'll need to check out the audio, but as a guide, if I'm sliding from the 3rd to 4th fret, I don't just slide up – I drop down a bit *before* sliding up. This is impossible to notate, but it's key to getting Ry's sound.

Example 2c

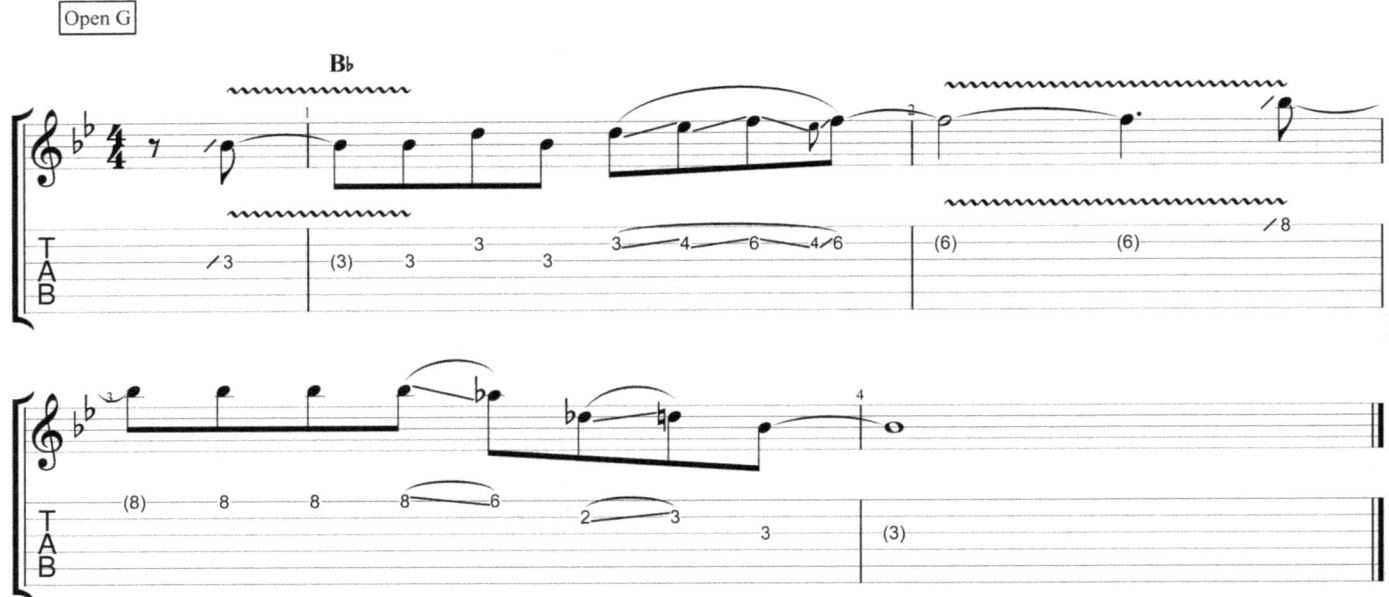

Here's a lick that's a little slower and gives you the chance to really milk the slides between notes. It's similar to what Ry might play on something like *Dark End of the Street*.

This idea sticks strictly to the G Major Pentatonic scale (G, A, B, D, E) and comes to rest around the home position barre at the 12th fret.

As with the last lick, when sliding between multiple notes, dropping down a bit before sliding up to the next note really adds some expression to the lick.

Example 2d

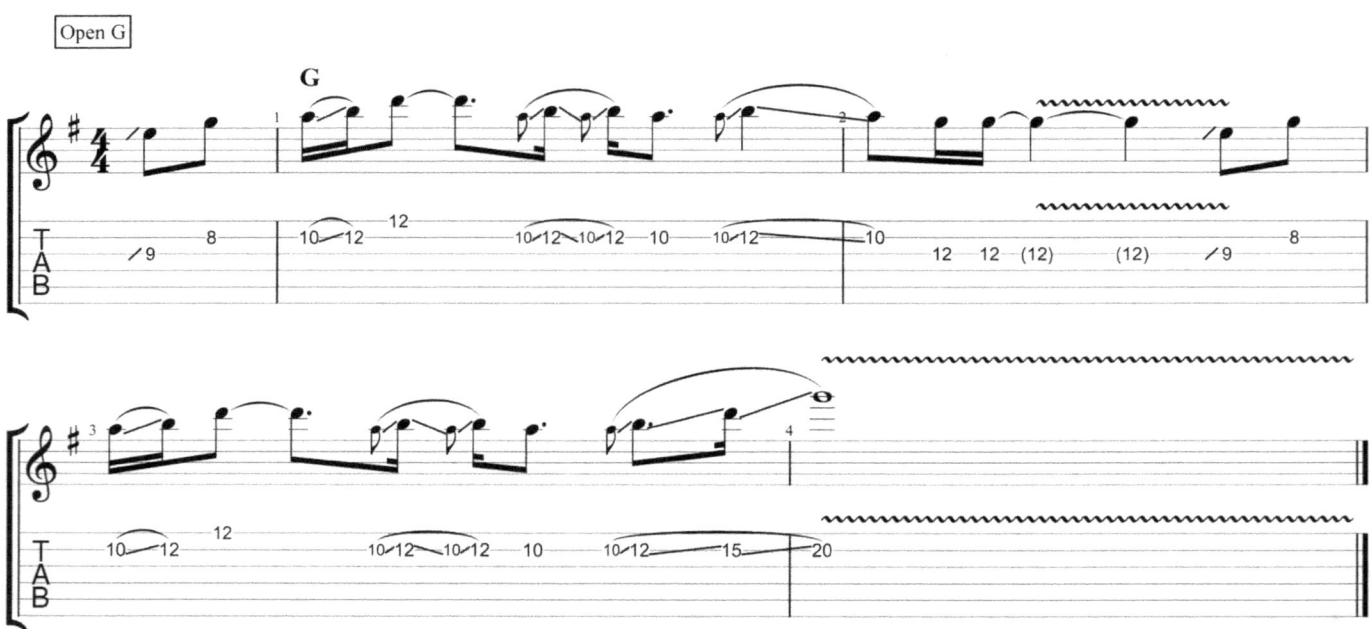

The final lick exploits this single-string sliding concept by covering an entire octave using the G Minor Pentatonic scale (G, Bb, C, D, F).

Begin at the 8th fret and be careful with the intonation when sliding up the scale (and dropping down a bit before sliding up!)

Example 2e

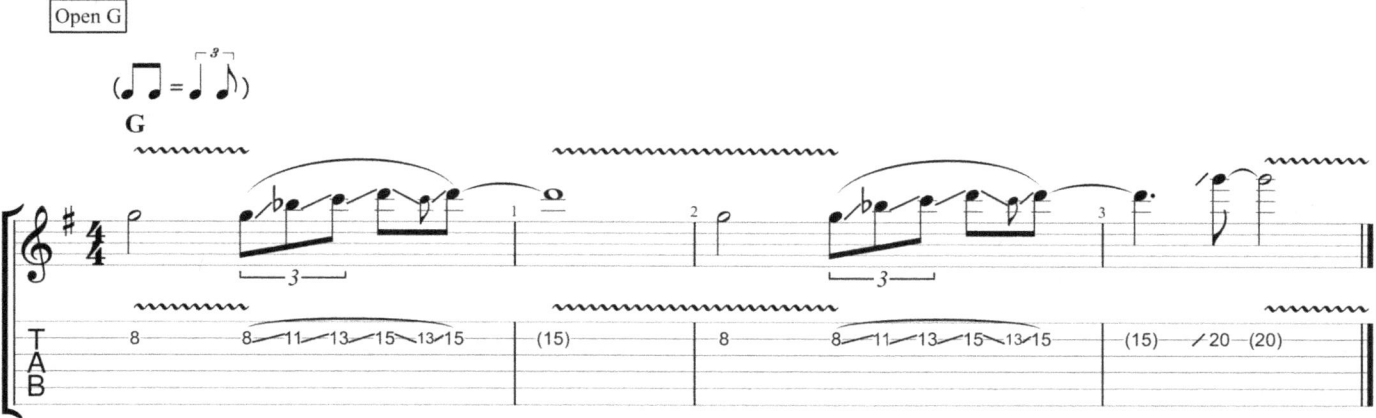

Ideas like this can (and should) be fully exploited. Try different scales, ascending and descending. Play them quietly; play them loud. It's all about developing accuracy of intonation, control and vibrato. Slide guitar is one of the most expressive ways to play music, so explore every nuance as much as possible.

I can't stress this enough: Ry's playing is so broad and unique, it's impossible to cover him in just five licks. It would be easy to fill a whole book on his style and even then we'd only be scratching the surface. Go and listen to his music and catch the bug!

Chapter Three – Brett Garsed

Born in Victoria, Australia, in 1963, Brett Garsed is one of the obvious wildcards included in this book. After almost 40 years on the scene, Garsed is best known as one of the fathers of modern rock fusion and legato playing, more than a slide player. Yet he's a wonderful slide player with unique things he brings to the table. Garsed was the reason I personally decided to take up slide playing.

Brett picked up the guitar aged 12 after listening to Deep Purple, but it was hearing Ric Formosa playing on the Little River Band track *Every Day of My Life* two years later that encouraged him to buy a chrome slide to try to get that sound.

In Brett's own words, "The results were absolutely terrible, as I was in standard tuning and had no idea about anything like intonation, vibrato and muting."

This first attempt knocked Brett back until he saw a video clip of Joe Walsh playing *Rocky Mountain Way*. The footage was good enough to see exactly what Walsh was doing. On the advice of a friend, Brett picked up a cheap Les Paul copy, tuned it to open E and began to play more seriously.

After developing some control of the technique required to play with the slide, he went back to standard tuning and quickly realised that the tuning between the G and B strings made playing 3rd intervals quite difficult. As he wears the slide on his middle finger, he tried angling the slide and this did a great job. Suddenly he could access a lot of the classic open tuning ideas in standard tuning.

Other influences included Sonny Landreth's technique of fretting behind the slide and the playing of Rory Gallagher, but in his own words,

"When I play slide, the guy I hear in my head is David Lindley. I loved how he played beautiful, soaring slide in a 'non-blues' context with Jackson Browne. So as well as just showing me how it's done, he also made me realise that slide guitar could be used in any musical context. I now know that this is obvious, but for a kid living in an isolated part of Australia with no one around to ask for advice or guidance, this was a moment of self-realisation that would have a huge impact on how I would play slide, when I would play it and how I would make it work in a variety of musical situations."

As a recording artist, Brett's list of credits is extensive: from sideman work with John Farnham and Nelson, to seminal fusion recordings like *Centrifugal Funk* (with Frank Gambale and Shawn Lane). *Quid Pro Quo* (with 8-finger tapper TJ Helmerich), and his solo albums, with 2002's *Big Sky* being a masterpiece.

Regarding guitars, Brett is a long-time endorser of ESP guitars, who have released two signature models. Sticking mostly with standard tuning, he uses 11 gauge strings with a medium action, wearing his glass slide on the middle finger.

Let's explore some Garsed licks!

Wearing the slide on the middle finger is an integral part of this first lick, inspired by the stellar playing on his track *Drowning,* as you'll need the other three fingers for fretting notes. In order to achieve this, wear the slide down to the second knuckle, so you're still able to bend the finger.

Play the ascending scale with your fingers, then transition to playing with the slide for the final note in the second bar. This note is held and allows you to use expressive slide vibrato before going back to playing fretted notes.

As with most things slide, this really isn't designed to be notated, so pay attention to the text above the notation and listen to the audio!

Example 3a

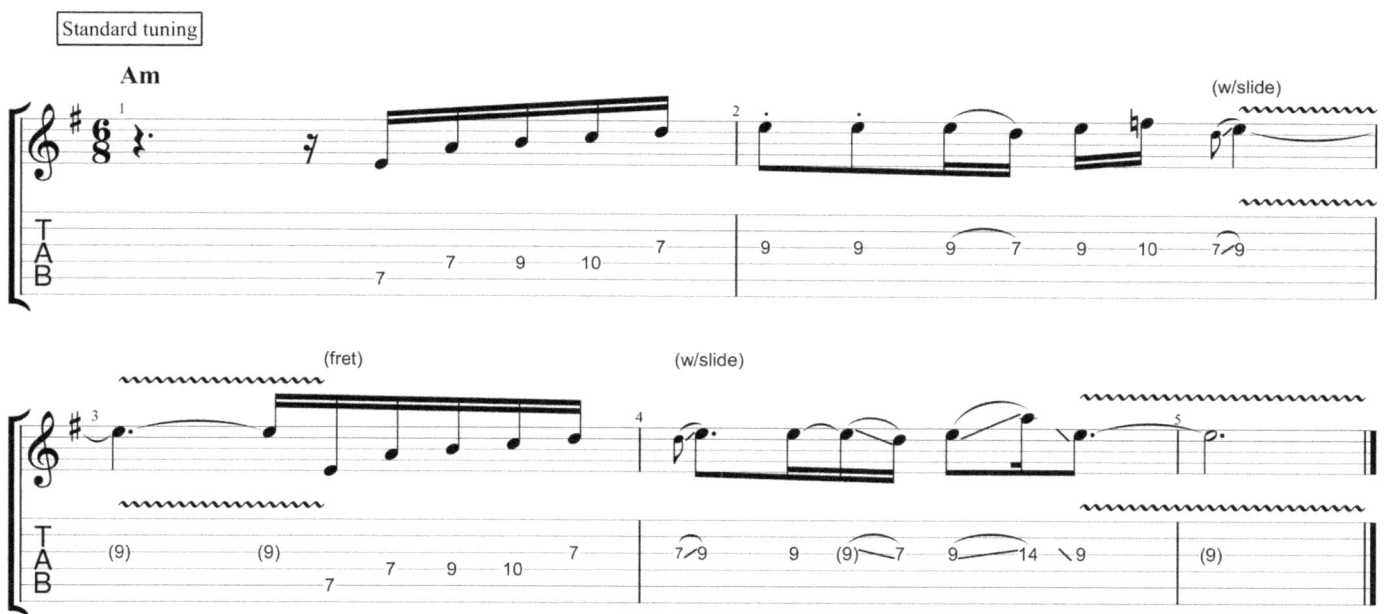

An interesting aspect of Garsed's playing is how he exploits aspects of standard tuning to give the impression of a more common open tuning as the next example illustrates.

When barring on the D, G and B strings, the notes form a major triad with the 3rd on top. So, any time you're going to play the 3rd of a chord on the B string, you can rake into it with the notes on the D and G strings, because they're going to be in that chord too.

Notice the rake into the 12th fret in the first bar of Example 3b, implying a G Major triad, then a C Major triad in the final bar.

Example 3b

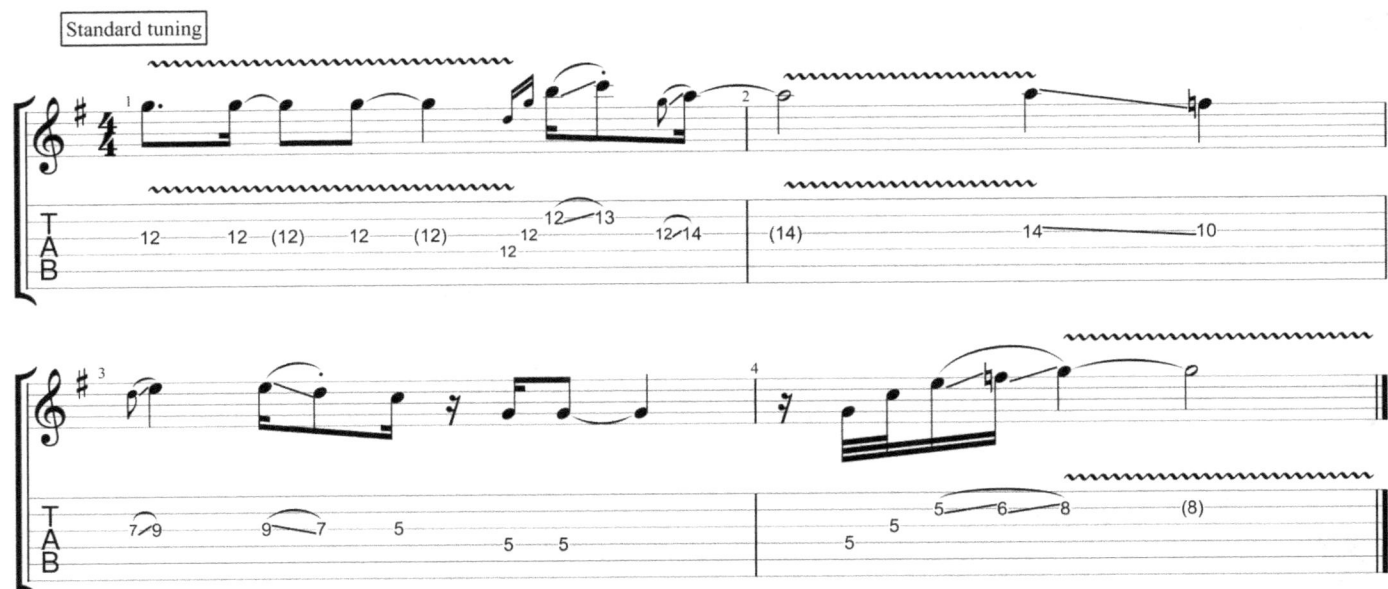

Example 3c covers a huge range of the guitar, from the 24th fret all the way down to the 4th. If you're playing a guitar that doesn't have that many frets, don't fret (sorry!) Actual frets aren't needed to make notes with the slide, so you can just slide up to where the 24th fret would be.

The main focus of this lick, and a unique feature of Brett's playing, occurs in the second bar. Towards the end you'll see I've put the note played at the 14th fret on the G string in brackets. This note isn't played with the slide. Instead, Brett would fret this with the pinky finger of his fretting hand – kind of like a backwards Sonny Landreth! It's very cool and a great way to work around the limitations of slide playing with standard tuning.

Example 3c

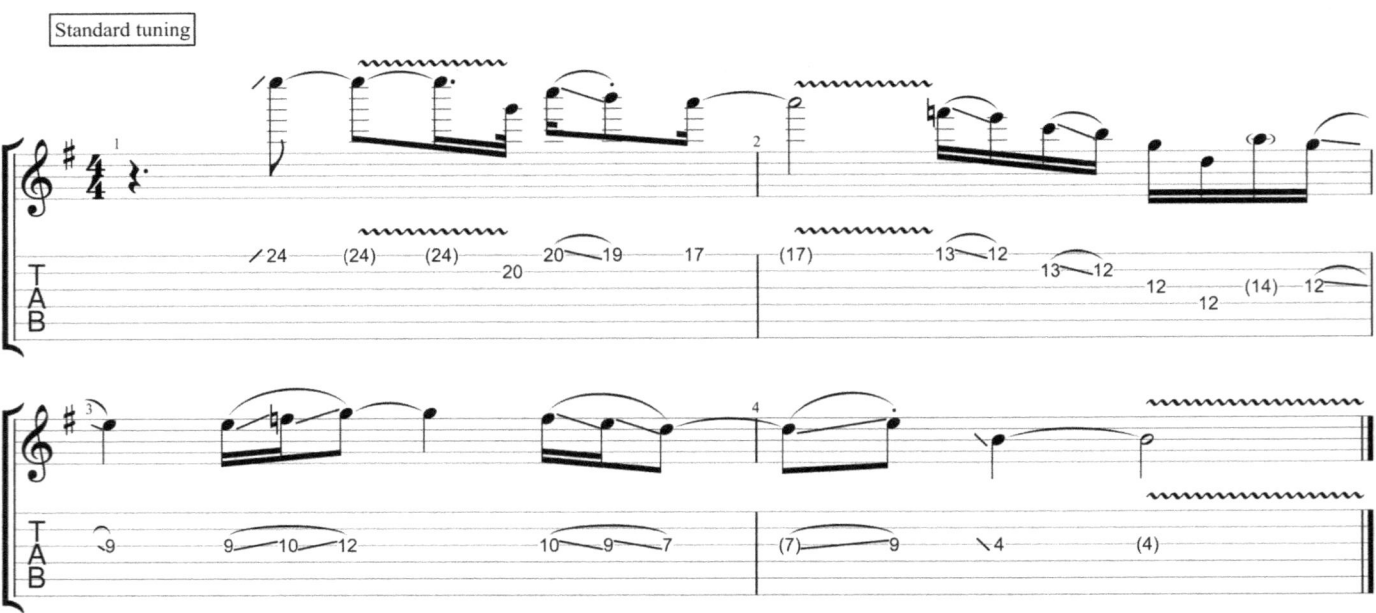

The next example takes the technique of fretting while playing slide even further, playing notes both in front of, and behind the slide.

Begin with the slide barred at the 9th fret, playing the D, G and B strings, then hammer on with the ring finger at the 10th fret before returning to the slide. The second bar sees you hammer from the 9th fret (played with the slide) to the 11th fret with the finger.

This sound has an undeniable pedal steel influence, so use your bridge pickup, a good clean tone, and some heavy compression to imitate this incredible instrument.

Example 3d

The final example showcases Brett's fluency in angling the slide to play double stops that are not located on the same fret. This technique is almost impossible to pull off with the slide on any finger other than the middle one, so don't kill yourself with frustration trying this with the slide on the pinky!

Begin by playing with the slide parallel at the 14th fret and, as you slide down, begin to angle the slide to allow you to play the 11th and 10th frets simultaneously.

A similar idea occurs in the next bar. Hold the slide at the 14th fret for the A Major triad, then slide up to the 18th and 17th frets to play two more notes in that A Major triad.

As with the previous example, this gives the impression of a pedal steel guitar. Obviously, this has its limitations, but if you need a low rent pedal steel sound, this will get you close enough.

Example 3e

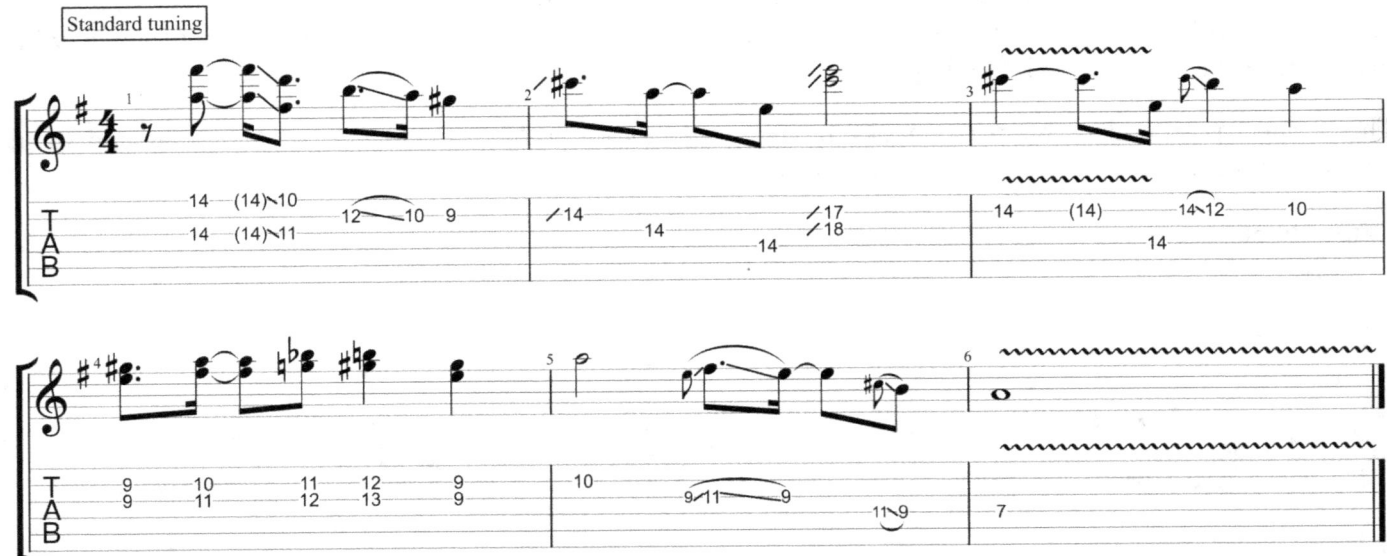

225

Chapter Four – A.J. Ghent

A.J. Ghent is another odd choice for this book as he's not strictly a "slide guitarist". He does, however, give us an excellent opportunity to talk about lap and pedal steel guitarists and their influence on slide guitar. Not to mention that A.J. is an outrageously talented musician who continues to influence musicians of all backgrounds.

Ghent is definitely one of the younger names in this book, being born in Florida in 1986.

Considering the rich musical heritage in A.J.'s family (which includes steel guitar pioneers such as Willie Eason and Henry Nelson, who brought the "Sacred Steel" sound to the world) Ghent took an interest in the instrument at the relatively late age of 12.

After some time in Florida, Ghent relocated to Atlanta, Georgia, where he was taken under the wing of the legendary Colonel Bruce Hampton (best known for Aquarium Rescue Unit). This brought him immediate legitimacy as Hampton invited him to front his then band, Pharaoh's Kitchen. Being part of the jam band scene, Hampton's fans are avid archivers, so there are plenty of bootleg recordings to be found from this period.

As a solo artist, Ghent released *Live at Terminal West* in 2015 and his debut studio album, *The Neo Blues Project*, in 2018. Both have a somewhat cult following on the blues scene.

Despite being namechecked by top players like Jimmy Herring and Derek Trucks, it was a viral YouTube video (AJ Ghent and his Singing Guitar) that brought A.J. to the attention of the wider public. This short clip showcased a live solo filmed at his album release party. To this day I've yet to hear anything closer to the sound of the human voice played by a slide guitarist. Despite being able to see him playing, every time I watch it, I keep thinking a singer is in the background doing her best Beyoncé or Mariah Carey impression!

As mentioned above, A.J. actually plays a hybrid of slide guitar and lap steel, so it's worth talking about the lap and pedal steel tradition he comes from.

The lap steel guitar is played with the strings parallel to the ground and a metal bar that acts like a slide. There's no fretting of the strings. The instrument often has 8 or 10 strings and is tuned to an open tuning.

The pedal steel guitar is an answer to the limitation of these open tunings and takes advantage of the stationary nature of the instrument. It has a series of foot pedals and knee levers that allow the player to change the pitch of strings while playing. This enables you to create beautifully expressive parts without being limited by the open tuning you're using. Players like Buddy Emmons, Paul Franklin Jr, and Robert Randolph are shining examples of the instrument and I urge you to check them out immediately.

A.J.'s main guitar is a custom built 8-string that looks like a cross between a Telecaster, a Stratocaster, and a Les Paul, with a set of Lollar steel pickups thrown in for the authentic sound. He uses a tuning that is a hybrid of open D, with a B and E on top, but Ghent does mix this up depending on the song.

As for the slide, A.J. uses a heavy steel bar and plays with his hand over the top of the neck. This is interesting, but his technique can obviously be adapted to a more traditional slide guitar approach. For the sake of continuity, I've recorded these examples with a traditional slide on my ring finger.

Let's take a look at those licks!

The first example instantly gives you an idea of how hard these licks are to play on a standard slide guitar. In theory, this is a simple single-string lick in A Major, but getting it to sound like a human voice (or even just getting the intonation spot on for the faster 16th note runs) seems impossible!

There's no avoiding it: this will just take time.

Example 4a

Here's a shorter example, again on the high E string. This time the challenge comes with the addition of the chromatic passing note at the start of the 16th note run. The goal here is to achieve good definition between each note, rather than aimlessly sliding between pitches.

Example 4b

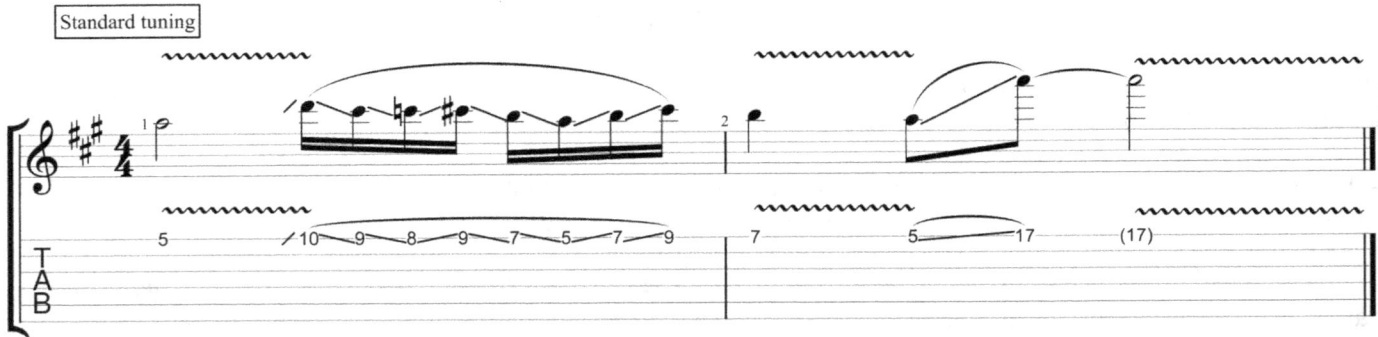

The next example expands on the theme of the last two licks but adds more complex rhythmic ideas.

One of the signs of a confident improviser is not needing to start on beat 1 of a bar, and in this case you begin on the second 1/8th note triplet of beat 2. This might take some time to get comfortable with, but it will give your licks a more laid-back feel.

Example 4c

Example 4d ramps up the difficulty with a long scalar run that spans most of the second bar. Aside from accuracy with the intonation, the other challenge here is keeping the note sustaining. This can be achieved with a compressor pedal, or some overdrive to help the notes sing a bit.

As with each example in this chapter, the notes are pretty basic, all coming from the A Major scale (A, B, C#, D, E, F#, G#). It's all about how well those notes are executed which brings the music to life.

Example 4d

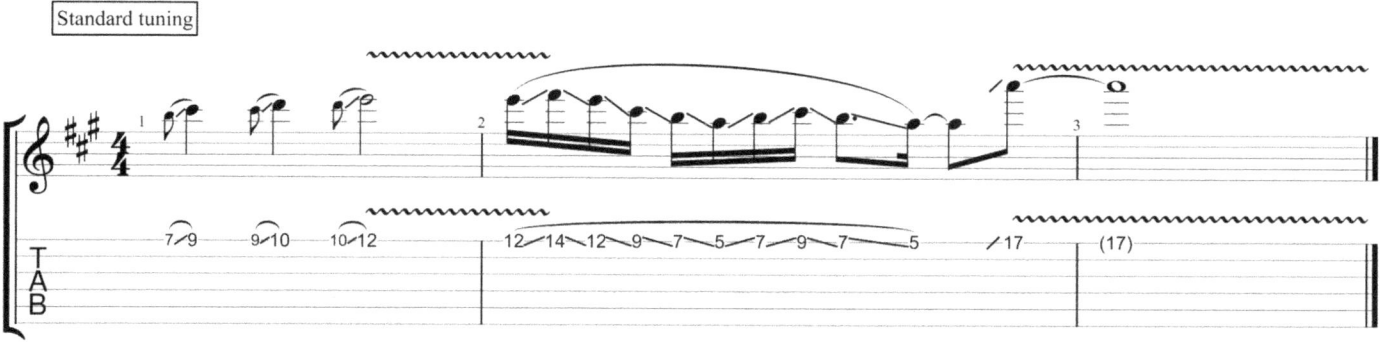

For the final example, I've decided to look at some of A.J.'s rhythm work, inspired by a clip of him playing a standard 6-string guitar tuned to open E.

One of the benefits of playing with your hand over the top of the neck is that you can fret a chord like A Major at the 5th fret, but allow the B and high E strings to ring open, thus turning a garden variety A Major into Aadd9. Do the same when moving the chord up two frets to B Major, and the open strings create a Badd11.

Each note here is played with the slide, so you'll either need to have your slide over the top of the neck, or ensure it's not touching the first two strings to execute those chords.

Example 4e

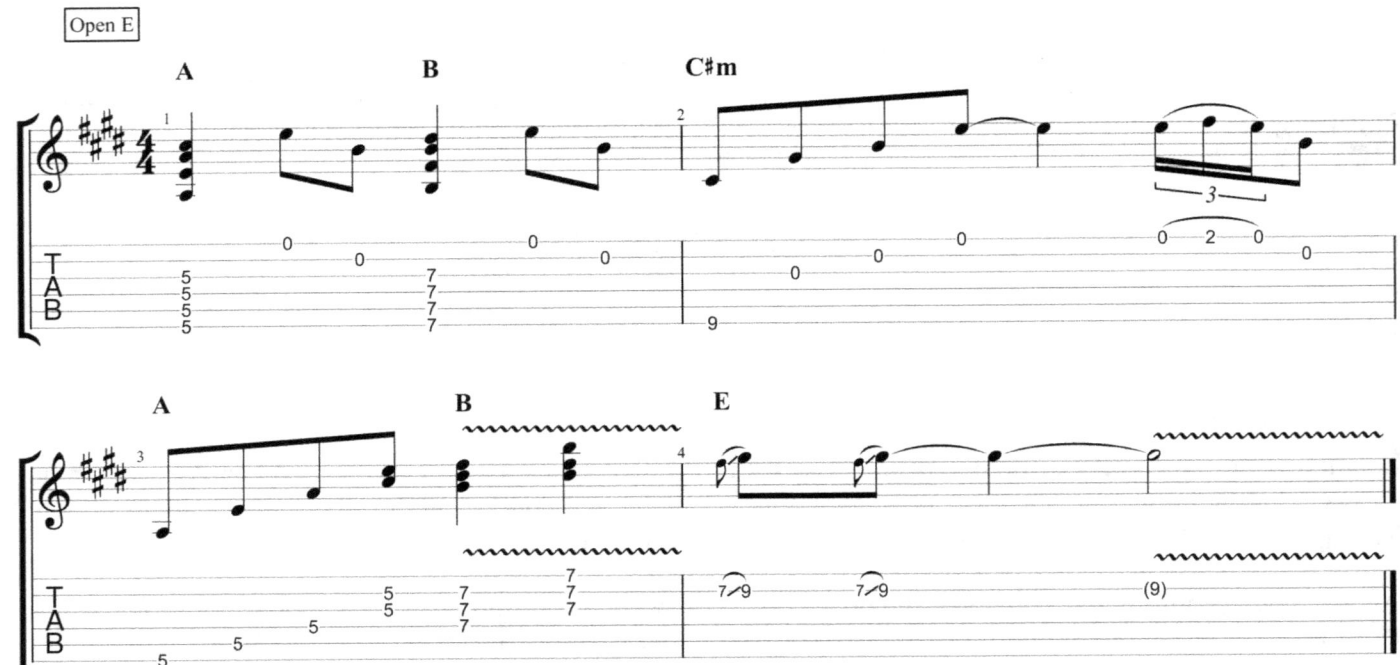

Chapter Five – Billy Gibbons

Born in Texas in 1949, Billy was the son of musical parents (his father was a concert pianist and conductor) who bought him a Gibson Melody Maker for his 13th birthday.

Billy played in many bands in his youth but found success before he was 20 when he released his first record, *Flash*, with the group Moving Sidewalks.

Despite this group showing promise, Gibbons would cement his legacy by forming ZZ Top in Houston in 1969, where Billy, Dusty Hill and Frank Beard (ironically un-bearded!) have stayed for an incredible 50 years.

ZZ Top's First Album, released in 1970 was a solid blueprint for what would follow and you can instantly understand why the group has been so popular – from Billy's unmistakable vocal style to the rocking rhythm section and tasty blues rock soloing… There's even some pedal steel guitar on *(Somebody Else Been) Shakin' Your Tree*!

Billy's playing style is a blend of many influences, from the authentic blues he grew up on, like B.B. King and slide maestro Muddy Waters, to the sounds of '60s guitar icons such as Eric Clapton in Cream and Jimi Hendrix (Jimi and Billy actually became good friends).

Slide makes a debut on the group's 1972 album, *Rio Grande Mud*, on the track *Just Got Paid*. It's something Billy comes back to time and again on songs like *Tush* (from 1975's *Fandango!*), *Dust My Broom* (1979's *Deguello*), and *Sharp Dressed Man* (1983's *Eliminator*).

There's not much information available on Billy as a slide player. He's never been much of a teacher and if you ask him a question, his long-time tech Elwood Francis says you're likely to get a "colourful story". Aside from the obvious influences then, it's hard to say how Gibbons landed on his particular style. I can tell you that he has a signature slide produced by Dunlop, the Rev Willy Slide, which is made from porcelain with thick walls for superior sustain, and back in the day he used a medicine bottle style slide. Regardless of the material, his slide is worn on the middle finger.

To say Billy has a large collection of guitars is an understatement. But, with many hundreds of stage guitars in the ZZ Top warehouse, it really comes back to two guitars: his '59 Les Paul (Pearly Gates) and his "Billy-Bo" Gretsch Jupiter Thunderbird. These are strung with extremely light stings (7s!). It's hard to say which he prefers for slide. It would be reasonable to assume he's sticking to 7-gauge strings as he most often plays slide in standard tuning or open E.

When it comes to amps, Billy has the stadium power rock setup. There might be a huge rack, but it really comes down to a Marshall style amp with some delay, and some Hendrix style octave fuzz with EQ.

In 2015, Billy released his first solo album, *Perfectamundo*, which he followed in 2018 with *The Big Bad Blues* (with his slide making an appearance on *Standing Around Crying*). It shows that after almost 50 years since getting started, he's still full of music.

Let's take a look at some of his licks.

First up is a riff in the style of *Just Got Paid Today*. The key here is wearing the slide on the middle finger to allow you to play fretted notes with the other fingers. This is a big part of Billy's slide playing as he seeks to integrate the slide with his normal playing.

Beginning in open E, there is a driving rhythm on the open strings before a slide up to the 12th fret and down to the 10th. While sitting on this D Major chord, a light vibrato can be applied as you arpeggiate the chord.

This is followed by a classic rock riff, with all the notes fretted, and the slide is reintroduced for the final slide up to the 12th fret.

Example 5a

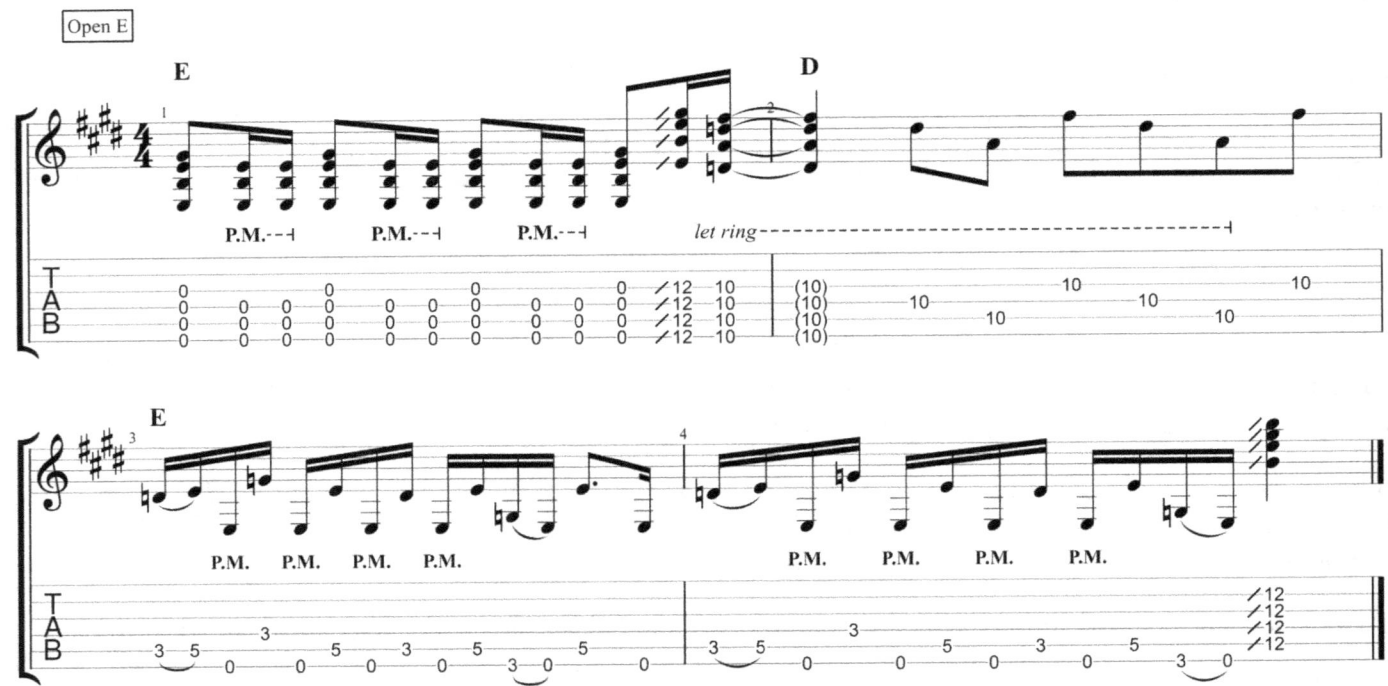

When it comes to soloing, Billy's style is incredibly simple. Instead of choosing to milk as much as he can from some simple, well-integrated ideas, he usually relies on going to areas of the neck where he can play all the notes under the slide.

Example 5b is also in open E tuning and relies on sliding repeatedly between the 17th and 12th frets. With the 12th fret as home, sliding to the 17th fret on the B and G strings highlights the 6th (C#) and root (E) of the underlying E Major chord, both of which sound great.

In the last bar I've indicated a slide down from the 12th fret on the 3rd string. This should be played really slow to give you a mean blues sound.

Example 5b

Another excellent example of sticking to barred positions is this slick little melodic idea that alternates between D Major and A Major, before resolving back to E Major.

An idea like this would be next to impossible in standard tuning, but exploiting the open tuning and using the slide often results in some really easy ways to make music.

Example 5c

By contrast, the following example, inspired by *Sharp Dressed Man*, milks the barred home position to the max, in the same way Duane Allman would have approached it.

The lick is played at the 8th fret over a C Major chord, but you can easily move it to work over other chords (at the 5th fret over A Major, or the 10th fret over D Major, etc).

Refer to the audio to get a feel for just how slow some of the slides are between notes. This is how to make this sound like the blues.

Example 5d

The final example shows how Billy might stray from the barred position when looking for a melody. In this case we are dealing with the turnaround of a 12-bar blues on a faster tune like *Tush*.

Although the chord progression is D Major – C Major – G Major, Billy might treat this as though it's all over a G chord and play the same basic two-fret pattern common to blues rock slide players. The addition here is the shift up three frets to the 18th position on the high E string for a bluesy bend. This note can always be added above your basic home barred position.

Example 5e

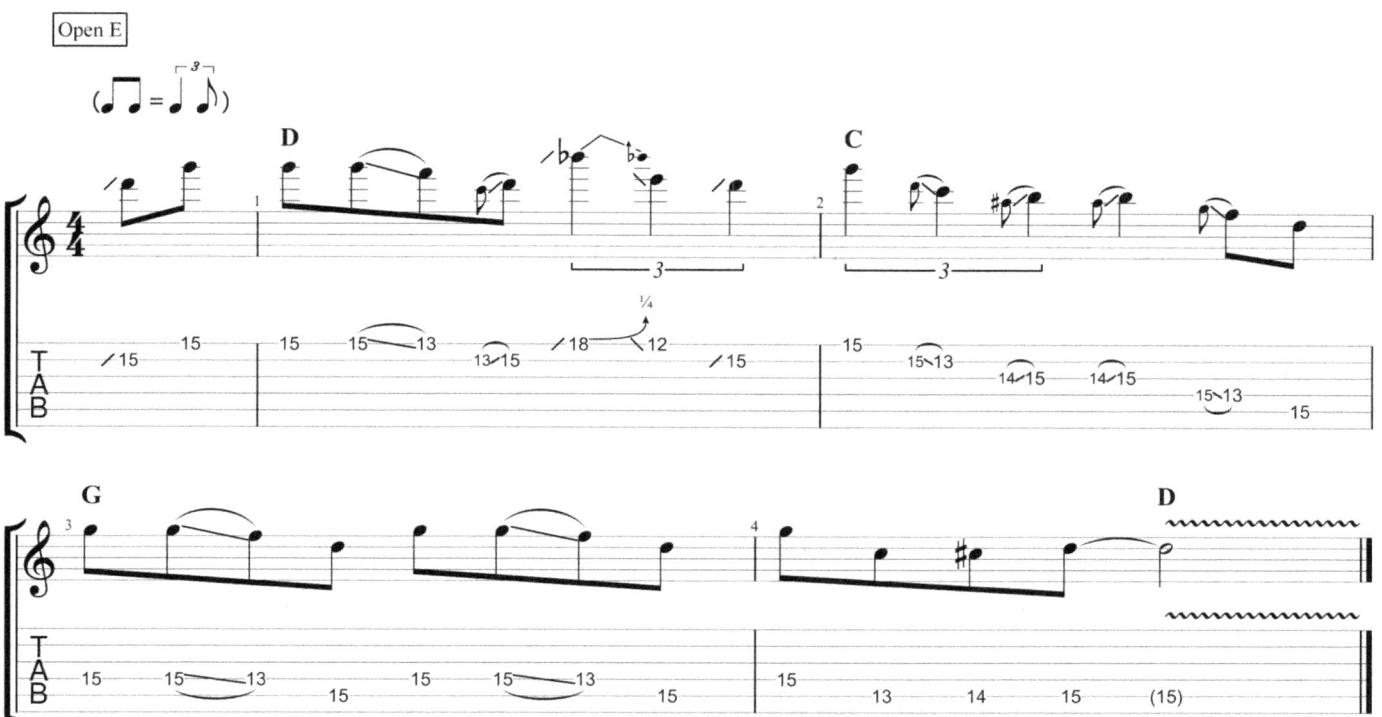

As you've seen, Billy's slide playing isn't advanced by any stretch of the imagination, but that's the beauty of slide guitar: you don't need a whole lot of tricks up your sleeve to create one hell of a sound!

Chapter Six – Warren Haynes

Born in North Carolina in 1960, Warren Haynes grew up on the sound of soul music and as a child sang along to the records of artists like Wilson Pickett and Otis Redding.

He picked up the guitar at the age of 12 and quickly became enamoured with the playing of Eric Clapton. As a singer, Warren was drawn to players who sang through their instruments: "When I listen to Bonnie Raitt or B.B. King, their voice is an extension of their instrument. All my life I have been looking for a guitar sound that is compatible with my voice."

After playing extensively in his home State, at the age of 20 Haynes landed a gig with Country music legend David Allen Coe. The gig lasted for 4 years and during this period Haynes rubbed shoulders with many industry pros and friends of Coe, one of whom was Dickey Betts, the surviving guitarist from the Allman Brothers (who had been in hiatus since 1982).

This friendship would result in Haynes joining Betts on his 1988 album, *Pattern Disruptive*, and becoming the obvious choice for guitar when Betts and Gregg Allman reformed the Allman Brothers in 1989 for their 20th anniversary. During this period the group released three studio albums: *Seven Turns* (1990), *Shades of Two Worlds* (1991) and *Where it All Begins* (1994), along with multiple live albums.

While this period of the group's history brought them to the attention of a new generation of music fans, relationships in the band were tense as both Betts and Allman spiralled out of control. This was exacerbated by an extensive touring schedule.

During this time Warren disbanded his Warren Haynes Band (with whom he'd released *Tales of Ordinary Madness* in 1993), and formed Gov't Mule with Allman Brothers band bassist Allen Woody. The Southern rock jam band found popularity with their self-titled 1995 album, which would lead to Warren opening Allman Brothers shows with Gov't Mule, then going on to play with the Allman Brothers later that night.

However, the internal friction in the band was enough to force Warren to leave the Allman Brothers, and he went out to make it with his new outfit.

While on his travels, Haynes got to play with Phil Lesh of the Grateful Dead (the iconic American jam band where Jerry Garcia made his name), and this eventually led to the reformation/evolution of the band under the moniker of The Dead, with Warren taking on guitar duties.

Warren re-joined the Allman Brothers after Betts left, this time alongside slide maestro Derek Trucks. Together they released just one studio album, 2003's *Hittin' the Note*, but as a band they would regularly perform right up to their final gig in 2014. When all is said and done, Warren played with the Allman Brothers for 22 years – as long as founding member Dickey Betts! So as far as having an influence on the group, Warren was very much a part of their DNA.

Warren owns a wide array of guitars, but much of his collection consists of Gibsons. While he can be seen with a Firebird, SG, or ES-335, Haynes is a Les Paul guy at heart and often plays his own signature model by Gibson, strung with 10-46 strings.

For amplification, he generally uses a Marshall style amp – usually a Diaz CD-100 and a Soldano SLO-100.

Warren favours a glass slide on his ring finger and uses a selection of tunings, but often opts for standard tunings, which he says, "…gave me more of my own voice. I could play stuff that was less conventional and less traditional."

Now, onto the licks!

First is a rock riff in standard tuning that uses the G Minor Pentatonic scale (G, Bb, C, D, F) with a combination of fretted notes and the slide. While this could easily be played with just the slide, Warren would use his fingers for more precise double stops, then the slide when he wants to add vibrato.

In the notation/TAB here, the notes with vibrato are played with the slide, while the rest are fretted. The key to nailing this lick is to make sure the slides into the notes are at the right speed for maximum effect.

Example 6a

In Warren's lead playing, you'll see a wonderful combination of traditional Allman-style slide influence and some of his own cool ideas.

The following example works over a typical rock jam in E Minor, using notes of the E Dorian mode (E, F#, G, A, B, C#, D) and can be seen as two separate ideas.

First is the open position lick part, sliding a picked note down a scale tone, then executing a pull-off to an open string. It takes a while to get the hang of pulling-off with the slide, but don't skip over this technique.

The second part of the applies pull-offs to an ascending line on the high E string. While this could obviously be fretted, using the slide allows you to subtly slide into the notes before the final slide up with vibrato.

Example 6b

Playing in standard tuning often means that some of those classic open tuning licks require a bit more work with the slide, as demonstrated in the next example.

This D Major pentatonic lick will give you an idea of how Warren deals with the limitations of standard tuning. The first measure translates pretty well, but the second measure (a classic Duane Allman style lick) is much trickier in this tuning. When you listen to Warren, his playing is rarely pitch perfect, but that's all part of the attitude.

The final part of the lick demonstrates Warren's willingness to fret notes when the slide presents too many problems. Fret the double stop-before sliding up to end the phrase higher on the neck.

Example 6c

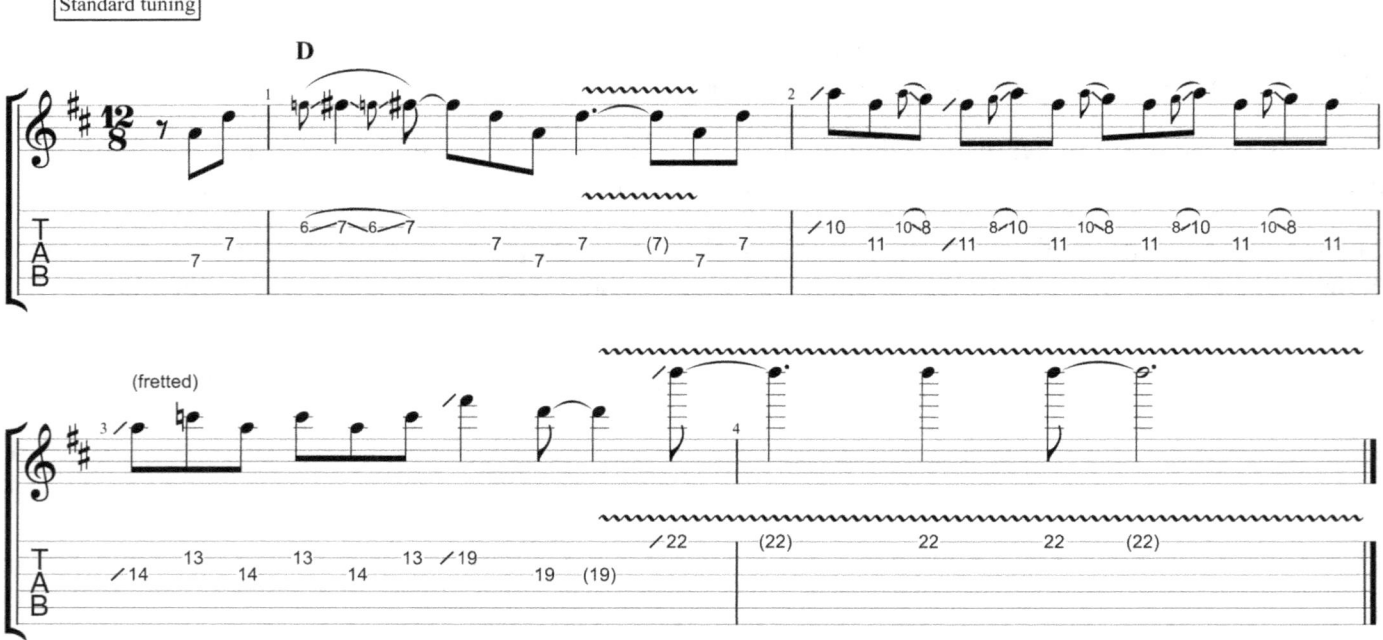

Here's an idea Warren might play over some diatonic chord changes: F Major – C Major – G Major.

Despite all the chords belonging to the key of C Major, it's the G Major that feels like "home". But rather than picking one scale to fit over everything, here it makes sense to treat each chord as a new harmonic event. Analyse things a bit deeper and you'll see that over the F Major chord, the line slides into an A note (the 3rd of the chord). Over the C Major, there is a slide to an E (the 3rd of C Major), and over the G chord, a slide to a D (the 5th of G Major). Each time a chord lands, the note that is played happens to be in the chord and sounds good… there might be something to this!

Example 6d

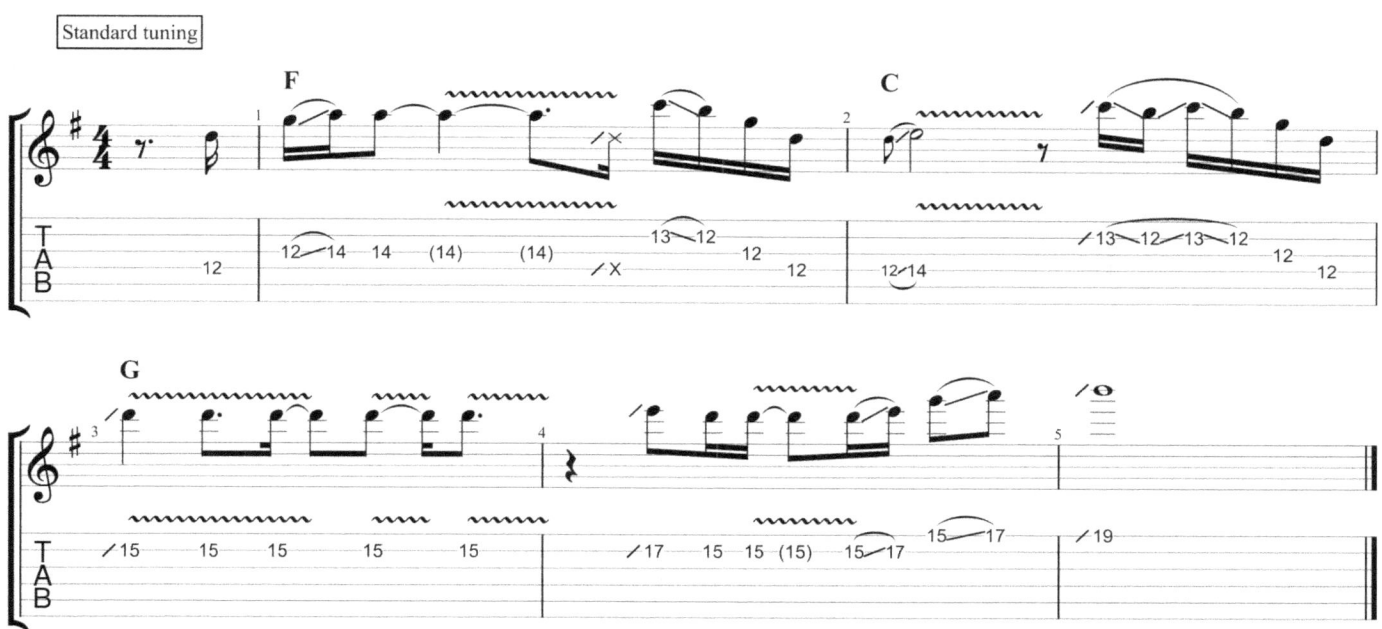

The final example repeats the previous chord progression, but showcases the extreme range Warren likes to use when soloing, often going way beyond where his fretboard ends.

In bar 4, as the melody moves towards the F Major chord, it makes sense to land on an F note – the root of the chord. This moves down a semitone and leads nicely to E, the 3rd of C Major, followed by a slide way up to the 27th fret and a G note (the root of the G Major chord).

A nice aggressive vibrato is essential here. It will help to mask the pitch you're aiming for and make the listener's ear do some of the legwork.

Example 6e

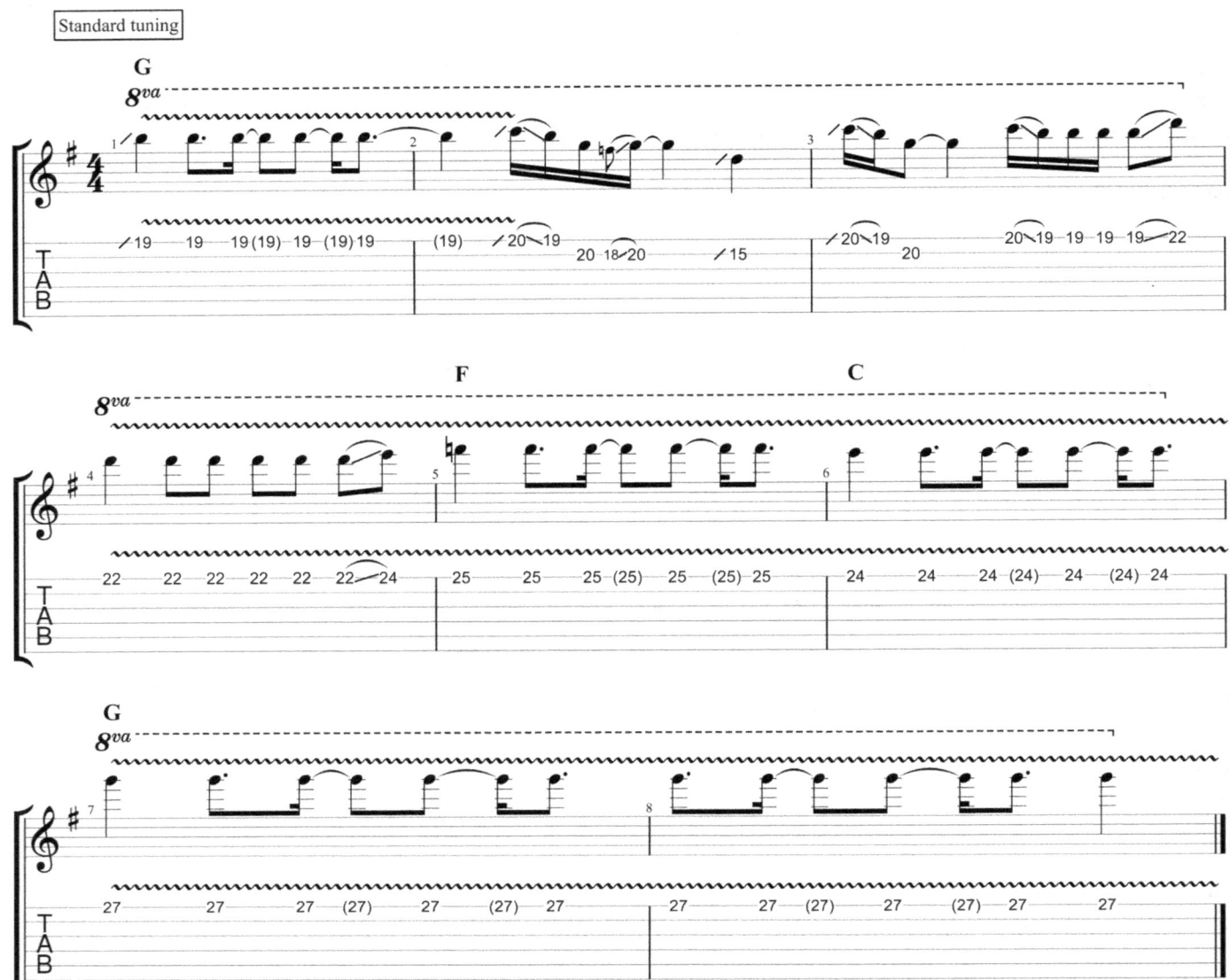

239

Chapter Seven – Son House

Eddie James "Son" House Jr, was born in Mississippi in 1902, making him one of the undeniable fathers of the slide guitar tradition.

House led an interesting life and grew up in an time where there were still people who had lived through the era of slavery. Like many people with similar roots, religion became a big part of his identity. Verifiable records of his youth are hard to come by (as we'll see), but we do know that he worked as a preacher and had a disdain for secular music. He said, "I didn't like no guitar when I first heard it. Oh gee, I couldn't stand a guy playin' a guitar. I didn't like none of it."

Nevertheless, Son picked up the guitar around the age of 25 and, after making a little bit of money, he would focus his efforts into a career in music.

With music came drink, however, and in 1928 House shot a man dead at a party and was convicted of murder.

Somehow he managed to get out of his sentence after just a year, on condition that he left town. He relocated to Clarksdale and formed a friendship with fellow Delta blues guitar legend, Charley Patton. While the two shared a mutual love of music and booze, it's said that they were very different men and would argue often. Ultimately their respect for each other won through and Charley helped launch House's career when he joined him for a recording session for Paramount in 1930.

While these recordings weren't a huge success at the time, they were enough for respected ethnomusicologist Alan Lomax to seek House out in 1941 to record more for the Library of Congress.

The first thing you may notice here is more than a decade elapsed between these records. It's widely thought that House all but put the guitar down during this period. Some would say it was due to the constant internal struggle of being a man of God playing "the Devil's music". Others say it was a combination of missing fame and his friend Patton dying in 1934.

Such gaps weren't uncommon in House's history, and after making these recordings Son disappeared again, only to be found onve more by a group of blues enthusiasts and researchers in 1964! Having clocked up 20 years away from the guitar (Son seemed quite cheerful about this), the group eventually managed to persuade Son House to be Son House again.

He remained reasonably active in music from this time until Alzheimer's and Parkinson's disease forced him to hang up his guitar in 1976. He settled down in Detroit and passed away in the October of 1988, succumbing to cancer of the larynx.

When it comes to his sound, House's trademark was his National resonator guitar. Aside from this, it was just Son's fingers and a metal slide (worn on the middle finger) that did all the talking. He was known to play in both open G and open D tuning.

Son was a man who lived the blues. When he performed it, he wasn't playing a scale he read in a book, he was telling his story. There's nothing more authentic than that. Son House WAS the blues.

Let's take a look at some of his licks!

I want to preface these examples by saying that Son's playing is the hardest to emulate in this entire book. Not because of its technical challenges, but because his playing is so loose that it's easy to sound TOO clean when playing in his style. My advice is, just let it all ring out!

First up is a riff similar to that heard on his iconic *Death Letter Blues*.

Bend the note on the 3rd fret with your finger before switching to the slide for all other notes. When sliding into the 5th fret on the 1st string, let it ring out and play the 5th string against it to drive the rhythm on. This isn't exactly what House played, but the focus here is playing a note on the high string with a slide and letting the other strings ring out.

Example 7a

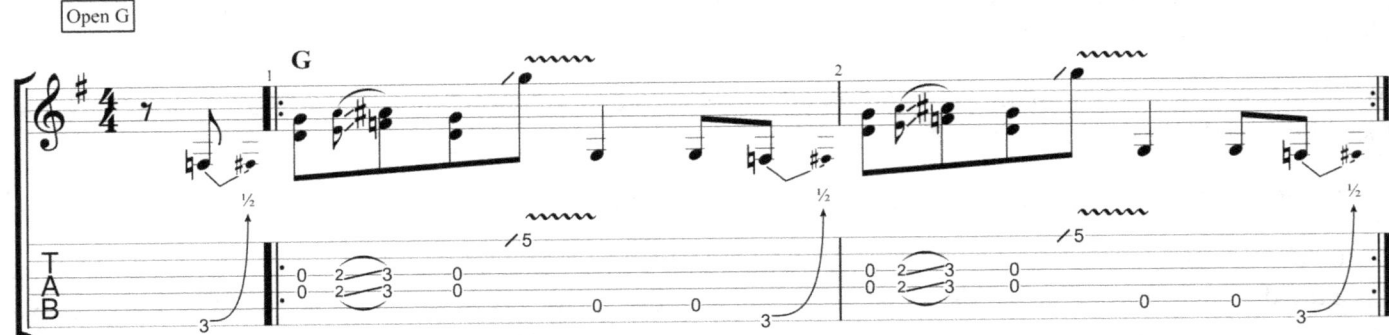

The next example is almost identical to the previous one, but attempts to capture some more of the flavour of House's playing.

Whereas in the previous example each note was picked with precision, here I'm strumming with my index and middle fingers, and putting an aggressive accent on the downstrokes.

When the slide note rings out, you can dig in and add some real noise underneath it to push the riff along.

Example 7b

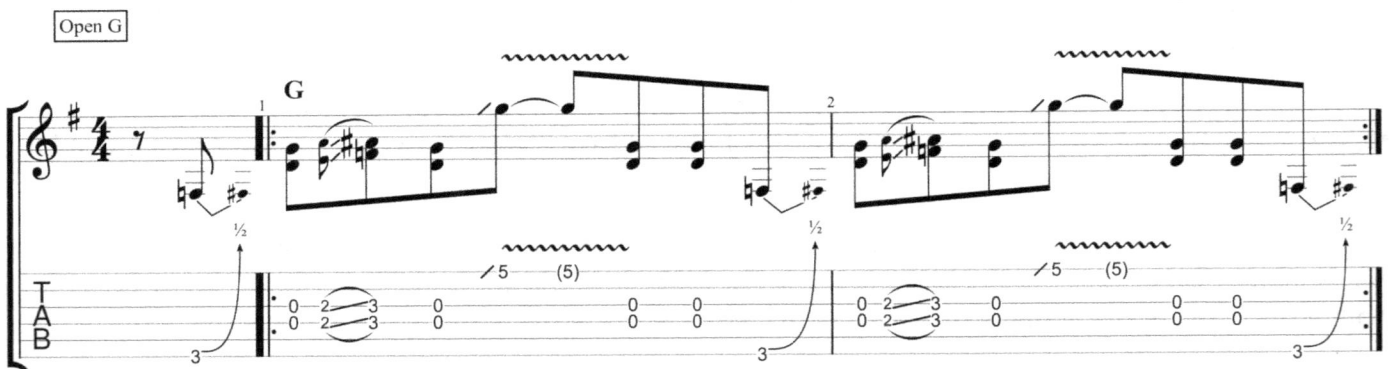

Here's another slow blues riff, now in open D tuning.

The goal here is to really *hit* the guitar. Make noise. On its own this can sound a little odd, but in context – with Son's powerful voice bellowing over the top – it's quite a sound!

Example 7c

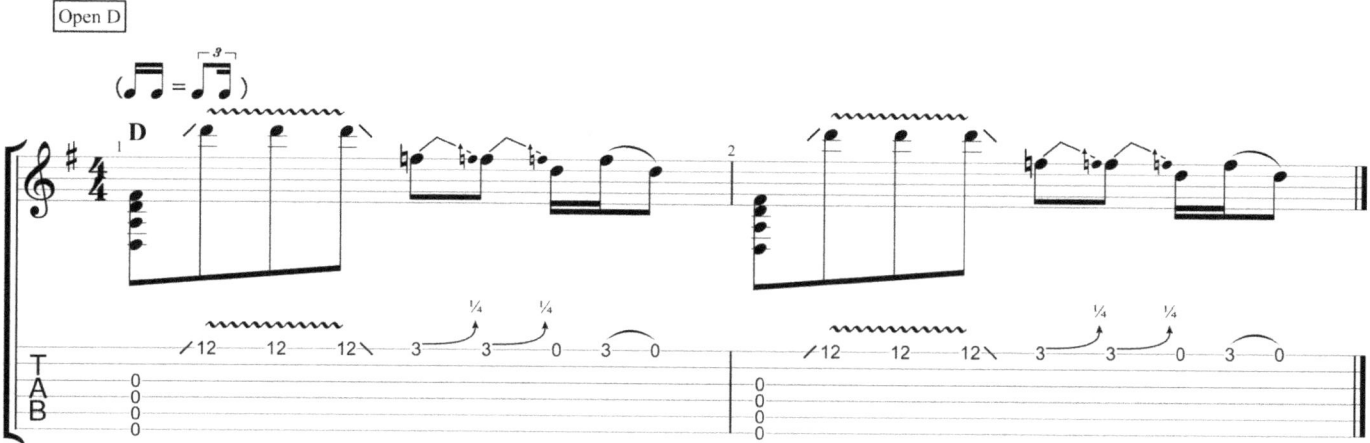

While Son's ideas are difficult to execute in the same he would have played them, it doesn't mean they are complicated, as demonstrated by the following lick.

This is similar to something Son might sing over. The idea simply requires you to repeatedly slide into the 12th fret and add a decent amount of vibrato. This doesn't need to be in tune, it just needs to be played with passion!

Example 7d

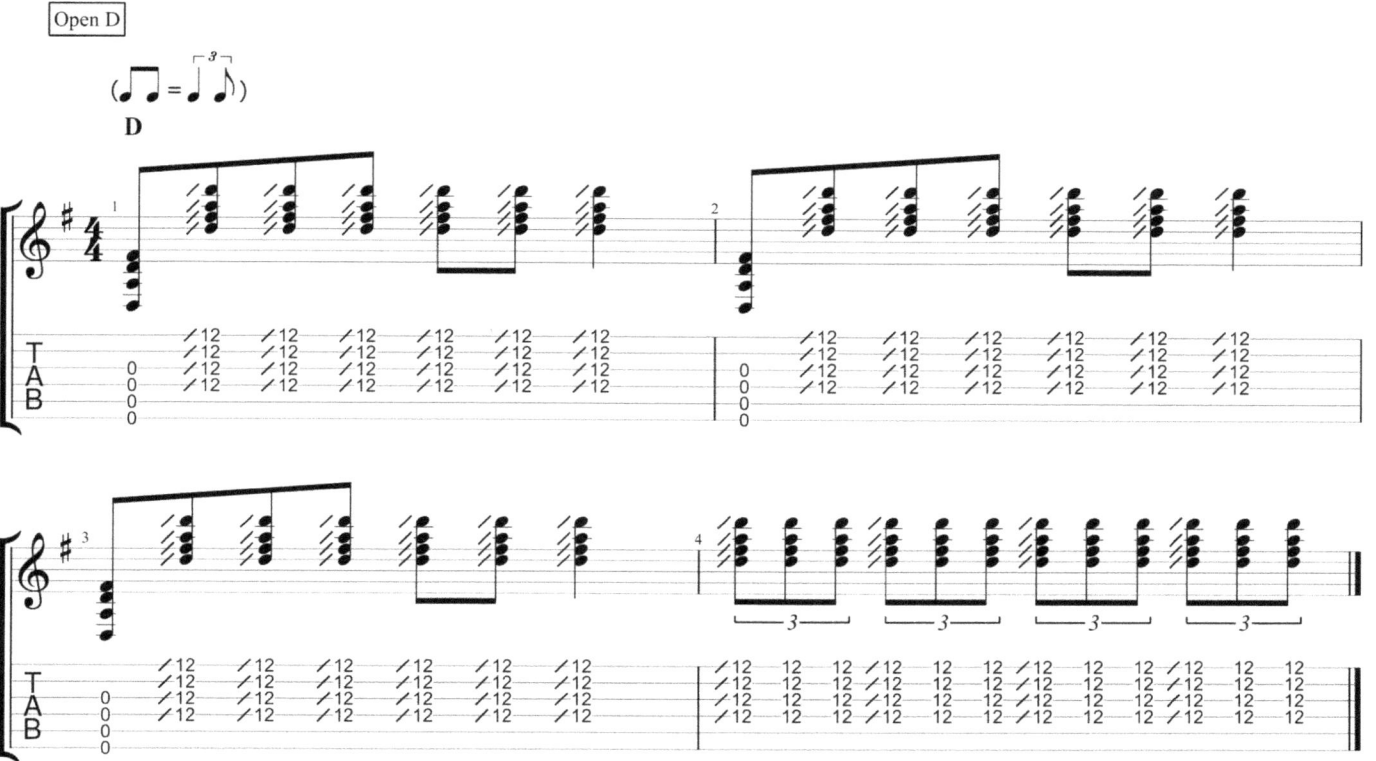

The final lick shows House's simple approach to outlining chord changes, this time in open G tuning.

In the key of G Major, we're moving from the IV chord (C), back to the I (G). In order to do this, Son would slide into the 5th fret area (home position for the IV chord), then down to the open position for a simple two note blues lick.

Example 7e

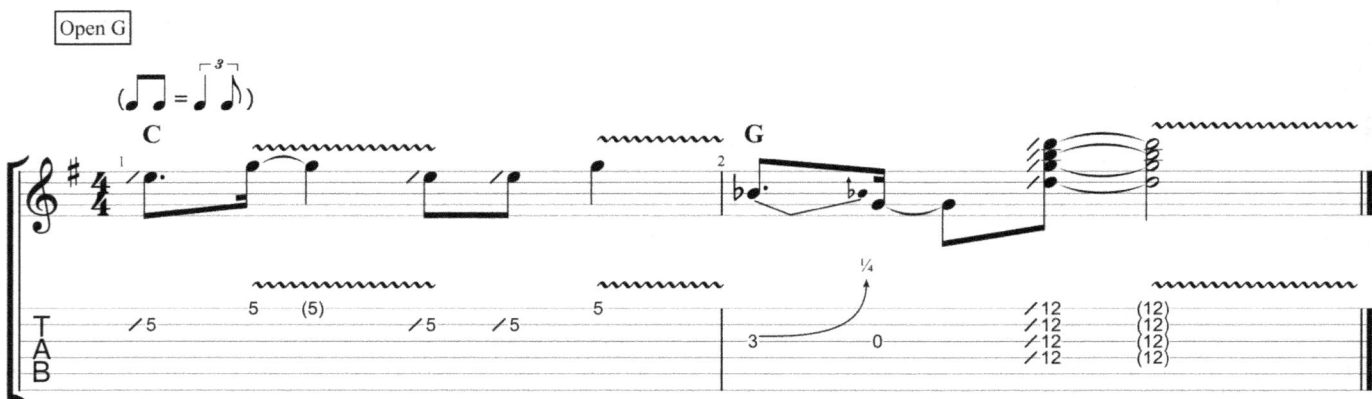

There's no denying the simplicity of Son's guitar playing, but if you spend some time listening to his recordings, you'll quickly understand how the power of his voice carried his career. As far as Delta blues guitarists go, there's not many better than Son House.

Chapter Eight – Elmore James

Elmore James (originally Elmore Brooks) was born in Mississippi in 1918.

James picked up music around the age of 12, playing the diddley bow (a single-string instrument consisting of a string stretched over a wooden board). By 14 he was out playing on the weekends and finding his sound by developing the ideas of those who influenced him, such as Robert Johnson and Tampa Red.

Despite playing regularly, James's recording career didn't begin until 1950, after the war (where James served in the Navy).

His first record was *Dust My Broom*, released in 1952, which was a surprise success. In large part this was due to the unique sound he'd crafted for himself, due to his work as a radio repairman. His skills allowed him to modify amplifiers to run at breaking point.

James bounced from record label to record label, recording 29 singles in total, but this was enough to land him the title of The King of Slide Guitar among music fans of the day. He was an influence on early Rock 'n' Roll music and the blues explosion of the '60s. One only needs to listen to a record like *The Sky Is Crying* to get a feel for just how ahead of his time he was.

Unfortunately, he wouldn't be around to see the extent of his huge influence, as he passed away of a heart attack in 1963 aged just 45.

There are very few pictures of Elmore, but we can see that he played a Silvertone 1361 and he appeared to wear a brass slide on his pinky finger. He often used open E and open D tunings.

James's slide influence is undeniabl. Many of the licks he pioneered became staples, played by everyone who picked up a slide after him.

Let's look at some of them!

It would be impossible to talk about Elmore James and ignore his most influential lick: the classic intro to *Dust My Broom*.

Begin by sliding into the 12th fret on the top 4 strings and apply a subtle vibrato as you continue to pick the chord. After you've created a strong sense of the underlying chord, it's time for a simple, single-note melody using the 12th fret home position and notes found two frets below. The licks aren't particularly refined, it's about sliding into that 12th fret knowing that it sounds good.

Example 8a

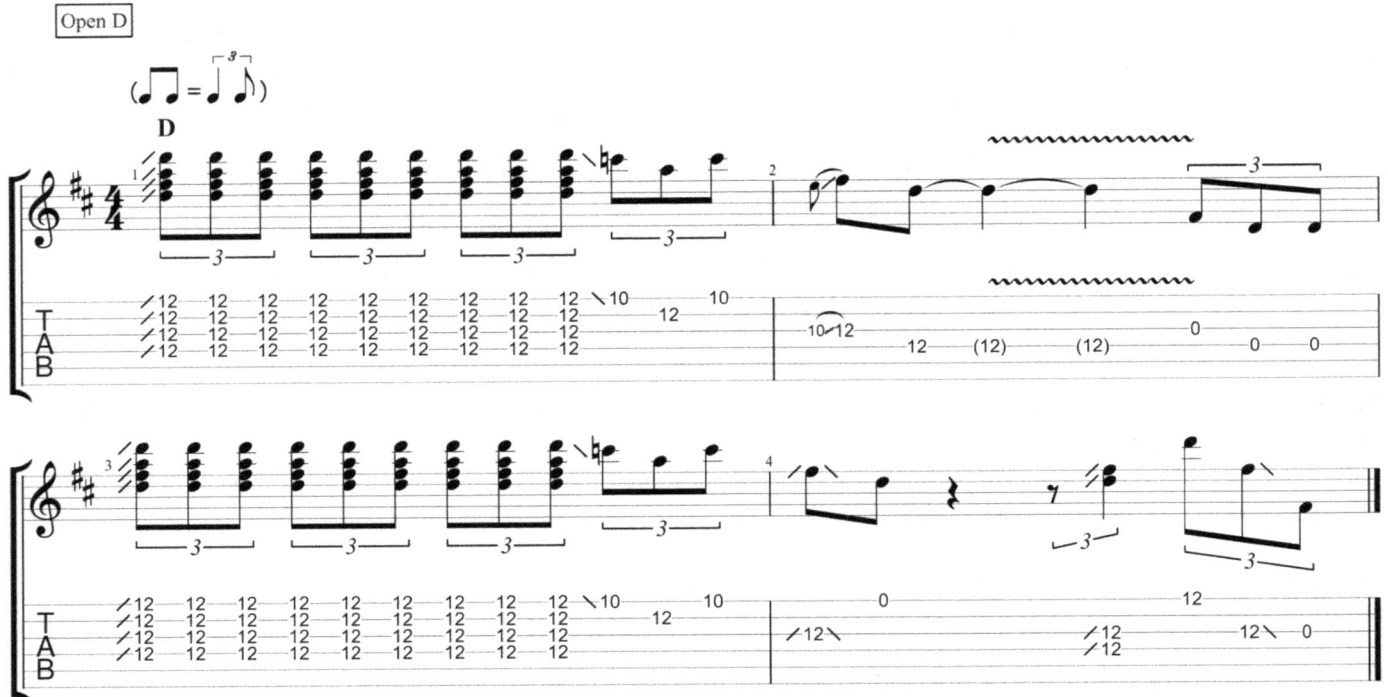

As one of the pioneers of single-note slide guitar soloing, James' licks are far from complicated. Most often he would stick to the basic home position and approach these notes from two frets below.

The following example would usually be played over the first four bars of a blues, though you could play this over the second four bars too.

The secret to making something like this your own is how you phrase it. Elmore slides so slowly between notes that using slides in the TAB felt wrong. Instead I opted for bends, but it's still all slide!

Example 8b

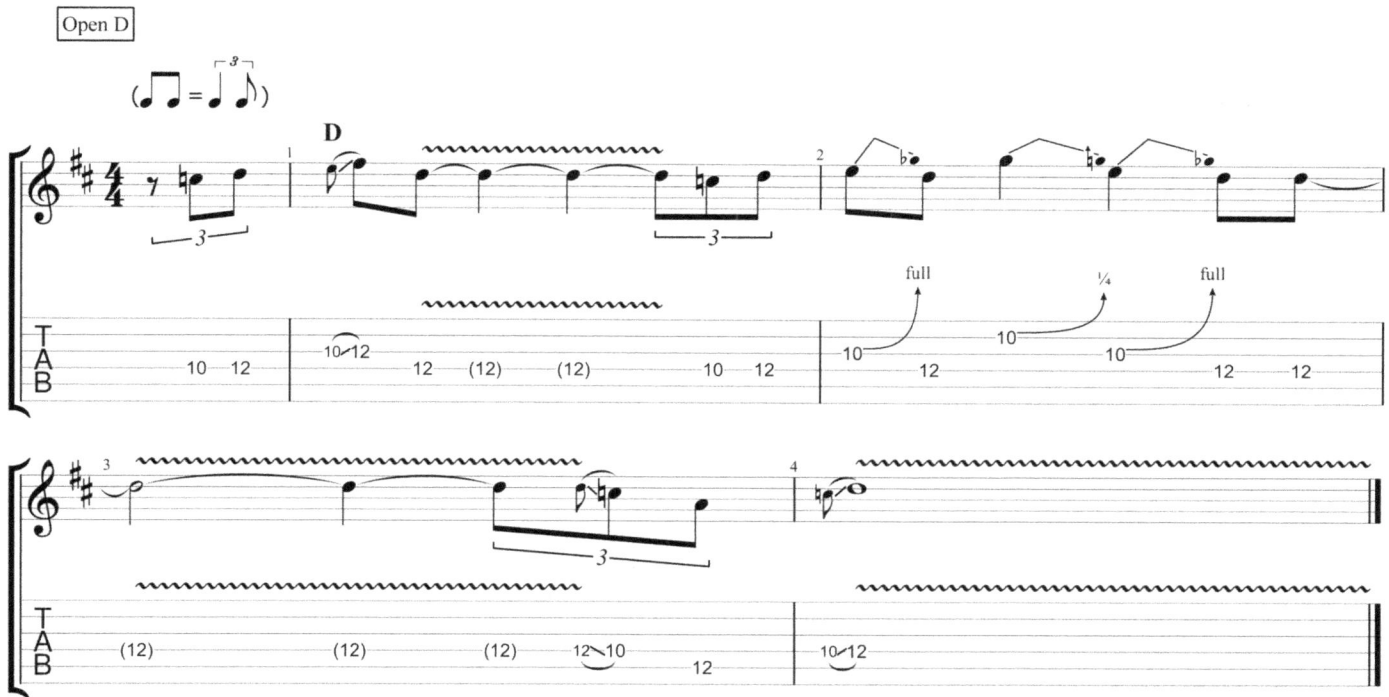

The next example is played over the last four bars of our blues in D Major and combines the same two-fret pattern from before with a great little turnaround/ending in the last two bars.

In bar 3, the descending chromatic note on the 5th string should be fretted. This will allow you to play the open 1st string against it before using the slide again to slide up to the 11th and 12th frets.

The lick finishes with a typical ending, but if you wanted this to be a turnaround, then instead of sliding to the 11th and 12th frets to play the root note, you can slide to the 6th/7th frets to play the V chord which pulls you back to the start of the blues progression.

Example 8c

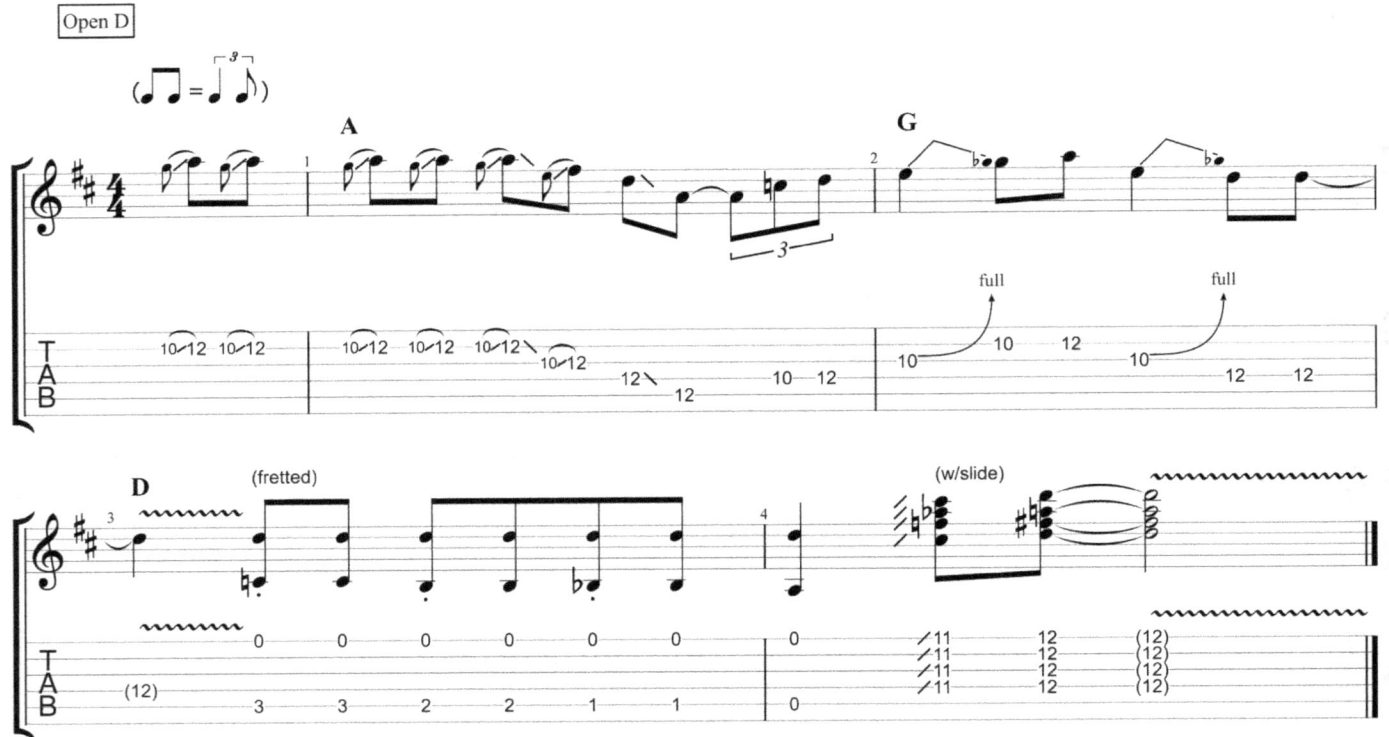

Here's another blues intro in D using nothing more than the home position at the 12th fret and the notes found two frets below. Again, I've opted to use a combination of slides and bends in the notation, with the bends indicating a slow, bluesy slide.

Regarding the rhythms, I've notated this in 12/8 time and used some 4:3 tuplets. This is all very complicated and not something Elmore would have thought about – it's just a way of trying to explain what's happening. Nothing is set in stone here, just push and pull with the rhythm and express yourself.

Example 8d

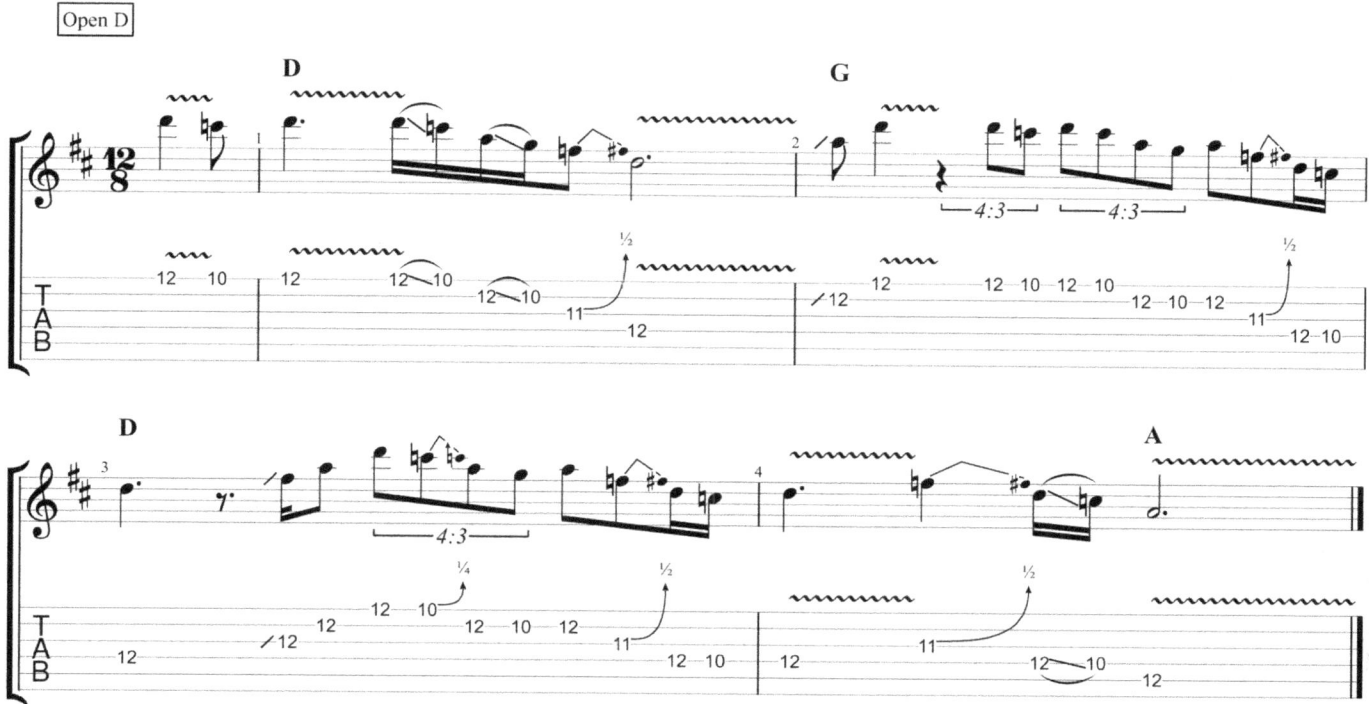

Here's one final idea, this time showcasing one of Elmore's faster repeating licks leading to a blues turnaround. We're still sticking to the home position and adding notes two frets below.

In essence the idea is simple: play the 12th fret, move down to the 10th, then pick the 12th fret on the second string. While easy in theory, doing this with the slide introduces a lot of noise. However, this should be celebrated! It's the noise of transitioning between notes that make this a lick to play and not a great lick to notate!

Example 8e

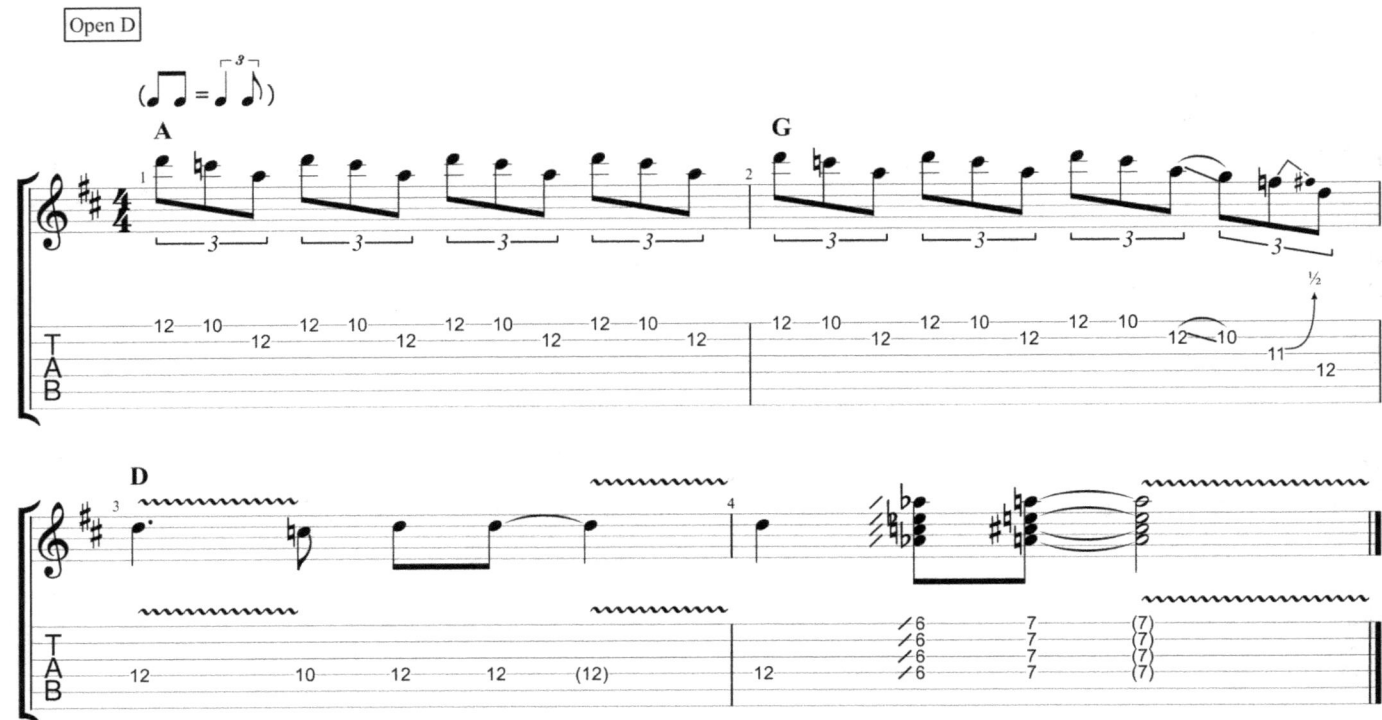

249

Chapter Nine – Robert Johnson

Born in Mississippi in 1911, Robert Johnson is the pinnacle of the Delta blues and wrapped up in the mystery that surrounds the genre.

Despite being widely regarded as a legend, most of what we know of Johnson's life has been pieced together from document research and the people who claimed to have known him, or who knew people who knew him.

It's hard to say when Robert began playing, but we do know that he was hounded for playing secular music – the "Devil's music" as it was known. Robert would eventually let this idea grow, when it became rumoured that his astonishing guitar playing skills and gaunt appearance were a direct consequence of making a deal with the Devil (or perhaps the Haitian Vodou icon Papa Legba) at the crossroads.

From November 1936 to June 1937, Johnson is credited with 41 known recordings, featuring just 29 songs – and that was it. Just as suddenly as he appeared, he was gone. He died of unknown causes in August 1938 at the age of just 27. Nothing was reported at the time and we only know this to be the case because three decades later a musicologist researching Johnson's life discovered his death certificate.

Although his musical output was small, his influence is undeniable, and every great blues guitar player that followed would namecheck the man.

Robert's playing was as steeped in mystery as the man himself. We can't say for certain what guitar he played (though it's widely assumed to be the Gibson L-1 he held in one of only two confirmed authentic pictures of him). It's also impossible to say for certain what type of slide he used or which finger he wore it on. If you want that information, you'll need to go down to the crossroads…

Let's take a look at some of those trademark licks!

First up is a *Crossroads* style turnaround which I've written in open A tuning (though I believe Robert played the original in open A with a capo on the second fret, making everything sound a tone higher).

Begin with a slide into the 12th fret on the top strings, before sliding down to the open position for the classic two note Delta blues lick.

The second half of the lick is a classic Robert Johnson turnaround idea. Fret the notes in bar 3 with the index finger, then shift back to the slide in the final bar.

Example 9a

The thing that fascinates me most when listening to *Crossroads* is something Johnson does in the final two bars – playing a simple slide melody against a steady palm-muted note in the bass. This example explores that idea in a way that will facilitate looping.

First get used to playing a palm-muted open 5th string with your thumb to a metronome. Next, work on adding the melody against that pulse. It will come as no surprise that the melody notes all come from the home position at the 12th fret.

Example 9b

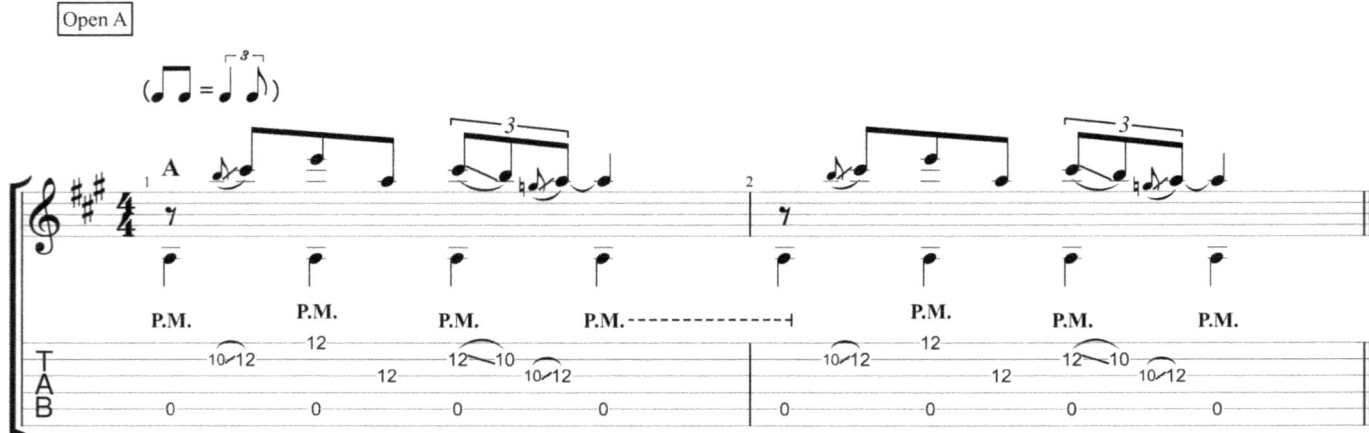

Example 9c explores this idea further, now with a melody that lasts for 2 bars.

As with the previous examples, I've recorded this in open A tuning. If you want to add a capo at the 2nd fret, that will bring you closer to Robert's sound.

Example 9c

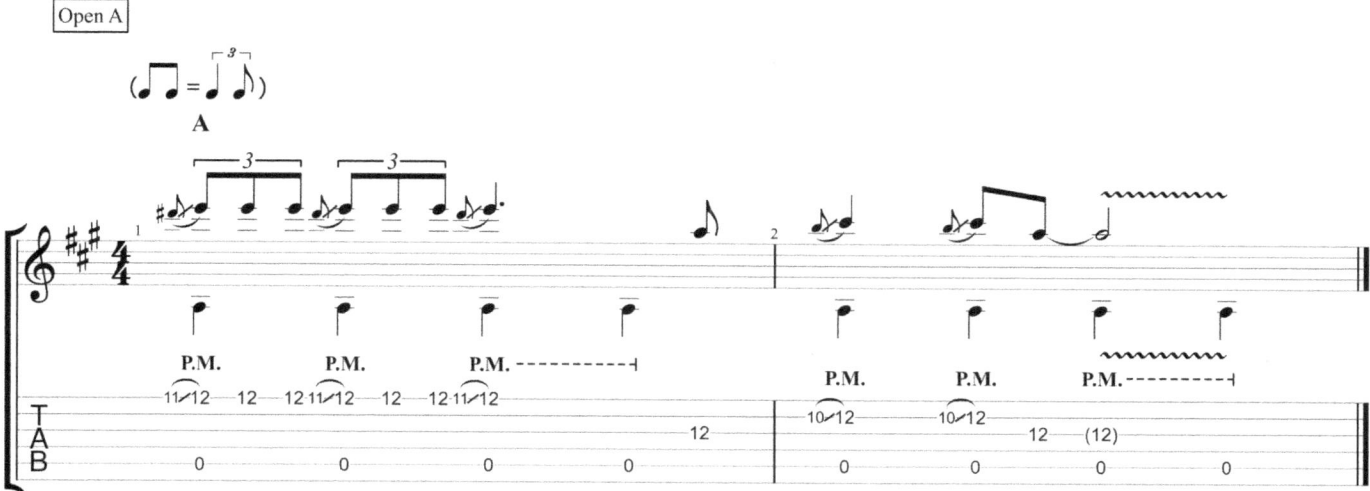

The next lick continues with this idea. It's a turnaround in the style of *Come On In My Kitchen* in open G tuning.

Instead of playing the open 5th string on each beat, this time it's added underneath each of the high melody notes.

Begin by sliding into the 12th fret while playing the open bass note. Then slide down to the open position for a bluesy double-stop idea. This turnaround features the same descending chromatic note, but it's ringing out against the open high string.

Example 9d

The final example draws influence from *Ramblin' On My Mind,* and showcases Robert's love of combining slide melodies at the 12th fret with open position fretted riffs.

Apply a palm mute to all the notes in the open position and use the fretting hand index finger to play the notes at the 2nd fret. Apart from that, each note should be played with the slide.

Example 9e

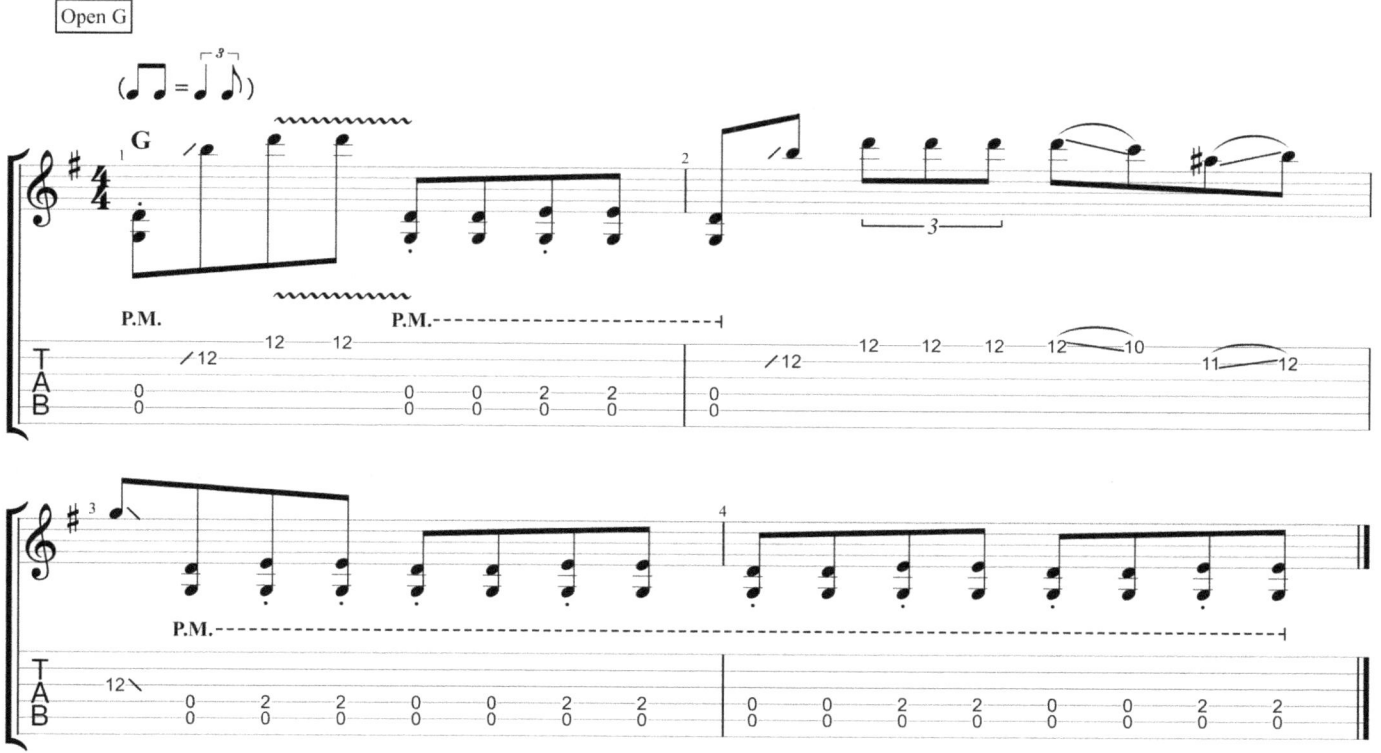

As with each of the true Delta players in this book, it's impossible to nail their styles in just five licks, so do check out my book *Delta Blues Slide Guitar* to dig deeper into this fascinating style.

Chapter Ten – Sonny Landreth

Clyde "Sonny" Landreth was born in 1951 in Mississippi. After spending a few years in Jackson, his family relocated to Lafayette, Louisiana.

Taking his early influences from Scotty Moore and Chet Atkins, Sonny would go on to pioneer modern slide guitar playing, pushing the boundaries of technique as he developed his highly influential style.

Sonny got his start in the mid-to-late 70s as a session player, playing guitar and dobro for many artists including Tommy Bolin, Freddy Fender, Zachary Richard and Marti Jones.

Working in the Louisiana music scene brought a strong *zydeco* influence (a Cajun/Creole jazz blues fusion) to his playing, which can be heard on his 1981 debut, *Blues Attack*.

Landreth would go on to release 16 more albums, with notable efforts including 2008's *From the Reach*, and 2012's *Elemental Journey*.

As a slide player, Sonny is best known for his extensive use of fretting behind the slide to overcome the limitations of open tunings. His playing is that of someone with immense creativity and with the skill to express it to the listener.

Landreth's influence is far reaching and fans include Mark Knopfler, Warren Haynes, Johnny Winter and Eric Clapton. Each has worked with Sonny on record, with Clapton featuring him on multiple Crossroads Guitar Festivals.

For gear, Landreth is a big fan of the Stratocaster and Dumble amps. He uses multiple tunings on his records, but we can say for sure that he's a fan of the Dunlop 215 heavy glass slide, which he wears on his pinky finger.

Let's look at some Landreth-style licks.

First up is an example using Sonny's "Melodic tuning" – an interesting hybrid consisting of the notes E, A, E, A, B and C#. This one is a lot of fun, as the top three strings are tuned to the first three notes of the A Major scale, making melodies very easy to play.

In this example you'll need to lift the fingers behind the slide up, then use the picking hand to pluck the notes between the slide and the nut. This results in a unique, ethereal sound as you add the sympathetic resonance on the other side of the slide. Listen to the recording and you'll see what I mean.

Example 10a

Now we're going to apply a simple Travis picking pattern to this tuning to show just how easy it is to add a great melody to a picked bass pattern.

Use the thumb to alternate between the 5th and 4th string with a palm mute. Pick out the melody over the top, letting it ring, and apply a light vibrato.

The magic of this tuning is that playing the middle 4 strings gives you a sus2 chord. Adding the top string brings the 3rd into play and gives you an add9 chord.

Example 10b

Next up is a slick little solo idea in open G tuning that showcases Sonny's fretting behind the slide style.

Begin by sliding into the 12th fret on the top string. To play the note on the 10th fret, keep the slide positioned at the 12th fret and use the index finger to press the string down behind the slide. Each time you see a note in brackets in the TAB, that's requires fretting behind the slide.

Example 10c

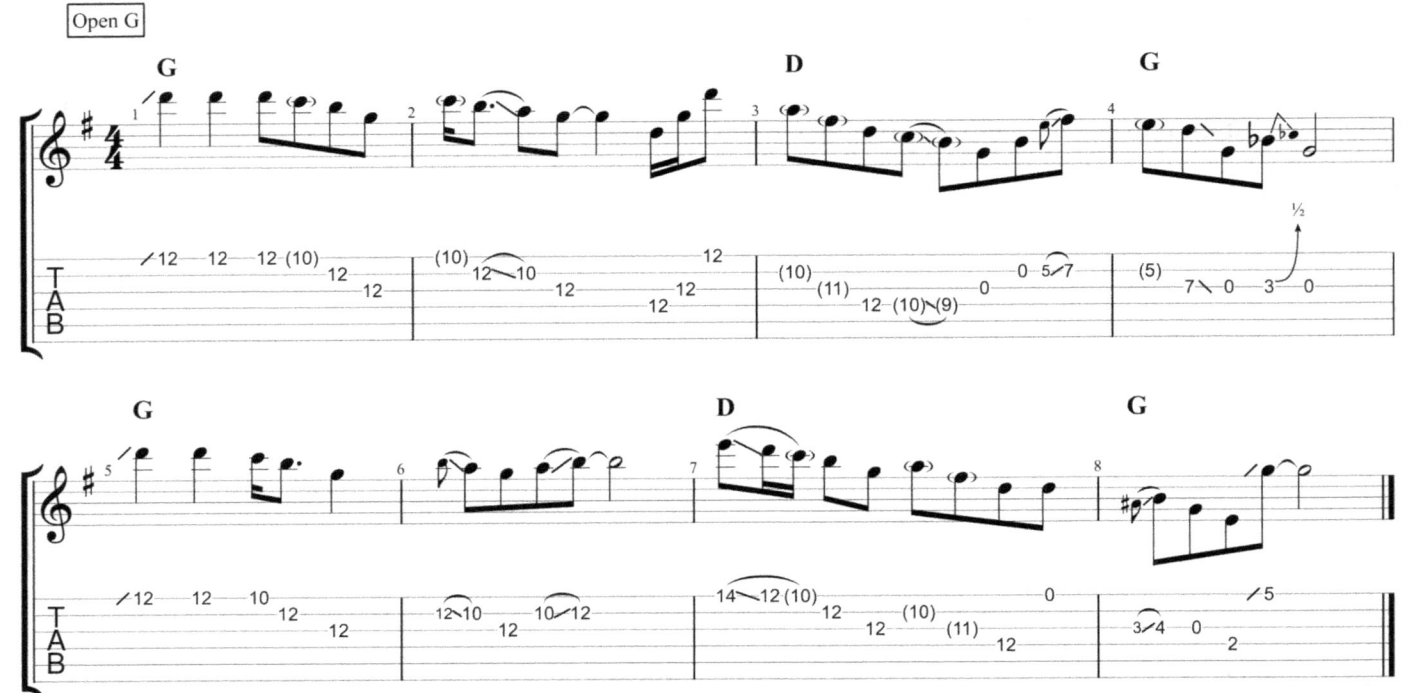

Example 10d takes this idea even further and applies the concept to whole chords!

This is almost impossible to pull off with the slide on any finger other than the pinky, so give it a go. Pay careful attention to the TAB and fret everything in brackets behind the slide. This should be relatively obvious as (thankfully!) the slide stays at the 12th fret.

Add some light vibrato to taste and prepare to wow your friends.

Example 10d

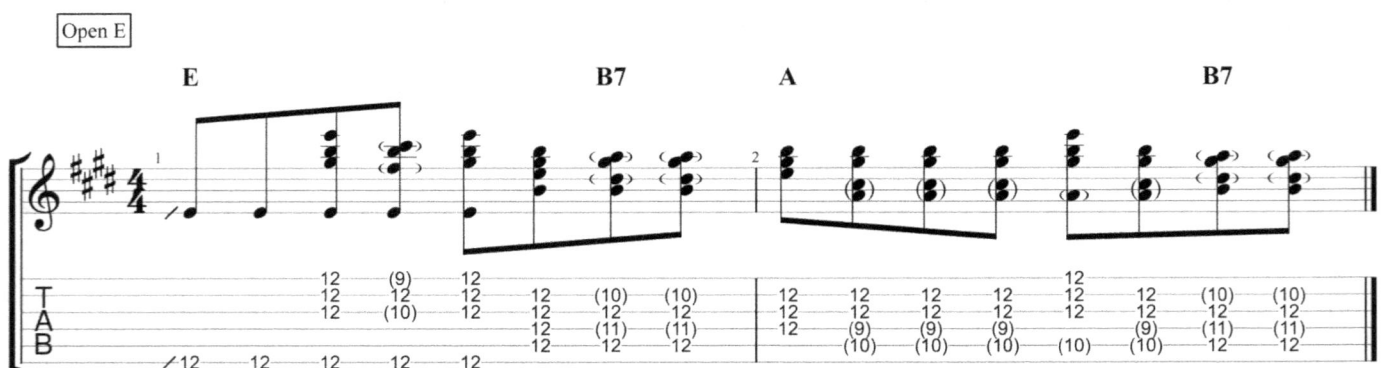

Our final lick showcases just how awesome fretting behind the slide can be when you want to add a burst of speed to a solo.

Begin by tuning to open G Minor (D, G, D, G, Bb, D).

The trick here is to pull off from the note behind the slide before returning to the slide – that's right, a pull-off! Although the pitch is going up, in order to execute this cleanly you need to really pull off from the fretted 10th fret note, rather than just lifting your finger.

Aside from this technical aspect, the lick is relatively simple… it's just very fast! Take your time with it and get to grips with the fingering slowly, then build up speed over time.

Example 10e

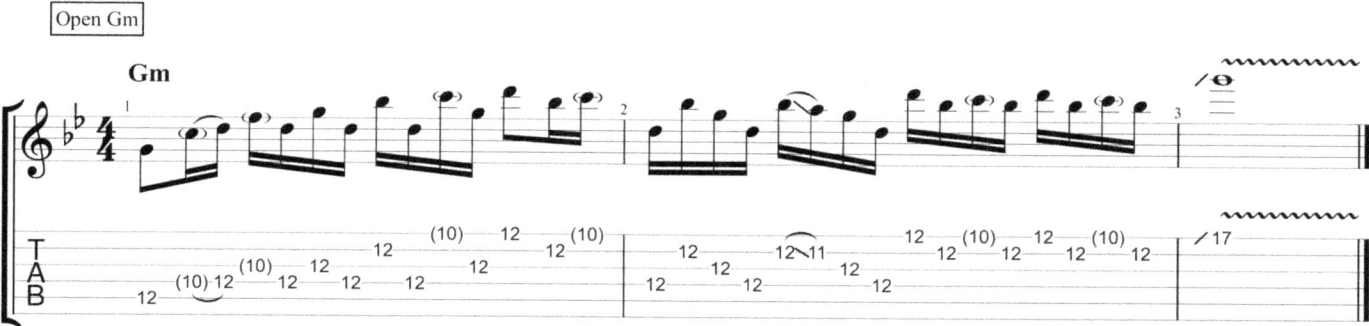

Chapter Eleven – Joey Landreth

Another of the young, promising stars of slide guitar, Joey Landreth (amazingly no relation to Sonny Landreth!) was both in 1987, in Winnipeg, Canada.

Another child prodigy, Joey picked up the guitar aged around 7, when his father salvaged a Maya Telecaster.

Joey worked hard and found himself a niche as a desirable session musician due to his unique sound on the guitar, but fame came when he formed The Bros Landreth with his brother David. The group released *Let it Lie* in 2013 and picked up an American distribution deal in 2014. This would result in heavy touring around the US and Canada, finding an audience anywhere they went.

While this was happening, Joey continued to write and would release his own EP, *Whiskey* in 2017, and follow it up with his debut album, *Hindsight*, in 2019.

Although he's not been around for long, Joey exists in a time where access to music is easy. It's easy to find incredible live-in-the-studio videos and gear demos with a quick search on YouTube. Look up Joey Landreth and you'll find it's absolutely worth your time, as he's one of the most incredible musicians walking the earth. I appreciate that sounds like hyperbole, but give him a chance…

Joey mostly plays guitar in an open C tuning, though not the common C, G, C, G, C, E. Instead, he takes open D as his starting point and moves it down a tone, resulting in C, G, C, E, G, C – a trick he picked up from fellow guitar player Champagne James Robertson.

His choice to play in an open tuning at all times means he's had to learn how to get by playing covers, no matter what the chords. As such, he's developed an incredible ability to play harmony in the tuning, and not be slowed down by the slide. He's fluent in playing over changes and makes extensive use of fretting behind the slide to make this work when not playing a major chord. For strings, he's using 19, 22, 26, 42, 52 and 65 with a regular high action. He wears his signature Rock Slide brass slide on his pinky finger.

Let's look at his incredible playing!

First up is a typical rhythm guitar example Joey might play. It showcases how fluently he frets while playing slide, and also his impressive chord vocabulary (the open major tuning doesn't get in the way of any chord sound!)

The lick begins with some resonant vibrato at the 12th fret. Just place your slide there and apply vibrato without picking. The chord will sound, but very quietly.

The next two bars require you to play with the slide at the 12th fret, while fretting behind the slide at the 9th and 10th frets. Again, I've used brackets around these notes to help indicate the use of a fretting hand finger.

After sliding into an F chord, three bars are played without the slide. Here you'll find a great minor triad voicing for this tuning, along with a beautiful open string melody which you can really let ring.

Finally, when you get back to the low open string, it's back to the slide for a typical open position blues lick.

Example 11a

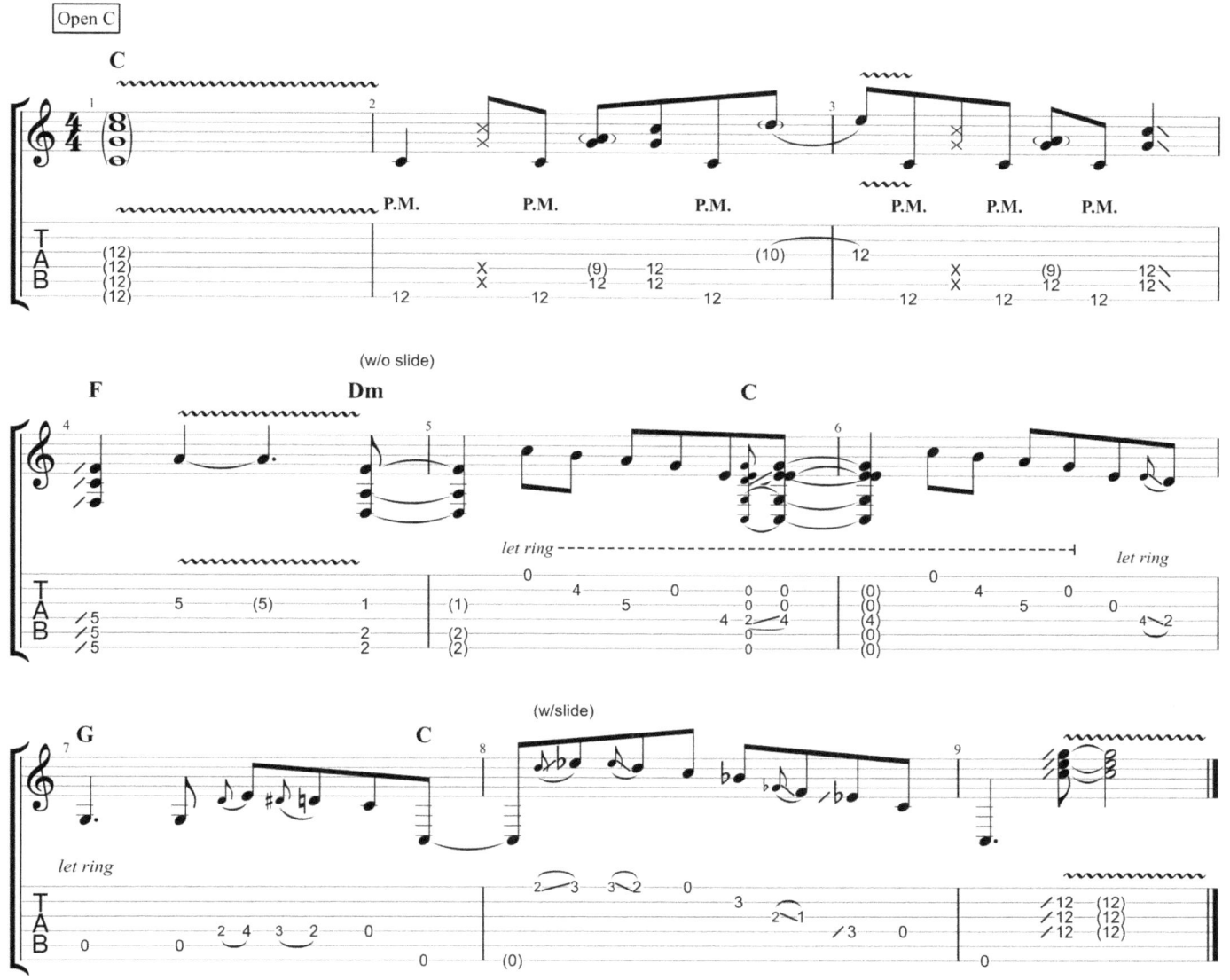

Next up is a lick that really focuses on fretting behind the slide. As with the previous example, any notes in brackets are fretted with a finger behind the slide and everything else is played with the slide.

There's a lot going on here, both technically and harmonically. Joey doesn't treat his tuning as a limitation and has a firm grasp of the harmony needed to get by in pop, rock, even jazz. This licks sounds like something between Bach and Charlie Parker… but with a slide! Take your time with it and focus on accurate intonation.

Example 11b

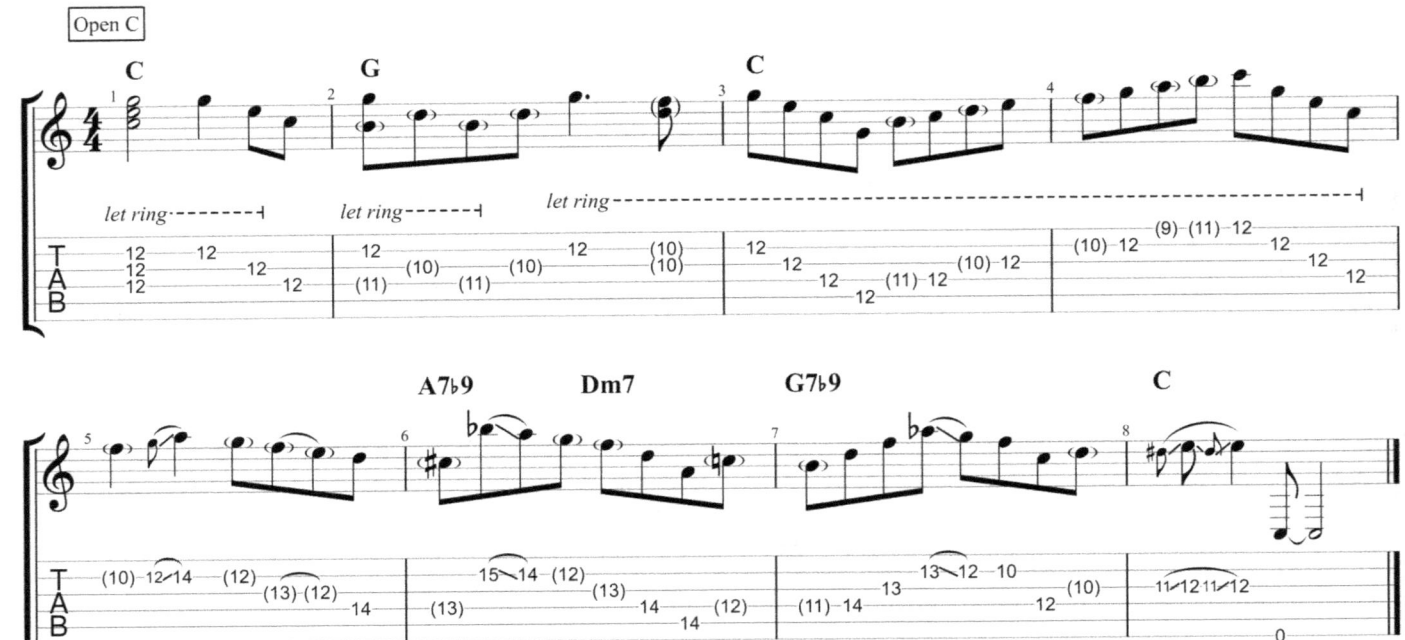

Now you've developed some basic proficiency in fretting behind the slide, here's a lick that takes you from the IV chord (F Major) back to the I chord (C Major) via the iv minor (F minor). Playing these minor triads with the slide alone is impossible, but removing the option from your vocabulary altogether would be a shame.

Bar one sits on an F chord at the 5th fret and features a percussive slap on beats 2 and 4 (indicated in the notation with the * symbol). Next, move up the neck playing the three F minor chord inversions shown, playing the notes in brackets with a fretting hand finger behind the slide. Apply a light vibrato to these chords to imitate a pedal steel guitar.

Example 11c

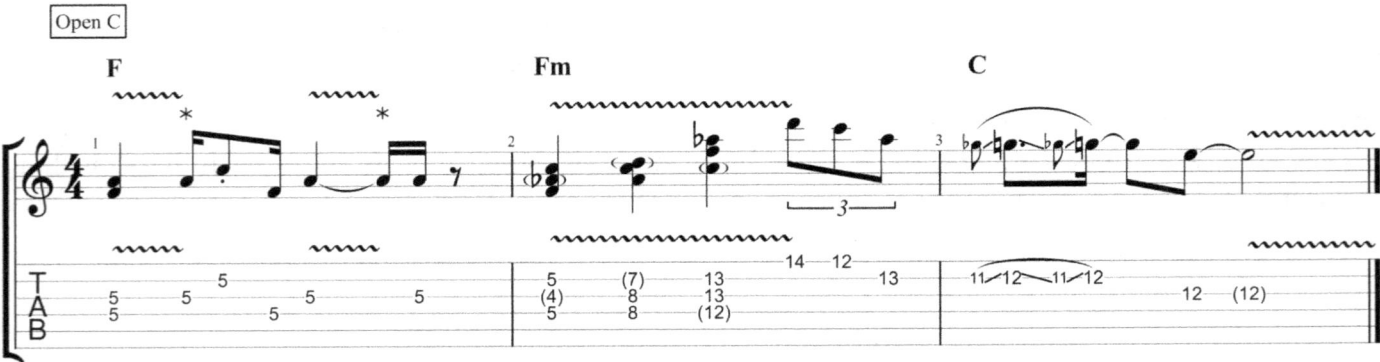

261

Now we have a beautiful jazzy/Gospel chord progression that takes the fretting behind the slide concept to the extreme.

The most important part of the technique of playing behind the slide is understanding that the slide itself must be kept straight in its position. For most chords it's obvious where the slide should sit, but with the F7/A chord it's easy to miss the fact that the slide sits at the 12th fret.

The best part of this idea is the slick movement from the Bb in bar 3, moving though chords back to the Bb. In the bass notes here there's a great descending movement of Bb (over the Bb chord), Ab (over Bb7), G (Eb/G), then Gb (Ebm/Gb). This descending chromatic movement using inversions is beautiful and something you'll absolutely never see from an average slide player.

Example 11d

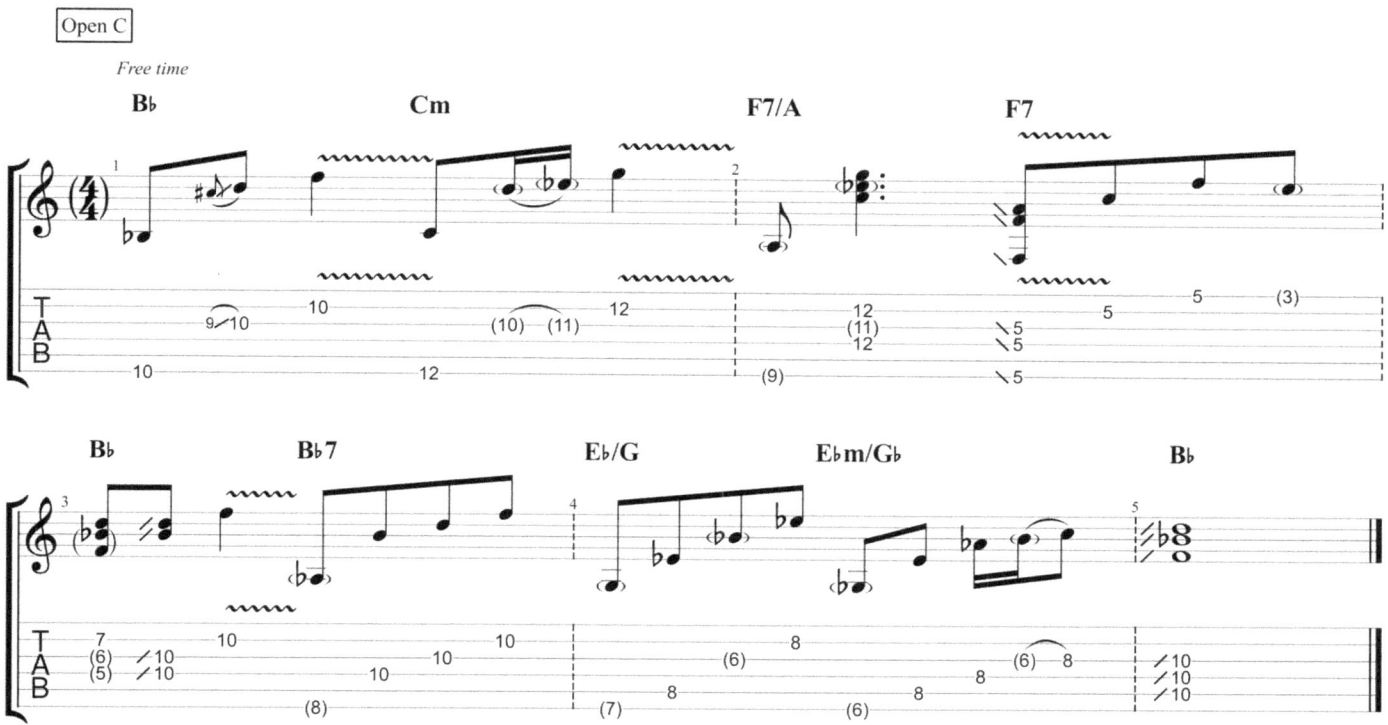

Finally, we move away from fretting behind the slide to look at a lead idea played completely with the slide.

The interesting technique here is the sliding artificial harmonic at the end of the second bar. Place the slide over the 5th fret as normal, but place the index finger of the picking hand on the string over the 17th fret. With the picking finger in place, pluck the string with either the thumb or ring finger. This will create an artificial harmonic an octave higher than the slide. From here, use the slide to shift this note up an octave by sliding up to the 17th fret. This will result in an outrageously high-pitched note that's guaranteed to grab attention.

Example 11e

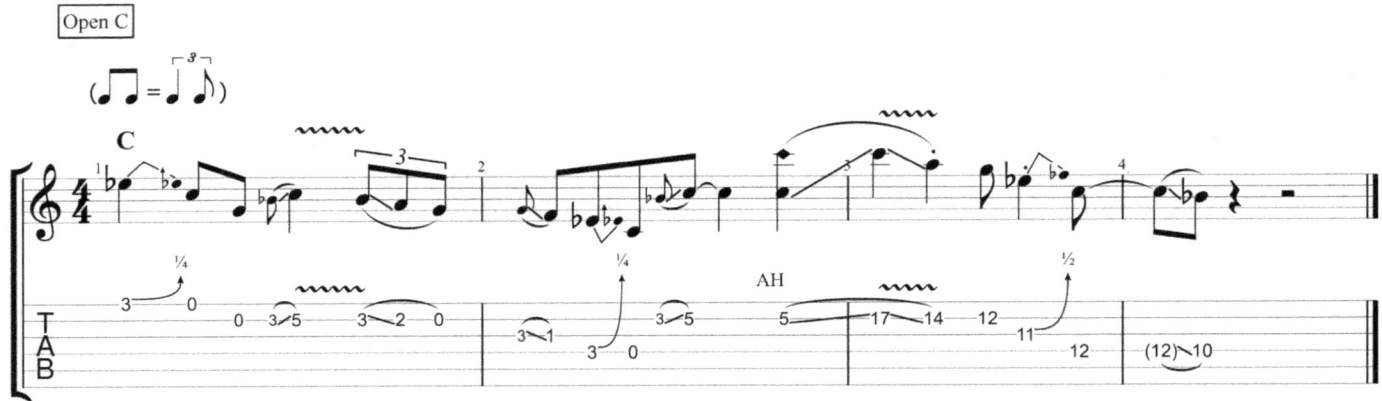

We're only scratching the surface here of what Joey is capable of. I hold him in the highest regard and think he's one of the most talented guitarists alive today. There's a treasure trove of things you can learn from him, so get to work!

Chapter Twelve – Bonnie Raitt

Born in California in 1949, Bonnie Raitt went on to become the first lady of slide guitar with a career spanning almost five decades and counting.

Raised in a musical family (her father was a Broadway music star and her mother a pianist), Raitt picked up guitar aged 8 and progressed quickly, taking an interest in slide playing early on.

As a singer/songwriter, Raitt's influences weren't just guitar players. Instead she took inspiration from the folk scene of the day, and artists such as Pete Seeger, Joan Baez, Woody Guthrie, Bob Dylan and Janis Joplin to name a few. This was combined with a love of the traditional blues slide players. She even opened gigs for Muddy Waters and John Lee Hooker in her early days.

Despite trying to avoid a career in music, Bonnie was eventually snapped up by Warner and handed a record deal. She released her self-titled debut album in 1971, and followed this up with 1972's *Giving it Up*, 1973's *Takin' My Time*, 1974's *Streetlights*, and 1975's *Home Plate*. Each of these albums was received well critically, but none were the big commercial success a label really looks for.

This all changed with the release of 1977's *Sweet Forgiveness*. Suddenly the dynamic in the record industry changed and big money was being thrown around to secure the next big act. With big money behind her she could take things to the next level, but as that happened, the positive critical reception died down. It seemed that success just wasn't meant to be.

In fact, it took more than 10 years before the magic happened. 1989's *Nick of Time* (her 10th album) achieved the critical and commercial success everyone knew she was capable of. This album secured Raitt a Grammy, went to number one on the US charts, and all these years later still makes it onto Rolling Stone's 500 Greatest Albums of All Time list.

She would go on to record 7 more albums, with the most recent (at the time of writing) being 2016's *Dig in Deep*. At the age of 69, she continues to write, record, and inspire generations of young musicians to see what's possible when you keep working and never give up.

Gear wise, Bonnie is a big user of the Stratocaster (being the first female to receive a signature model back in 1996). Her main axe is a combination of a '65 body and an unknown neck which she picked up for just $120 back in 1969. She's used that guitar on every gig since.

She uses a glass bottleneck style slide on her middle finger, and while she's used many tunings, the most notable is open A tuning (E, A, E, A, C#, E) – open G tuning shifted up a tone.

Let's take a look at some of her licks!

Example 12a is an open position lick that sits somewhere between A Major and A minor. With any new tuning, a great starting point is to get to grips with the bluesy minor pentatonic sound in the open position.

Example 12a

Next up we have some more melodic vocabulary around the home position at the 12th fret. As expected, Raitt draws a lot of her vocabulary from the home position and the notes two frets below.

The real treat here is the inclusion of the D note in bar 3. This nice passing tone takes us from major pentatonic to something more akin to the A Major scale.

Example 12b

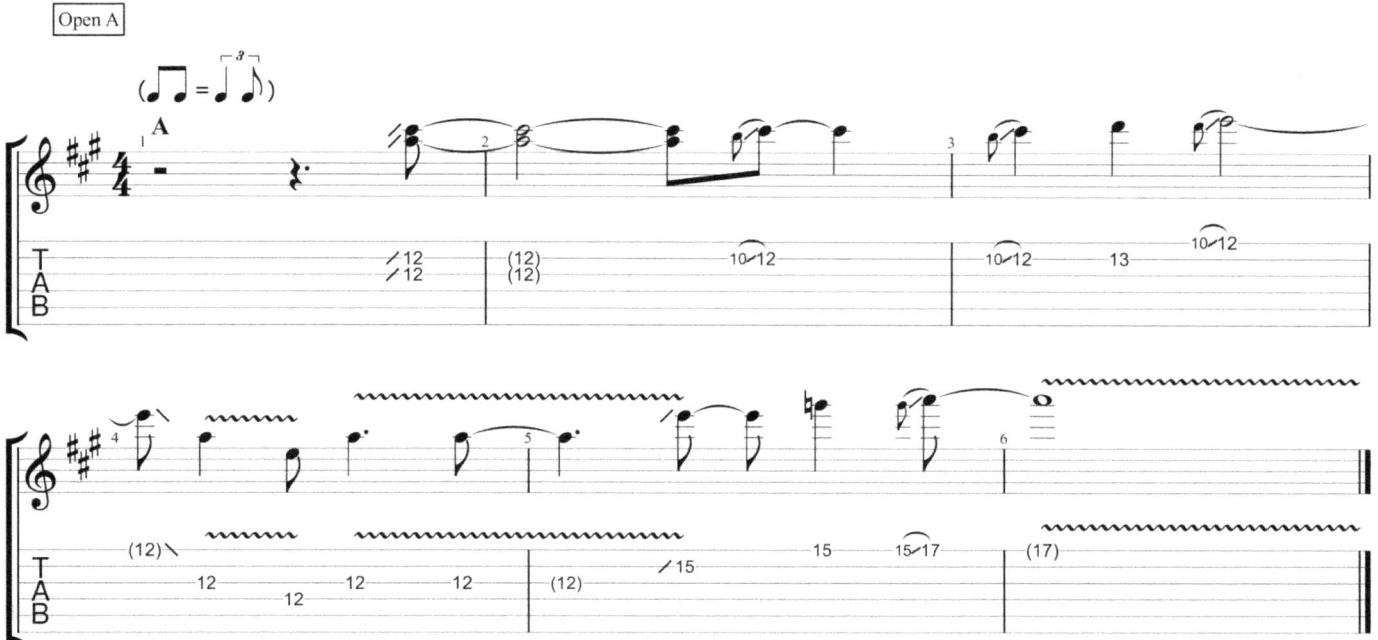

Example 12c takes the previous idea and explores it a little further with another lick in A Major.

Begin at the 17th fret and move down to the home position at the 12th fret. Everything else is a mixture of the home position and notes two frets below.

Example 12c

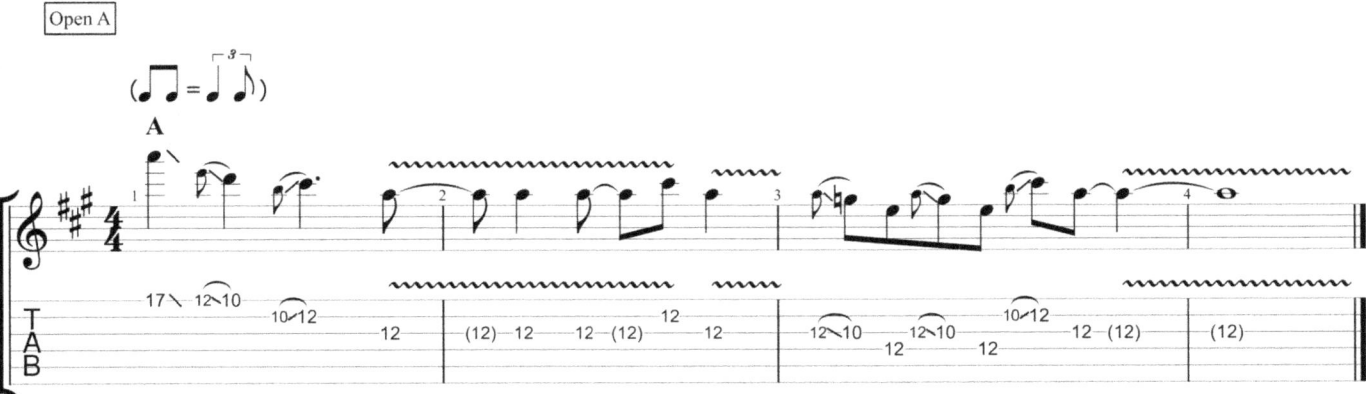

The next example begins on the root note on the 5th fret of the high string, then moves up the A Major scale before it resolves to the home position at the 12th fret.

Bonnie has a wonderful vocabulary of major scale licks that are perfect for pop songs that have shifted away from a straight-up blues vibe.

Example 12d

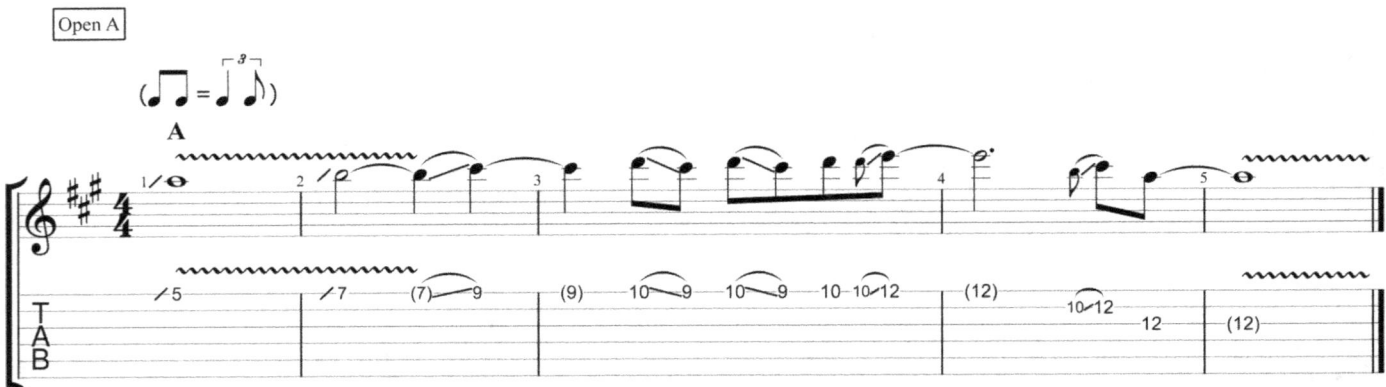

The final example shows how Bonnie might play around a chord other than the A Major she's tuned to. In this case it's a melodic idea around an E Major chord. The solution is relatively simple – treating the 7th fret position as home and adding basic scalar ideas around this area.

Example 12e

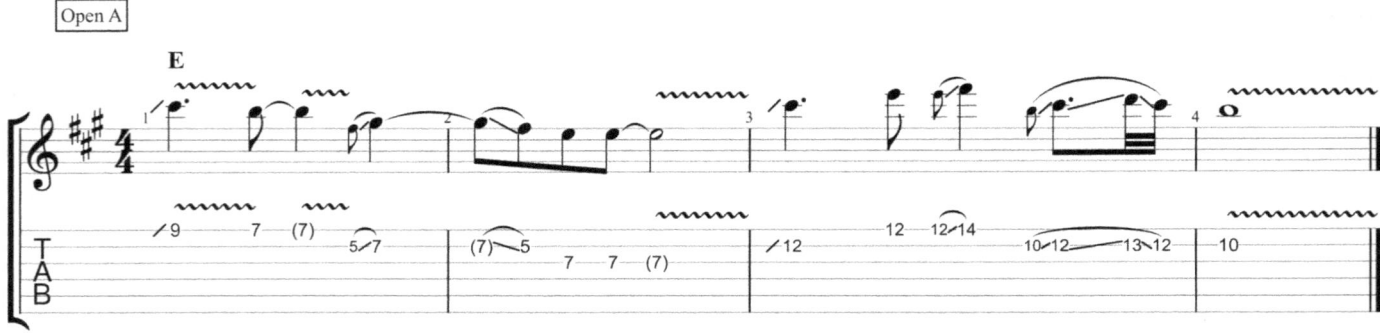

Chapter Thirteen – Chris Rea

Born in Middlesbrough, England, in 1951, Chris Rea is the only guitarist featured in this book from my side of the pond. To his credit, it's a position well deserved – his impact as a composer and a slide player has influenced a generation of young English guitar players.

Impressively, Rea didn't pick up the guitar until his early 20s, when he found a deal on a 1961 Hofner V3 for just £32! Upon hearing Charley Patton, Chris sought out more experienced guitarists in his area to explain how Patton was getting the sound from the guitar. The answer was, of course, "a slide", so in Chris's own words, "That was it for me. I was gone from that day on."

Rea worked with a selection of bands in his early years, even recording guitar on Hank Marvin's 1977 release, *Hank Marvin Guitar Syndicate*. His debut album, 1978's *Whatever Happened to Benny Santini?* didn't see much success in the UK, but *Fool (If You Think It's Over)* would be Rea's biggest success in the US, reaching #12 on the Billboard Hot 100. The downside was that it didn't feature Chris playing any guitar!

His next few albums were anything but hits and Chris would often argue that this was due to the record label trying to smooth out his harder blues side for more commercial appeal. Eventually, Rea realised this wasn't going to work and in 1983 he released *Water Sign*. This album wasn't an immediate success, but with strong touring support across the UK and Europe, the album suddenly caught on and sold half a million copies.

His next record, 1985's *Shamrock Diaries* was the start of major success and from here, each successive album sold extremely well. Ultimately, while Chris was never considered "cool" with the youth, he managed to find a solid market. While that market might have been dads driving in their cars, the fact was they were reliably buying records. Chris had made it.

When it comes to guitars, Chris is a Strat man (having his own signature model at one point). His main axe is a '62 Candy Apple Red (affectionately known as "Pinkey") that he has played since the beginning of his career. He uses a pair of Fender Blues Juniors on stage with drive coming from a tube screamer, a compressor, and occasionally a delay or chorus pedal.

His main tuning is open E and he plays with a glass slide on his pinky finger.

Let's look at some of Chris's licks.

First up is a typical Rea chord progression which falls more in line with pop than blues. This is cool because it requires a different approach to playing than simply the minor pentatonic in home position.

Having said that, Chris's approach is clear. Handling the Am chord with a double-stop at the 20th fret (highlighting the 5th and b7th), there is a shift down to the same intervals for the Dm chord at the 13th fret.

Next is a G Major chord, achieved by sliding up two frets to the home position for G Major, highlighting the 3rd and 5th.

Example 13a

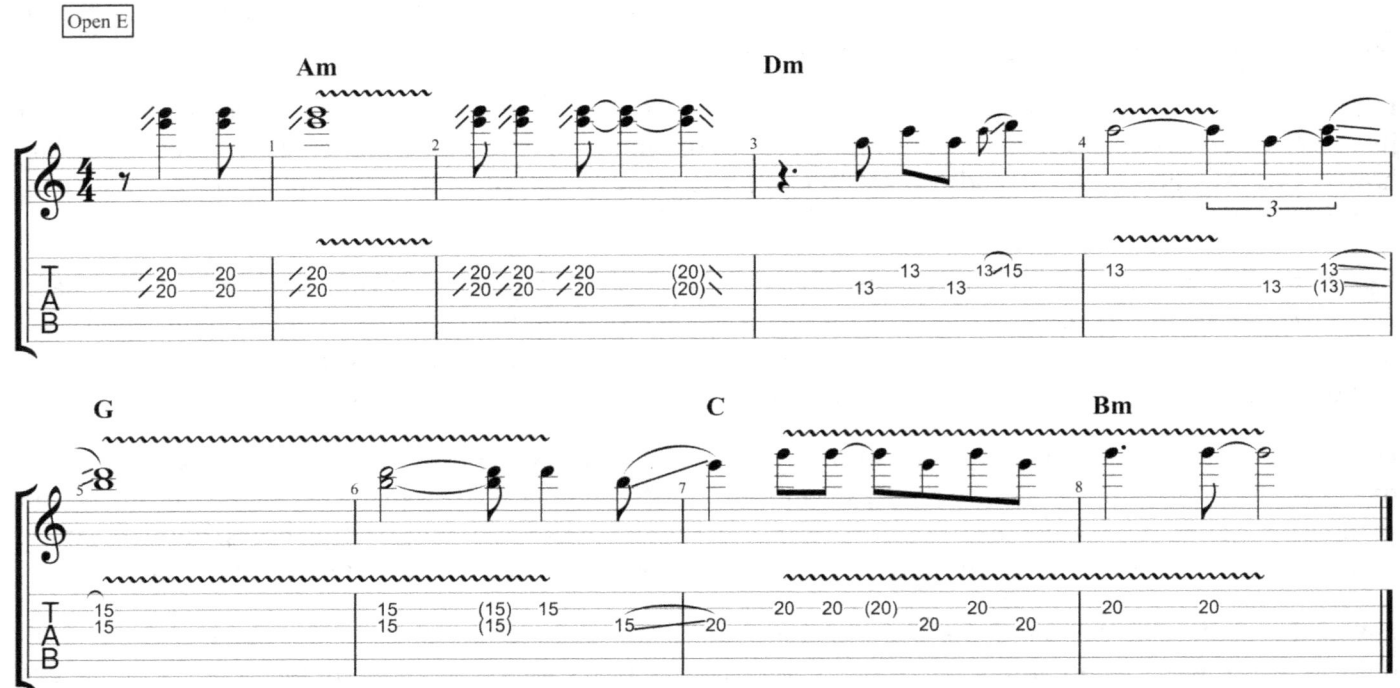

The next example continues with the second part of the chord progression and adds an ending using F Major and E Major chords.

As in the previous example, Chris would find a single position for each chord and stick relatively closely to it.

The other interesting thing to note is how Chris approaches the A minor chord. Playing in an open major tuning makes minor chords a little tricky. Chris plays notes at the 20th fret which we would normally think of as C Major. C Major is the relative major of A minor. Look at a C Major chord's construction (C, E, G) and you'll see it has a lot in common with A minor (A, C, E). Add an A note under your C Major triad (A, C, E, G) and you create an Am7 chord.

Example 13b

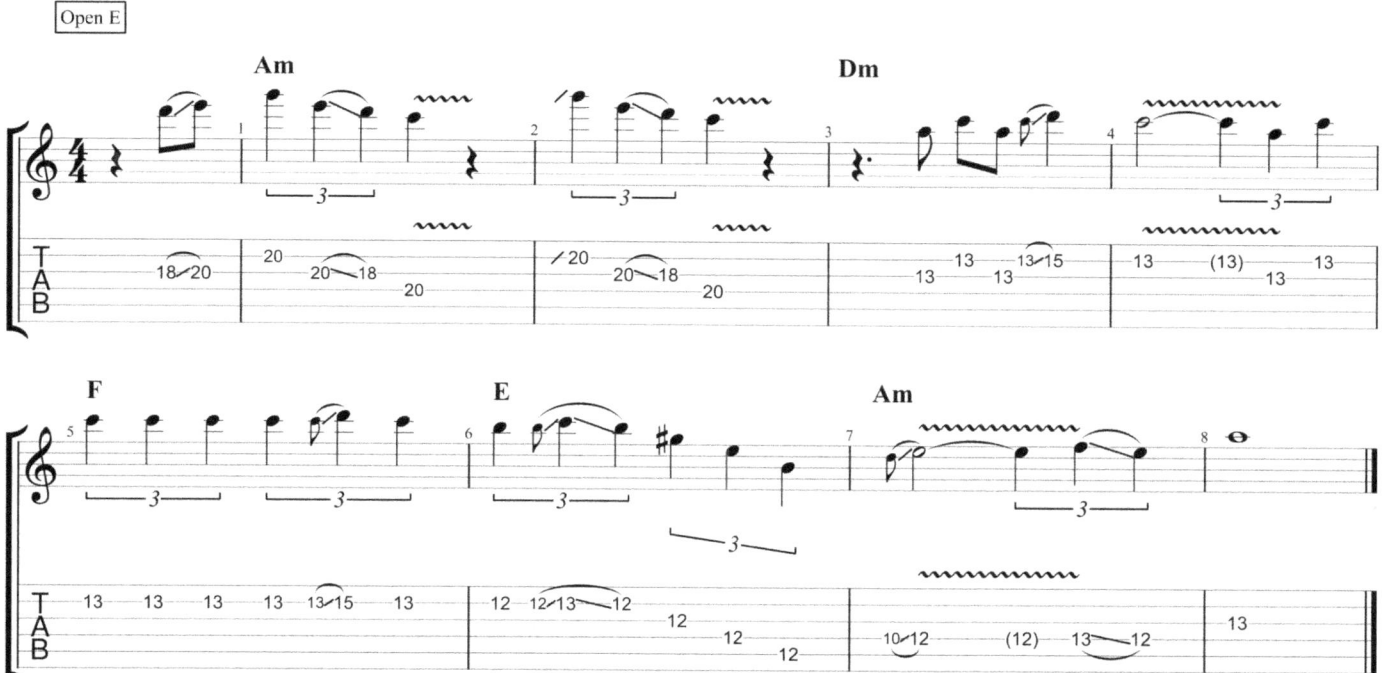

For the next example, I've taken the entire passage and played double-stops in each position, applying vibrato. It showcases how simple, yet effective, slide playing can be. This sort of idea is great for a lead player to play during a verse.

Example 13c

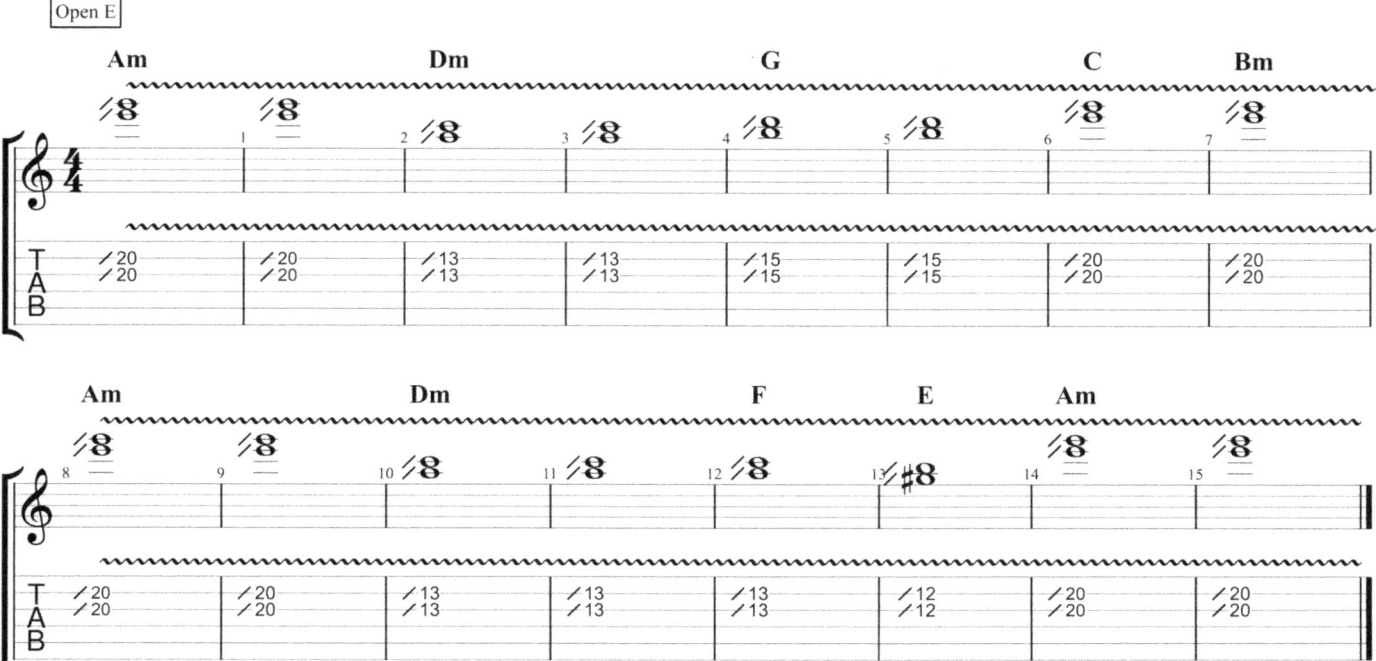

Of course, Chris still plays the blues! The next lick demonstrates his approach with a line that works well over a blues in E. As with many slide players, milking vocabulary from a single string is an effective way to make a melody.

Example 13d

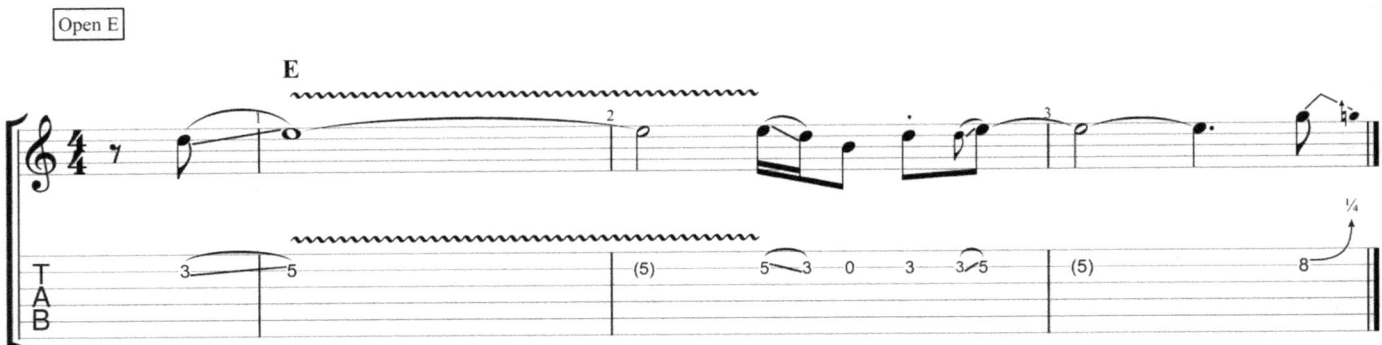

Finally, here's a single-note blues idea that works well on the IV to I chord movement in a 12-bar blues. In this case it's A Major going back to E Major. There's nothing wrong with the open position!

Example 13e

Chapter Fourteen – Tampa Red

Born Hudson Woodbridge in Georgia, 1903, Tampa Red would go on to be one of the early Chicago blues influences, having an impact on Robert Nighthawk, Muddy Waters, Elmore James and more.

Red moved to Florida at a young age and picked up guitar skills from his brother and local musicians. He relocated to Chicago in the 1920s, now with a unique approach to slide guitar, and was set to start his career.

His first real gig was accompanying the mother of blues, Ma Rainey. He went on to record his music with Georgia Tom as the Hokum Boys, and with Frankie Jaxon, as Tampa Red's Hokum Jug Band.

From here his career grew steadily, both as a band leader and session musician. Alongside the Chicago Five, he pioneered the "Bluebird Sound" when recording for Bluebird Records and continued putting record out right into the 1950s.

In the early '50s Red's wife passed away, and during this period he turned to drink. This would take him away from music for a while, until the blues revival of the late '50s and early '60s when he resurfaced to make a few more select recordings before hanging up his guitar for good.

Tampa Red had a long career which went through the electric revolution, so his sound changed a lot. He began on acoustic, moved onto a resonator guitar (a gold one, earning him the name "The Man With The Golden Guitar"), and eventually dabbled in electric guitar, showing that your sound is what you make it. He played in a few tunings, but open D appears to have been the most common.

Like many of these early pioneers who were lost to time, it's hard to say for sure what type of slide Tampa used, or what finger he wore it on. All we can say is that his unique approach to single-string slide improvising was a precursor to the Rock 'n' Roll that would come later.

Now, onto the licks!

First is a simple melody that Red might play in between some fingerstyle chordal work.

There's nothing complicated here, so just focus on the articulation. This is a melody and it should be treated as such. Focus on the vibrato and sliding in and out of notes. Make it sing!

Example 14a

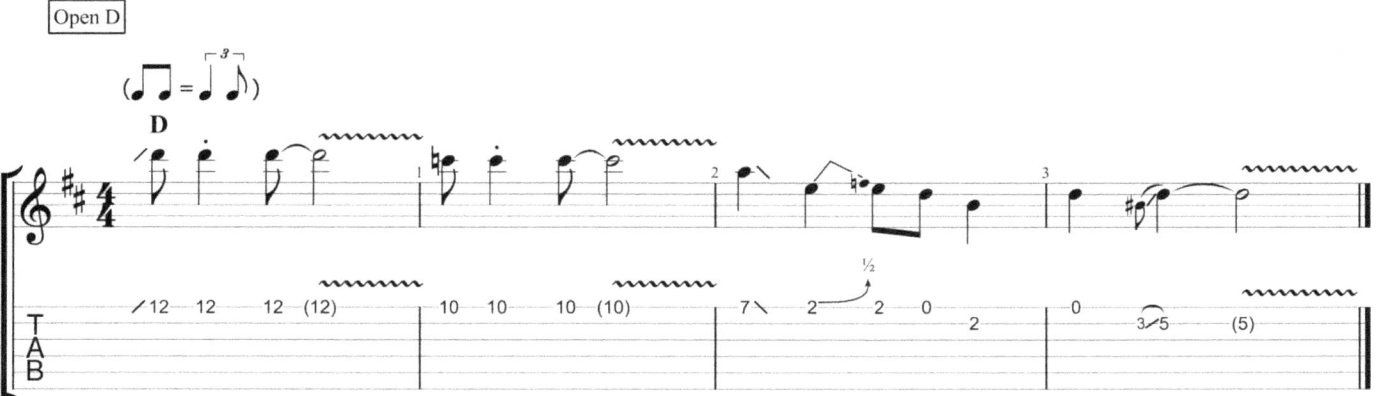

Tampa was keen on both open D and open E tuning, but would often use a capo to change key. This example stays in open E and uses a capo at the 4th fret to raise the key to F# Major. You could just as easily play this in open D with a capo at the 2nd fret.

This line is a little faster and uses triplets, but your main focus here should be the use of the slide and the fingers of the fretting hand. Two notes need to be fretted with the index finger (indicated in the TAB with brackets).

Example 14b

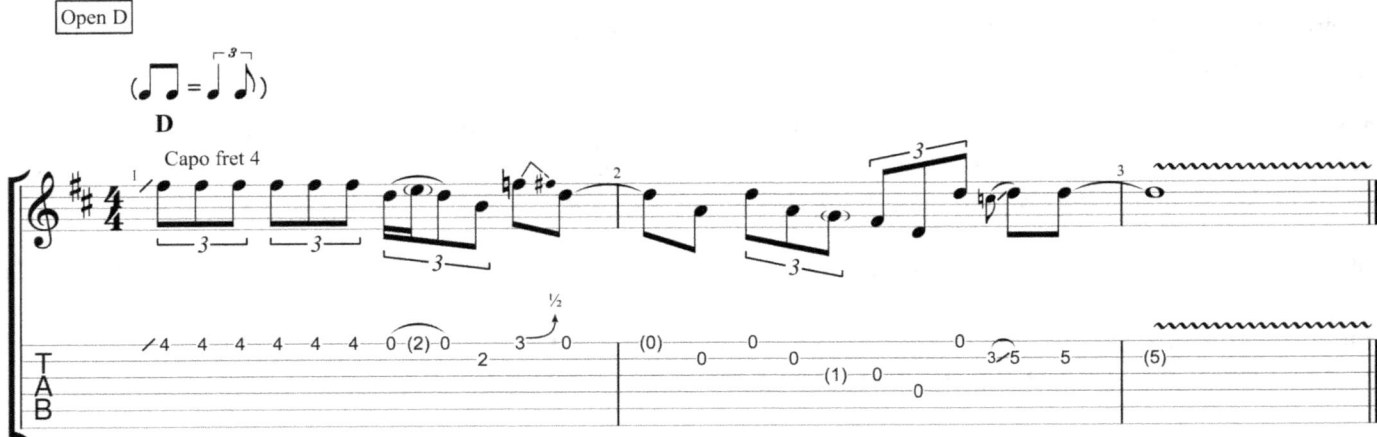

Next is a great turnaround lick that subtly outlines the chord changes. Pay attention to which notes should be played with the fretting hand. They all occur in bar 3.

Example 14c

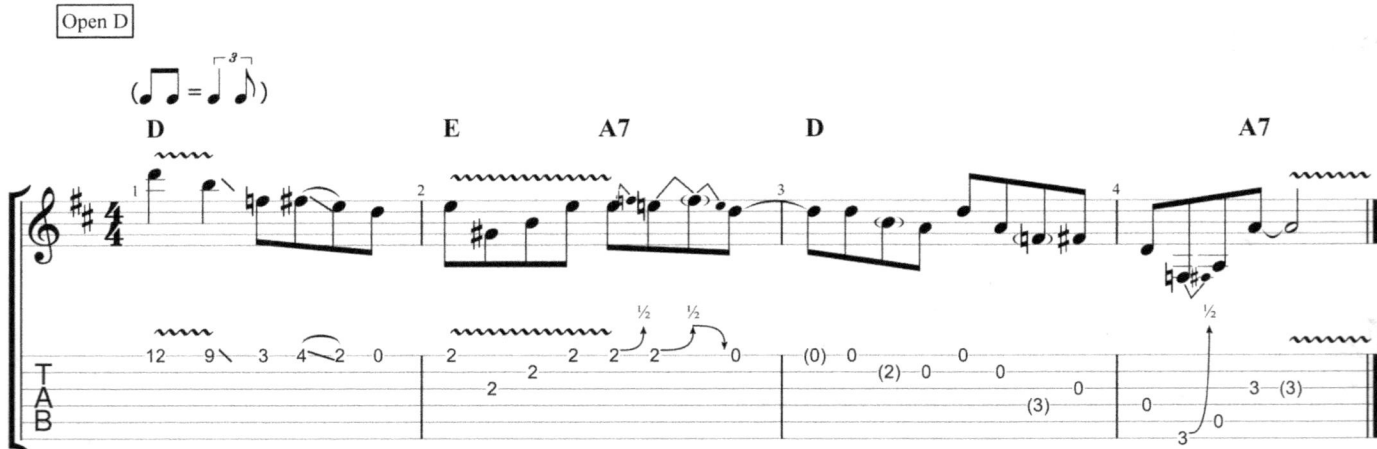

This example only uses the slide on notes indicated by a bend – everything else is played with the fretting hand fingers. I know this seems like an odd example for a slide guitar book, but being a good slide player means being able to get by with things other than single-note melodies. The chords in the turnaround are an excellent example of this skill.

Example 14d

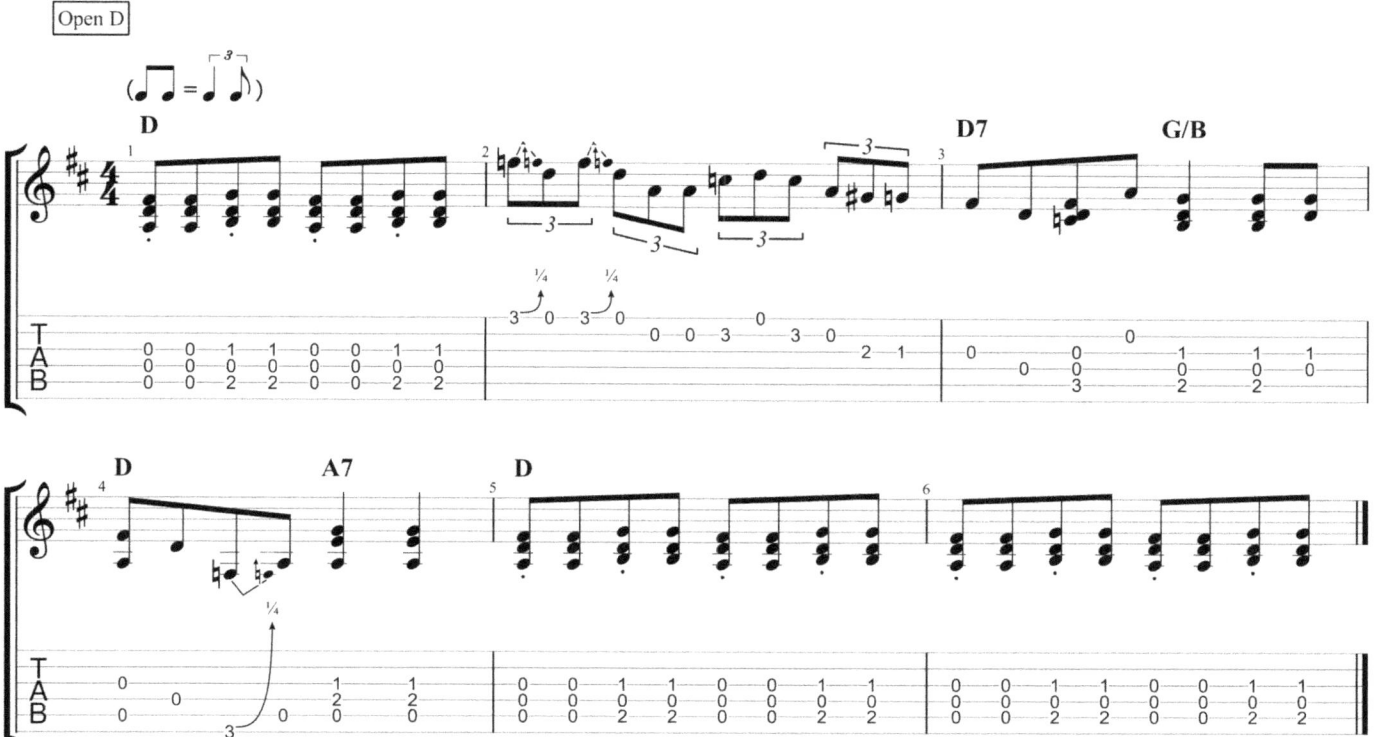

The final example shows more of a solo guitar part. It takes a simple melody in D played on the high string, set against a thumping pedal note on the low string. In bar 3 there are some more fretted notes indicated by the brackets.

Example 14e

Chapter Fifteen – Gary Rossington

Born in Florida in 1951, Gary Rossington has the odd distinction of not playing an astonishing amount of slide guitar in his career, while having played slide on one of the most iconic rock tracks of all time.

After getting some experience playing drums, Rossington picked up the guitar aged 14 (a Sears and Roebuck Silvertone). He played in a band with friends and after several line-up changes the group eventually came to be called Lynyrd Skynyrd.

Influenced by rock and blues music of the time, and bringing a classic southern twist, Rossington admired slide players like Duane Allman (who the band used to go and see), Al Wilson, and Brian Jones, but learned to play as well as he could in standard tuning.

The group released their debut album *Lynyrd Skynyrd (Pronounced 'Lĕh-'nérd 'Skin-'nérd)* in 1973. The album contained favorites such as *Gimmie Three Steps*, *Simple Man*, and the guitar epic, *Free Bird*. Aside from the legendary guitar solo, the prominence of the slide guitar part is often overlooked in this track. It was a sound Rossington would come back to time and again.

If you watch a video of the band playing *Free Bird* live, you'll see Rossington has a piece of heavy green electrical wire placed under his strings around the first fret to push the action up and make slide playing easier. This is a great trick used by many players over the years who just need to play slide for one track, so don't carry a second guitar.

The group followed their success with 1974's *Second Helping* (containing the band's best known song, *Sweet Home Alabama*), 1975's *Nuthin' Fancy*, 1976's *Gimmie Back My Bullets*, and 1977's *Street Survivors*.

At this point the band couldn't have been more successful, but tragedy hit just days after the release of *Street Survivors*. The band were involved in a plane crash that killed lead singer Ronnie Van Zant, guitarist Steve Gaines, backing singer Cassie Gaines and key members of the band's crew. The members who survived were seriously injured and Rossington broke his pelvic bone, multiple ribs, bones in his feet, both wrists, both arms and both legs.

Gary made a return with both The Rossington-Collins Band and later The Rossington Band, with each group releasing their fair share of music.

In 1987, Skynyrd would reunite with Ronnie's younger brother Johnny on vocals. The group are still active today and releaed a further 9 albums. Gary has also continued to release music as a band leader, most notably under the "Rossington" moniker, and his most recent album is 2016's *Take It On Faith*.

Gary is a long time Les Paul user, though he has been known to use a Firebird and an SG from time to time. In his current setup he has a black Les Paul with slightly higher action that he uses for slide playing. He wears a glass slide on his middle finger, and plays in standard tuning often, though he occasionally uses open E and open G tuning.

Let's take a look at some of his licks!

Of course, it would be impossible to talk about Gary's playing and not lean heavily on *Free Bird*, so the first lick is based around the slide melody from that iconic recording.

This example is an interesting one to study as the chords in the progression (G Major, D/F#, E minor, F Major, C Major, D Major) don't all come from the same key. Therefore, a single scale will not fit over the top! When soloing, our approach needs to be based around the individual chords.

In Example 15a then, the first note played on each chord is a note from the chord itself. G is the root of G Major, F# is the 3rd of D/F# and G is the b3 of E minor. Using this approach, we play an F root note when we reach the F Major chord in bar 5 that does not occur in the key of G Major and everything sounds great.

Example 15a

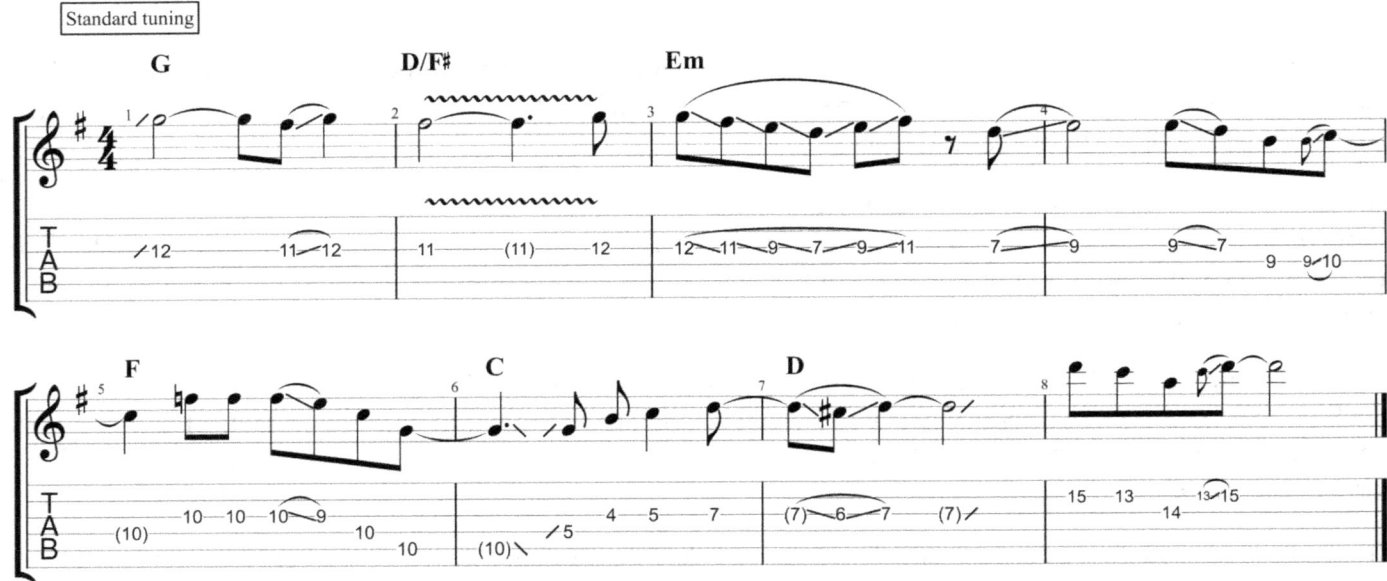

The second lick showcases how Rossington might play slide lead guitar lines behind a singer. The chord progression is the same, but there is a lot of space in the phrasing.

Example 15b

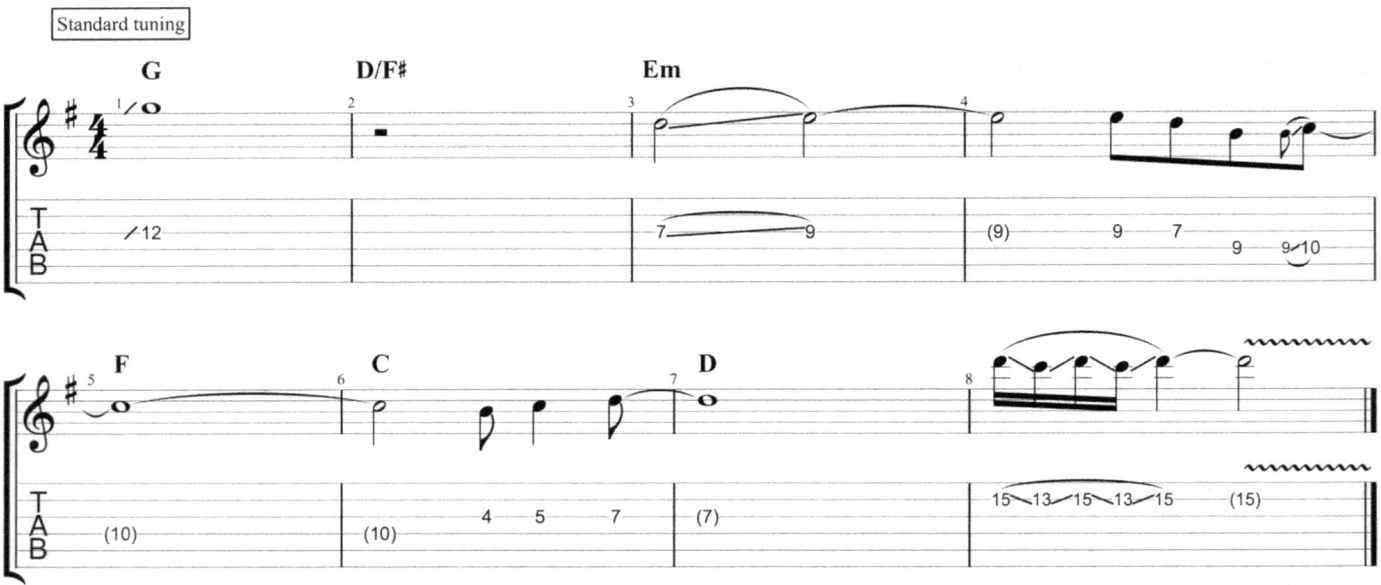

The next example develops this idea over the chorus progression – a repeating F Major, C Major and D Major.

The melody sticks closely to the chords, taking few risks. The excitement in the lick is produced by including almost random slides up the neck between phrases. These are never played the exact same way twice, but that's not important – what's important is exploiting the unique aspects of the slide.

Example 15c

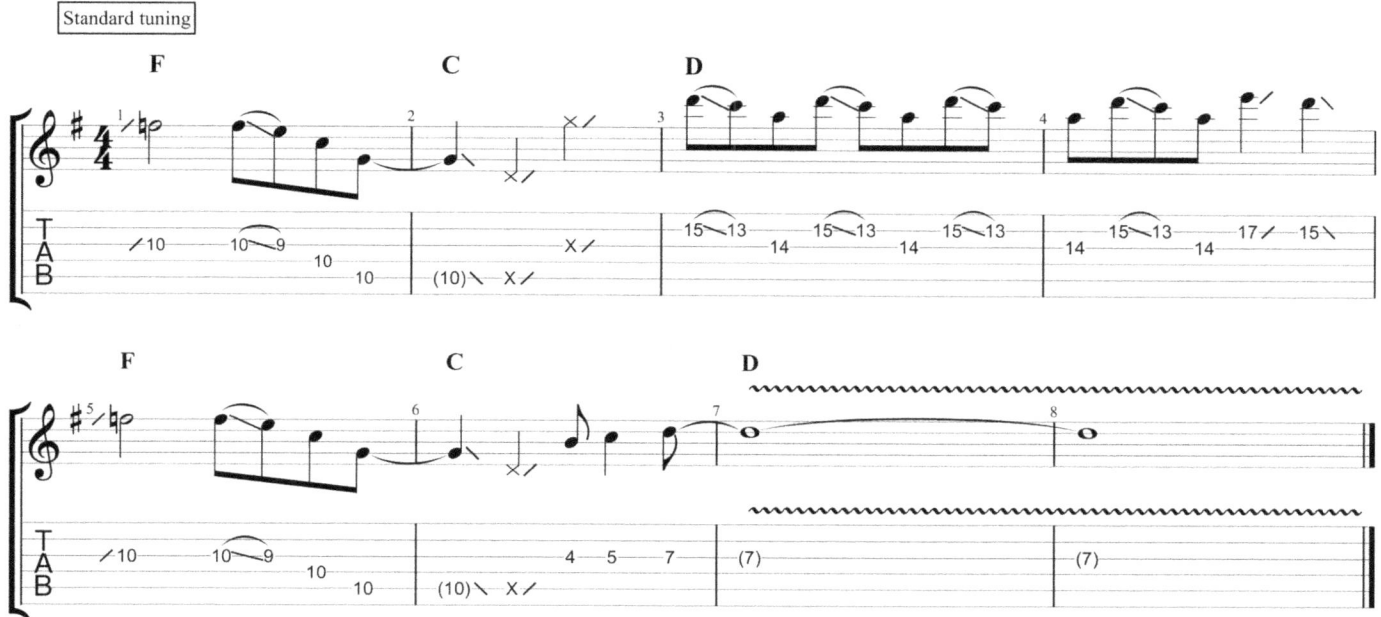

The following lick walks the same path as the last, but now ramps up the intensity in the final two bars by playing the exact same notes as the last idea, but with a 1/16th note rhythm instead of tamer 1/8th notes.

The beauty of a lick like this is that, at speed, it can never be as cleanly executed as it would if it was fretted, but this adds to the chaotic magic of slide!

Example 15d

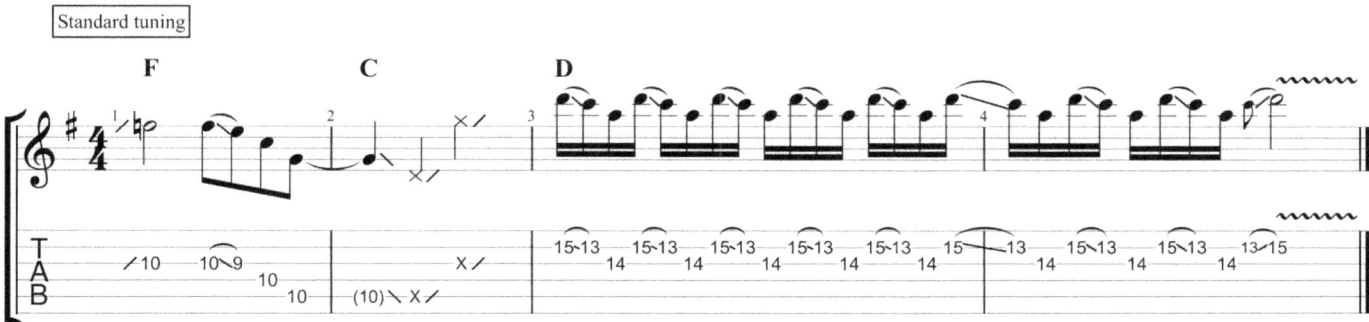

Our final example demonstrates something Gary might play on a track in E Major, now using just the notes of the E Major Pentatonic scale (E, F#, G#, B, C#). Something like this is much tricker to play in standard tuning, but it's beyond the realms of possibility.

Gary isn't a particularly advanced slide guitar player – he's not full of theory or chops – he just plays basic melodies, but with lots of expression. Experiment with the scale and see what happens.

Example 15e

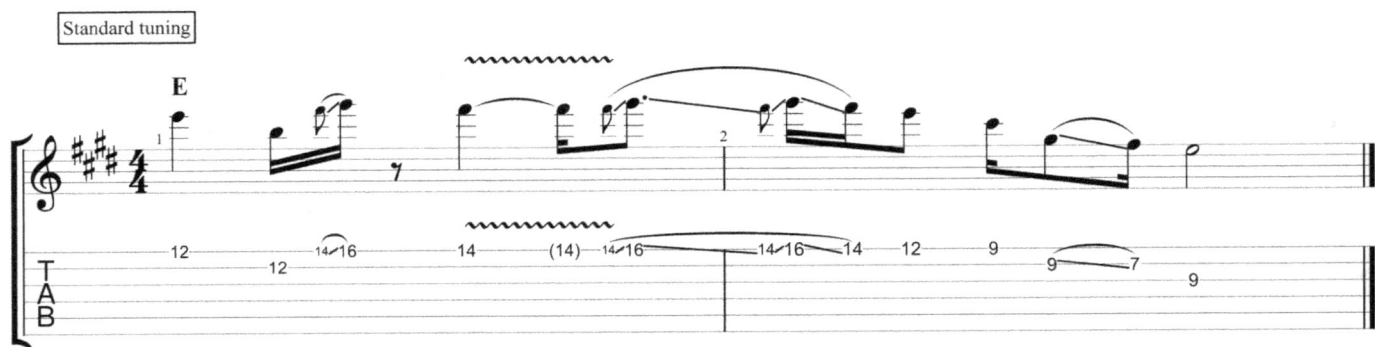

Chapter Sixteen – Derek Trucks

Born in Jacksonville, Florida, in 1979, Derek Trucks would quickly become one of the pioneers of electric slide guitar, influencing endless guitarists to pick up a bottleneck.

Born into a musical lineage (his uncle was Butch Trucks, the long serving and original drummer in the Allman Brothers Band), Derek picked up guitar at the age of 9 when he found a beat-up acoustic guitar in a yard sale for $5.

Attracted to the sound of Duane Allman on the *Live at Fillmore East* and *Layla* records, and spurred on by his father's Elmore James records, Derek instantly understood the power of slide guitar and the way it emulated the human voice.

To describe Derek as a prodigy may be an understatment as he was out playing shows aged just 11, and even sitting in with the Allman Brothers when he was 13. Footage of these gigs is available on YouTube and it's clear that Derek could probably outplay anyone, even that early in his life.

In 1994 Trucks formed the Derek Trucks Band, which would go on to record multiple albums (and from a personal persepctive, some of my favorite albums of all time!), winning a Grammy for 2009's *Already Free*. If you have some time, 1998's *Out of the Madness* and 2002's *Joyful Noise* are must-hear albums for fans of slide guitar.

In 1999 Trucks became an official member of the Allman Brothers Band alongside Warren Haynes. He recorded just one studio album with the band, 2003's *Hittin' the Note*, along with several live releases and endless bootlegs. He spent 15 years with the band before their final show in 2014.

In 2014, Derek formed the Tedeschi Trucks Band with his wife Susan Tedeschi. To date, the group have released five studio albums, each being an absolute masterclass in expression, and one official live release. Their latest offering, 2019's *Signs*, continues to showcase what a great future Derek has in music.

Derek's slide style is extremely expressive, but technically straight ahead. There's no need for crazy advanced techniques – it's just him and a glass slide on his ring finger doing his best to imitate the human voice.

Gear wise, Derek is a long time Gibson SG user, having his own signature model. He's a straight into the amp kind of guy, riding his volume knob for maximum expression. Just like his hero, Duane Allman, he tunes almost exclusively in open E, using a set of 11s and always has an unwound 3rd string.

Let's take a look at his incredible licks.

First up is a killer lick demonstrating Derek's fluidity with the traditional tuning, coupled with his ability to play outside of the "key of the tuning" by ripping out a lick in Eb Major.

There's a hint of the familiar with some home postion based playing, though his particular sense of phrasing is incredible. It takes a considerable amount of control to play licks at this speed and still be able to slide down from notes (in this case the 11th fret on the 2nd string) so go slowly – it's essential to nail this to create the right feel.

The real twist here is the extensive use of the 6th note (C) located at the 13th fret, 2nd string. Most often players will stick to the notes two frets below the home position, but this note adds a sweet major pentatonic flavor to the lick.

Example 16a

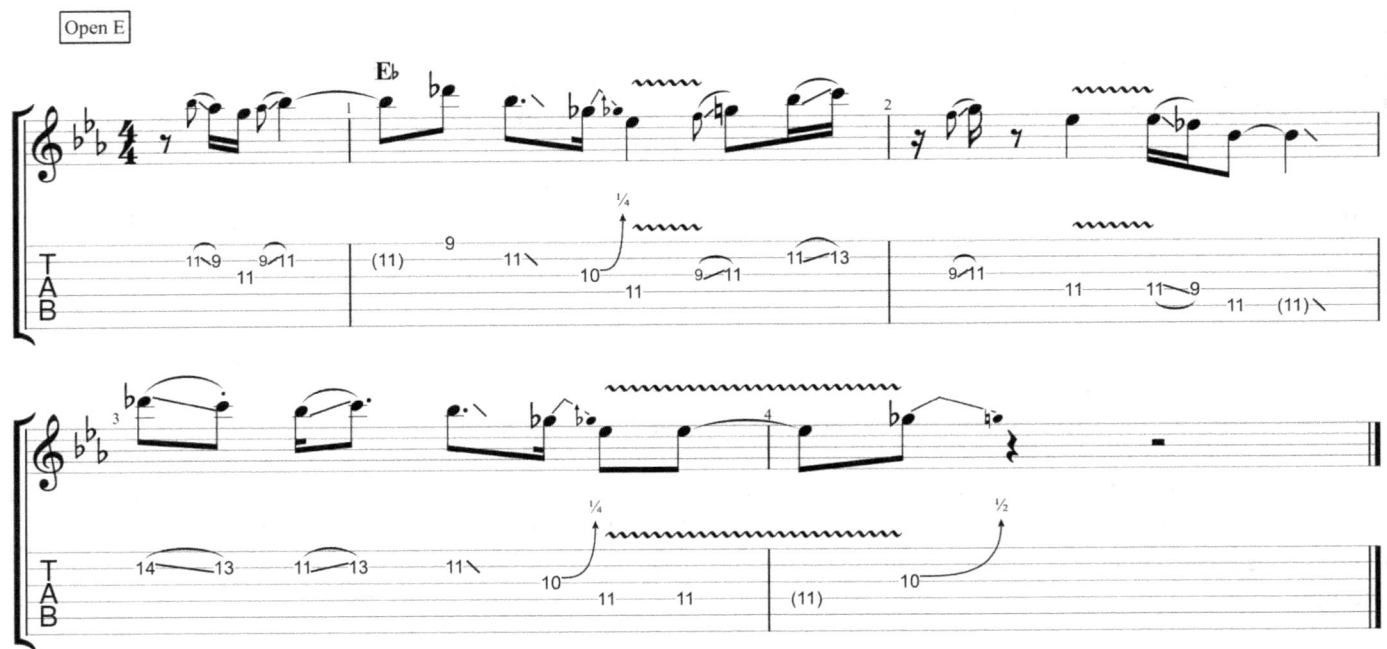

Continuing with this Eb vibe, the following lick is played over a Gospel-type chorus that moves between Ab Major, A diminished 7 and Eb Major (or even an Eb/Bb chord if you want that sweet ascending bassline!)

Considering the jazzy undertones provided by the diminished chord, Trucks' approach to soloing in a setting like this still sticks closely to blues roots. He would likely play a mix of Eb Major Pentatonic (Eb, F, G, Bb, C) and Eb Minor Pentatonic (Eb, Gb, Ab, Bb, Db). Not all of these notes are used here, but that blend of the 6th (C) from the major and b3rd (Gb) from the minor gives this lick a sophisticated sound.

Example 16b

The next example takes inspiration from a viral clip of Derek playing with B.B. King. It keeps the blues phrasing, but is played over a chord progression more in line with Gospel and soul music.

Despite having a wonderful set of chords to play over, Derek would stick closely to the major and minor pentatonic scale from the key of the piece (in this case Ab Major). So while there is some moving around on single strings, eventually the focus is the home position at the 16th fret.

The tricky part of this lick is the timing. It's worth pointing out that Derek wouldn't be counting when playing a lick like this. Instead he's just pushing and pulling time for dramatic effect, so don't get too bogged down thinking about the rhythm. That said, if you want to take something from this lick, the tuplet of 4:3 requires you to play 4 notes in the space of 3!

Example 16c

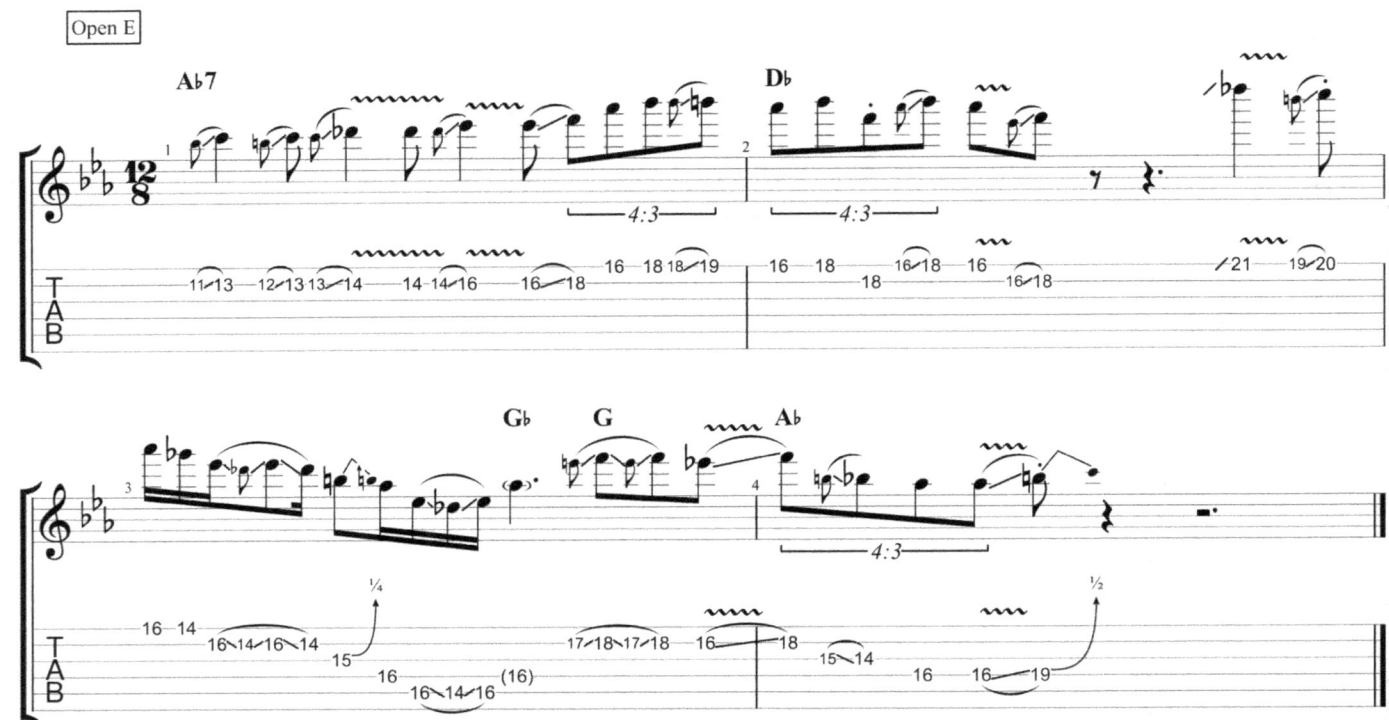

Example 16d explores some of Derek's incredible single-note playing, similar to that heard on *Down In The Flood*.

Taking place over a C7 type vamp, Derek would combine both C Major Pentatonic (C, D, E, G, A) and the C Blues Scale (C, Eb, F, Gb, G, Bb) to create something bluesy and soulful.

The first four measures are a simple melody based around the idea of descending chromatically from G to Gb to F. That Gb is pretty spicy!

The next four bars showcase more of Derek's fluid single-note style. Ideas like this can be problematic, as getting clean notes on the top two strings with slide can be tricky without a high action. An interesting aspect of Derek's style is that he will fret with the slide from time to time when sliding between notes. It's hard to say if this is by design or something that just happens, and has become part of his sound. Either way, it's cool!

Example 16d

The final example shifts into a more up-tempo setting, this time with a 1/16th note shuffle feel. In terms of note choices, the line sticks close to the underlying G7 chord, but with a cool slide from the b5th (Db). The key to this lick is sitting on a note and repeatedly sliding down and back into it, without losing a sense of the intended pitch. Take it slow and build up accuracy of intonation.

Example 16e

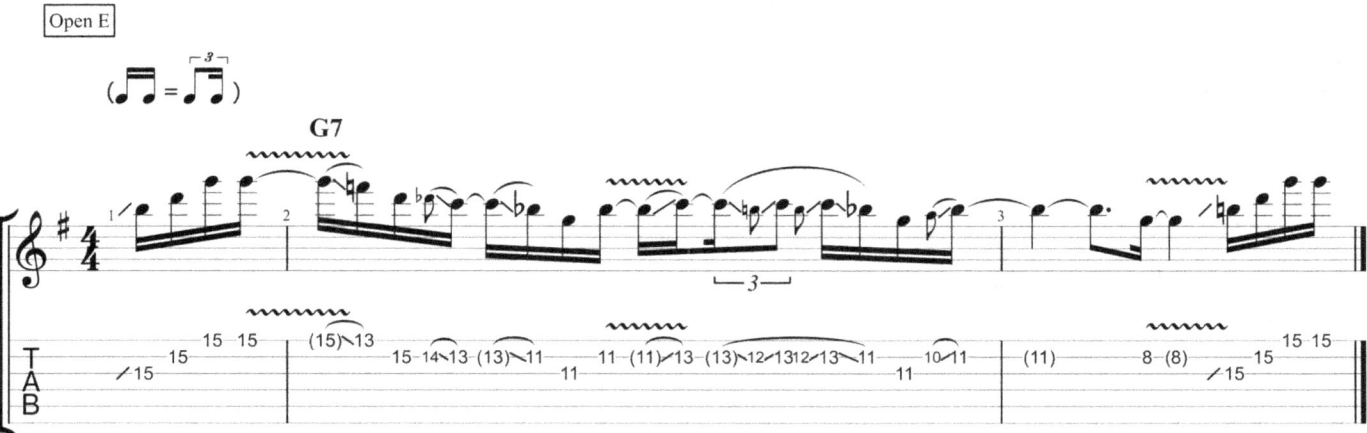

Derek is undeniably one of the greatest slide players to walk the planet and it would be impossible to capture what he can do in just five licks. You would do well to go and listen to his music right now and start working out some of the cooler licks!

Chapter Seventeen – Joe Walsh

Born in Kansas, 1941, Joe Walsh has achieved a lot in his musical career. Most notably he has played a major role in the fifth bestselling band of all time, the Eagles.

Walsh was given his first guitar at the age of 10 and very quickly decided he wanted a career as a musician after he learnt *Walk Don't Run* by The Ventures.

His first recordings came with a band called The Measles, releasing two singles between 1965 and 1966. He stepped up the career ladder when he joined The James Gang in 1968. Joe remained part of the group when they became a trio and took on vocal duties. The group's debut album *Yer* was released in 1969, followed by *James Gang Rides Again* in 1970 and *Thirds* in 1971. Despite releasing classic songs like *Funk #49*, Walsh felt the group had their limitations and left in 1971.

He followed The James Gang up with Barnstorm. Despite this being a band, the group were often billed simply as "Joe Walsh". The group's self-titled debut was released in 1972 and was received quite well. It would be their 1973 follow-up record, *The Smoker You Drink, The Player You Get*, that would really show what Walsh was capable of. It was on this record that the world was introduced to *Rocky Mountain Way*. Joe also played slide guitar on Joe Vitale's debut album, *Roller Coaster Weekend* in 1974.

In 1975, Joe joined the Eagles, appearing on the groups 1976 hit record, *Hotel California*. This was followed up in 1979 with *The Long Run*. Both albums sold many millions of copies and showcased Walsh's ability to fit in with the classic Eagles sound, but bring a rockier edge when they needed it.

The group split suddenly in 1980 due to relationship tensions between Don Felder and Glen Frey and suddenly Walsh was out on his own again. Fortunately, Walsh never stopped recording his own albums, so he continued with this to great success, releasing 10 more albums between 1974 and 2012, and recording guitar parts on many collaborations, including work with Randy Newman, Ringo Starr and The Foo Fighters.

The Eagles would reunite in 1994 and, after several lawsuits, released *Long Road Out of Eden* in 2007, their first studio album in 28 years.

Joe has used almost every guitar under the sun, so it's hard to link one particular guitar to his playing, but a Les Paul in open E tuning is going to get you close enough. He uses both glass and brass slides, and wears them on his middle finger.

Now, onto his licks!

First up is a *Rocky Mountain Way* style melody in E Major.

Walsh has never been a revolutionary slide player when it comes to his approach, but he took ideas he learned from Duane Allman and applied them to his own classic tunes, as demonstrated by this simple idea that sticks strictly to the home position at the 12th fret and the notes two frets below

Example 17a

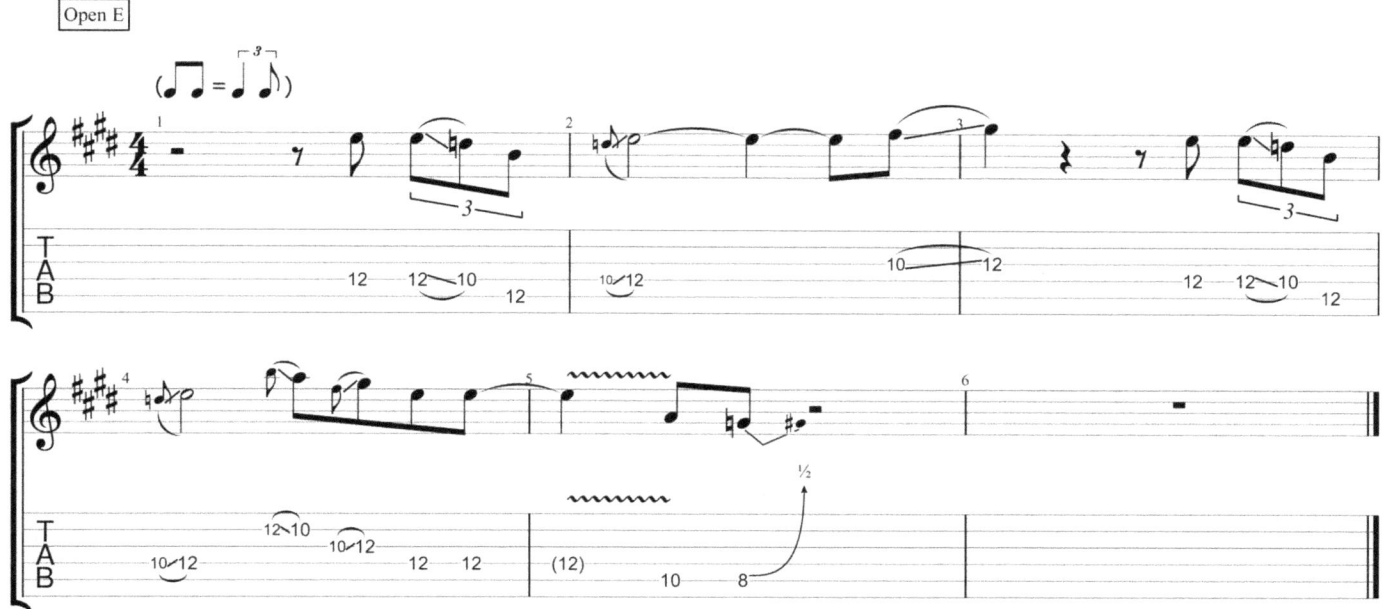

Next is an idea in a similar vein that adds a note three frets higher than the home position on the 2nd string. Sliding into this note creates a cool variation to the basic two fret pattern which is so often played. Nothing here should present a challenge, just play with some passion!

Example 17b

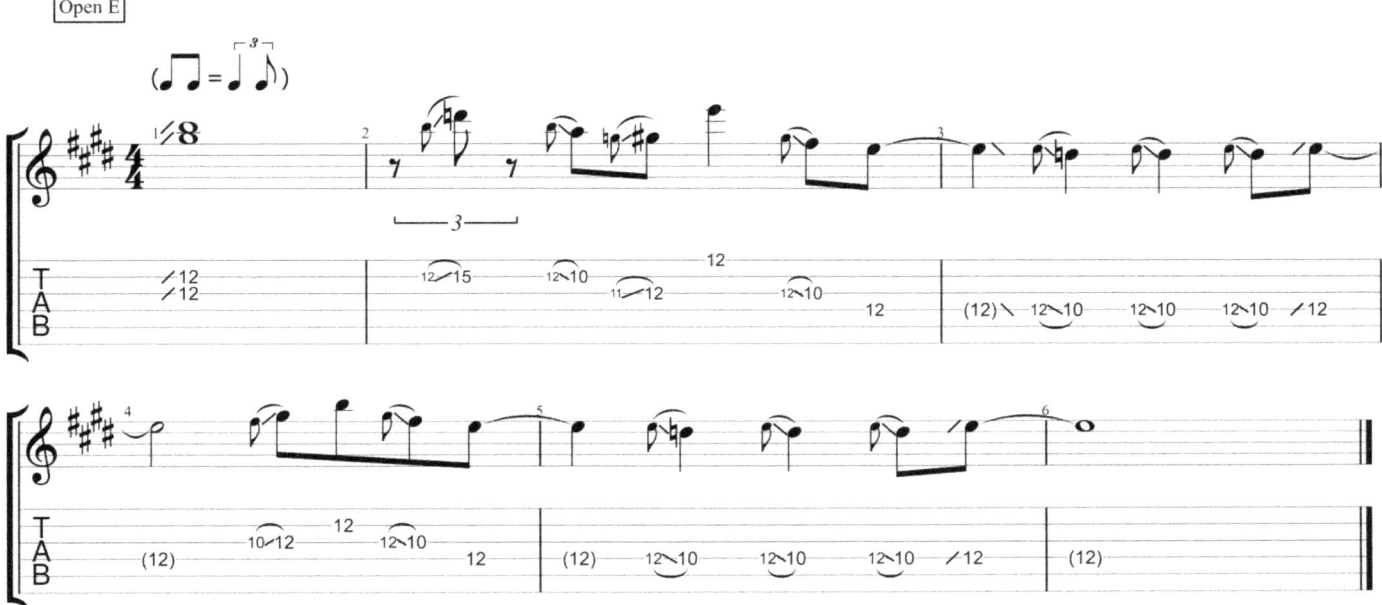

The next example sticks with the E Major setting, but adds some more exciting ideas like slides up and down the neck, open strings, and some faster triplets around the 15th fret.

While there are certainly a few more notes in this lick, the notes are still all from either the E Major Pentatonic scale (E, F#, G#, B, C#) or E Minor Pentatonic scale (E, G, A, B, D).

Example 17c

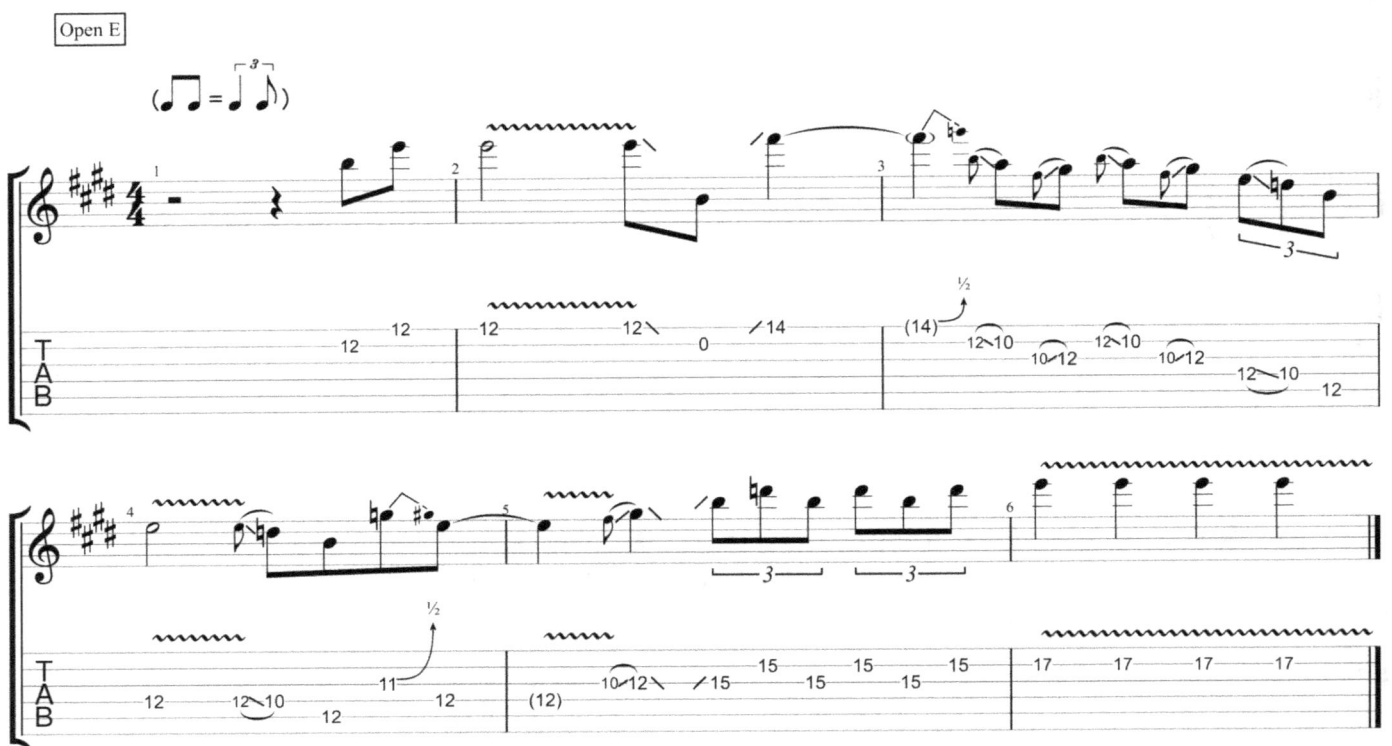

Moving away from static chord vamps, the next lick moves between an A Major and E Major chord. While you could use some theory to work out the best scale for both chords (and all those things the best players do. Hendrix himself was a well-known Berklee graduate…!), you could just take the Joe approach and base your ideas around A Major at the 17th fret and E Major at the 12th fret. It's a considerably easier way to do things, and it sounds great!

Example 17d

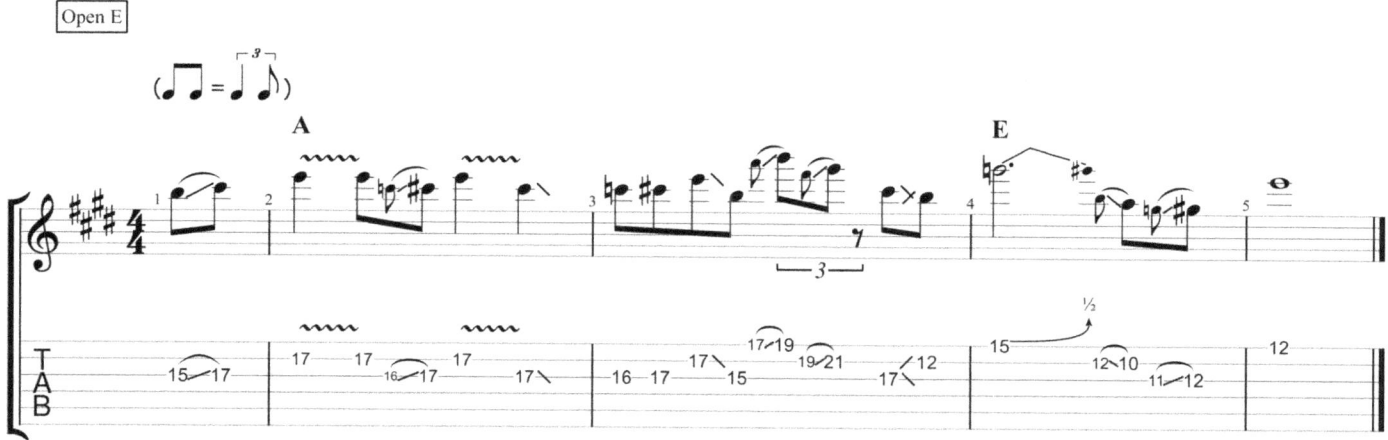

Our final lick shows the build towards the end of a solo, using an A Major, B Major, and E Major chord progression.

Walsh would begin by playing the A Major chord around the home position at the 17th fret. As the chord changes, he would switch to something based around E at the 12th fret to create a bluesy, pentatonic "one scale fits all" vibe to end.

This mixture of giving the chords their due, but adding tension with long sections of minor pentatonic is common in all blues playing, so slide should be no different.

Example 17e

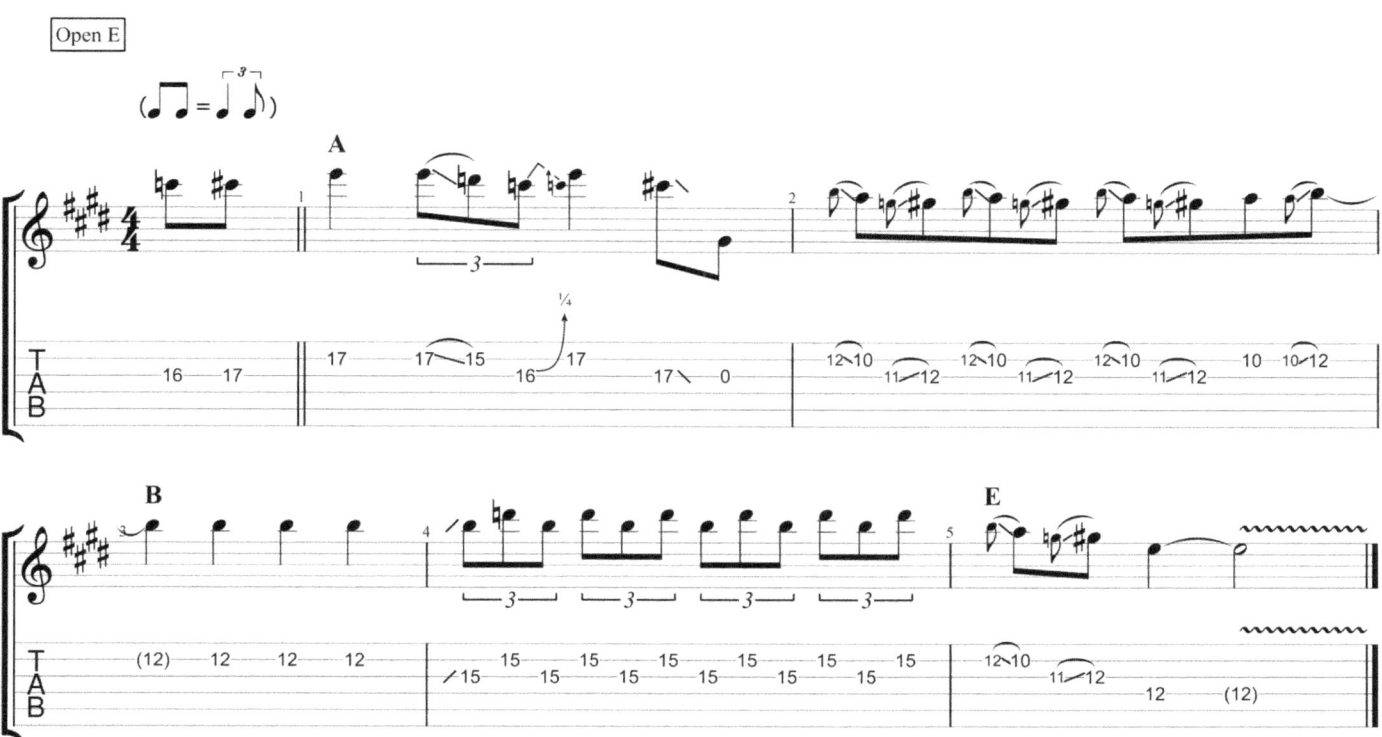

Chapter Eighteen – Muddy Waters

Born in Mississippi in 1913, the name McKinley Morganfield might leave many scratching their heads. Muddy Waters, however, the man he would become, would go on to be a household name in blues.

Waters was raised around music in his Baptist church, so singing came naturally. It wasn't until he was 17, however, that he acquired a guitar – a Stella from Sears-Roebuck that he paid just $2.50 for.

Muddy played around his local area, singing and playing guitar without any real recognition until 1941, when Alan Lomax went to Waters' house for the Library of Congress and recorded him. The result was $20 in Muddy's pocket and a record that would spur him on. As he recalled, "I carried that record up to the corner and put it on the jukebox. Just played it and played it and said, 'I can do it, I can do it.'"

In 1943, Waters moved to Chicago. Despite not yet owning an electric guitar (he would buy one the following year), Muddy quickly found a place in the scene, regularly opening for Big Bill Broonzy.

After a few years, Muddy had really begun to develop a sound and was recording for a few labels, but success would come when the guitarist partnered with Aristocrat Records, who would go on to be known as Chess Records. Singles like *I Can't Be Satisfied, I Feel Like Going Home, Rollin' Stone, Hoochie Coochie Man* and *I'm Ready* launched Muddy into commercial success, making him a must-see act on the club scene.

In the late 50s, Waters travelled to Europe and changed everything when he played loud electric blues and slide guitar to audiences who were expecting traditional acoustic blues material. While this was offputting to many (music has always had that sub-section which rejects change), many also found this new Chicago blues sound exciting and changed their own musical direction.

As his career continued, so did his success. Between 1972 and 1980, he won six Grammy awards for Best Ethnic or Traditional Folk Recording. Three albums during this period, beginning with 1977's *Hard Again*, were produced by Johnny Winter!

Waters died of heart failure in his sleep in 1983, but his influence would go on forever, both as a forefather of the blues music that followed and as a cultural icon.

Muddy played many guitars over the course of his career, but was best known for playing a Telecaster. He would tune this to open G most often, and wore a brass slide on his pinky finger.

Let's look at some of his best known licks!

First up us a riff idea based on the classic hit, *I Can't Be Satisfied*.

The idea with this line is to alternate between high notes for the melody and open position notes to create a rhythm guitar vibe.

Pay close attention to the audio recording on this one as Waters' style is pretty reserved compared to many others in this book. There's a precision to his playing with a subtle controlled vibrato.

Example 18a

When watching any live footage of Muddy, you'll quickly notice just how much he can milk out of a single string, as shown the following example illustrates.

The other thing of note here is just how slow some blues tracks are. This one clocks in at 50bpm, which leaves you a ton of space to play with, but for this style, less is definitely more.

In open G tuning, the highest string isn't tuned to the root of the G chord, instead it's the 5th (D). The root note is found at the 5th fret, so this will always sound like home.

Example 18b

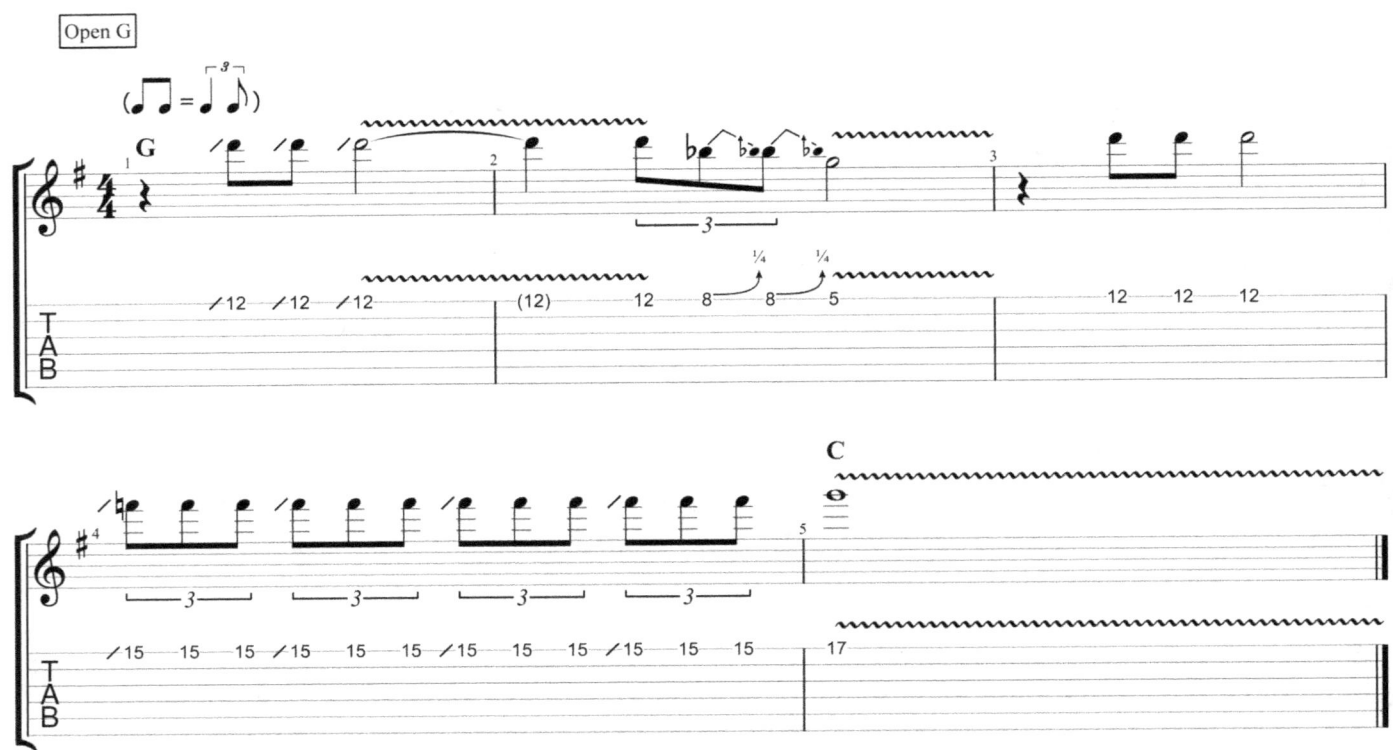

Another noteworthy aspect of Muddy Waters' playing is his use of the slide in conjunction with fretted notes. The following outlines the last four bars of a 12-bar blues in G Major and features a classic Waters turnaround lick. Fretted notes played with the finger descend chromatically, played against an open string. Aside from this one measure, the rest is executed with the slide as normal.

While I've notated this as only having an open 3rd string, it will sound just as good if you leave the 2nd string open too. Experiment and have fun!

Example 18c

Here's another take on the same turnaround lick. This time it's been dressed up with a few more single note ideas.

One fascinating aspect of Waters' playing on a lick like this (not to mention all the old blues guys) is just how out of tune some of the slides can be. When you're reading a book on technique, you might find this hard to deal with, but those old blues slide players weren't concerned with our nice neat 12-tone system. It was all about expression, so when you're sliding to a note (like the 3rd fret in this lick), you're really playing some-where *between* the 3rd and 4th frets.

Example 18d

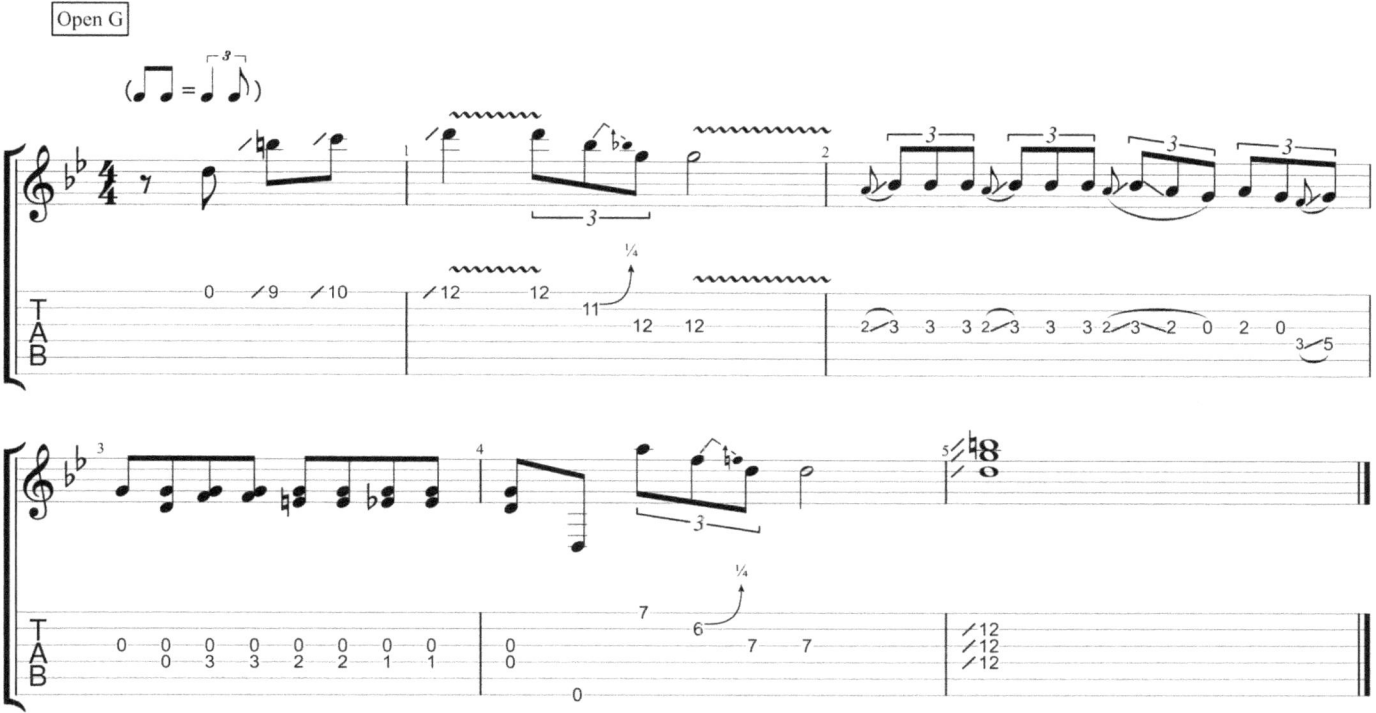

The final example mixes thing up a little with a turnaround on a blues in D. (It's worth noting that the track that inspired this lick was played with a capo, making the key Bb. Waters often played with a capo).

This idea sticks largely to a single string and shifts between pitches in a bluesy manner. The only part to take note of here is that the final measure is fretted with the fingers, not played with the slide!

Example 18e

Chapter Nineteen – Bukka White

Born in Mississippi, 1906, Bukka White would forge a legacy as one of the iconic Delta blues guitarists of the golden era.

Like many musicians of this era, the details surrounding White's early life are speculative. In fact, his date of birth and location are often debated – and not by a day or two, but by 8 years! Some have reported that he got his first guitar aged 9. He had music lessons, but his grandmother made it very clear that she didn't want anyone playing "that Devil music" so he kept his passion hidden.

Realising that playing guitar brought him attention from the opposite sex, a 14-year old White began to take music a lot more seriously, and things gathered momentum when he met Charley Patton.

In the '30s and '40s White had flirtations with success, but this was marred by circumstances and he was imprisoned for shooting a man. Despite spending three years locked away, he continued to further his career. Everyone he met, from inmates to guards, were drawn to his personality and music.

After serving his sentence he recorded his most loved sessions for Lester Melrose. During this time he recorded *Parchman Farm Blues, Good Gin Blues, Bukk's Jitterbug Swing, Aberdeen, Mississippi Blues, Fixin' to Die Blues*, and more. All would go on to be considered classics of the Delta blues genre.

Unfortunately, the war took White away from music and, like several artists in this book, he just disappeared for a long time. During the '60s he was unearthed when John Fahey and Ed Denson posted a letter addressed to "Bukka White (Old Blues Singer), c/o General Delivery, Aberdeen Mississippi" and somehow it managed to filter through to him via a family member.

This '60s period saw a huge resurgence for White as he donned his suit and went out to play regularly. He thrived on the attention and recorded three albums, but it wasn't until he took the time to go back and listen to the original Melrose recordings and relearn how "classic White" played that he really became the man his audience had imagined.

White died of cancer in 1977 in Memphis.

Despite yearning to give electric guitar a try in later life, Bukka never strayed far from his National resonator guitar, which he tuned to many chords, but most notably open D minor (D, A, D, F, A, D), sometimes called cross note tuning. He played with a metal slide on his pinky finger. As for his music, he simply played what he lived.

Let's check out some of his ideas.

First is a classic Delta slide style riff, alternating the 6th and 4th strings with the thumb and playing a melody on top with the slide.

Use the slide for the notes on the high string. You'll probably find fretting the note on the 2nd string easiest.

Example 19a

The second lick takes the same thumping rhythm concept, but now with a melody using the D Minor Pentatonic scale (D, F, G, A, C).

Playing in a minor key makes a lot of sense given Bukka's tuning, but in this case you're not actually playing the F string, so this lick will work fine in open D *or* D minor.

Example 19b

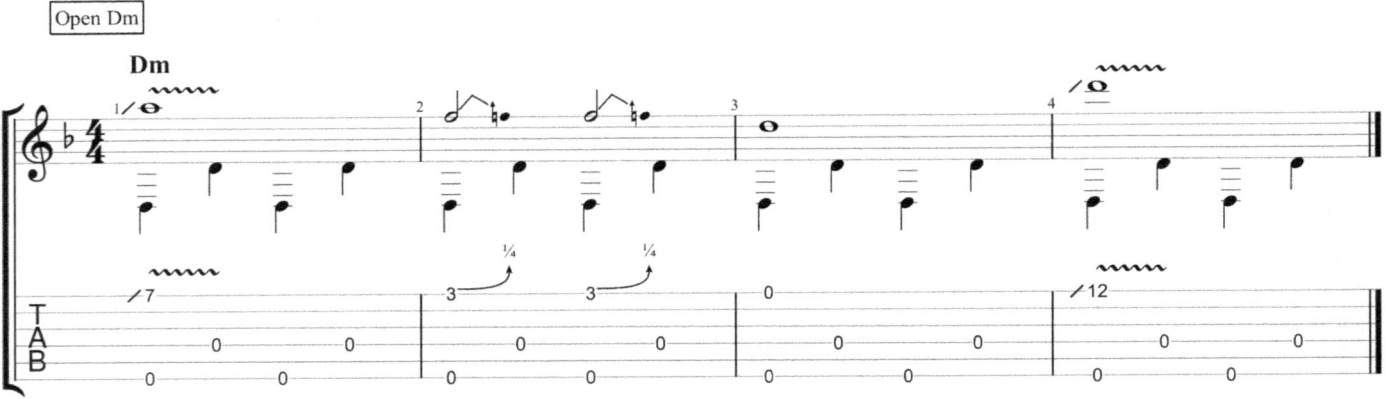

The next example employs the same basic idea as the last two examples, but adds more notes on the upbeats between the notes played with the thumb.

While there are many ways to execute this idea, Bukka would have just used his thumb for the notes in the bass and index finger for the melody notes. Other than that, keep the note with the slide ringing throughout.

Example 19c

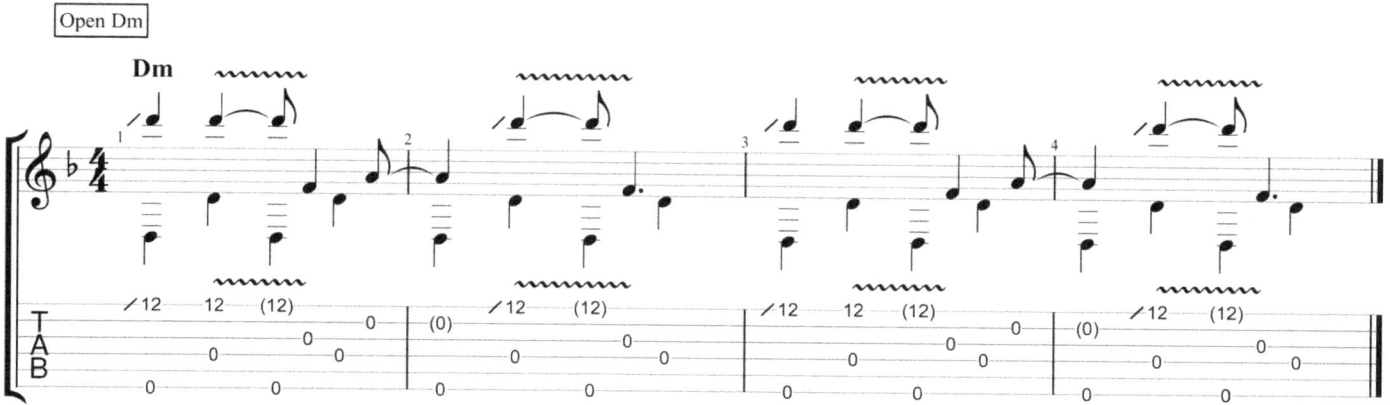

Next we'll attempt to get wild, the same way Bukka would when he played solo slide parts. There is still a separation between chord and melody parts, but this example is strummed quite wildly! Bukka would use a thumbpick here to get the upstrokes on beat 3. The thumb is going: down, down, down up, down… over and over, like a riff, but the slide melody is added over the top.

Example 19d

Our final example showcases how Bukka uses the slide to slide between notes in a melody. Like the previous examples, keep the thumb going while adding the melody on top. Note that the 2nd fret on the 2nd string is fretted with a finger rather than the slide.

Example 19e

Bukka White had one of the wildest, unrefined sounds of anyone in this book, and learning to play like him will never come from words on a page. You need to go and listen to his music and do everything you can to copy the attitude of his playing.

Good luck!

Chapter Twenty – Johnny Winter

Born in Texas in 1944, Johnny Winter was raised in a musical family, with a father who played saxophone and guitar at various public events. This clearly appealed to Johnny and his brother, as by the age of 10, they were performing on children's shows with Johnny playing ukulele.

After some minor success in his late teens, in 1968 Johnny decided to focus his efforts on blues-rock. After releasing *The Progressive Blues Experiment* locally, things changed when Rolling Stone Magazine wrote a glowing review of Johnny and his playing, calling him the next big thing. This was enough to attract serious management and, before he knew it, labels were fighting over him. In the end, CBS won out with a record breaking $600k advance – the most the label had ever shelled out on a new solo artist.

Winter's first two albums on Colombia (1969's *Johnny Winter* and *Second Winter*) were big successes, and even landed him a spot at Woodstock.

Despite being dogged by heroin addiction, the '70's were still a successful period for Johnny, both with his new backing band, and through producing three Grammy award winning albums for one of his guitar idols, Muddy Waters.

From here he continued to record album after album for various labels, until he was found dead in his hotel room in Switzerland in 2014. Until this point, Johnny's only success at the Grammys was with Muddy Waters, but 2014's *Step Back* was posthumously awarded Best Blues Album.

Winter was an influence to many, and did much to help the careers of the people he looked up to. This spirit of positivity is still heard in his music by fans today.

Johnny was a long-time fan of the Gibson Firebird, with his main guitar being a '63 V model. The V model differed from previous offerings as they featured the mini-humbucker, something Johnny was particularly fond of. "It feels like a Gibson, but it sounds closer to a Fender than most other Gibsons," he said. "I was never a big fan of humbucking pickups, but the mini-humbuckers on the Firebird have more bite and treble."

He played with a thumbpick and his fingers, and used the same piece of metal pipe as a slide, worn on his pinky finger, for his entire career. Now that's impressive!

Let's look at some of his legendary licks.

This first idea is inspired by Johnny's classic *Highway 61 Revisited*. It showcases some slick open position ideas in open D tuning.

There's nothing revolutionary here, just a good combination of D major and minor pentatonics, all executed with some attitude.

Example 20a

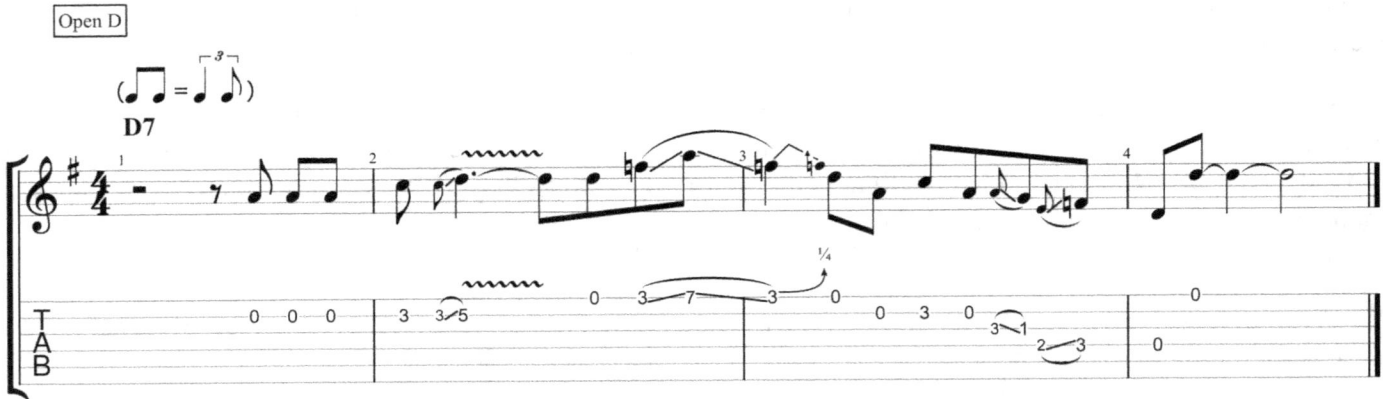

Example 20b continues the idea, but jumps from higher up the neck to the same basic riff seen before.

Slide into the 2nd and 3rd strings at the 15th fret, and let them ring out with some vibrato to add excitement. Then play the open position lick before sliding back up the neck to the 12th fret home position.

Example 20b

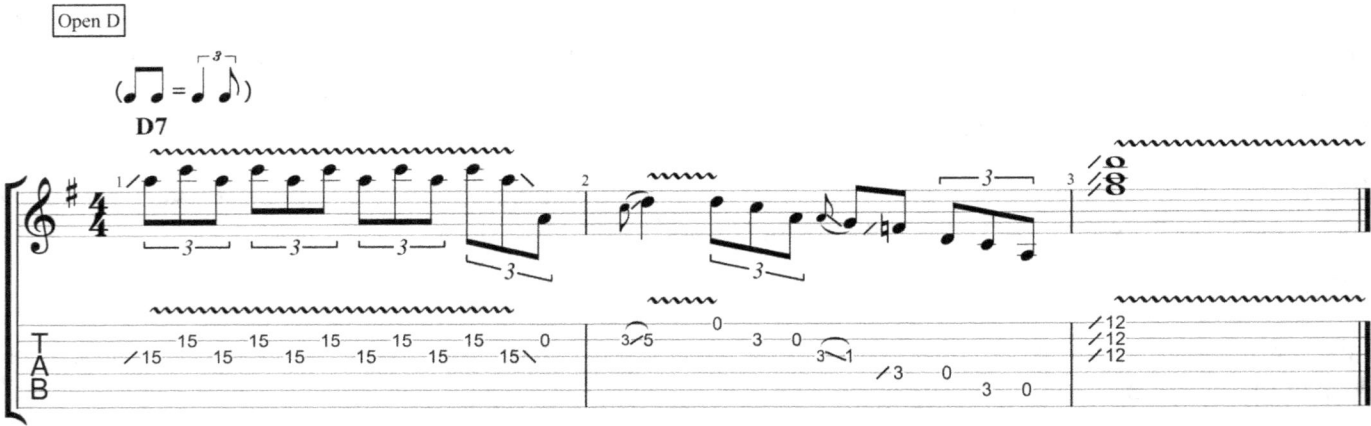

The next example shows how much mileage Johnny can get out of one idea, this time offsetting the open position idea by a few beats (playing it early) and extending it out at the end.

After the fast-paced lead part, shift up to the 7th fret for the V chord (A), then back to the 12th fret home position for the I chord (D).

Example 20c

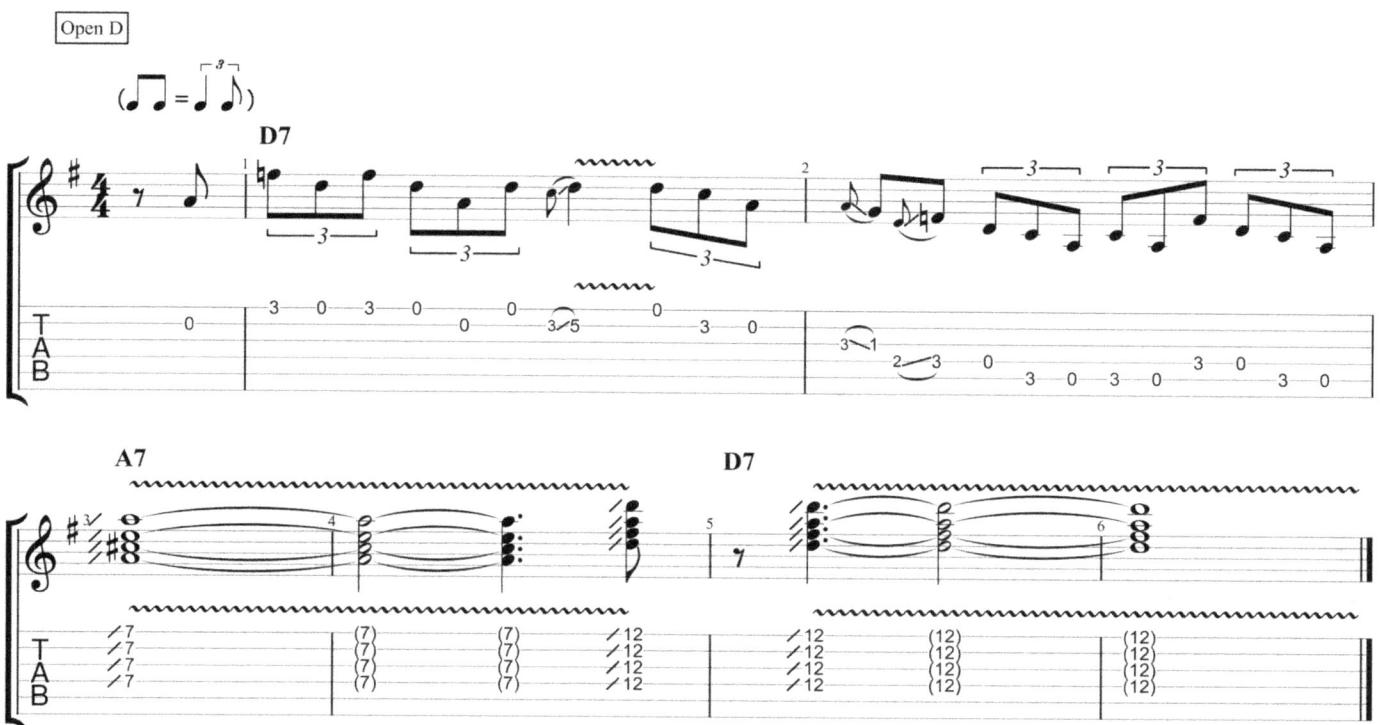

When it comes to soloing, Johnny was no stranger to playing around the home position of whatever key he was in, as demonstrated in the following example.

The twist here is offsetting the higher notes against open strings. This technique created huge intervallic leaps in his licks and elevated Winter above average position-based slide players. They're also quite tricky to execute at speed. I recommend picking the first note with the middle finger, then the next with the index, followed by the thumb on the 2nd string. Take your time with the mechanics of the lick and build up speed over time.

Example 20d

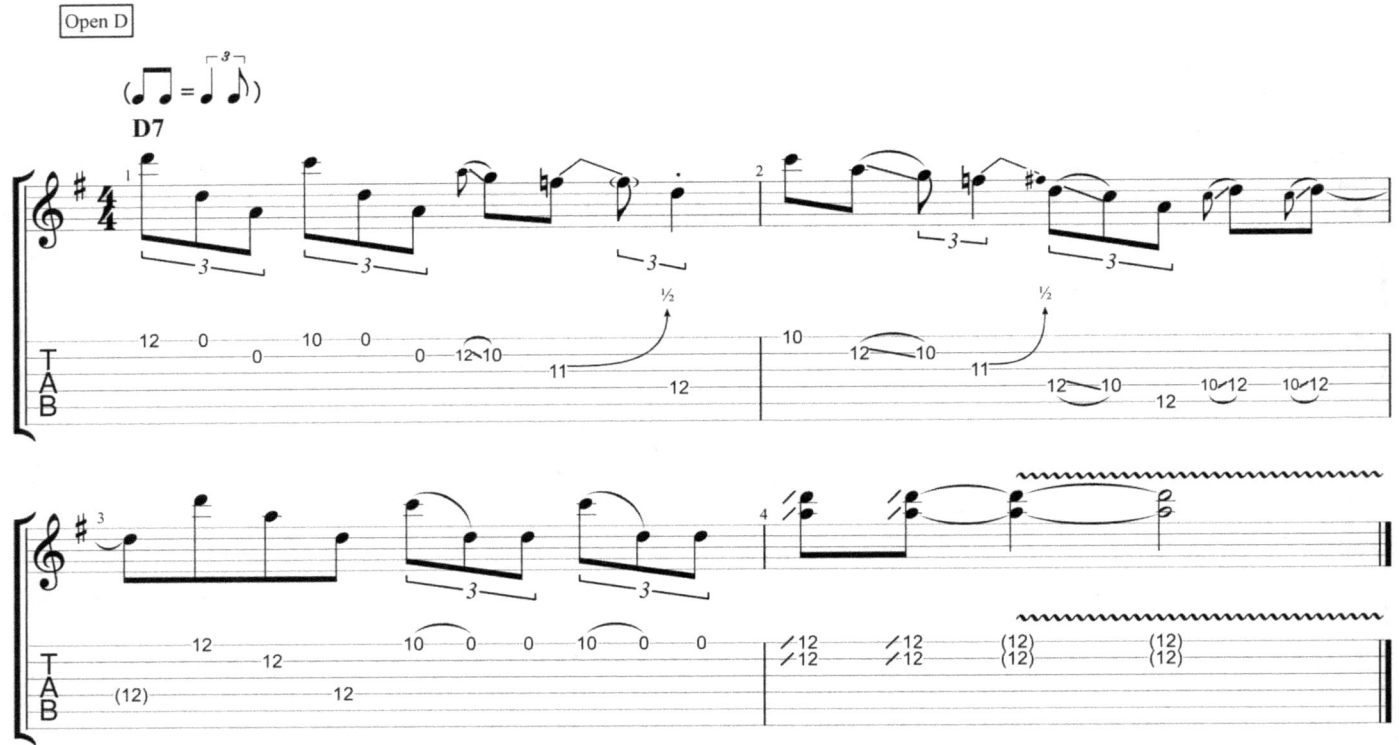

The final example takes the idea of Example 20b but adds high string into the ringing notes for some real high energy blues rock.

After two bars of playing around the 12th fret area, you're back to the open position for an idea similar to each example in this chapter. The point here is that it's possible to milk endless musical ideas out of just a few basic patterns. The masters of this style often had limited vocabulary, but their mastery lay in how they used that vocabulary to express themselves – so get to work!

Example 20e

302

Other Books by Levi Clay

Country Guitar for Beginners is a complete guide to help beginners master elements of the country genre. Split into two sections, this book is designed to develop chord playing, rhythm guitar skills and lead guitar solos.

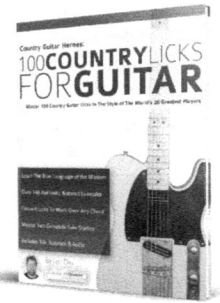

100 Country Licks for Guitar goes way beyond most normal 'boring' lick books… you will learn authentic country guitar licks "In the style of" the 20 greatest country guitarists…ever. What's more, you'll learn how to form their licks into your own personal language… in any key and in any style.

The Country Fingerstyle Guitar Method is the perfect way to master finger picking on the guitar. Part One tackles the techniques and skills needed to build confidence, speed and articulation when playing Country Guitar. Part Two takes a detailed look at the evolution of Country Guitar Fingerstyle and studies the styles and idiosyncrasies of artists Merle Travis, Chet Atkins and Jerry Reed. Each artist's approach to Country Guitar is dissected and through multiple 'in the style of' examples.

Country Guitar Soloing Techniques takes you on a journey of discovery that teaches you authentic country guitar soloing using the actual techniques of the masters. With over 100 notated audio examples, every essential technique, scale and approach is dissected and developed into musical licks and exciting, flamboyant solos.

The Complete Country Guitar Method Compilation is a collection of three best-selling books that teach the essential skills, techniques and theory required to move from absolute basics to astonishing country guitar solos. With 278 jam-packed pages and 400 notated audio examples, this is the most comprehensible guide to country guitar playing ever.

www.ingramcontent.com/pod-product-compliance
Lightning Source LLC
Chambersburg PA
CBHW051147290426
44108CB00019B/2636